Who Guards the Guardians and How

Who Guards the Guardians and How
Democratic Civil-Military Relations

EDITED BY THOMAS C. BRUNEAU AND SCOTT D. TOLLEFSON

University of Texas Press Austin

Requests for permission to reproduce material
from this work should be sent to:
    Permissions
    University of Texas Press
    P.O. Box 7819
    Austin, TX 78713-7819
    www.utexas.edu/utpress/about/bpermission.html

♾ The paper used in this book meets the minimum
requirements of ANSI/NISO z39.48-1992 (R1997)
(Permanence of Paper).

Library of Congress Cataloging-in-Publication Data

Who guards the guardians and how : democratic civil-military relations /
edited by Thomas C. Bruneau and Scott D. Tollefson.— 1st ed.
    p.   cm.
  Includes bibliographical references and index.
  ISBN 0-292-71278-2 (cloth : alk. paper)
  1. Civil supremacy over the military. 2. Civil-military
relations. I. Bruneau, Thomas C. II. Tollefson, Scott D.
JF195.W56   2006
322'.5—dc22

2005032406

For our children and grandchildren.
May their dreams be realized.

Table of Contents

Part Three Issues in Civilian Control of the Military

Foreword

DAVID PION-BERLIN

I F democracy is to survive and flourish in today's world, it must strike a balance between controlling the armed forces and ensuring their effectiveness. This is often easier said than done. In the Third World, newly democratizing states struggling to overcome legacies of military interventionism are often tempted to consolidate their power over the military by weakening it. After all, a smaller, less well financed military has less weight to throw around, permitting the civilian government then to divert scarce resources to programs that bring it greater electoral dividends. But even the older, more established democracies face their own civil-military dilemmas. The more able the armed services become, the more exclusive command they have over information that precludes civilian overseers from really understanding what they need to control. Politicians may want a greater say over the conduct of war so that their foreign policy objectives are fulfilled, while militaries resent the intrusion, setting up some daunting means-ends debates. And a well-oiled military machine may exude supreme confidence in its own abilities while harboring skepticism about whether the politicians are up to the task of defense leadership.

The editors and contributors to this volume believe that the military can be outfitted with what it needs to perform well while also ensuring that civilians have the upper hand. But translating these goals into successful outcomes demands that the right ideas, incentives, and institutions be in place. Officers and civilians must understand each other, be properly motivated to interact in a mutually beneficial way, and be able to work within well-designed defense-related organizations. Although these are the keys to improved civil-military relations, this book places particular emphasis on institutions, which are the foundations and building blocks for civilian control. Locating themselves within a long, distinguished intellectual tradition of institutional analysis that dates back to Max Weber, the contributors to this book peer into the military and civilian bureaucracies where vital decisions are made regarding defense recruitment, education, strategy, roles and missions, budgeting, intelligence gathering, oversight, and restructuring. Their analyses of these subjects provides a level of detail seldom achieved in previous civil-military studies.

The focus on defense-related functions within institutional settings is long overdue, and the attention paid to defense ministries and legislative oversight in particular is especially welcome. Defense ministries usually lie within the chain of command and at the heart of civil-military relations. Nowhere else do so many actors from the two sides meet and work together on a daily basis. Meanwhile, the legislature is, in theory, the only branch of government that can ensure that civil-military relations become democratic, by holding executive officials accountable to the public and their representatives. Despite these facts, I am aware of only one other English-language book devoted solely to the subject of central defense organizations published in the last three decades. And my survey of the lead interdisciplinary journal on civil-military affairs, *Armed Forces and Society*, from 1994–2004 reveals a total of only four articles devoted primarily to executive branch defense organization, and just one article to the legislative branch. Along with my own work on institutions and civil-military affairs, *Who Guards the Guardians and How* helps fill this void in a compelling manner.

It is within the central defense-related bureaucracies where power relations between civilians and soldiers are negotiated, settled, routinized, and enforced. Who has the authority to make what kinds of decisions? Who is accountable to whom? How are roles defined and resources allocated? And how is labor divided up, information shared, and blame assigned? These are questions raised by the authors, questions that would be important in any era. They are more so in today's world, where the dividing line between things military and things civilian is blurry. In the post–cold war, post-9/11 environment, threats to national security, development, and well-being seldom come packaged in the form of an invading army. Nations are often besieged from within, the victims of ethnic or religious hatreds, internal civil wars, and insurgencies. From without, they may be vulnerable to cross-border guerrilla raids or to the operations of sophisticated networks of narcotics traffickers and terrorists. None of these threats is purely military or civilian in nature; they are both.

The military is being called upon to assist in suppressing these threats, maintaining the peace once achieved, and rebuilding strife-torn societies. These unorthodox missions demand a wide range of coercive and non-coercive skills—everything from clearing minefields to clearing the air between erstwhile enemies. Soldiers cannot go at it alone; they must cooperate with civilian specialists if such missions are to be accomplished.

And ultimately, they must submit to political oversight if civilian control over these missions is to be achieved. It is especially critical that civilians maintain the upper hand over sensitive operations that pull combat units into urban areas or other population centers where innocent noncombatants could inadvertently become victims. Such operations may succeed in military terms but fail in political terms if the larger battle is not won: the battle for the hearts and minds of the inhabitants who happen to live in these war zones. Unfortunately, the situation in Iraq reminds us of how things can go awry. All too often our combat operations there, though successful within the narrow confines of armed engagement, fail to win the peace, for lack of guidance from our leaders. The Iraq quagmire demonstrates how a great power rushes to use its instruments of violence without first carefully calculating and then recalculating the political effects of doing so. Political calculation, leadership, collaboration, and compliance—all of these begin at home, inside the military- and civilian-led defense institutions of state. It is there that a meld of policy, strategy, and tactics must be engineered and then continuously reassessed to the satisfaction of politicians and warriors alike. And it is to those institutions that the contributors to this volume wisely direct our attention.

One of the distinctive features of *Who Guards the Guardians and How* is that it is based on firsthand observations about a vast array of regions and countries. The book itself does not comprise country case studies. Instead, it culls experiences from across the world, finds patterns, and then derives some generalizations. In fact, a fascinating and controversial assertion of this book is that despite the extraordinary diversity among the consolidating democracies of the world, their civil-military problems are quite similar in nature. So too are the solutions.

Why would that be the case? For one thing, democratic systems would be expected to face a set of common challenges such as accountability and transparency. These goals pertain to the democratic system as a whole and to the civil-military relation in particular. For instance, politicians are held responsible for allocating and spending taxpayers' monies wisely. But they cannot do this in defense unless they are privy to what often are rather secretive budgetary details and unless they are able to hold military officials accountable for how they use public resources. Hence, consolidating democracies must find the will and the way to make defense expenditure a more transparent, scrutinized phenomenon.

For another thing, the economic forces of globalization might be creating greater convergences among nations that would otherwise retain distinctive features. For example, international institutions like the World Bank and the International Monetary Fund have concluded that excessive military spending is harmful to economic development. As these agencies routinely apply pressures on aid recipients to reduce their fiscal deficits, they also now regularly urge them to put costly, wasteful military programs on the chopping block. Thus, many developing democracies are motivated to solidify civilian control so they can reduce military expenditures while ensuring—in fact, demanding—military compliance with those measures as well.

If there are common problems, are there common solutions? While not quite advocating a one-size-fits-all, the authors do give us a set of similar ideas on how best to engineer defense-related institutions to perform better. This convergence is not coincidental but the result of a greater cross-national fertilization of ideas among specialists from dozens of countries across many continents. These exchanges have been institutionalized in the form of courses and consultations organized by key learning centers, including the Center for Civil-Military Relations (CCMR) at the Naval Postgraduate School in Monterey, California. The editors, Thomas Bruneau and Scott Tollefson, along with the rest of the contributors to this volume, have all been affiliated with CCMR and, in that capacity, have offered their professional assistance to countries wishing to civilianize defense ministries, rethink military roles and missions, formulate strategy, and in general improve civil-military relations.

Through intense interactions with defense ministers and employees, military general staffs, think tanks, and legislators, they have been able to absorb valuable information from those "on the ground" in many corners of the globe, converting that data into informed observations and generalizations about civil-military affairs. From that unique vantage point, they are convinced that in fact common threads run through all the democracies that wish to consolidate their control over their militaries. As the editors argue in the introduction, civil-military issues in democracies old and new involve ongoing conflict, negotiation, and compromise between those who hold power by virtue of free and fair elections and the organizations to which society has granted a monopoly on the means of violence.

In the final analysis, the relationship between civilians and officers is a political one. What this book does, and does well, is to give us a window into the institutional dimensions to that political relationship. It also gives us a greater hope that when parties to civil-military conflicts come to a meeting of the minds, challenges of all sorts can be overcome to the enormous benefit of democratic systems worldwide.

David Pion-Berlin is a Latin Americanist widely known for his research and writings on civil-military relations, military regimes, military political thought, political repression, and human rights.

Acknowledgments

The chapters in this volume were generated from the research and teaching programs of the Center for Civil-Military Relations (CCMR) at the Naval Postgraduate School in Monterey, California, since the center's founding in 1994. All of the contributors are closely associated with CCMR in researching and delivering seminars on various aspects of democratic civil-military relations in either the United States or one or more of the forty other countries where CCMR offers seminars annually. In addition to the ongoing research and teaching functions of CCMR, several of the authors also benefited from a research and publishing program funded by the United States Agency for International Development (USAID) between 1999 and 2001. The funding was provided to a partnership that brought together CCMR, the National Democratic Institute for International Affairs (NDI), the Institute for Strategic and Development Studies (ISDS) in Manila, and a nongovernmental organization, Seguridad Estratégica Regional en el 2000 (SER in 2000), in Buenos Aires, which has played a very important role in promoting democratic civil-military relations in Argentina and elsewhere in Latin America. The partnership, which was managed by Professor María José Moyano Rasmussen for CCMR, allowed us to write first drafts of several of the chapters included in this volume. We would like to acknowledge the support of the director of CCMR, Mr. Rich Hoffman. We want to express our sincere thanks to Elizabeth Skinner for her dedicated and efficient work throughout the project. Without her professional competence and commitment to seeing this project through to completion, we would have lost momentum and direction. We finally owe a great debt of gratitude to those military officers, civilian officials, and representatives of civil society (universities, NGOs, think tanks, and the media) with whom we have worked during this past decade in our seminars. We can only hope that they have learned as much about democratic civilian control and military effectiveness from us as we have from them.

Who Guards the Guardians and How

Introduction

THOMAS C. BRUNEAU

Quis custodiet ipsos custodes?
JUVENAL, *Satire VI*

THE spread of democracy among nations continues apace in the early part of the twenty-first century, with some two-thirds of the almost two hundred independent countries of the world more or less following this once-rare political format. In most of the newer democracies of the so-called third wave of democratization that began in 1974 with Portugal's upheaval, one of the biggest challenges to democratic consolidation and deepening has been to find the proper balance between the civilian and military sectors. If on the one hand the balance of power is tipped in favor of the military, which can occur when military leaders continue to enjoy prerogatives—for instance, in finances, control over promotions, or the handling of intelligence—left over from a previous nondemocratic regime, democracy probably is still in the process of consolidation. If on the other hand civilian leaders have subsumed the military and either politicized it through promotions of political cronies or crippled it with severe budget cuts, then the country will be left without a critical resource in such areas as humanitarian and disaster relief, counterterrorism and counter–drug operations, international peacekeeping, and, most important, national defense.

Although the "proper" balance between democratic civilian leadership and military effectiveness in achieving roles and missions will clearly vary from country to country and era to era, in the view of this volume's contributors striking that equilibrium is fundamental to the success of authentic democratic governance. It is the purpose of this volume to describe the variety of ways in which a wide range of institutions structuring civil-military relations may achieve a balance between democratic civilian control and military effectiveness.

Breaking New Ground

Studies by the leading scholars of democratic consolidation call attention to the centrality of civil-military relations in the transition to functioning democracy. Unfortunately, beyond highlighting the importance of the topic, these works do not go into any detail about the issues, actors, and institutions involved. This is the case, for example, in the now classic studies by Adam Przeworski and Philippe Schmitter. In *Democracy and the Market: Political and Economic Reforms in Eastern Europe and Latin America*, Przeworski states: "Obviously, the institutional framework of civilian control over the military constitutes the neuralgic point of democratic consolidation."[1] Having said that, he fails to revisit this tantalizing assertion anywhere else in the book. Schmitter summarizes twenty years of research on democratic transitions in "The Consolidation of Political Democracies: Processes, Rhythms, Sequences, and Types," in which he asserts that "the submission of the military to civilian control" is one of four necessary processes of democratization.[2] Schmitter, like Przeworski, does not then pursue the issue in that chapter or any later work.

An exception to this gap in the literature is a book by Juan J. Linz and Alfred Stepan, *Problems in Democratic Transition and Consolidation*.[3] Although we regard Linz and Stepan's approach and observations to have been insightful and accurate when they first appeared almost ten years ago, they are less relevant today as the tides of domestic and international politics have pushed the issues and challenges in directions the older work does not adequately capture. This problem of datedness is particularly obvious in Chapter 5, "Actors and Context," which contrasts hierarchical and nonhierarchical militaries to draw a distinction that does not seem useful today. In the same chapter, a list of international influences on domestic decision making is so limited as to be misleading, in comparison with the level of outside involvement and influence that takes place today around the globe. It is worth noting that during the "bad old days" of dictatorships and authoritarianism, there was a rich and diverse literature on military coups, the military as a political actor, and military-dominated regimes. Later, with the transition to democracy in outheastern Europe, Latin America, sub-Saharan Africa, East-Central Europe, and parts of Asia, a few excellent studies of the role of the military in the transitions and early consolidation phases of these new democracies were published.[4] There is a fundamental gap in the literature, however, in the area of civil-military relations—that is, the roles, responsibilities, and rights of the armed forces and the elected government in consolidating democracies. This void is precisely what our book seeks at least to address.

We maintain that in all democracies, new or old, issues of civil-military relations are fundamentally the same. They involve ongoing conflict, negotiation, and compromise between those who hold power by virtue of free and fair elections and the organizations to which society has granted a monopoly on the means of violence. Once a country has consolidated its governing format—in this case, democracy—then it becomes a matter essentially of negotiating on the margins. In his magisterial work "Military Organization and the Organization of the State," Otto Hintze asked, "What place is occupied by the organization of the army in the general organization of the state?"[5] If leaders honestly can answer that it is just one part of the state bureaucracy and, like all others, is under the control of democratically elected civilians, then further issues of civil-military relations will be similar to those in other democracies throughout the world. They become "management" problems revolving around the balance of power and force and the inherent tension between democracy and expertise. We take the standpoint that it is how governments deal with these issues that constitutes the crux of civil-military relations and will determine not only how successful civilians are in controlling the armed forces but also how effective these forces will be in fulfilling the increasingly varied roles and missions that are assigned to them.

Schmitter makes an excellent point regarding the applicability of some of the literature in comparative politics as a country's democracy is becoming consolidated.[6] He notes that these works, which by their nature seek patterns that can be generalized across cases, are of limited value until a democratic regime reaches the stage scholars currently term "consolidation." The literature and findings on democratic transitions tend to differ to the degree that each country's political transition is unique, but this does not appear to be the case in democratic consolidation.[7] Once that certain phase is reached, then general findings on political parties, electoral systems, bureaucracies, and the other institutions of democracy become relevant, albeit with necessary adaptations.

We believe the same point applies to civil-military relations. This is not to assume that democratic consolidation is inevitable, assured, or complete in any given case; rather, the assumption is that the challenges will be the same in both newer and older democracies. How these challenges are defined and resolved is fundamental for democratic consolidation and civil-military relations, if the armed forces are actually to serve the needs of the nation and not their own goals or those of a small clique or political party. These practical similarities are not coincidental. There are a finite number of tasks that any country has to handle in any sector of public administration, be it in health, education, transport, or national defense, although this does not imply that all countries will deal with these tasks in a similar fashion. The authors in this volume discuss many of these challenges with an eye to identifying lessons—and obstacles— that may be useful to both scholars and officials seeking to understand civil-military relations in new democracies.

The literature on civilian control of the military in established democracies that will be most valuable to post-transition democratic states is not the now classic theoretical works of Samuel Huntington or Morris Janowitz, which have been more than sufficiently reviewed and criticized over the years.[8] These studies offer a level of generalization too broad to be very useful under current circumstances. We look instead to that body of literature dealing with the renegotiation and adjustment of relations between civilian leaders and the armed forces in those democracies where there is no issue about who has a right to rule—that is, the "consolidation" stage that many of the newer democracies are currently approaching. This approach is epitomized by Michael J. Hogan's *A Cross of Iron: Harry S. Truman and the Origins of the National Security State, 1945–1954*, which details the creation of the national security system in the United States at the end of World War II; James Locher's *Victory on the Potomac: The Goldwater-Nichols Act Unifies the Pentagon*, which describes and analyzes the political process whereby this same system was reformed forty years later; and Hew Strachan's *The Politics of the British Army*, on the consolidation of civilian control in Great Britain.[9]

Findings from this literature are relevant for the newer democracies as they seek to reform and restructure their military establishments and the relations between civilian politicians and ministries because their militaries have tended more and more to be structured in similar fashion since the end of the cold war. Furthermore, democratic decision makers are compelled to formulate policy from a widely accepted, well-defined selection of roles and missions along a spectrum from national and territorial defense to counterterrorism to peacekeeping to delivering humanitarian assistance. On top of these implicit policy constraints, the more-established democracies—singly and through organizations such as the North Atlantic Treaty Organization (NATO), Partnership for Peace, and the Organization of American States, to name only a few—seek explicitly to shape the military structures, missions, and civil-military relations in the newer democracies in their own image. These include the already proven institutions such as ministries of defense, defense committees, oversight of intelligence, and so on, which are now part of democratic civil-military relations. Furthermore, once one of the newer democracies has reached a certain stage in its consolidation, as Spain did in the late 1980s, Argentina in the early 1990s, and Hungary in the late 1990s, it then becomes a proponent for these very same policies and institutions, sending experts abroad and hosting seminars in-country on these topics for the yet even newer democracies.

The trend toward homogenization of the main issues in democratic civil-military relations raises more considerations as well. The United States, Great Britain, Argentina, and Canada, among many others, have established organizations in other countries—such as the U.S. Department of Defense regional centers and the Center for Civil-Military Relations—that rely on funding from governmental organizations (U.S. International Military Education and Training and the Geneva Centre for the Democratic Control of Armed Forces, for example) and nongovernmental organizations and think tanks created explicitly for these purposes. These centers, which actively network among themselves to ensure cooperation and coordination, promote very similar agendas with reference to these very similar issues. Officials in the newer democracies are often eager to join the international community of democratic states and thus are receptive to such agendas. It is not surprising, then, that a limited range of topics receives scrutiny and that decision makers are encouraged to resolve them in predictable ways. This does not mean that all leaders will do so, or will do so at the pace prescribed to them, but the definition and analysis of these issues across countries are intentionally homogenous and geared toward an almost universally desired outcome.

Taking the Next Step toward a Useful Analysis

Despite these more or less well-intentioned efforts to control the outcome of democratic consolidation, the question remains: How do we first conceptualize and then analyze civil-military relations as they really exist in these post-transitional democracies? The first and fundamental point in any democracy is to understand where the power lies.[10] Who in fact is in charge of a country? If the country is a democracy, then the answer must be the democratically elected civilian leaders. If the answer is ambiguous or if there is an ongoing struggle for control as in Iran and Pakistan, then the subject—civil-military relations—will be the same, but the terms of analysis will be different.

In the course of our research, writing, and teaching on civil-military relations in the United States and abroad, we have found that the methodology that guides our inquiries in the right direction is an updated version of Max Weber's groundbreaking work on political power and bureaucracy.[11] The approach Weber employed to understand the military and its locus within state and society leads us to take a closer look at and emphasize the structure of bureaucracy as it relates to civil-military relations. After all, the military not only constitutes a complex and hierarchical bureaucracy in itself but also, in the modern state, interacts and is integrated with other bureaucracies, domestic and foreign. Without this kind of stable structural support, armed forces would be unable to fulfill the ever-increasing numbers and kinds of roles and missions they face in the new millennium. The contemporary version of Weber's approach is known as New Institutionalism. The various subtheories that together loosely constitute New Institutionalism "all seek to elucidate the role that institutions play in the determination of social and political outcomes."[12] In other words, an understanding of the roles of institutions is indispensable to this or any study of how actors manage power relations within a society. Therefore, we need to highlight a few of the main elements of this model.

First and most important is the meaning of the term "institutions." Peter Hall and Rosemary Taylor define institutions as "formal or informal procedures, routines, norms, and conventions embedded in the organizational structure of the polity or political economy."[13] This broad definition is vital to the present volume because it forces us (if we are faithful to the approach) to focus on the institutions that determine civil-military relations, such as ministries of defense, legislatures, the military as a profession, control of military budgets, the means by which intelligence is gathered and applied, military education, and the recruitment system. Each author looks closely at the institutions relevant to his or her discussion and seeks to explain their responsibilities and operations—and liabilities—in ways that will assist our understanding of the sum total of civil-military relations.

This understanding is important not only because virtually all democracies are facing dramatic changes in their civil-military relations, but also because few researchers are prepared to undertake the work necessary to understand the civilian government side of the equation, let alone the military side. Such an in-depth grasp of both institutions is necessary before we can begin to analyze their impact on one another and on society as a whole. This research agenda is challenging but possible and plausible through basic academic research enhanced by active engagement.

Once we know what an institution is, we need to analyze what influences that a given institution may exert on actors and processes. This book therefore focuses on the many institutions that exist to manage national security and civil-military relations. Throughout, the authors grapple with the problems of effectiveness, to see whether the military can actually fulfill the roles and missions assigned to it by the civilian leadership, and the means by which a democracy exercises civilian control over its armed forces.[14] As the authors in this volume agree, there is an integral relationship between these two dimensions.

Another key aspect of New Institutionalism is attention to the origins of institutions, which can be understood in two parts. First, we must look to the goals and motivations of the actors involved in creating these institutions, keeping in mind the concept of "unintended consequences." Civil-military relations must be understood as a set of institutions. Creating only one part—for example, a ministry of defense—will not necessarily result in either civilian control or military effectiveness. Second, we must remain aware that, again in the words of Hall and Taylor, we live in "a world replete with institutions."[15] The chapters underscore that there are a finite number of models for democratic civil-military relations; the challenge for scholars is to analyze the extent to which a model copied from one country and one context does in fact translate into an institution in another country and context.

Finally, it is worth reiterating that the process of creating and implementing institutions is all about power, and institutional power relations therefore are a primary concern of New Institutionalism. Some actors have the power to adopt and implement new institutions, whereas others wield authority to resist this adoption—or, more often, implementation.[16] The importance of power relations to the balance between civil and military institutions cannot be overemphasized. Not only have scholars of New Institutionalism recognized the critical part that the creation of institutions plays in structuring relationships of power, but based on the experience of researchers at the Center for Civil-Military Relations, military and civilian actors from around the world also are very much aware of the implications for their own countries. The conditions under which an institution forms will have a strong impact on who determines the rules of the game and how those rules will be implemented. New Institutionalism directs our attention to the centrality of institutions in structuring relations of power, through the conditions of their creation, the interests of those involved in creating them, and the influence of preexisting institutional models.

The institutional relationships that must be included in any useful analysis of civil-military relations cover a broad range. In most societies military institutions were established with the founding of the nation, extend throughout national territory, are intertwined with multiple levels of the executive and legislative branches, are linked closely with society and the economy, and engage in a variety of international contacts and negotiations. The book's chapters illustrate and analyze how these institutional relationships come together for most of the issues of democratic civilian control and military effectiveness.

The Center for Civil-Military Relations

The Center for Civil-Military Relations (CCMR) at the Naval Postgraduate School in Monterey, California, was founded in 1994 to provide military officers and civilian policymakers from emerging democracies around the world with the knowledge and tools they need to work together to establish sound, stable, and democratic relations between the military and civilian sectors. This volume reflects the commitment of CCMR and its members to the promotion of healthy civil-military relations, both for democratic consolidation and for the fostering of military effectiveness in carrying out the roles and missions assigned by civilian leaders. The authors' open advocacy of particular policy choices arises from their professional experiences in assisting other countries' work through the process of ensuring that democratically elected civilians are in control of a military that implements its tasks effectively. This does not, we are convinced, detract from the objectivity and soundness of the descriptions and analyses included here. On the contrary, this work is all the more relevant, given that each author has seen the impact that success—or failure—in these critical areas can have on a newly consolidating democracy and is thus in a uniquely knowledgeable position to comment on it. The authors have been encouraged therefore to include suggestions on how to establish and implement new institutional arrangements.

Unlike most of the literature in the field of civil-military relations— which in the case of the United States is heavy on theory and richly supported by concrete information, but for other countries and regions tends to be legalistic and devoid of theory or original data—we seek to marry up our extensive empirical findings with the theoretical approach of New Institutionalism. The data utilized here are collected from traditional interdisciplinary academic research, including primary and secondary source documents, the World Wide Web, and interviews, and also through the intense and intimate involvement of all the authors in CCMR programs. These one- or two-week seminar programs typically focus on themes that are determined by the sponsoring organizations, which include ministries of defense, general staffs, legislatures, war colleges, think tanks, NGOs, and others, which means that the programs are of great interest to the participants and offer the instructors the opportunity to learn as much as they teach. In addition, CCMR has now been asked to assist several countries in certain key areas such as restructuring ministries of defense (Colombia), strategy formulation procedures (Moldova and Estonia), staffing a ministry of defense with civilians (Taiwan), roles and missions of the armed forces (Guatemala), and intelligence sector reform (Argentina and Romania). These kinds of cooperative programs offer CCMR staff unusual levels of access to a country's civilian and military decision makers and helps the staff gain valuable insights into how governments are attempting to deal with these critical issues.

The approach in this book is interdisciplinary. The authors are political scientists, historians, and even one soldier-philosopher. Four have extensive military backgrounds, one is still on active duty, and all are part of military academic programs in several countries. Chapter 1, "Military Professionalism in a Democracy," and Chapter 9, "Professional Military Education in Democracies," draw heavily on the U.S. experience of professionalization as a basis for comparing other countries' policies. The other chapters use extensive research from a variety of countries. Several of the chapters, particularly 1, 3, and 4, highlight the centrality of tensions between and among civilians and officers in most aspects of civil-military relations. These authors make the case that this tension is normal and, indeed, that it would be surprising if there were not disputes over so many key issues of political power and military roles and missions, many of which involve the threat of violence and loss of life. These are by definition issues worth fighting over.

With the publication of this volume, the members of CCMR are turning to topics for future collaborations, including intelligence reform in third-wave democracies; case studies in U.S. civil-military relations; and eventually, case studies in civil-military relations in more recently established democracies such as Romania, Colombia, and South Africa.

The Chapters

The book is divided into three sections. The first deals with the key actors in democratic civil-military relations: the military, the executive branch (particularly the ministry of defense), and the legislature. The three chapters in this section provide a basic understanding of how these actors function and interact in a democracy. The second section addresses the roles and missions of the military, beginning with the development of strategy and then surveying different elements of the broad variety of roles and missions that contemporary nations assign to militaries. These chapters link the actors reviewed in the first section with the decisions, captured in the idea of strategy formulation, for employment of the military. Section three delves into some of the most important issues in democratic civilian control of the military: oversight of intelligence organizations, budgeting, types of recruitment systems, and professional military education. Together these areas, dealing as they do with both control and effectiveness, constitute the heart of institutionalized democratic civilian control.

Thomas-Durrell Young starts us out with a description and analysis of the military as a profession. Following from Weber, and consistent with the New Institutionalism, professions are viewed as institutions. Through his work with CCMR, Young understands the value of educating civilian decision makers about the nature of the military profession, with which they likely have had little contact, as well as the value of giving military officers a conceptual yardstick for comparing and contrasting their organization with an ideal model of the profession. In the present work, Young highlights several of the tensions that arise from the very different cultures and perspectives of officers and politicians. Although these tensions never disappear, he suggests several ways to mitigate them in order for officers and civilians to be able to cooperate for the common goal of national security.

Jeanne Giraldo, in Chapter 2, uses data from several consolidating democracies to review the roles and responsibilities of the legislature in national security and defense. While highlighting the many positive aspects of legislative involvement in democratic civil-military relations, Giraldo notes that in most countries the legislature in fact plays a very limited role. She provides extensive insights into how the relationship between a legislature and the armed forces can be regularized and stresses the need for legislators and what staff they may have to cultivate expertise in things military. The author further suggests ways in which dysfunctional situations can be changed and improved through the formation of new institutions.

In Chapter 3, Thomas Bruneau and Richard Goetze provide a rare discussion of the possible roles a ministry of defense might have in national security, defense, and civil-military relations. In the course of their in-country research, the authors found that answering the question of who determines these policies must precede any analysis of the policies themselves. Besides Spain and Portugal, their study covers several newer democracies where CCMR is working, including South Africa, Ukraine, Brazil, and Nicaragua, which recently established or reconstituted ministries of defense, and Colombia, which is restructuring its defense ministry. Bruneau and Goetze further emphasize the relationships that defense ministries must cultivate with other sectors of the executive, the legislature, the armed forces themselves, and international actors. Again, the critical importance of civilian expertise becomes apparent.

Eminent military historian Douglas Porch, in Chapter 4, introduces the topic of strategy and the tensions between the civilian and military sectors inherent in its planning. In addition to raising the classic questions of strategy formulation, Porch provides insights into how different leaders in different eras have attempted to deal with those institutional disputes. The challenge in a democracy, he concludes, is to determine how best to manage and live with these inevitable tensions.

In Chapter 5, Paul Shemella grapples with the fundamental questions of why societies create armed forces and what kinds of missions they direct them to undertake. He provides a framework for understanding the definition of roles and missions, along with insights on how to think about them. In doing so, he raises two critical points. First, many countries have never had a public debate about the purposes of the armed forces, without which it is difficult to establish legitimacy for the military or to generate sufficient resources to support them. Second, the variety of roles and missions that modern militaries are asked to assume is daunting and has only expanded since September 11, 2001. Even in small, recently stabilized countries, such as those in Central America, the armed forces may be simultaneously involved in traditional defense, international peacekeeping, counter–drug operations, counterterrorism, counterintelligence, and humanitarian and disaster assistance. Unless policymakers grasp the wide spectrum of possible roles and missions the military may be assigned, it will be difficult for them to comprehend the real challenges of civilian control and the requirements of resources, recruitment, and training.

Tom Bruneau joins Kenneth Dombroski in Chapter 6 to examine the intelligence sector, including counterintelligence, or "state security." They pay particular attention to the military's role in intelligence, which can pose a serious challenge to democratic consolidation. An unreformed intelligence organization left over from a previous nondemocratic regime, they warn, can exert undue influence on elected politicians and thus undermine efforts to democratize governmental institutions. If, by contrast, a government lacks an effective intelligence service, it will find itself virtually blind in the face of organized crime, terrorism, and impending threats to national defense. The authors emphasize the importance of professionalization of intelligence officers and their functions as a means to mitigate those dangers.

In Chapter 7, Jeanne Giraldo turns to the pivotal role that money plays in democratic civil-military relations. In a democracy, not only is the budget the main mechanism for civilian control of the military, but it also enables civilian leaders to define roles and missions for and to ensure transparency and accountability in the military organization. Giraldo stresses that in order to exert the necessary controls through budgeting, however, not only legislators but also officials in the executive, including the ministry of defense, must have an interest in becoming knowledgeable about military matters.

The final two chapters deal with different aspects of the structure and culture of the military itself. In Chapter 8, Austrian Army brigadier general and philosopher Edwin Micewski explores the importance of recruitment methods—conscription and volunteer—not only for the ability of the military to implement its roles and missions but also in terms of the armed forces' relationship with society as an institution and of its members as individual citizens. He highlights several of the key problems and considerations inherent in both types of force and makes clear that no single choice will serve every society equally well, whether it be conscription, an all-volunteer professional force, or some combination thereof. As with most of the issues covered in this volume, the reader is urged to think in terms of "lessons learned and best practices" rather than to expect to find hard-and-fast solutions to these complex relations.

In Chapter 9, Karen Guttieri deals with another extremely important issue that has received little attention in the scholarly literature outside the older democracies: professional military education (PME). As Young and Micewski note, military and civilian leaders bring unique perspectives to questions of civil-military relations arising from quite different cultures and expectations. These differences are no less apparent in decisions of how best to educate officers both to win wars and to advise their civilian counterparts on the best way to do so. Probably the key element in molding and maintaining professionalism in all branches of the armed forces—including intelligence, as Chapter 6 reminds us—is education and training. Besides exploring many of the key issues in professional military education (PME) and training, Guttieri also highlights the importance of civilian control in this area. Although civilian control may predominate in the United States, in most other countries PME remains chiefly the responsibility of the military itself.

We undertook this book project to address what we consider to be a critical gap in the literature on how consolidating democratic regimes can use institutions to establish civilian control over and manage relations with their militaries so that roles and missions can be implemented effectively. The contributors have found in the course of a decade of research and teaching with the Center for Civil-Military Relations, both in the United States and mainly abroad, that the available literature on civil-military relations is currently out of touch with the reality we have witnessed in the third-wave democracies. It is our intention not only that readers should better understand how to think about democratic civil-military relations but also that this volume will inspire scholars and practitioners alike to consider what the next steps should be in ensuring democratic consolidation.

Notes

1. Adam Przeworski, *Democracy and the Market: Political and Economic Reforms in Eastern Europe and Latin America* (New York: Cambridge University Press, 1991), 29.

2. Philippe Schmitter, "The Consolidation of Political Democracies: Processes, Rhythms, Sequences, and Types," in *Transitions to Democracy*, ed. Geoffrey Pridham (Aldershot: Dartmouth, 1995), 562, and illustrated in figures 1 and 3.

3. Juan J. Linz and Alfred Stepan, *Problems of Democratic Transition and Consolidation: Southern Europe, South America, and Post-Communist Europe* (Baltimore: Johns Hopkins University Press, 1996).

4. See for instance Felipe Aguero, *Soldiers, Civilians, and Democracy: Post-Franco Spain in Comparative Perspective* (Baltimore: Johns Hopkins University Press, 1995); Anita Isaacs, *Military Rule and Transition in Ecuador, 1972–92* (Pittsburgh: University of Pittsburgh Press, 1993); David Pion-Berlin, *Through Corridors of Power: Institutions and Civil-Military Relations in Argentina* (University Park: Pennsylvania State University Press, 1997); and Alfred Stepan, *Rethinking Military Politics: Brazil and the Southern Cone* (Princeton, NJ: Princeton University Press, 1988).

5. Felix Gilbert, ed., *The Historical Essays of Otto Hintze* (New York: Oxford University Press, 1975), 181.

6. Schmitter, "The Consolidation of Political Democracies," 536.

7. For an excellent review of the literature and the issues, see Doh Chull Shin, "On the Third Wave of Democratization: A Synthesis and Evaluation of Recent Theory and Research," *World Politics* (October 1994): 135–170. For a

review of some competing explanations for democratic transitions, see Samuel P. Huntington, *The Third Wave: Democratization in the Late Twentieth Century* (Norman: University of Oklahoma Press, 1991), chapter 2.

8. For two excellent reviews, see Peter D. Feaver, "The Civil-Military Problematique: Huntington, Janowitz, and the Question of Civilian Control," *Armed Forces and Society* 23, no. 2 (1996): 149–177; and Eliot A. Cohen, *Supreme Command: Soldiers, Statesmen, and Leadership in Wartime* (New York: Free Press, 2002), 225–248.

9. Michael J. Hogan, *A Cross of Iron: Harry S. Truman and the Origins of the National Security State, 1945–1954* (New York: Cambridge University Press, 1998); James R. Locher III, *Victory on the Potomac: The Goldwater-Nichols Act Unifies the Pentagon* (College Station: Texas A&M University Press, 2002); and Hew Strachan, *The Politics of the British Army* (New York: Oxford University Press, 1997). See also Charles C. Moskos, David R. Sega, and John Allen Williams, eds., *The Postmodern Military: Armed Forces after the Cold War* (New York: Oxford University Press, 2000).

10. Felipe Aguero concurs, "The basic assumption is that the central issues in civil-military relations in transition periods of the kind studied here are issues of power." Felipe Aguero, *Soldiers, Civilians, and Democracy*, 11. We would argue, however, that this is true not just in transition periods but always.

11. For the most accessible literature by Weber on these issues, see H. H. Gerth and C. Wright Mills, *From Max Weber: Essays in Sociology* (New York: Oxford University Press, 1958). See esp. the essay "Politics as a Vocation."

12. Peter A. Hall and Rosemary C. R. Taylor, "Political Science and the Three New Institutionalisms," *Political Studies* 44 (1996): 936. See also Sven Steinmo, Kathleen Thelen, and Frank Longstreth, eds., *Structuring Politics: Historical Institutionalism in Comparative Analysis* (New York: Cambridge University Press, 1992); and W. Richard Scott, *Institutions and Organizations* (Thousand Oaks, CA: Sage Publications, 1995).

13. Hall and Taylor, "Political Science," 938.

14. Our purpose is broader than David Pion-Berlin's in his excellent work on Latin America, in which he and his contributors review the state of theory on civil-military relations in Latin America, test current prominent theories in comparative politics, and illustrate their findings with empirical data. See David Pion-Berlin, ed., *Civil-Military Relations in Latin America: New Analytical Perspectives* (Chapel Hill: University of North Carolina Press, 2001).

15. Hall and Taylor, "Political Science," 954.

16. Ibid.

Part One Actors and Institutions

Chapter 1
Military Professionalism in a Democracy

THOMAS-DURELL YOUNG

DEMOCRATIC states, like other forms of states, struggle with the challenge of defending themselves against external aggression. The models of military organization that democracies have tried range from a loosely constituted citizen militia to a highly institutionalized standing army, with many variations in between. The explosion in technologies and the development and spread of nationalism have forced all democracies to confront the need for a professional military, as opposed to a reserve-based one. This trend toward all-volunteer forces in turn has often produced something like a modern soldier "caste." The professional officer throughout history has had the imposing task of becoming an expert in the "management of violence,"[1] a unique skill that distinguishes the military professions from their civilian counterparts. There are key requisites, however, that legitimate the use of force and violence by a soldier in a democracy: force and violence are employed only in a rational way, for a public purpose and with public consent.

The analysis in this chapter is based on the New Institutionalist framework and regards the military profession as an institution. This midlevel analysis, between grand theory and empiricism, seeks to suggest ways in which the twin goals of a professional military and civilian control of the military can be attained. The objective here is to define and discuss what constitutes the military profession in a democracy, with an eye to encouraging the implementation of the principles it presents. The chapter also identifies sources of civil-military tension—a given in any democracy—and describes how they can be mitigated. Finally, the chapter examines how democracies traditionally have sought to create practices and procedures that will ensure civilian control of the military.

Elements of Military as a Profession

Definitions vary as to what constitutes modern military professionalism. In its simplest form, the term "military profession" describes volunteers who choose to serve, as distinct from conscripted soldiers. A more expansive definition of the military profession includes normative orientations. For example, in the words of Anthony Forster, Timothy Edmunds, and Andrew Cottey, professional soldiers are those who

> accept that their role is to fulfil the demands of the civilian government of the state and are capable of undertaking military activities in an effective and efficient way, and whose organisation and internal structures reflect these assumptions.[2]

In his classic study, *The Soldier and the State*, Samuel P. Huntington argues that the "distinguishing characteristics of a profession as a special type of vocation are its expertise, responsibility, and corporateness."[3] The following section of this chapter is organized around these themes. Huntington's focus on the "vocation of officership" echoes Max Weber's notions of politics as vocation and bureaucracies as features of modern societies.[4]

Huntington argues that the emergence of the military profession since the nineteenth century makes possible the "achievement of objective civilian control" of the military. According to Huntington, that objective civilian control is attained by "militarizing the military, making them the tool of the state," and by "professionalizing the military, by rendering them politically sterile and neutral." Objective civilian control of the military, therefore, is intimately linked to military professionalization and is possible only in modern societies "in which the division of labor has been carried to the point where there emerges a distinct class of specialists in the management of violence."[5]

Huntington therefore does not view military professionalization and civilian control of the military as trade-offs. Instead, they are inextricably linked together—and actually reinforce each other—as features of modern societies and modern bureaucracies. Huntington warns, however, that it is very difficult, even for modern Western societies, to attain a high level of objective military control of the military.[6] In large measure, this difficulty results from the inevitable tensions between the cultures of politicians and military officers. The challenge for policymakers, therefore, is to structure institutions in such a way that those tensions are moderated, in order to achieve the goal of objective civilian control of the military.

Expertise

The best way to understand what constitutes military as a profession is to examine its principal elements as they apply in a democracy. The most obvious requirement for any professional is expertise. The exercise of effective command and control over complex modern military organizations requires not only tactical and operational proficiency in one's area of specialization but also mastery of bureaucratic and organizational skills. Military professionalism is the systematic creation of a class of people for whom war is a profession and who pursue general and subspecializations in the art and science of conflict. Although this definition applies throughout history, it has acquired greater meaning since the end of the eighteenth century, when the rise of nationalism made possible the drafting of mass conscript armies during the French Revolution and thus invalidated Louis XIV's claim that war was simply ultima ratio regum (the final argument of kings).

War had become a concern of "nations" that were contained in increasingly efficient modern states with effective military organizations. Rapid technological advances (e.g., railway, telegraph, repeating rifles, steam-driven warships), starting in the mid-nineteenth century, demanded much more exacting selection, training, education, and promotion procedures for military professionals. Being sufficiently well-bred became a far less relevant qualification for promising young officers than had been the case in the past, at least in those states with more forward-thinking leadership. Where political necessity did keep the military under aristocratic domination, as in Prussia (and later the German Empire), the general staff found a practical solution. The most intelligent, and proven, junior officers received rigorous education and training in the disciplined science of warfare, at the completion of which they became general staff officers. As chiefs of staff, young German officers provided inter alia, at least until the end of the empire, "adult" supervision to often "dodgy" aristocratic commanding generals. Their carefully cultivated scientific knowledge and expertise were likewise essential to establish, maintain, and execute vastly complex mobilization and deployment operations in the event of conflict.[7] This tradition of professional military education spread throughout the world in the late nineteenth century; currently it takes the form of staff and defense colleges with mandatory curricula that prepare officers to achieve high rank.

Essential Duties

The definition of essential duties is another indispensable element of military professionalism. The demands of empire forced ancient kingdoms and republics alike to create professional military organizations, instead of relying for either defense or conquest on traditional citizen militias or ad hoc formations. A fundamental change in the Roman Legions followed the Second Punic War, with the rising demand for highly trained (that is, professional) soldiers and especially officers who could execute maneuvers in an effective and disciplined manner on the battlefield.[8] This shift to a professional military constituted a major social, economic, and political change in Roman society.

It is even more difficult for modern democracies to base their national security upon a largely reserve or militia structure than it was for Rome. Officers in democratic militaries must be competent across a range of skills in force and formation management. Many of these skills have been transformed completely by new technologies. This is particularly true in democracies that aspire to deploy forces outside of national borders and participate in high-intensity warfare.[9]

The first area of competence for an officer is organization. The high speed of communications and operations means that "command" can now be expected to extend from national political leaders down to the lowest tactical units, thanks to the widespread use of microchip technology. High-speed communications allow the coordinated rapid movement of land, air, and sea assets, thereby complicating the exercise of effective command, particularly in coalition operations.[10] Only through extensive education, realistic training, and frequent exercises can officers today hope to succeed on a high-intensity modern battlefield.

Second, military professionalism increasingly dictates that officers at least be well aware of the latest technological advances in their respective specialties and services, even if they do not master the technology themselves.[11] The development of rapid target acquisition capabilities, precision-guided munitions, and diverse delivery systems, for example, makes the modern battlefield a death trap to any platform with a "signature" (i.e., an inherent characteristic that exposes the platform to enemy sensors). The more officers know about the dangers they face and the assets they control, the more likely they are to complete their mission and keep their soldiers alive.

A third essential area of competence is training to established tasks, conditions, and standards. A modern defense force cannot maneuver effectively, let alone maintain a static defense in a demanding combat environment, without systematic training to established tasks. These tasks are derived from the missions themselves, while commanders judge the conditions their forces are likely to face and train accordingly.

Standards objectively measure the success or failure of units and platforms to perform their tasks.[12] Here also, technological advances have placed a heavy burden on the officers and noncommissioned officers (NCOs) who must be capable of conducting and participating in such training.

Fourth, military leaders must be able to plan operations in the field. A professional officer must be able to carry out complicated but essential responsibilities that could include operational planning, effective use of intelligence, interpretation of doctrine, development of operational or mobilization plans, and creation of accurate logistic support plans, all of which must entail complex organizational relationships and operating arrangements.[13]

Finally, the professional officer must demonstrate the ability to command formations and lead forces—personally, if necessary.[14]

Responsibility

Although professional soldiers perform an essential service to the client, which is the state, their "management of violence" can be considered legitimate today only in the context of service to the democratically elected government. Thus, the military professional constitutes a sui generis "moral unit" and, as such, has a singular social responsibility to the state and civil society. Should an officer employ his or her skill of arms for personal benefit, then that officer is immediately transformed from society's protector into a criminal threat to social stability. The Roman Republic provides a chilling example of the use of the military for personal gain. At the end of the Third Punic War, several military leaders (for example, Gaius Marius and L. C. Sulla) launched bloody struggles to become *primus* in Rome. To achieve their ends these generals raised and maintained armies for the benefit of their personal rise to power, not for that of the Roman Republic. Thus, long before the Principate of Octavianus Augustus, normally associated with the end of the republic, the constitutional principles of democratic rule upon which the Roman Republic had been founded were fundamentally compromised.[15] As all professions have clients, the client of the military professional in the democratic state is the democratically elected government. This responsibility is formulated in today's world by swearing an oath of allegiance to the constitution or other basic institutions of these states.

Corporateness

Soldiers, by definition, constitute a class who live apart from general society. To be effective in battle, soldiers must learn to give their loyalty to their organization first and to put personal considerations aside for the good of the group with which they serve. The degree to which this ethic is manifested varies, but it exists even in long-standing democracies with impeccable histories of stable civil-military relations. The soldier's sense of isolation from society must be mitigated in a democracy, but not so as to compromise the military's morale or effectiveness. There are five steps that democracies have taken to ensure that their military stays integrated in society. Although they may be applied generally to all democracies, these steps are undertaken according to a particular society's norms if they are to succeed.

The first step is to establish requirements for entry, particularly for the officer corps. High intellectual capabilities and demonstrable adherence to the moral standards of the society must be preconditions to selection for commissioning.[16] Second is the military education system. Prospective military leaders need to undergo a rigorous educational program that comprises, besides the science of modern warfare and the history of the art of war, liberal arts that will enable officers to develop a cosmopolitan appreciation for the broader society and world of which they are a part. A liberal education provides the added benefit of allowing the officer corps to claim "professional" status within their society and, therefore, to attain social advancement.[17]

Promotion standards are the third way a democracy nurtures loyalty to itself among military personnel. The criteria by which officers, non-commissioned officers, and other ranks are promoted must be based on objective standards, known to all, that are applied in a fair and unbiased manner. Nothing undermines morale and the willingness of high-quality personnel to remain in service faster than the appearance or even suspicion of favoritism. Notwithstanding its reputation for advancement based upon merit, the officer corps of the Imperial and Royal Army of the Austro-Hungarian Empire, for example, was made up of more Germans than Magyars or Slavs. This ethnic favoritism, by decreasing morale and stoking ethnic nationalism in the force, undermined the effectiveness of the army in the First World War.[18]

Fourth is the creation, education, and training of a professional military staff. The general staff in a democracy is a public, bureaucratized profession, an essential for a modern military to perform its duties.[19]

Finally, a democratic society must honor esprit de corps while preserving democratic values and respect for human rights within the military culture. The officer corps needs to cultivate the unique values, traditions, attitudes, and perspectives that are integral to the practice of the profession of arms.[20] History has shown time and again that such moral cohesion is essential for success on the battlefield.[21]

Sources of Tension in Civil-Military Relations

The fundamentally different cultural norms and conditions that exist between political leaders and military officers will always be a source of tension in a democracy. Politicians thrive on ambiguity and uncertainty and achieve success when they are able to master such conditions.[22] Military officers, by contrast, seek clarity of mission and certainty of conditions. In war, the lack of either can result in bad decisions with devastating consequences.[23]

The military's focus on equipping and training to win wars inevitably will conflict with the need for elected officials to serve the wider policies of the state. Civil-military harmony requires political institutions that are capable of formulating a rational foreign policy and maintaining a military establishment adequate to support state policy.

Tension between the soldier and the politician generally arises from the former's dissatisfaction or disappointment with political leadership. Most typically, senior military officials may conclude that they have been given insufficient resources (i.e., limited defense spending) to meet the national security requirements established by the state. Soldiers in turn may fear that they will be unable to do their job or carry out their assigned missions properly.

There are also important differences between the political and military strategic cultures within a democracy.[24] Officers may come to the conclusion that governing elites are antimilitarist and that their ideology is alien to the military's professional ethos of political neutrality.[25] As a result, official efforts to keep the military loyal to what may be perceived to be a hostile regime could undermine the military's efficiency and sense of corporateness, as well as its ability to serve its political masters with professional military advice.[26]

Another frequent source of tension relates to the issue of responsibility. If they come to the conclusion that public morals are decaying or political culture is corrupt, military leaders may determine that they possess one of the few moral institutions in society and, as a result, are compelled to rescue society from corrupt or incompetent government officials through a coup d'état. Finally, tension between the military and political authorities can stem from a failure of military corporateness. The institution of the military can break down when personnel become divided over policy (such as the French Army over the war in Algeria), resources (the British armed services during the interwar period, for instance), or strategies (as with the U.S. Army over the conduct of the war in Vietnam).[27] In some countries, these differences can also take the form of social, ethnic, or tribal divisions.

Traditional Mechanisms of Civilian Control

In a democracy, the military's activities and missions are established, controlled, and limited by political authorities through mechanisms such as a constitution, laws, policies, and regulations. The actual "control" of the military in peacetime and war can entail a variety of institutional techniques and practices, each of which carries its own particular advantages and disadvantages. The seven most common and effective means that polities use to restrain the power of the military professional are important to understand in detail. As will become clear, none of these seven in itself is sufficient, and each may generate at best a counter limitation or at worst a dilemma.

Limits on the Mission

Politicians will seek to limit the military's mission as a means to ensure that the military refrains from activities that might bring it into conflict with the civilian authorities. Stationing armed forces in distant locations and burdening personnel with nonmilitary (that is, non-combat-oriented) missions can also act to keep them from becoming too involved in domestic political and social affairs. For instance, the U.S. Army was established largely to pacify the frontier and to undertake civil engineering projects.[28] As such, it rarely had garrisons in or near large metropolitan areas—a tradition that continues to this day. The advantages of clearly defined, benign tasks are to keep the military from the temptation to encroach on, or intervene in, the affairs of state. Moreover, such missions work to enhance the state's development (the U.S. Army Corps of Engineers).[29]

There are, however, serious disadvantages to such policies. Armed forces that concentrate on largely noncombat, internal security missions are unlikely to be competent at wartime tasks. They will have too many ongoing domestic operations to be able to "train to fight" in a conflict against a professionally trained and well-armed adversary (e.g., the Argentine Army in the Falkland Islands War).[30] From the perspective of civil-military relations, it is unclear in the context of limited missions where "technical expertise" ends and "professionalism" of the armed forces begins. Indeed, this is exactly what happened in the U.S. Army as a spirit of corporateness took over in the late nineteenth and early twentieth centuries with the expansion of the military's missions.[31]

Limits on the Size

Another way to keep control of the military is to limit its size. Britain, because of its long history of internal conflicts between monarchs and nobles, traditionally has been suspicious of a standing army and has maintained only a small force, usually deployed or stationed abroad. Even today the British-dominated NATO Rapid Reaction Corps headquarters and the First UK Armoured Division remain stationed in Germany, fifteen years after the end of the cold war.[32] The advantages of this method are obvious. Size matters, and fewer trained soldiers under arms mean less internal danger to a society. Such a policy also allows a country to direct more of its resources to other needs. The disadvantages, unfortunately, are equally obvious. Armed forces, depending upon their envisaged missions, must attain a certain size in order to achieve a "critical mass," below which they cannot develop and maintain certain key capabilities. For example, armies find it very difficult to develop the expertise necessary to maneuver larger formations (divisions and corps) on the battlefield unless they have a body of trained and experienced commanders and staff officers who have worked extensively together during peacetime in field training and command post exercises.[33] History is replete with examples of armies that were forced to learn how to maneuver on the battlefield and paid for their education in blood.[34]

Furthermore, a small military that finds itself unable to meet an impending threat may be seduced into supporting domestic opposition political leaders who promise it larger budgets (as happened in the German Reichswehr in the interwar period).[35]

Limits on the Budget

As suggested in the discussion above, and as will be dealt with in comparative details in Chapter 7 on the legislature, a third method of control is through access to funding. A government may exercise the "power of the purse" by limiting defense budgets and dictating the ways in which appropriated money can be spent by the military. In the United States, committees in both houses of Congress keep tight control over the four defense budgets (one for each of the three military departments and one for defense agencies) and determine how the military and the Department of Defense expend resources.[36] In some former Communist countries in Central and Eastern Europe, the beginnings of effective civilian control over the military came only after a ministry of defense was established, which allowed civil authorities to scrutinize how funds were being spent on and by the military. This topic is dealt with in greater detail in Chapter 3.

A system of strict control over defense expenditures has the advantage of keeping the military under close observation. The prospect of higher spending on defense also can be used as a quid pro quo for "good behavior." Equally important, the appropriation and execution of the defense budget are a useful means by which a congress or parliament can maintain regular communications with the military general staff. Unfortunately, many countries do not possess a civilian cadre of experts in their legislatures or ministries of defense who are capable of making informed decisions about defense expenditures. This official ignorance can stoke resentment among officers over what they consider inept civilian oversight and control, thereby polarizing and politicizing civil-military relations.

Constitutional and Legal Limitations

A democracy may circumscribe the military's power through various constitutional and legal instruments. There are no inherent or systematic advantages or disadvantages to the employment of such mechanisms. Different models simply reflect a democratic society's fundamental characteristics. In the United States, the armed forces are controlled through the constitutional separation of powers in the federal government. Military oversight is divided between the president as commander in chief and Congress, which appropriates money and approves the commissions and promotions of officers. In the European "continental" system, each government's cabinet exercises control over the military in a centralized fashion. No system of legal control over the military, however, is foolproof. In the United States, the military departments and elements of the Department of Defense (such as the Joint Staff) play Congress off against the president to get what they want, or they appeal directly to supporters in the U.S. electorate.

Since the end of World War II, European ministries of defense, and particularly general staffs, have seen their previous positions of influence and prestige diminished through limited budgets and closer governmental oversight.[37] The United Kingdom's armed forces, for example, have tended to be active politically, despite a long tradition of effective control by civilian authorities.[38] Senior officers have even been known to "revolt" against impending defense cuts. The military of France has been subjected to varying degrees of legal and constitutional control, with equally varying degrees of success, ever since the French Revolution of 1789. The Fifth Republic, established by General Charles de Gaulle in 1958, developed effective controls over the military in answer to a series of crises in civil-military relations, such as the army revolt in Algeria in 1961. Today the French armed forces and the Ministry of Defense are almost completely subordinated to the Ministry of Foreign Affairs and the president. (The question of whether it is actually the president or the prime minister who oversees and tasks the French military, however, was raised again by the 1985 sinking of the Greenpeace vessel *Rainbow Warrior* by French special agents while it was moored in New Zealand waters. A political fiasco ensued, and the episode culminated in an $8 million decision against the French government.)[39]

Culture of Professionalism

The fifth type of control is the professionalism imposed by military culture itself. Samuel Huntington, in *The Soldier and the State*, argued that military professionalism will act to constrain soldiers from transgressing democratic norms. If a democracy's armed services have a strong sense of mission and ethics, they will develop an organizational culture based on self-restraint and respect for civilian authority and law, what Huntington calls "objective control."[40] The advantage of these internal controls lies chiefly with placing responsibility for self-restraint directly on officers. In some young democracies, particularly those with a long history of political corruption and a weak civil society, it may be easier to inculcate discipline in the military than to depend on politicians to behave responsibly. Strongly moralistic military officers, when faced with what they perceive to be a decadent polity, however, may conclude out of a sense of "professionalism" that the integrity of their institution, or even the salvation of the nation, requires military intervention in the political arena. The real challenge in most new democracies is precisely how to establish the institutions, including that of the military as a profession, that will lead to the culture that Huntington places at the center of his analysis.

Societal Norms

The social and political constraints that the society imposes on a military organization are the sixth way a democracy maintains control over that organization. While democracies must recognize the legitimacy of the military as a necessary tool of statehood, the prestige of the military in turn rests upon general societal approval. Armed forces based on recruitment of volunteers (professionals) and those manned by conscripts nurture very different kinds of ethos, each of which has advantages and disadvantages for democratic control. The professional military in a democracy should be raised to reflect the social, ethnic, and geographical composition of society. Ideally, democracies will develop policies that encourage citizens of all backgrounds to consider serving for a period or making a career in the military. To encourage such inclusive policies, the military must inculcate in its members the values of the larger society.[41]

Conscription, as shown in Chapter 8, is generally disdained by the professional military because an army of draftees requires large amounts of resources for the amount of military capability that it produces. Militaries based on conscription often function largely as training institutions, which in some cases—western Europe, for example—are maintained at the expense of modernization.[42] Conscription can act to limit military independence, however, because the citizen-soldier gives his or her primary loyalty to the state rather than the institution of the military. In the 1990s the Federal Republic of Germany, for example, found that the political need to maintain the Staatsbürger in Uniform (citizen in uniform) outweighed the need for a professional military, let alone modern power-projection capabilities.[43]

A Free Press

Finally, freedom of the press in a democratic society is a critical tool that citizens and their representatives use to keep a grip on the reins of military power. Access by journalists to the military and its activities (within the legitimate requirements of operational security) enables public oversight, encourages public debate over reform, and ensures that the military is accountable to society at large rather than a few interested elites. In effect, the press ideally can play an important role in restraining military power by seeing that its soldiers are not allowed to retreat into a physical or spiritual ghetto of institutional attitudes and practices but, rather, conform to mainstream values.

Conclusion

This chapter has argued that an effective professional military and civilian control of the military are not incompatible but actually mutually reinforcing. To exert control, however, civilians must gain expertise on issues related to the military. Civilians must also provide the means necessary to maintain an effective military able to fulfill the roles and missions they assign to these forces.

For newer democracies emerging from authoritarianism or state socialism, the establishment of professional armed forces will improve military efficiency and effectiveness, as well as create better-educated and -socialized soldiers. None of the techniques or approaches suggested in this chapter alone will guarantee civilian control in all instances. Politicians and soldiers alike must choose instruments acceptable to the society they serve, which will ensure the military's obedience to political authority and loyalty to the state according to the state's legal foundation. This requires the military to cultivate high standards of professionalism and respect for civilian authority—particularly when civilians appear to be "wrong." To govern in a democracy, politicians need the flexibility sometimes to be ambiguous, especially with regard to foreign policy. The members of the armed forces must accept that their institution exists to serve the state, not its own parochial interests. Likewise, politicians must respect the military's indispensable contribution to the state and become skilled at managing the soldier's need for certainty in an uncertain world. Political leaders can take steps in this direction by ensuring that the missions of the military are compatible with national interests, that national policy enjoys popular support, and that the missions of the armed forces are within their technological and operational capabilities. History has shown that these will be challenging goals in any democracy.

Notes

1. A term first coined by Harold Lasswell and used extensively by Samuel P. Huntington in *The Soldier and the State: The Theory and Politics of*

Civil-Military Relations (Cambridge, MA, and London: Belknap Press of Harvard University Press, 1957); see particularly 11–12.

2. Anthony Forster, Timothy Edmunds, and Andrew Cottey, "Introduction: The Professionalisation of Armed Forces in Central and Eastern Europe," in Forster, Edmunds, and Cottey, eds., *The Challenge of Military Reform in Central and Eastern Europe: Building Professional Armed Forces* (Basingstoke: Palgrave, 2002), 6.

3. Huntington, *The Soldier and the State*, 8.

4. Ibid., 11.

5. Ibid., 83–85.

6. Ibid., 85.

7. See Walter Goerlitz, *History of the German General Staff, 1657–1945* (New York: Frederick A. Praeger, 1963). For its particular application to the Bundeswehr, see Christian O. Millotat, *Understanding the Prussian-German General Staff System* (Carlisle Barracks, PA.: Strategic Studies Institute, 1992).

8. See Hans Delbrück, *Warfare in Antiquity*, vol. 1 of *History of the Art of War*, trans. Walter J. Renfroe Jr. (Lincoln: University of Nebraska Press, 1975), 412–413.

9. Morris Janowitz, *The Professional Soldier: A Social and Political Portrait* (New York: Free Press, 1960), 21–37.

10. See Jon Whitford and Thomas-Durell Young, "Command Authorities and Multinationality in NATO: The Response of the Central Region Armies," in Thomas-Durell Young, ed., *Command in NATO after the Cold War: Alliance, National, and Multinational Considerations* (Carlisle Barracks, PA: Strategic Studies Institute, 1996), 53–78.

11. See Lawrence Freedman, "The Revolution in Strategic Affairs" (Adelphi Paper 318, Oxford University Press for the International Institute for Strategic Studies, London, 1998).

12. In the U.S. Army, tasks, conditions, and standards are contained in individual unit mission-training plans.

13. See Cathy Downes, "Leadership Challenges of RMA Technologies, and Their Familiar and New Battlespaces" (paper presented at the annual conference of the Australian Defence College, Canberra, May 10, 2001); and "Ethos-Directed Armed Forces for the 21st Century" (paper presented to General Dennis Riemer, Chief of Staff, U.S. Army, Washington, DC, November 1997).

14. See Martin Van Creveld, *Command in War* (Cambridge, MA: Harvard University Press, 1985).

15. See A. H. Beesley, *The Gracchi, Marius, and Sulla* (New York: Scribner's, 1913); and Arthur Keaveney, *Sulla, the Last Republican* (Dover, NH: Croom Helm, 1982).

16. See Cathy Downes, *Special Trust and Confidence: The Making of an Officer* (London: Frank Cass, 1991).

17. See Martin Edmonds, *Armed Forces and Society* (Leicester, UK: Leicester University Press, 1988).

18. Johann C. Allmayer-Beck and Erich Lessing, *Die K. u. K. Armee, 1848–1914* (Vienna: Prisma Verlag, 1974). For a fascinating novel set in the prewar years of the "K. u. K. Armee," see *The Panther's Feast*, by Robert Brown Asprey (New York: Putnam's Sons, 1959), and its film version, *Oberst Redl* (1985). Interestingly, one ethnic minority, Italians, did disproportionately well in "service to the emperor," despite numerous wars and almost continuous tensions between the Austro-Hungarian empire and the Kingdom of Italy. See Lawrence Sondhaus, *In the Service of the Emperor: Italians in the Austrian Armed Forces, 1814–1918* (Boulder, CO: East European Monographs; distributed by Columbia University Press, 1990).

19. James Donald Hittle, *The Military Staff: Its History and Development* (Harrisburg, PA: Military Service Division, Stackpole Co., 1961).

20. For example, see Donald Abenheim, *Reforging the Iron Cross: The Search for Tradition in the German Armed Forces* (Princeton, NJ: Princeton University Press, 1988).

21. See Correlli Barnett, *Engage the Enemy More Closely: The Royal Navy in the Second World War* (New York: W. W. Norton and Co., 1991).

22. See Douglas L. Bland, *Chiefs of Defence: Government and the Unified Command of the Canadian Armed Forces* (Toronto: Canadian Institute of Strategic Studies, 1995), 15–16.

23. For a discussion of the differences between the norms and requirements of politicians and those of generals, see Correlli Barnett, *The Sword Barriers: Supreme Command in the First World War* (Bloomington: Indiana University Press, 1975); Bob Woodward, *The Commanders* (New York: Simon and Schuster, 1991); and Michael R. Gordon and General Bernard E. Trainor, *The Generals' War: The Inside Story of the Conflict in the Gulf* (Boston: Little, Brown, 1995).

24. See Alastair I. Johnston, *Cultural Realism: Strategic Culture and Grand Strategy in Chinese History* (Princeton, NJ: Princeton University Press, 1995); and Elizabeth Kier, *Imagining War: French and British Military Doctrine between the Wars* (Princeton, NJ: Princeton University Press, 1997).

25. See Douglas Bland, "A Unified Theory of Civil-Military Relations," *Armed Forces and Society* 26, no. 1 (1999): 21.

26. Bland, *Chiefs of Defence*, 18–24; particularly 20 and 24, on the situation in Canada during the Trudeau years.

27. For more on each of these examples, see Alexander Harrison, *Challenging De Gaulle: The OAS and the Counterrevolution in Algeria, 1954–1962* (New York: Praeger, 1989); R. P. Shay, *British Rearmament in the 1930s: Politics and Profits* (Princeton, NJ: Princeton University Press, 1977); and David Halberstam, *The Best and the Brightest* (New York: Random House, 1972).

28. Russell F. Weigley, *History of the United States Army* (New York: Macmillan, 1967), 105–106.

29. See *The History of the U.S. Army Corps of Engineers* (Alexandria, VA: Office of History, Headquarters, U.S. Army Corps of Engineers, 1998).

30. See Max Hastings and Simon Jenkins, *The Battle for the Falklands* (New York: W. W. Norton and Co., 1983); and Lawrence Freedman and Virginia Gamba-Stonehouse, *Signals of War: The Falkland Islands Conflict of 1982* (Princeton, NJ: Princeton University Press, 1991), 357–412.

31. Weigley, *History*, 313–341.

32. For details on the ACE Rapid Reaction Corps and some of the political fallout from its presence in Germany, see Thomas-Durell Young, *Multinational Land Formations and NATO: Reforming Practices and Structures* (Carlisle Barracks, PA: Strategic Studies Institute, 1997), 29–31, 49–50.

33. For the NATO example, see Thomas-Durell Young, "Multinational Land Forces and the NATO Force Structure Review," *Royal United Services Institute Journal* 145, no. 4 (2000): 45–52.

34. For a study on the role and place of the "corps" in the future of the U.S. Army, see D. Robert Worley, *W(h)ither Corps?* (Carlisle Barracks, PA: Strategic Studies Institute, 2001).

35. See F. L. Carsten, *The Reichswehr and Politics, 1918–1933* (Berkeley and Los Angeles: University of California Press, 1966).

36. To see how the system works under the Quadrennial Defense Review, see George Wilson, *This War Really Matters: Inside the Fight for Defense Dollars* (Washington, DC: Congressional Quarterly Press, 2002).

37. Catherine McArdle Kelleher, "Defense Organization in Germany: A Twice Told Tale," in Robert J. Art, Vincent Davis, and Samuel P. Huntington, eds., *Reorganizing America's Defense: Leadership in War and Peace* (Washington, DC: Pergamon Brassey's International Defense Publishers, 1985).

38. See Hew Strachan, *The Politics of the British Army* (Oxford: Oxford University Press, 1997). For a novelistic but accurate view, see Patrick O'Brian's Jack Aubrey novels, particularly *The Yellow Admiral* (New York: W. W. Norton and Co., 1996).

39. For a discussion of civil-military relationships in France, see Michael M. Harrison, *The Reluctant Ally: France and Atlantic Security* (Baltimore: Johns Hopkins University Press, 1981), 49–71.

40. Huntington, *The Soldier and the State*, particularly 80–97.

41. For the Australian Defence Force's experience, see Anthony Bergin, R. Hall, R. Jones, and I. McAllister, "The Ethnic Composition of the Australian Defence Force: Management, Attitudes, and Strategies" (Working Paper 11, Australian Defence Studies Centre, Australian Defence Force Academy, Canberra, 1993).

42. See David C. Gompert, Richard L. Kugler, and Martin C. Libicki, *Mind the Gap: Promoting a Transatlantic Revolution in Military Affairs* (Washington, DC: National Defense University Press, 1999).

43. The inability of successive German governments to abolish conscription in order to free resources for crisis reaction capabilities began shortly after unification and continues to this day. See Thomas-Durell Young, "Defense Planning and the Bundeswehr's New Search for Legitimacy," in *Force, Statecraft, and German Unity: The Struggle to Adapt Institutions and Practices* (Carlisle Barracks, PA.: Strategic Studies Institute, 1996), 49–70; and Martin Agüera, "Ambitious Goals, Weak Means? Germany's Project 'Future Bundeswehr' Is Facing Many Hurdles," *Defense Analysis* 17, no. 3 (2001): 289–306.

Chapter 2
Legislatures and National Defense: Global Comparisons

JEANNE KINNEY GIRALDO

DEMOCRATICALLY elected representatives in a country's legislature have an important role to play in controlling the military; formulating defense legislation, policy, and budgets; and monitoring their implementation (i.e., oversight). Although there is widespread agreement on this point, there is little consensus on what exactly the legislature's role should be. How to balance the legislature's and executive's responsibilities in policy formulation and oversight is a central question for every democracy and is resolved differently from country to country. This chapter evaluates the factors that shape the legislature's participation and its impact on civilian control and defense policy outcomes.

Little is known about the role that legislatures play in the defense sector outside of the United States, which in many ways is a deviant case. Instead, much of the existing work on "parliamentary control of the armed forces" is normative and prescriptive, designed to answer the questions of actors in new democracies about why the legislature should play a role in the defense sector and how it might play a role.[1] As such, that work focuses on the possible contributions the legislatures might make to the policy process, as well as the wide range of constitutional powers the legislature might conceivably employ to make a contribution. The existing literature is more ambiguous about the role the legislature should play, although there is agreement that, whatever its role, the legislature should exercise it in an informed and expert manner. Accordingly, this chapter considers the institutions at the heart of legislative involvement in the defense sector in detail: the defense committee and the institutional mechanisms and resources at its disposal that allow members to cultivate the information and expertise necessary to make responsible decisions. The following five sections of the chapter review these widely discussed issues of why the legislature should play a role, how it might play a role, what role it should play, and the institutions and resources necessary to play an informed role.

The second half of the chapter, in contrast, enters into largely uncharted territory in an effort to describe the role that legislatures in consolidating democracies actually play in the defense sector, to explain the factors that account for differences in the legislature's role, and to assess the impact that variations in the legislature's role have on civilian control of the military and defense policy outcomes. Although most experts rightly lament legislators' lack of interest and expertise in defense issues as an obstacle to legislative involvement, legislatures in many consolidating democracies nevertheless have played an important role in shaping defense legislation. This lack of interest and expertise can be explained by differences in the willingness and ability of legislatures to engage in the activities with which they are tasked. Most legislatures tend to be more willing and able to formulate laws than to oversee policy; they are least likely to possess the resources or incentives to create institutionalized mechanisms for carrying out these activities. The chapter then draws on the broader literature concerning legislatures to shed light on the extent to which institutional factors like presidentialism, parliamentarism, electoral rules, and the nature of the party system affect the incentives for the legislature to engage in policymaking. Finally, the chapter shows that the literature says little about the impact of legislative involvement in the defense sector on civilian control of the military and effective democratic governance, and it provides some guidelines for evaluating the relationship among these factors.

Possible Contributions of the Legislature to Effective Democratic Governance of the Defense Sector

Scholars argue that the participation of the legislature in the defense realm (as in other issue areas) enhances the accountability, quality, transparency, and legitimacy of the resulting policies in both established and consolidating democracies.[2] There are several reasons for this effect. First, democratic accountability is strengthened when policymaking receives input from all democratically elected officials, not just those in the executive branch. The needs of society and the military are more likely to be balanced when representatives from all segments of society are consulted in the policy process. Legislative debates on defense issues can help contribute to the growth of an informed public that will be able to participate constructively in future policy discussions. Second, although consultations with legislators may be more time-consuming than a policy process dominated by the executive, the end result is usually better (and longer-lasting) policy. The policies produced tend to be better because the interested parties in both the executive and the military are forced to defend their positions publicly. Legislative oversight can determine whether laws are being effectively implemented and whether they do in fact work in the way they were intended. Lawmakers can thus identify policy failures within a reasonable time (at least theoretically) and change laws accordingly. The public nature of legislative oversight—the investigation of mistakes and wrongdoing—can help deter the executive and the military from shirking their duties.

Third, open consultation on important issues also helps develop a national consensus on the direction that policy should take and decreases the chances that defense policies will suffer serious modifications with a change in government. Policy stability is particularly important since key aspects of defense, such as procurement decisions or the establishment of a credible deterrent posture, can be carried out effectively only over the long term. Fourth, transparency within this process of debate and decision making legitimizes both the armed forces and the defense policy, thus contributing significantly to policy stability. Finally, legislatures may act as a check on executive misuse of the military.

Possible Powers of the Legislature in the Defense Sector

A wide array of powers is potentially available to the legislature that would help it exercise its role in the defense sector. These can be grouped into two categories: general powers that affect the legislature's ability to make and oversee laws in all policy areas; and powers specifically delineating the legislature's responsibility on defense-related issues (e.g., procurement, deployment of troops). Initial studies of the extent to which legislatures in established and consolidating democracies possess these various powers reveal a great deal of variation from country to country, although much more work remains to be done in both describing and explaining the variation.

Powers to Make and Oversee Budgets, Decisions, Laws, and Policies

The legislature can act at two key stages of the policy process: during the formulation of budgets, decisions, laws, and policies, and in the oversight of their implementation. The legislature's ability to participate in the formulation stage is shaped by formal powers that govern the legislature's right to initiate legislation, amend legislation proposed by the executive, and make changes to the budget. The writing of defense-related legislation tends to be a fairly episodic task, potentially reducing the significance of this stage of the policy process for regular legislative participation in the defense realm. The passage of the budget is an annual event, however, and, as such, introduces a measure of regularity to the consideration of defense issues. (How meaningful this participation is will depend upon the special rules governing the budget process—the kinds of changes the legislature is allowed to make, the amount of time permitted for review of the budget, and the level of detail provided in the defense budget.)[3] Also, in some countries the legislature may be called on to participate in and approve policy decisions that do not require new pieces of legislation—for example, the purchase of weapons or the issuance of a national defense strategy. The legislature's influence over policy at this stage is more direct than at the formulation stage and potentially provides the opportunity for more involvement, particularly if the executive consults legislators during the drafting of bills and policy or if the amendment powers of the legislature are significant.

The term "oversight" refers to the legislature's ability to monitor the implementation of budgets, laws, and policy decisions passed during the formulation stage.[4] Oversight has two functions: first, to hold the government and the military accountable for their actions and, second, to see if laws are working the way they were intended. Legislatures monitor executive and military behavior in two main ways, through the use of what have been called "police patrols" and "fire alarms." The "police patrol" approach, as the name suggests, involves an active search for mistakes and wrongdoing and typically takes the form of defense committee hearings or written or oral questioning of government ministers. "Fire alarm" monitoring occurs when actors outside congress supply information to the legislature about executive and military behavior. Congress itself frequently is responsible for creating the fire alarm, most often through audits carried out by independent agencies and the reporting requirements written into legislation. In other instances, nongovernmental groups interested in a policy area, such as the news media or concerned citizens, raise the alarm about misguided policy or actions. An alerted legislature would then convene hearings or conduct inquiries into the issue. Both forms of oversight function primarily by using the legislature's powers (which vary from country to country) to summon ministers, public servants, military officials, and civilian experts to testify and provide documents and to carry out investigations whose results would be made public. The impact on policy and behavior is largely indirect: the threat of exposure might deter unlawful behavior, and, more importantly, legislative scrutiny of executive or military actions might lead to corrective measures, such as new laws from the executive or the legislature to deal with the problems at hand.

Powers in Defense-Related Policy Areas

In addition to its general powers to make and oversee policy in all issue areas, the legislature may also have specifically delineated powers in a broad range of defense-related issue areas, such as procurement; the deployment of troops at home and abroad; general defense and security policy planning; personnel management; and the approval of international treaties related to defense. Scholars have made important advances in cataloging the *possible* powers that legislatures might possess in each of these issue areas. For example, with respect to defense personnel management, the legislature might have the following powers: to approve or reject the personnel plan; to fix ceilings for manpower; and to approve or reject the highest military appointments (such as the chief of staff). For procurement decisions, the executive may be obligated to inform the legislature of those decisions; the legislature may have the right to approve or reject contracts; and the legislature may have the right to review documentation that specifies the need for new equipment, the selection of a manufacturer, and offers for compensation and offset. These are just two items on a comprehensive checklist that has proven useful in nascent efforts to document the *actual* variation in defense-related legislative powers across countries, through surveys and comparative case studies.[5]

What Should the Role of the Legislature Be?

Scholars and policy practitioners generally agree that, by definition, democratic civilian control of the armed forces requires that democratically elected representatives in the legislature participate in some fashion in the defense realm. Since some form of power sharing between the executive and legislative branches is at the heart of democracy, no one branch of government may completely monopolize oversight of the military if civilian control is to be labeled "democratic."[6] The amount of power shared and the mechanisms for doing so vary greatly from country to country, depending on institutional arrangements and political traditions. In every democracy, however, the function of the legislature is to contribute to the accountability, legitimacy, and transparency of the policy process and, in so doing, to serve as a check on the power of the executive and contribute to the "effective democratic governance" of the defense sector.

Although there is a consensus that the legislature and the executive share responsibility for the defense sector, there is little agreement on how much of a role the legislature should play at different stages of the policy process and across the wide range of defense issues. Although this topic has not engendered much overt debate or disagreement among scholars, four general strands of thought are evident (often in the same work). I have labeled these arguments as "no best practices," "informed expert," "informed expert plus core powers," and "ideal type." It is important to understand these arguments because they not only shape the policy prescriptions offered to legislatures in consolidating democracies but also affect the research that has been done to assess the impact of different institutional arrangements on civilian control and effective governance of the defense sector.

"No Best Practices"

Aware of the diverse ways in which established democracies structure their legislative-executive relations, scholars argue that it is impossible to define any "best practices" for legislative oversight of the executive and the military. In different countries, legislatures contribute to democratic accountability, transparency, and legitimacy in different ways, depending on constitutional, political, and legal choices such as the nature of the government, the nature of the party system, and the rules that govern legislative procedures. Each country has the right to organize its legislative-executive relations as it sees fit—"no one model fits all."[7]

Although most studies of the legislature's role in the defense realm begin with the disclaimer that there are "no best practices," they all then proceed to describe a set of "best practices" to be followed if the legislature is to carry out an oversight role. These prescriptions focus on the institutional powers and resources that defense committees should cultivate (the three options sketched below).

"Informed Expert"

Whatever responsibilities the legislature might be assigned in a polity, scholars universally agree that they should be met in an informed and expert way, preferably by a legislative committee that focuses on defense-related issues. Although a dizzying array of institutional arrangements shapes the legislature's role, the institution that almost all legislatures have in common is an internal committee to address defense issues. The section below entitled "Cultivating Information and Expertise" summarizes the institutional and other factors that affect the ability of legislators to maximize their influence within the constraints of a given system of legislative-executive relations. This approach, as well as the following two, stresses that legislators must display the "political will" to put their knowledge (and powers) to work, but none of these approaches discusses the conditions under which political will might be maximized.

"Informed Expert Plus Core Powers"

The third approach argues that defense committees should not only be informed experts but also possess a minimum set of powers if they are to exercise effective parliamentary oversight. What these core powers should be varies by study, but most scholars include control over the budget, appointments of high-ranking military and political leaders, and the deployment of troops.[8] Unfortunately, the authors offer little justification for the inclusion of these powers (and the exclusion of others) on the legislature's "must have" list.

"Ideal Type"

In many ways, the ideal-type approach is a how-to guide for legislators interested in increasing their influence over the defense sector. It describes the conditions and mechanisms for creating "effective parliamentary oversight" (defined as legislative influence over outcomes): the legislature should possess the full range of potential powers cataloged in the previous section, the resources necessary to act as an informed and expert participant, and the political will to exercise its powers. (This might also be called the "informed expert plus full range of powers" approach.) Although this approach could be narrowly construed as a catalog of the legislature's options, without any advocacy of what part the legislature should play, it is often understood more expansively to describe an ideal type to which legislatures should aspire.[9] Parliamentary oversight is said to confer a number of benefits on defense policy such as accountability, transparency, and legitimacy, and oversight will be "effective" if the conditions and mechanisms listed above are in place. The implicit conclusion is that the maximum benefits of oversight will be obtained by maximizing the influence of the legislature.

In sum, scholars rightly stake out the normative position that a country is not a democracy if the legislature does not exert influence in the defense sector. Though seemingly uncontroversial, this claim is often challenged in practice by an executive branch and a military that are reluctant to cede any of their power to legislators whom they often criticize for their lack of knowledge about defense issues. Promoters of "parliamentary control of the armed forces" acknowledge lack of expertise as a central dilemma but note that the only appropriate conclusion to draw from this is that the legislature's access to information and expertise should be enhanced, rather than its role diminished. Legislators in new democracies seeking to enhance their influence with the defense sector would find many useful recommendations in the existing literature (the primary focus of which, after all, is offering policy prescriptions to this group). All three approaches sketched above stress the kinds of institutions that should be put in place for the legislature to have influence: a defense committee with institutionalized access to information and expertise (including legal powers to request information at hearings, and adequate legislative staff and research services). These institutions are discussed more fully in the two sections immediately following.

The literature on the legislature's role in the defense sector, given its prescriptive focus, is far less useful in accounting for the conditions under which legislatures are likely to possess the political will to play a role or to create the institutionalized oversight mechanisms so essential to this role. It also does little to assess the impact of variations in legislative power on civilian control of the military and effective democratic governance of the defense sector. Those issues are addressed at the end of the chapter.

Defense Committees: The Key Institutions

While constitutional, legal, and political factors account for variations in legislators' power from country to country, one commonality is the way that legislators have organized internally to handle their main tasks of shaping legislation and overseeing the defense budget and policy.[10] In every democracy, the legislature faces the same hurdle to participation in the policy process—an asymmetry of information and expertise relative to the executive branch. And in most democracies, legislatures have embraced similar institutional solutions to this challenge: the creation of legislative committees that specialize in selected policy areas whose jurisdiction typically matches that of the executive ministry they shadow, such as defense, economy, or education.[11]

Legislators themselves typically form these committees according to their needs and implement them through either legislation or congressional protocol (standing orders). In very rare cases, committees enjoy constitutional status. (In Germany, for example, the defense committee is the only legislative committee mandated by the constitution.)[12] Sometimes temporary committees might form to tackle pressing issues that require highly specialized knowledge or action (for example, a committee monitoring negotiations over a border dispute) or to investigate wrongdoing in high-profile cases.

Committees are able to examine legislative proposals more closely than the entire chamber, and their smaller size usually facilitates compromises on policy formulation among representatives of different parties or points of view. In theory, a seat on a committee should give legislators the incentive to develop expertise in a topic; the prestige of being a committee member and the control over policy that committees exert in many systems encourages their members to invest in the accumulation of specialized knowledge that will enable them to carry a debate. In many legislatures, the workload handled by the committees is so impressive that they have been called the "engine room" of the lawmaking body.

Usually, the defense committees themselves are also charged with oversight. In some cases, special subcommittees devote themselves solely to the job of oversight in a given policy area (this often is true in the United States Congress but is much less common in other countries). In others, a separately created committee will handle oversight of one dimension of policy, such as finance, across issue areas (public accounts committees in Westminster systems are an example of this arrangement). The latter system, however, cannot foster the kinds of expertise in a given policy area that are often essential to oversight.

The amount of influence that committees are able to exercise over the legislative process relative to the executive and to their colleagues on the floor will depend in large part upon the parliamentary procedures in place. It is generally believed that the greater the influence of the committee, the greater the overall legislative capacity of the chamber. Committees have the most influence over the legislative process (relative to the floor) when they can control which bills will be considered by the legislature (as in the U.S. Congress). By contrast, committees have the least influence when bills are not required even to pass through their doors but can be treated directly on the floor of the legislature. Most committees fall between the two extremes. They respond to a legislative agenda set by the executive alone or with party (or faction) leaders within the legislature, amend legislation drafted by the executive, and submit a report to the floor on the new law and proposed changes.[13] By discussing the merits of the policy and revealing the positions taken by different committee members, these reports provide guidance to the rest of the legislature on how to vote.

Cultivating Information and Expertise

One of the main challenges the legislature faces in exercising whatever jurisdiction it may have over policy formulation and oversight is to overcome the dominance of the executive branch, which has much greater access to expertise and information than lawmakers do. While the executive's near-monopoly control over information applies to most policy areas, in the defense arena the deck is even more stacked against legislative influence. Secrecy laws exacerbate the natural information asymmetry between the legislature, on the one hand, and the executive and the military on the other; the latter have only to invoke "national security" to withhold information and thus effectively deny the legislature jurisdiction over certain issues. This asymmetry of information and expertise charactcrizes even the U.S. case, where the combined expertise of the president's political advisers, the administrative staff of the Department of Defense, and the ranks of professional soldiers in the military allows the executive to dominate, even though Congress has far more constitutional powers than the president in the field of defense. The obstacles to a legislative role would seem to be far greater in countries transiting away from authoritarian regimes with a history of secrecy, military prerogatives, and executive dominance of the policy process.

Faced with this reality, legislatures must find ways of cultivating the knowledge base necessary to challenge executive domination of defense decision making, to participate effectively and credibly in constructing laws that will regulate the military's role, and to monitor implementation of those laws. Regardless of any formal rules governing the passage of legislation, lawmakers are more likely to be consulted by the executive at the law formulation stage, and their recommendations heeded at later stages, if they are knowledgeable of the issues involved. In short, committees must have access to sources of information and expertise, both inside and outside the government. In this enterprise, defense committees in consolidating democracies face many of the same opportunities and constraints as other committees: the same formal powers to hold hearings and solicit documents; the same ability to draw on independent auditing sources for information; and a relative paucity of legislative staff. In addition, defense committees face some special challenges that legislators in most other policy areas often do not: executive and military reliance on secrecy laws to withhold information from the legislature, and a relative lack of experts or interested groups on which to rely for information and advice.

Power to Solicit Information: Hearings and Documents

Many legislatures have provisions for the entire body to question ministers, either in person (the so-called Question Time in Westminster parliaments) or through petitions for information sent by individual representatives (or small groups) to the ministry. Most often this kind of questioning is used to score political points, by embarrassing the minister and/or demonstrating to constituents that their representative is active in their behalf. It is less effective as an oversight mechanism, for the questions can easily be dodged (in the case of Question Time) or ignored (in the case of written petitions, even when laws require a response).

Consequently, it is important that committees have formal powers both to request such information and to enforce the requests. These powers include the right to review government documents, summon witnesses (including ministers), and hold public hearings. Congressional invitations to testify are taken seriously in the United States, because Congress has the power to subpoena witnesses and to cut the budgets of noncomplying agencies. In most other countries, committees do not have the legal power to require the attendance of ministers, civil servants, or other witnesses. (One survey of European parliaments found that legislative committees had the power to compel testimony in only five of eighteen countries.)[14] The best they can do is try to embarrass the executive politically for noncompliance. Legislators also face challenges when they solicit independent, expert testimony on executive proposals from members of the military, who are by definition subordinate to the executive as commander in chief of the armed forces. This contrasts with other issue areas, where both career civil servants from the relevant ministry and particularly the affected interest groups (for example, farmers, teachers, and labor unions) often give testimony critical of the executive project. In the case of defense, the affected party is usually the military, and, in many cases, the military supplies much of the expertise within the ministry of defense.

Democracies must decide whether or not military personnel should be allowed to provide dissenting opinions to the legislature. In the United States prior to 1940, the military limited itself for the most part to echoing the president's position in testimony before Congress.[15] After World War II, however, Congress insisted that military leaders be free to present their views directly to the congressional committees, a change that was codified in the National Security Act as amended in 1949.[16] The armed forces of many other countries, however, represent only the government's view before the legislature. In Great Britain, independent testimony by members either of the ministry of defense or of the armed services carries with it an implicit requirement for resignation. Dissenting views by German officials or officers may be delivered informally but not in official testimony.[17] Complaints about Spain's military budget or other issues are lodged with the executive rather than the parliament.[18]

Auditing Agencies

Legislators often use reporting requirements and audits to keep track of defense policy—in other words, they create the "police patrols" to root out systematically malfeasance and policy mistakes. Legislation in the United States frequently requires an agency to inform a congressional committee before or after it makes a policy decision, or requires the Government Accountability Office (GAO, an arm of the Congress) to carry out audits and other evaluations.[19] Of the 5,704 GAO staff employed in 1979, 1,200 (20 percent) were tasked with defense auditing, and 230 of 983 reports submitted in fiscal year 1979 were on defense issues (23 percent of the total).[20] Like the Congressional Research Service, the GAO plays a proactive role in monitoring the implementation of legislation. Since 1974 it has been authorized to inform Congress of problems and concerns on its own initiative.[21] By contrast, the Comptroller and Auditor General of Great Britain is an officeholder of the Crown (the executive) and as such does not conduct inquiries at the request of the committees of the House of Commons. Unlike the GAO, it makes no recommendations or criticisms in its reports.[22] Between 1965 and 1978, it conducted only forty-seven inquiries on defense issues, an average of less than three and a half per year.[23] The inspectors general located within executive agencies may also be a useful source of information for the legislature. In addition, a number of consolidating democracies have followed Germany's example and created the office of ombudsman, designed to address the human rights concerns and other grievances of members of the military.

Legislative Staff and Research Services

Legislators have varying degrees of access to three main kinds of staff and research assistance: a general research staff that provides assistance to the entire chamber; a committee staff that should offer specialized policy expertise in relevant issues; and a personal staff that often primarily attends to petitions from constituents but may also provide policy advice. In some cases, party experts may constitute an additional source of staffing within the legislature. In the case of the U.S. House of Representatives, each of the nineteen standing committees is authorized to hire eighteen professional staff assistants and twelve clerical aides (plus one additional staffer allotted to each subcommittee).[24] The House Armed Services Committee employs around eighty-one staffers, and its Senate counterpart fifty-one; many of these have a military or civilian background in the Department of Defense.[25] In 1985, the 435-member House of Representatives employed 2,146 committee staff members, 7,528 personal staff, and 2,595 research staff (counting the Government Accountability Office, the Congressional Research Service, and the Congressional Budget Office).[26] Committee staffers often play a proactive role, negotiating and working to build coalitions, while the Congressional Research Service provides Congress with a list of subjects and policy areas that committees might analyze in depth. A host of think tanks and nongovernmental groups covering the ideological spectrum monitor government policy on a wide range of defense-related issues.

The nature and level of staffing of the U.S. Congress stands in stark contrast to that available to defense committees in other countries. To the extent that committee and research staffers elsewhere are trained professionals, they tend to be librarians or lawyers rather than experts in defense matters. Since gaining a recent increase in staff resources, the British defense committee can now rely upon four retired military staffers and two academic advisers. The committee staff for South Africa's entire National Assembly was increased in late 1995 from twenty-five to sixty, most of whom are professionals trained in law.[27] In Argentina, committee staffs usually number about half a dozen—one by assignment and the others provided by the party leadership.[28] South Korean committees also are typically advised by half a dozen policy specialists.[29] The South Korean legislature as a whole has a decent-sized reference staff, but it tends to be underutilized and bureaucratic.[30] A survey of defense committees in twenty-nine European countries revealed staff resources varying from one person (in Ireland, Iceland, and Norway) to ten (in Ukraine). Interestingly, in a number of cases, defense committees in newly democratizing Central and Eastern European legislatures were as equally well staffed as, or better staffed than, those in Western Europe.[31]

The German Bundestag perhaps comes closest to the United States in employing a serious-minded professional staff to assist in the legislative process, yet even there the numbers pale in comparison to Washington. In 1987, German research services staff numbered 234, or about one-tenth those in the United States. The 519 delegates to the Bundestag employed 2,200 personal staff members,[32] approximately 10 percent of whom were academics or legislative experts.[33] Committee staff levels are quite low, comparable to other Western European parliamentary democracies. In 1982, every standing committee in the Bundestag had one executive-rank civil service secretary, one senior assistant, and one or two clerical staff.[34] Unlike the U.S. Congress, most of the funding for Bundestag staff positions is channeled through party groups (Fraktionen) rather than the committees themselves, and these groups employ most of the policy experts. Fraktionen employees numbered 619 in 1987.[35]

In some cases, the limited funds that are available for congressional staff may not be used to increase levels of expertise within the legislature. For example, the party leadership may use committee staff positions to reward the party faithful, or members may prefer to spend their resources on personal staff, the majority of whom perform administrative or constituency services, rather than on professional staff who focus on policy development. Although personal staffers are a large majority in the U.S. Congress (outnumbering committee staff by a ratio of more than three to one), the proportion in developing countries is often much more skewed (in 1993, the ratio of personal to committee staff in the Argentine House was approximately twenty-six to one).[36]

A number of factors may account for the discrepancy in levels of staffing between the United States and other legislatures. In some cases, particularly in developing countries, the level of resources available to the legislature is simply much lower than in the United States. This cannot, however, explain the differences in staffing between countries at similar levels of development, such as the United States and Western European countries. Nor can it explain the similarities in staffing levels between countries with different levels of wealth, for example the parliaments of Western and Eastern Europe. Politics, not resource levels, best explain the institutionalization of legislative power through mechanisms like high staffing levels. The incentives and ability of legislators to institutionalize the legislature will be discussed in more depth in the section "Accounting for Variations in the Role of the Legislature," below.

Relative Weakness of Nongovernmental Organizations in the Defense Sector

Given the general lack of resources available to most legislatures, and the low likelihood of increased funding in countries facing lean economic times, many legislatures in developing countries find (at least in the short to medium run) that the most effective way to develop expertise may be to increase their reliance on think tanks outside of parliament. Unfortunately, there is a relative lack of civilian national security experts in many countries, especially in new democracies where defense topics have traditionally been the sole preserve of the military. In countries with strong parties, the think tanks may be party based, with funding coming from international party organizations, such as the Socialist International or the Christian Democrat International, rather than the central government. In other cases, independent think tanks, most often funded by international organizations, may play a central role in advising legislators. These international organizations provide general expertise on security matters and the framing of legislation but are typically less able to provide the country-specific information necessary for oversight.[37] (The defense budget would be an exception to this, as international organizations have devoted a great deal of energy to collecting and disseminating information on defense spending.)

Not all groups need to have expertise in national security matters to contribute to the legislature's ability to formulate and oversee policy. For example, nongovernmental organizations, such as mothers' and youth groups and human rights groups, may conduct fire alarm monitoring on government policy concerning issues such as human rights and conscription. Despite their efforts, however, fire alarm monitoring in defense-related areas tends to be less effective than in other policy areas, because the number of independent groups in civil society with the ability and interest to monitor defense tends to be fewer than the number of those involved in other policy areas.

Handling Secrets

Executive and bureaucratic reluctance to reveal information to the legislature is exacerbated in the defense arena, where policymakers and especially the military have been accustomed historically to operating behind a veil of secrecy and unaccountability. This applies both to established democracies, where norms of secrecy developed around the cold war have been reinforced by current concerns with terrorism, and to newer democracies.

While many consolidating democracies (particularly in Central and Eastern Europe) have been able to pass "freedom of information" legislation, at the same time some have placed increased restrictions on the circulation of defense information in order to meet the requirements for joining the North Atlantic Treaty Organization (NATO).[38]

Defense committees are necessary to balance the right of the public in a democracy to be informed with the need for secrecy that governs some activities and policies in the realm of national security. Committee members, if they have the appropriate security clearances, are delegated the responsibility to make decisions on behalf of their fellow legislators and the public as a whole. Unfortunately, in many new democracies, current or former members of the military who serve on the defense committee are more likely to have security clearances than their civilian counterparts, thus giving them a certain monopoly over policymaking on reserved issues. In a number of countries, mistrustful legislators are wary of the possible sanctions that an overly secretive or hostile executive branch might impose on the holders of security clearances. For example, civilian defense experts on the Russian Duma's Defense Committee do not hold clearances, because they want to retain the right to travel abroad without restriction.[39] Brazilian legislators opposed a provision of a bill on intelligence oversight that had been proposed by the government of Fernando Collor de Mello, because it imposed stiff penalties on those who disclosed information (five to ten years for intentional disclosures and three to five years for unintentional leaks).[40]

In addition, defense committees may hold closed hearings on issues that involve secret information. Although public hearings are usually desirable for their contribution to transparency and a public debate on the issue at hand, closed hearings designed to protect secrets are preferable to allowing the executive a pretext for marginalizing the legislature from policymaking or oversight. In a survey of fifteen defense committees, eight held public meetings at least on occasion, whereas the remainder never held them.[41] Interestingly, the tendency to avoid public hearings is not a unique characteristic of defense committees: in a survey of seventeen European parliaments, committees in nine of them always or normally held private hearings.[42]

The Personal Expertise of Committee Members

In theory, committee members—as a result of their special powers and responsibilities in the legislative process—should have more incentives than other members of the legislature to cultivate the information and expertise necessary for making and overseeing policy. In practice, this is not always the case. Although some committee members may have a personal interest and expertise in defense, the majority are likely to be novices who lack the time or interest to develop their expertise.

Committee seats typically are divided among the various political parties in proportion to their share of seats in the legislature and then are assigned to members by their party leaders, in large part based on their individual requests. Since legislators usually self-select into committees in this fashion, at least some members of the defense committee are likely to have a personal or electoral interest in defense. Active-duty or retired officers holding seats in the legislature are the most likely to request positions on defense committees. This is the case in the defense committee of the Russian State Duma, which is frequently chaired by an officer, and whose military members often are the only ones with security clearances. Other members on a defense committee may be civilians who have been involved in defense issues and civil-military relations, either as academics or as members of the government.

Committee members without a military background or prior experience in defense issues will need to develop their expertise on the job. At a very practical level, committee members need to have time to do this. Legislators realistically can expect to participate effectively in only one or two committees; those assigned to multiple committees are unlikely to develop credible expertise in all of them. A certain stability in committee membership is also necessary, so that individuals are in their post long enough to learn the material and establish key relationships with the ministry staff, as well as with other, independent experts in the defense field. This stability is undermined if there is a high turnover at election time, as is often the case in many developing countries where the electorate does not strongly identify with parties or where membership in the legislature is a stepping-stone to other goals and is not valued as a desirable career in and of itself. In some cases, an overall shortage of qualified personnel may lead to executive poaching of committee experts to fill government positions, thus undermining levels of expertise within the legislature.[43] In some countries, the practice of rotating committee chairs and memberships among party representatives, so that all spend some time in the more "desirable" committees—often those that provide access to state resources or address policy issues of interest to constituents—militates against the development of expertise.

More generally, legislators are said to lack the political will necessary for developing their expertise and playing an independent role in making and overseeing defense policy. This is most often attributed to two factors: legislators belong to a majority party that backs the executive, and defense issues are not electorally important. Overall, the "informed expert" approach that dominates the prescriptive policy literature tends to stress legislators' lack of interest and expertise in defense matters, a theme echoed in the few individual case studies of consolidating democracies that have been done. The next section attempts to reconcile this theme with the apparent protagonism of legislatures on defense issues in many new democracies. The chapter then provides a more systematic discussion of political will—that is, the factors that account for variations in the incentives that legislators have for taking part in the formulation and oversight of defense policy and for variations in the development of the institutionalized mechanisms for oversight discussed in this section.

Assessing the Role of Defense Committees in Consolidating Democracies

Civil-military relations appeared at one point or another on the political agendas of most consolidating democracies in the 1980s and 1990s. In many countries of Latin America and elsewhere—where the military as an institution played a key role in the preceding authoritarian regime or was involved in efforts to suppress an internal armed conflict—a fundamental restructuring of the way in which the military is inserted into society and overseen by civilians not only is a central task of the transition to democracy but also often remains on the agenda long after the transition is over.[44] In a majority of countries of Central and Eastern Europe, where the military was under civilian control during communist rule, civil-military relations tended not to be a high priority during the transition to democracy but gained importance during the consolidation phase, as countries sought to bring their institutions into line with Western models as part of an effort to meet NATO and the European Union (EU) accession requirements.

Particularly in countries where the military functioned as an appendage of the preceding authoritarian regime, politicians active in the process of democratization usually revise those constitutional provisions and laws that regulate the roles, rights, and obligations of the armed forces so that they conform to the basic democratic principles of accountability to elected leaders and respect for civil liberties.[45] These reformers seek to rein in the behavior of militaries that may have grown accustomed to acting without regard to these principles, operating autonomously within the defense arena, intruding in non-defense-related areas of civic and political life, and violating human rights under the sanction of the previous regime. Often legislators adopt constitutional provisions that establish the principle of civilian supremacy over the military, and they write legislation to institutionalize this principle through the creation of a civilian ministry of defense. Argentina's congress, for example, made significant contributions to the elaboration of the Ley de Defensa Nacional, which redefined the military's role five years after the transition to democracy.[46] In South Africa, the defense committee played a key part in the restructuring of the military and, given the importance of the military issue, was one of the more influential legislative committees in the first years of the new democracy. The Polish Sejm resolved a dangerous dispute between the president and the defense minister concerning jurisdiction over the armed forces. In many of the Central and Eastern European countries, parliaments engaged in a flurry of lawmaking, designed to reshape the defense sector in order to qualify for membership in NATO.

How can this important role for the legislature in the crafting of defense legislation be reconciled with the finding that most legislators in consolidating democracies lack the interest and expertise to operate effectively in the defense realm? First, laws governing civil-military relations are usually made when events—a transition to democracy, a recent war, accession to a regional alliance—shine a spotlight on the inadequacy of the existing rules and make the crafting of new rules a legally and politically salient enterprise. Although defense issues may not retain political and electoral importance over the long term, there will be periods when they greatly matter. The question is whether the legislature will be equipped with sufficient expertise to act when those moments arrive.

Second, the legislature often is able to assume a protagonist's role in restructuring civil-military relations because this task depends far less on the kind of expertise in defense issues and institutionalized mechanisms of oversight that are in short supply in new democracies. Unlike the body of knowledge needed to establish systems of planning and budgeting or for administrative restructuring of the ministry of defense, many civil-military reforms are a matter of democratic principle or involve political decisions; they do not require judgments based on an extensive and specialized knowledge of defense issues. This is the case, for example, with reforms establishing the principle of civilian supremacy, limiting the political activities of military personnel, and establishing the parameters of military involvement in internal security missions. In each case, knowledge of the issues at stake is necessary for responsible and effective decision making, but this knowledge can be gained relatively easily through the study of model legislation. In contrast, the specialized knowledge necessary for restructuring the military or carrying out effective oversight of defense policy and budgets is more difficult to develop.

Accounting for Variations in the Role of the Legislature

Nascent efforts to catalog variations in the formal defense-related powers of legislatures in both established and consolidating democracies and to understand cross-national variations in the role of the legislature in the defense realm have been useful, given the paucity of information on the topic. Nevertheless, such studies could benefit from the institutionalist focus that has characterized recent work on legislatures.[47] This literature evaluates a wide range of institutional factors that shape the role that the legislature plays vis-à-vis the executive in any polity. Although the parliamentary or presidential nature of the regime has long been viewed as one of the most influential factors, I argue that subregime factors like the size and discipline of political parties and the schedule and rules of elections are more important in shaping the extent to which there is unity or divergence of interests between the executive and legislative branches. Legislators have incentives to play more of a role where their interests diverge from the executive, although they may not always have the power to do so.

Presidentialism versus Parliamentarism

The "separation of powers" that characterizes presidential systems is based upon the separate origin and survival of the elected representatives in the two branches. The voter has two "agents"—the president and the legislature. Each branch can claim democratic legitimacy in its own right, setting up the basis for conflict between the two (and hence checks and balances). In contrast, the "unity of powers" in parliamentarism is based upon a single unbroken chain of principal-agent relationships from the voter (the principal) to the executive:

> Parliamentary systems in their purest form consist of a single chain of nested principal-agent relationships. . . . Voters make only one voting choice: they select a candidate (or list of candidates) to

represent them in parliament. Parties serve as screening mechanisms for voters, enabling them to select legislators who will in turn select cabinet ministers who share their policy preferences. . . . The executive enjoys no constitutional independence from the legislature and no direct connection to the electorate. It is instead a pure agent of the parliament and accountable to that majority in the most simple and direct way: subject to ouster at any time by a vote of no confidence.[48]

Thus, the constitutional design of a parliamentary regime provides few incentives for conflict of interest between voters, legislators, their parties, and the executive. Should a serious conflict arise, the government can be dissolved and new elections held to create a new equilibrium where the interests of all actors are aligned.

For decades, the marginalized British parliament and the powerful United States Congress were cited as prototypical examples of parliamentarism and presidentialism, when in reality each should be considered more as a deviant case. Most parliaments have more power than the British example, and most congresses are weaker than their counterpart in the United States. In fact, many parliaments might fall closer to the U.S. Congress on the spectrum of influence than would chambers from other presidential systems.

This use of the British and U.S. cases as examples tended to confuse the impact of regime type with the effect of other factors on the relationship between the legislature and the executive, such as the size and discipline of political parties, and legislative procedures and powers, all of which vary independently of regime type.[49] The prime minister in Great Britain historically was backed by a disciplined party, which held a majority of seats in the parliament. In other established, parliamentary democracies, where the prime minister is backed only by a majority coalition of parties or by a minority of the parliament, the government is more constrained in its actions and the legislature tends to play more of a role. (More recently, disorder among parties in some of the new parliaments of Central and Eastern Europe provides evidence that lack of party discipline can also undermine the power of a prime minister whose party or coalition holds a majority of seats in the parliament).

Outside the United States, presidents often have much stronger constitutional powers (e.g., line-item veto, decree, and emergency powers) than the U.S. president and may dominate the legislature, especially if they enjoy the support of a disciplined party with a majority of seats in the legislature. In short, while regime type may be important for dealing with an untenable deadlock, it is unclear how much it determines the responsibilities of the legislature for formulating laws and overseeing the executive.[50] Instead, the power of the legislature will depend upon the relative powers and interests of the two branches, which tend to be affected more by subregime factors, such as the schedule of elections, electoral rules, and the party system, than by whether they operate under a parliamentary or presidential system per se.

Electoral Rules and the Party System

In the United States, the founding fathers' belief in the counterposed interests of the branches of government was based not just on the direct election of the president but also on the election of presidents and legislators at separate times and from separate constituencies and on the president's lack of involvement in legislative elections. Today, many scholars have elaborated additional theories about the factors that might generate a "separation of purpose" between the executive and the legislature, thus creating incentives for the legislature to play an independent role.[51] In general, it is believed that electoral systems based on proportional representation rather than winner-take-all principles, and those that are candidate-oriented rather than policy-oriented, are more likely to shape the number of parties, their level of discipline, and their programmatic interests in ways that create a separation between the branches. Where there is a majority, disciplined party whose members care more about policy than pork, the strength of the executive will be maximized and the role of the legislature correspondingly reduced. Proportional-representation electoral rules are more likely to encourage a multiparty outcome than winner-take-all rules, thus depriving the executive of the support of a majority party in the legislature. Candidate-oriented electoral systems provide incentives for legislators to act independently in pursuit of their own interests rather than toe the party or executive line. A wide range of other factors, including the historical development of the party system and its social context as well as internal party rules, will also affect the nature of the party system and, hence, incentives to act independently of the executive.

Impact on Lawmaking, Oversight, and the Institutionalization of the Legislature

In general, legislators face different incentives for formulating legislation, exercising oversight, and institutionalizing the legislature's own powers to carry out these activities. For example, legislators from the governing party or coalition have a variety of incentives to participate in making legislation, but they are often less motivated to engage in oversight, which usually involves criticizing the behavior of the government in power. Parties in the legislature may have incentives to exercise oversight of an opposition executive, but they are likely to be less willing to give up some of their power by creating neutral institutional mechanisms for oversight, like auditing agencies or a nonpartisan legislative staff. In all cases, the incentives for playing an independent role may not be matched by the capacity to do so. The executive usually has an interest in opposing any increases in the legislature's power and has many mechanisms at its disposal to prevent such an outcome.

MAKING LAWS Although members of the governing party or coalition tend to have less of an interest in oversight (and the public scandals often associated with this activity), they may have a strong interest in policy formulation. Loyal party experts can contribute to good governance (and hence government popularity) both by monitoring legislative proposals put forth by their own ministers to correct any miscues and by brokering compromises between parties within the committee. Often the committee is a place for aspirants to executive branch positions to develop and showcase their expertise in a given subject. In the case of a coalition government, committee experts are likely to pay special attention to the legislative proposals made by ministers from allied parties, to ensure that they respect the coalition "contract."

Despite these benefits of committee input, party or government leaders often use various means to discourage independent behavior by committee members and chairs. In many parliamentary systems such as Germany's and Great Britain's, members of the executive branch sit on committees and are able to influence the proceedings. Party leaders may exert influence through their control over the naming of committee members, while leaders in the executive branch solicit favorable outcomes through their power to appoint legislators to executive positions. In Great Britain, for example, the Whip's Office within Parliament (specifically tasked with ensuring party voting discipline), the Ministry of Defence, the Cabinet Office, and chairmen of the Defence Committee "collude" to prevent independent behavior by members.[52] "Subversive" chair holders are co-opted by being promoted to roles as parliamentary leaders (whips, for example) or ministers, where they are required to toe the party line.[53] In many consolidating democracies, norms of party discipline or the mechanisms to enforce such norms are less developed, leading at times to a more independent role for the legislature.

EXERCISING OVERSIGHT Parties in opposition to the executive are much more likely than members of governing parties to exercise oversight. It is commonplace to note that exercising oversight can be an extremely time-intensive and laborious task that tends to yield fewer electoral and policy benefits than the actual making of legislation. Systematic oversight must be conducted on a routine basis, in the shadows cast by other pressing issues. It is not clear, however, that oversight is politically unappealing—at least not given the way oversight is conducted by most legislatures. It is impossible for even the best-staffed legislature in the world to carry out systematic oversight of issues; the choices legislators make about which issues to oversee will depend upon their political salience. The scandals that often precipitate oversight yield both political spectacle and profit; in fact, "serious" legislators often criticize their gadfly colleagues for "grandstanding" on oversight issues and neglecting the careful formulation of laws and policy. Given this, we should expect to see opposition parties and legislators engaging in oversight as a means of upstaging the executive. To the extent that opposition parties are excluded from a meaningful role in formulating legislation, they will have more time and energy to devote to oversight.

INSTITUTIONALIZING THE LEGISLATURE As discussed above, legislatures rely on a number of institutions to help them carry out oversight, including committees, a research staff, and independent auditing agencies. A key condition for the professionalization or institutionalization of the legislature is time. It takes time for legislators to perceive the need for institutionalized mechanisms, put them in place, close any loopholes in their operation, and then strengthen them even further once they have established their initial usefulness. In countries where democracy is frequently interrupted by periods of authoritarian rule, the legislature is not likely to be institutionalized. Similarly, where politicians have very short legislative careers (for reasons discussed above), the possibility of institutionalization decreases.

Members of the executive and party leaders both have incentives to block efforts by rank-and-file legislators to strengthen institutions that would enable individual legislators to act independently of the party or the executive. Given this, it has been argued that the institutionalization of the legislature is more likely to occur where party leaders are "weaker."[54]

Not only are parties in such cases less able to control the actions of their members, but party members will also tend to have constituency or policy interests that diverge from those of the leadership. The "weakness of party leaders" hypothesis helps explain the comparable levels of staffing in many Western European democracies and the consolidating democracies of Central and Eastern Europe. Although the long-established parliaments of Western Europe have had much more time to institutionalize themselves than their counterparts elsewhere in Europe, the strength of political parties (and accompanying norms of party discipline) in most of Western Europe long discouraged this development. It was only in the mid-1970s and later that many parliaments created (or enhanced) committees to play a role in the political process. In Central and Eastern Europe, in contrast, the relative weakness of leaders in newly created political parties has made parliament an important center of activity from the start.[55]

Although the strengthening of legislative institutions is a gradual process that requires time, it also may be characterized by critical junctures that lead to important increases in the resources available to legislators. Dissatisfaction with the political process at a key point in time, and hence dissatisfaction with the executive and party leaders responsible for the status quo, can lead to cross-partisan coalitions of the party rank and file that press for resources to strengthen the legislature. In Germany in the late 1960s, for example, the Bundestag was under fire from the public for being unresponsive; at the same time, the majority of legislators were unhappy with the "establishment"—the few members of Parliament who were party leaders or members of the executive and, as a result, had access to resources. Increased funds were seen as a means to increase the strength of the parliamentary majority (made up of both Christian Democrats and Social Democrats) relative to the leadership. Since the demand crossed party lines (the Christian Democrats and Social Democrats had formed a so-called Grand Coalition in 1969), it was difficult to oppose the increase on partisan grounds.[56] In the end, individual legislators received more resources, and parties (in an effort to counter this new development and avoid excessive decentralization of the legislative process) fortified the system of federally financed party working groups within the legislature. Since then, party working groups in a given policy area meet individually before their members meet in the Bundestag committees to negotiate interpartisan agreements.

Similarly, staffing levels in the U.S. Congress underwent a significant increase in the early 1970s as rank-and-file members of Congress from both political parties became dissatisfied with the executive over Vietnam (and with the congressional leadership for failing to exercise vigorous oversight on this issue, among others). As in Germany, increased resources for individual legislators were offset by more funds for committees, in an effort to keep the balance of power from shifting too radically within the legislature.

Assessing the Impact of the Legislature's Involvement in the Defense Sector

The claims made at the beginning of this chapter about the potential benefits of the legislature's involvement in the defense sphere are just that: claims that must be subjected to further specification and evaluated in real-world cases. Under what conditions does the legislature actually contribute to the various goals of effective defense governance, that is, to the transparency, legitimacy, stability, and effectiveness of defense policies? Does the involvement of the legislature in the defense sector contribute to or undermine civilian control over the military?

Other than studies of the U.S. Congress, which in many ways is a sui generis case, little effort has been made to assess the impact of the legislature's involvement in defense on democratic civilian control of the military or the effective governance of the defense sector. In many ways, this is not surprising. The role of the contemporary legislature in general (much less in defense issues) became the subject of dedicated study only in the mid-1990s.[57] Scholars have been scrambling to understand the new developments on this front, in particular the emergence and operation of legislatures in consolidating democracies in Latin America and Central and Eastern Europe, along with the spread of committees throughout Western European parliaments in the late 1970s and 1980s. As a result, until recently, relatively little was known about the role of defense committees outside the United States.

Recent literature on defense committees has been more prescriptive than analytical, as scholars have focused on advancing a normative justification for a legislative role in the defense sphere and identifying the possible array of powers the legislature might exercise. Unfortunately, the prescriptive and normative frameworks developed for the practitioner (the four "approaches" described in the section "What Should the Role of the Legislature Be?") are less suited to the researcher interested in assessing the impact that the legislature has on civilian control and effective governance of the defense sector. Relying on these frameworks, most recent assessments of the impact of the legislature's role on the defense sector in consolidating democracies have been limited to determining whether it is playing the role it "should." Is the legislature acting as an informed expert? Is it exercising "effective parliamentary oversight"?—i.e., is it able to influence outcomes?[58] Presumably, the implication is that if the legislature is fulfilling its designated role, then it is contributing to civilian control of the military and effective governance of the defense sector. Few, if any, studies take the next step to determine what impact the legislature's expertise or ability to exercise effective parliamentary oversight has on levels of civilian control or the transparency, legitimacy, stability, and effectiveness of defense policies. To the extent that judgment is passed, it is based on the *belief* that the greater the level of legislative influence, the greater will be the level of effective democratic governance.

Finally, the normative framework of the prescriptive policy literature has led to comparative case studies that fall short of assessing the legislature's impact on the outcomes of interest to most observers. In these cases, scholars tend to limit themselves to observing cross-national differences in the responsibilities of the legislature rather than evaluating whether one set of institutional arrangements works "better" than another. As long as the legislature plays some kind of role, the notion of "no best practices" leads most scholars to conclude that it is performing its functions satisfactorily—after all, legislatures contribute to transparency and accountability in different ways in different countries. This conclusion, however, reveals a fundamental misunderstanding of the insight that there is no one democratic ideal. To acknowledge that countries structure their legislative-executive relations differently does not require the conclusion that these mechanisms work equally well, either in general terms or specifically in terms of producing legitimacy, democratic accountability, civilian control of the military, and effective defense policies. The choice of democratic institutions often involves trade-offs, and it is necessary to assess these trade-offs within the defense sector.[59]

Impact of the Legislature on Civilian Control of the Military

The prescriptive policy literature on parliamentary control of the armed forces, as well as individual case studies, focuses almost exclusively on the potential or actual contributions of the legislature to policy outcomes. There are very few hypotheses, and fewer studies, about how the legislature might contribute to civilian control of the military. By definition, of course, civilian control over the military is not deemed to be democratic unless there is at least some very minimal role for the legislature. Some enthusiasts of "effective parliamentary oversight" might even speculate that the more the legislature contributes to overseeing the defense sector, the more likely there is to be civilian control.

Studies of the U.S. Congress, however, reach the opposite conclusion. Decades ago, Samuel Huntington argued that the separation of powers was a "major hindrance to the development of military professionalism and civilian control in the United States," a view that has been echoed by most observers of the contemporary scene who highlight military efforts to sidestep the secretary of defense by appealing directly to Congress.[60] In one of the few comparative studies on this topic, Deborah Avant argues that the marginal role of Parliament in overseeing the defense sector in Great Britain led to greater levels of civilian control there than in the United States, where the Congress is much stronger. In the U.S. case, the existence of two civilian "principals" (the executive and the Congress) with often-conflicting views, allows the "agent" (the military) to play one off against the other and, in the absence of clear directions from civilians, to follow its own preferences.[61]

Despite the widespread agreement on the U.S. Congress's part in undermining civilian control, it is not clear to what extent this finding can be generalized to other cases. It is possible to imagine situations in which a role for the legislature in defense might strengthen the executive's hand in asserting control over the military. This would certainly occur when the two principals share preferences but the executive is too weak to assert control, as happened in Argentina in the 1980s. President Raúl Alfonsín was a leading critic of the military's violations of human rights under the authoritarian regime that governed from 1976 to 1983, but he was greatly weakened in his ability to act on this issue after his efforts to punish the military resulted in a number of coup attempts. The legislature had the power to participate in the officer promotion process and used this power to send a strong message about the kind of behavior that it expected of the military. On more than one occasion, the Argentine Senate refused to confirm Alfonsín's nominees to the high command, in order to underscore their repudiation of any officers involved in human rights violations. This worked in part because it is more difficult (though certainly not unheard-of) for the military to protest the actions of a collective body than to hold the executive personally responsible for actions taken "against" the military.

It is also conceivable that the legislature could contribute to civilian control even when its preferences diverged from those of the executive. For example, a centrist ruler might be too weak to act unilaterally to assert control over the military, but such a ruler could be strengthened to do so by a legislature that housed parties that desired an even more "radical" course of action—that is, a course of action that the military would find even more objectionable than that proposed by the executive. (Given the general centrism of U.S. legislators and the relative lack of party discipline, the U.S. military has often been able to find enough legislative allies whose preferences are closer to those of the military than the executive, thus undermining the executive agenda. This is not certain, or even likely, to be the case in other countries.) The legislature might also contribute to executive efforts to assert control over the military, even when the legislature and the executive disagree, if legislative oversight generates additional information about the behavior of the military that can then be used by the executive.

In cases where there are multiple principals in the executive branch (e.g., a president and a defense minister named by the prime minister) vying for control over the military—a not uncommon occurrence in the "hybrid" regimes of Central and Eastern Europe—the result may be weak civilian control of the military and, more dangerously, incentives for the politicization of the armed forces as part of any political conflict between the principals. In such a case, the legislature may be able to contribute to civilian control by resolving the conflict (as happened in Poland in the mid-1990s).[62]

Impact of the Legislature on Effective Democratic Governance of the Defense Sector

To acknowledge the right of countries to structure their legislative-executive relations as they see fit (as is the case in the "no best practices" approach) does *not* require the conclusion that these mechanisms work equally well, either in general terms or specifically in terms of producing legitimate, accountable, and effective management of defense policies and civilian control of the military. The choice of democratic institutions often involves trade-offs, and it is necessary to assess these trade-offs within the defense sector.

Little is known about the impact of the legislature's involvement in the defense sector on policy outcomes outside of the U.S. case. The impact of the legislature is likely to vary according to the policy value of interest, be it transparency, accountability, or stability, as well as the issue area, such as the defense budget or appointments. For example, an active defense committee might lead to more-transparent policies by increasing the amount of information available to the public (assuming that the defense committee does not exercise its powers behind closed doors), but it might lack the power to enhance accountability substantially. Trade-offs may also be involved. An influential legislature, for example, might contribute to the transparency of defense policy but undermine the speed with which policy decisions are reached, and their coherence.

Finally, studies would have to specify what is meant by "legislative involvement," because this can vary according to not only the level of influence but also its nature. The legislature's involvement in formulating laws and policy, for example, might have a different impact from its oversight activities. Involvement motivated by a concern with pork is likely to have different effects from involvement motivated by partisan policy concerns.

Notes

1. The subject of "parliamentary control of the armed forces" has begun to receive attention in recent years, primarily through international think tanks working to promote civilian control of the armed forces in consolidating democracies. The prolific analyst Hans Born, head of a project on parliamentary control of the military at the Geneva Centre for the Democratic Control of Armed Forces (DCAF), has almost single-handedly defined the field of study through his own publications and through collaborative projects he has overseen since the end of 1999. See the very good collection of studies at http://www.dcaf.ch/pcaf/. In 2003, DCAF and the Inter-Parliamentary Union (IPU) published a handbook for parliamentarians on this topic. Hans Born, Philipp Fluri, and A. Johnsson, eds., *Parliamentary Oversight of the Security Sector: Principles, Mechanisms, and Practices*, Handbook for Parliamentarians, no. 5 (Geneva: Inter-Parliamentary Union/Geneva Centre for the Democratic Control of Armed Forces, 2003).

2. See, for example, Born et al., *Parliamentary Oversight*, 24; and Andrew Cottey, Tim Edmunds, and Anthony Forster, "The Second Generation Problematic: Rethinking Democratic Control of Armed Forces in Central and Eastern Europe" (Civil-Military Relations in Central and Eastern Europe, 2000), http://www.bristol.ac.uk/Depts/GRC/CMR/TCMR%20Papers/TCMR%201.7.htm.

3. For more on the factors that affect the legislature's ability to influence the defense budget, see Giraldo, chapter 7 in this volume.

4. The literature commonly uses "oversight of the defense sector" to refer to all the activities of the legislature, including lawmaking and policymaking. This chapter opts for the less felicitous expression "the legislature's involvement in

the defense realm," in order to reserve the term "oversight" for activities that monitor the implementation of laws and policies.

5. For a checklist of possible defense-related powers, see Born et al., *Parliamentary Oversight*. For a survey of the powers that defense committees possess, see Wim F. van Eekelen, "Democratic Control of Armed Forces: The National and International Parliamentary Dimension" (Occasional Paper 2, Geneva Centre for the Democratic Control of Armed Forces [DCAF], Geneva, 2002), http://www.dcaf.ch/publications/publications%20new/occasional_papers/2.pdf. Van Eekelen reports findings from a survey of nineteen NATO countries carried out by DCAF Geneva and the NATO Parliamentary Assembly in Brussels. For case study comparisons, see Hans Born, "Between Efficiency and Legitimacy: Democratic Accountability of the Military in the U.S., France, Sweden, and Switzerland" (Working Paper 102, Geneva Centre for the Democratic Control of Armed Forces [DCAF], Geneva, 2002), http://www.dcaf.ch/publications/Working_Papers/102.pdf; and David Betz, "Comparing Frameworks of Parliamentary Oversight: Poland, Hungary, Russia, Ukraine" (Working Paper 115, Geneva Centre for the Democratic Control of Armed Forces [DCAF], Geneva, 2003).

6. Eva Busza, "Transition and Civil-Military Relations in Poland and Russia," *Communist and Post-Communist Studies* 29, no. 2 (1996): 167–174.

7. See Hans Born, "Learning from Best Practices of Parliamentary Oversight of the Security Sector" (Working Paper 1, Geneva Centre for the Democratic Control of Armed Forces [DCAF], Geneva, 2002): 3, http://www.dcaf.ch/publications/Working_Papers/01(e).pdf; and Cottey et al., "The Second Generation Problematic."

8. For example, Born et al., in *Parliamentary Oversight of the Security Sector*, stress the budget powers of the legislature, whereas Andrew Cottey, Timothy Edmunds, and Anthony Forster point to approval of senior military and political-military appointments and troop deployment. Cottey et al., "Introduction: The Challenge of Democratic Control of Armed Forces in Postcommunist Europe," in *Democratic Control of the Military in Postcommunist Europe: Guarding the Guards*, ed. Andrew Cottey, Timothy Edmunds, and Anthony Forster (New York: Palgrave, 2002), 9.

9. Born et al., *Parliamentary Oversight*.

10. See Lawrence D. Longley and Roger H. Davidson, eds., *The New Roles of Parliamentary Committees* (London: Frank Cass and Co., 1998). For more on the role of committees, see National Democratic Institute for International Affairs (NDI), "Committees in Legislatures: A Division of Labor," Legislative Research Series, Paper 2, Washington, D.C. (1996).

11. France is the most notable exception, with only six committees operating in its legislature. This limited number resulted from a deliberate effort to

weaken the legislature, which was deemed too strong during the French Fourth Republic. In other cases, committees sometimes form to cover the jurisdiction of two or more ministries—for example, a committee on foreign affairs *and* defense. The disadvantage of such an arrangement is that one committee will be unable to oversee the activities of the ministry of defense and the ministry of foreign affairs as closely as would two separate committees. Given that foreign policy decisions often have an impact on defense (and vice versa), however, this arrangement might facilitate the coordination of policy (and any necessary trade-offs) between the two areas. Countries with separate committees are usually able to solve the coordination problem quite easily by creating joint committees to handle legislation on issues under the purview of more than one committee. For more on the role of committees, see NDI, "Committees in Legislatures."

12. Article 45a, paragraph 1, of the Basic Law. All of Italy's legislative committees are designated by the constitution, an apparent reaction to attacks on parliament during the Fascist regime.

13. Committees need to have sufficient time to review the legislation before them, but they are not always given it—for example, when budget proposals are submitted only weeks before the budget must be approved. In a number of countries, executives have the option of assigning different levels of urgency to a bill, some of which can require the committee to consider the bill within a short time. Frequent use of this proviso can undermine the ability of the legislature to influence law formulation.

14. Kaare Strom, "Parliamentary Committees in European Democracies," in Longley and Davidson, *The New Roles of Parliamentary Committees,* 49–51.

15. Samuel P. Huntington, *The Soldier and the State: The Theory and Politics of Civil-Military Relations* (1957; repr., New York: Vintage Books), 414.

16. Ibid., 415–416. Of course, individual judgment and career considerations enter into whether military personnel actually express their personal views or not, but the legal provision for such free expression is in place.

17. Helmut Schafer and Christian von Stechow, "Control of Security Policy," in *The U.S. Congress and the German Bundestag,* ed. Uwe Thaysen, Roger H. Davidson, and R. Gerald Livingston (Boulder, CO: Westview Press, 1990).

18. Lynn M. Maurer, "Parliamentary Influence in a New Democracy: The Spanish Congress," *Journal of Legislative Studies* 5, no. 2 (1999).

19. Before July 7, 2004, the GAO's legal name was the General Accounting Office.

20. If classified reports sent directly to the Department of Defense were included, the percentage would be even higher. See Andrew Cox and Stephen Kirby, *Congress, Parliament, and Defence: The Impact of Legislative Reform on Defence Accountability in Britain and America* (New York: St. Martin's Press, 1986), 20.

21. For more on the evolution of the GAO's role, see "The Background of GAO," http://www.gao.gov/about/history.html.

22. Cox and Kirby, *Congress, Parliament, and Defence*, 12–13.

23. These reports were debated by only ninety-eight members of Parliament. Ibid., 13, 15.

24. NDI, "Committees in Legislatures," 15.

25. Bruce George and Alison Graham, "Defence Committees in Democratic and Democratising Legislatures" (paper presented at the Workshop of Parliamentary Scholars and Parliamentarians, Berlin, August 1994), 11.

26. Schafer and von Stechow, "Control of Security Policy," table 10 in appendix.

27. NDI, "Committees in Legislatures," 17.

28. Ibid., 16.

29. Chan Wook Park, "The National Assembly of the Republic of Korea," *Journal of Legislative Studies* 4, no. 4 (1998): 78.

30. Susan Webb Hammond, "Recent Research on Legislative Staffs," *Legislative Studies Quarterly* 21, no. 4 (1996): 543–576.

31. B. George and Graham, "Defence Committees," 13, 23. At the time of the authors' survey in 1994, the best-staffed defense committee in western Europe was Italy's, with five assistants. Numbers from a survey more than five years later reveal slightly different committee numbers, indicating that defense committees in western Europe may be slightly better staffed than in central and eastern Europe (see van Eekelen, "Democratic Control of Armed Forces"). The differences, however, do not seem that significant, and it would be possible to conclude that staffing levels are fairly comparable between the two sets of countries (with a great deal of variation within each set).

32. Schafer and von Stechow, "Control of Security Policy," table 11 in appendix. Elsewhere the numbers given are 500 party group employees and 1,800 personal assistants; regardless of the specifics, the general level is the same.

33. Suzanne S. Schüttemeyer, "Hierarchy and Efficiency in the Bundestag: The German Answer for Institutionalizing Parliament," in *Parliaments in the Modern World: Changing Institutions*, ed. Gary W. Copeland and Samuel C. Patterson (Ann Arbor: University of Michigan Press, 1994), 45.

34. Winfried Steffani, "Parties (Parliamentary Groups) and Committees in the Bundestag," in Thaysen et al., *The U.S. Congress and the German Bundestag*, 285.

35. Schafer and von Stechow, "Control of Security Policy," table 11 in appendix.

36. The ratio for the United States is calculated on the basis of the figures given earlier in this section. It is important to note that personal staffers may sometimes also play a policy role. The calculations of the Argentine numbers are

based on the figure of 6 staff members per 38 standing committees, and the 23 personal staffers allotted to each of the 257 deputies. NDI, "Committees in Legislatures," 16.

37. Hans Born, *An Inventory of Actors: Strengthening Parliamentary Oversight of the Security Sector in Transition Countries*, Geneva Centre for the Democratic Control of Armed Forces (DCAF), Geneva (2002), http://www.dcaf.ch/PCAF/inventory.pdf.

38. Alasdair Roberts, "NATO, Secrecy, and the Right to Information," *East European Constitutional Review* (Fall 2002/Winter 2003): 86–94.

39. David Betz, "No Place for a Civilian: Russian Defence Management from Yeltsin to Putin" (paper presented at the 41st annual convention of the International Studies Association, Los Angeles, March 14–18, 2000).

40. Wendy Hunter, *Eroding Military Influence in Brazil: Politicians against Soldiers* (Chapel Hill: University of North Carolina Press, 1997), 64. The law that was eventually passed in 1999 does not specify how much access legislators would have to secret information, nor the penalties that would be imposed in the case of an information leak. Priscila Antunes and Marco A. C. Cepik, "The New Brazilian Intelligence System: An Institutional Assessment," *International Journal of Intelligence and Counterintelligence* 16, no. 2 (2003): 349–373.

41. Van Eekelen, "Democratic Control of Armed Forces," appendix.

42. Strom, "Parliamentary Committees in European Democracies," 49–51.

43. In South Africa, for example, 122 of 400 National Assembly members and 13 of 27 committee chairs left their posts to take other government positions even before the first term ended in 1999. Richard Calland, ed., *The First Five Years: A Review of South Africa's Democratic Parliament* (Cape Town: IDASA, 1999), 10. This has happened to a lesser extent in other countries, such as Poland, where the government has drawn from the Sejm to fill vacant ministerial posts.

44. In many countries, there is a great deal of debate about when the transition is "over," because the end of the transition implies to some that the institutions in place at the time will no longer be subject to change. I use the end of the transition here in the way that it is employed in the introduction to the volume: regimes are considered to be past the transition stage and to have the status of "consolidating" democracies once there is no longer the immediate risk of the military overthrowing the process.

45. For a discussion of changes that need to be made to defense and military legislation in order to consolidate democracy, see Jeanne K. Giraldo, "Democratizing Civil-Military Relations: What Do Countries Legislate?" (Occasional Paper 7, Center for Civil-Military Relations, Monterey, CA, 2001). For a more general discussion of how legislation can be used to assert civilian control over the military, see James M. Lindsay, "Legislative Control of

the Military: Lessons from the American Experience" (Occasional Paper 12, Center for Civil-Military Relations, Naval Postgraduate School, Monterey, CA, 2000).

46. See José Manuel Ugarte, "La Comisión de Defensa Nacional: Un rol casi inédito," in *Defensa y democracia: Un debate entre civiles y militares*, ed. Gustavo Druetta, Eduardo Estévez, Ernesto López, and José Enrique Miguens (Buenos Aires: Puntosur Editores, 1990), 244–251. David Pion-Berlin notes that Argentine defense committees "have written important pieces of legislation on defense and security missions but have no authority over financial matters." Pion-Berlin, *Through Corridors of Power: Institutions and Civil-Military Relations in Argentina* (University Park: Pennsylvania State University Press, 1997), 136.

47. For these nascent efforts, see van Eekelen, "Democratic Control of Armed Forces"; Born, "Between Efficiency and Legitimacy"; and Betz, "Comparing Frameworks of Parliamentary Oversight." Wendy Hunter's work on Brazil is one of the few studies that draws on the institutionalist literature to explain the incentives that legislators face in overseeing the defense sector. See Hunter, *Eroding Military Influence in Brazil*.

48. Erika Moreno, Brian F. Crisp, and Matthew Soberg Shugart, "The Accountability Deficit in Latin America," in *Democratic Accountability in Latin America*, ed. Scott Mainwaring and Christopher Welna (Oxford: Oxford University Press, 2003), 85–86.

49. This is not to say that analysts did not cite these other factors as well, but simply that the excessive focus on Great Britain and the United States to illustrate the functioning of parliamentarism and presidentialism created misimpressions and understated the importance of subregime factors.

50. Parliamentarism, but not presidentialism, provides an institutionalized method (without having to wait for the next regularly scheduled election) for deposing an ineffectual leader who has lost the support of the population and his or her support coalition.

51. Stephan Haggard and Mathew D. McCubbins, eds., *Presidents, Parliaments, and Policy* (Cambridge: Cambridge University Press, 2001).

52. Cox and Kirby, *Congress, Parliament, and Defence*, 298.

53. George M. P. Bruce and J. David Morgan, "Parliamentary Scrutiny of Defense," *Journal of Legislative Studies* 5, no. 1 (1999): 10.

54. Malcolm Shaw, for example, argues that the power of parties and legislative committees are inversely related: "Where the committees are strongest . . . one finds the lowest level of party control over the committees." Shaw, "Conclusions," in *Committees in Legislatures: A Comparative Analysis*, ed. J. D. Lees and M. Shaw (Oxford: Martin Robertson, 1979), 394. Similarly, Scott

Morgenstern and Luigi Manzetti argue that legislators will be interested in professionalizing their organization when they are relatively independent of the executive and their party leaders and are interested in a legislative career. Morgenstern and Manzetti, "Legislative Oversight: Interests and Institutions in the United States and Argentina," in Mainwaring and Welna, *Democratic Accountability in Latin America.*

55. Philip Norton and David M. Olson noted in the mid-1990s that the new parliaments of Central and Eastern Europe "have proved to be more independent in determining public policy than most legislatures in established Western systems." Norton and Olson, "Parliaments in Adolescence," in *The New Parliaments of Central and Eastern Europe,* ed. David M. Olson and Philip Norton (London: Frank Cass Publishers, 1996), 242. If parties are weak in the sense of not having stable roots in society, however, this could lead to excessive turnover of legislators at each election, thus undermining the requisite corps of returning legislators with an interest in strengthening "their" institution.

56. Werner Blischke, "Parliamentary Staffs in the German Bundestag," *Legislative Studies Quarterly* 6, no. 4 (1981): 536.

57. See, for example, Lawrence D. Longley and Roger H. Davidson, eds., *The New Roles of Parliamentary Committees* (London: Frank Cass and Co., 1998); Olson and Norton, *The New Parliaments of Central and Eastern Europe;* and Scott Morgenstern and Benito Nacif, eds., *Legislative Politics in Latin America* (Cambridge: Cambridge University Press, 2002).

58. For example, chapters evaluating the state of civil-military relations in the countries of postcommunist Europe by necessity devote only a few pages to the role of the legislature in each country under study and typically provide this kind of "thumbs-up or thumbs-down" assessment. See Cottey et al., *Democratic Control of the Military in Postcommunist Europe.*

59. For example, Hans Born analyzes the legislature's role in the defense sector in France, Sweden, Switzerland, and the United States and concludes that the legislature is much stronger in the United States than in the other countries. No implications are drawn about the impact of the different strengths of the legislatures on either civilian control of the military or policy outcomes. Instead, all four legislatures are judged to be important for democratic legitimacy and accountability because they play more than a "rubber-stamp" role. The "no best practices" approach does permit analysts to criticize systems where the president is so strong that the legislature is marginalized (as is the case in Ukraine or Russia), since in these cases the legislature does not play the minimal role necessary for it to contribute to legitimacy and accountability. See Born, "Between Efficiency and Legitimacy"; Betz, "Comparing Frameworks of Parliamentary Oversight."

60. Huntington, *The Soldier and the State*, 177; Barry M. Blechman, "The Congressional Role in U.S. Military Policy," *Political Science Quarterly* 106, no. 1 (1991): 21.

61. Deborah D. Avant, *Political Institutions and Military Change: Lessons from Peripheral Wars* (Ithaca, NY: Cornell University Press, 1994). In particular, the strong reaction of members of the U.S. Congress to President Truman's firing of General Douglas MacArthur was said to have discouraged subsequent presidents from relying on this method of asserting control over the military. It was simply too politically costly, whereas in Great Britain the prime minister was free to fire generals at will and thus induce military compliance.

62. See Agnieszka Gogolewska, "Parliamentary Control of Security Policy: The Experience of Poland" (Working Paper 106, Geneva Centre for the Democratic Control of Armed Forces [DCAF], Geneva, 2003); and Betz, "Comparing Frameworks of Parliamentary Oversight."

Chapter 3
Ministries of Defense and Democratic Control
THOMAS C. BRUNEAU AND RICHARD B. GOETZE JR.

THE existence of a ministry of defense (MOD) is an important basic indicator of the quality of civil-military relations in a country. Although some of these ministries are hardly more than facades, with no power whatsoever, others have assumed increasingly important roles as catalysts and platforms for the consolidation of democratic civil-military relations. Some have worked closely with the armed forces' high command to develop national security strategies. This chapter situates the founding and development of ministries of defense in the context of the current post–cold war era of democratization. It explains why they are created and identifies those conditions and actions necessary for the ministries to formulate effective and efficient defense strategies while ensuring democratic civilian control.

A defense ministry is a core element in contemporary democratic civil-military relations. The MOD structure has become widely viewed as the best solution to the classic paradox, "Who guards the guardians?" If the accurate response is that democratically elected civilians should be the ones to do the guarding against a military takeover, then a MOD is the preferred mechanism to match the democratic legitimacy of elected civilians with the professional expertise of the military. Most important issues in civil-military relations during the present period of democratic consolidation are addressed within the form and functions of a MOD.

Despite the importance of this topic, very little has been written up to now about MODs and democratic consolidation. There is even less literature on developing national security and military strategies in the context of emerging democracies. Although some of the lessons learned since the creation of the U.S. Department of Defense in 1947 are relevant elsewhere, civilian control over the armed forces was never the challenge in the United States that it has been for many of the so-called new democracies.[1] Although most of the central issues in civil-military relations are generic to any democracy, differences in history, the security environment, and institutional structures can be so vast that the lessons learned in the older, more "mature" democracies often are not fully relevant to new ones. There is nothing in the current literature that defines what is required for a MOD to combine political goals and considerations with military needs and objectives in an emerging democracy.[2]

In this chapter we will draw data and illustrations from firsthand observations in countries creating, or re-creating, a MOD and from interviews with civilian and military officials involved in the process. The purpose of this chapter is to define the themes and issues surrounding the creation and role of MODs, rather than to suggest some kind of blueprint for quick success.[3] It will present an approach that others might develop further and apply to important contemporary cases such as Brazil, Bulgaria, Colombia, Spain, or South Africa, individually or through comparative studies.

New Institutionalism

An analysis of a bureaucracy such as a MOD must begin with Max Weber. In his classic essay "Bureaucracy," Weber explains,

> The decisive reason for the advance of bureaucratic organization has always been its purely technical superiority over any other form of organization. The fully developed bureaucratic mechanism compares with other organizations exactly as does the machine with the non-mechanical modes of production.[4]

Although this statement is basically correct, and Weber elaborates extensively on the conditions under which bureaucracies emerged, much hinges on the term "fully developed bureaucratic mechanism." The literature in New Institutionalism, discussed in the introduction, highlights a number of necessary considerations for understanding the topic.

The more important of these considerations center on the often-forgotten fact that bureaucracies, here referred to as institutions, are crafted by humans at particular times and with particular goals or purposes in mind. Scholars using this approach look to the conditions under which these institutions develop or wither, and their "stickiness," or resistance to change.[5] Put simply, no two MODs are the same in structure, process, or practices. It is important for the researcher to grasp whether a MOD does or does not have power and to know the real extent of its roles and reach. This chapter therefore looks at MODs as institutions that are either formal and without power or content, or alive and dynamic with the potential for further development. To do so, it first situates the MOD in a historical and political space by reviewing the contemporary global political and military environment.

The International Context

Three main features of the contemporary world are most important to the development of MODs. The first is the spread of democracy. The world continues to ride the so-called third wave of democratization that has seen a large number of dictatorships collapse, to be replaced by democracies with varying degrees of stability and popular participation. Although several of the emerging democracies in this third wave appear to be very fragile or even failing, but those few cases do not undermine the third wave concept. Since 1974 the world has experienced a trend in which authoritarian regimes, either run directly by or propped up by the armed forces, have been replaced by democratically elected civilian governments. The definition of "democracy" itself remains a matter of debate, but if "procedural democracy"—free and fair elections that in fact determine who governs—is used as the measure, then democracies have expanded from 27 percent of independent states in 1974 to 63 percent, or 121, of the 192 independent countries in 2000.[6]

The continuing spread of democracies, then, is the first element of the current picture. Of particular importance in the consolidation of democracy is the issue of accountability; that is, to what degree are the rulers accountable to the citizens they govern? Once the concept of accountability is introduced, then immediately the issues of structures and processes also emerge. By what means are the rulers held accountable? We look at a MOD in the same perspective; without one, how can civilians in government exercise control over the armed forces?[7]

The second, equally important and somewhat interdependent element is the end of the cold war. The cold war (1945–1991) defined the strategic relationship between the United States and the Soviet Union and their respective allies and enemies; furthermore, it also defined virtually all security relationships, including domestic security, throughout the world. The cold war was fought not only in Eastern and Central Europe, but also in Guatemala in 1954, Cuba after 1959, Chile in 1973, Angola in 1976, Afghanistan after 1979, and elsewhere, where the eastern and western blocs vied for ascendancy regionally and within countries. While the United States and the Soviet Union avoided global war, on the periphery the cold war accentuated regional tensions and increased the importance of states' armed forces. As a consequence, militaries in Latin America,

Asia, Africa, and the Middle East assumed a greater role than would otherwise have been the case for most of the period since 1945. Indeed, in the majority of these regions militaries *were* the government over that period.

With the end of the cold war, the prior rationale for security, and specifically for the size and centrality of the armed forces, disappeared. Today most militaries are scrambling to justify their budgets and configurations. Universal male conscription is increasingly being abolished. Historical enemies are forming new alliances and coalitions. In Iraq following the U.S.-British invasion in 2003, for example, troops from the Dominican Republic, El Salvador, Honduras, Nicaragua, Mongolia, and Bulgaria served alongside Poles, Spaniards, Americans, and Britons. In the midst of these changes, militaries are finding it difficult to define their current and future roles and missions. It is in this regard that the development of a national security strategy, which defines issues and identifies the range of possible responses, becomes critically important. If a national security strategy will be developed, it is most likely that it will be the MOD that does it.

The third and last element of the contemporary context is the international scramble for new relationships and new forms of influence in this democratizing, globalizing, unipolar post–September 11 world. Although nations and alliances continue to seek influence and ascendancy today, as they did during the cold war, they are applying different instruments and even have different goals. Democracy, free market capitalism, and cooperation in the global fight against terrorism are the current defining global themes. Today nations, international organizations, foundations, nongovernmental organizations, and even individuals (George Soros, Bill Gates, and Ted Turner, for example) are profoundly involved in providing models, resources, and technical assistance to politically evolving countries. These links and mechanisms for influence are not the monopoly of the bigger and wealthier actors but extend to regional players such as Spain, South Africa, and Argentina and the nongovernmental organizations within them.

Civil-Military Relations in Nondemocratic Regimes

To better understand the steps and challenges involved in establishing viable ministries of defense today, it is necessary to review briefly civil-military relations prior to democratization. By definition, the governments in question did not have functioning democratic institutions in place. Elections either were not held at all or were merely formal and ineffective. Those in power did not rely on popular support for their positions. Rather, they tended overwhelmingly to rule by force, possibly with reference to nationalism or some other kind of ideology, which required the threat of and capability for suppression of dissent.[8] While some authoritarian regimes were run by civilians (in Portugal, Spain, and the Soviet Union, for instance) and others by the military (in Argentina, Brazil, Chile, Indonesia, and Nigeria), in virtually all cases the armed services were a central element in the actual or potential use of repressive force. In most, though not all, countries, the primary function of the armed forces was domestic control. It could even be argued, from both theory and the empirical record, that the external conflicts in which these authoritarian regimes engaged were due largely to their nondemocratic characteristics.[9]

The cold war both directly and indirectly influenced virtually all military roles and missions and civil-military relations throughout most of the world. The war, though "cold," was still a war. As such, it provided a rationale that exaggerated the importance of the military. In a context of war, the armed forces of many nondemocratic countries found they could justify commandeering more resources, keeping a high degree of autonomy, and exerting great influence or even veto power over areas of state, economic, and civil decision making.

In their inflated and exalted positions, the armed services were not required to coordinate their activities, cooperate with civilians, or rationalize their use of resources through documents such as national security strategies. After all, open-ended preparation for some possible future conflict can justify almost any level of funding and autonomy. And within these largely authoritarian regimes there was no public pressure to coordinate and economize in order to achieve effectiveness and efficiency. These were largely alien concepts that did not figure into the public discourse, if there even was any.

Spread of Ministries of Defense in the Third Wave

In the contemporary era, most countries have created or reconstituted ministries of defense under at least formal civilian control. For example, Spain established a MOD in 1977 after the restoration of civilian rule in the country; in Portugal an old organization was redefined and brought under formal civilian control in 1982; Argentina put its MOD under civilian leadership in 1988; and Colombia's began to assume importance in 2000. In much of Latin America, establishment of defense ministries under civilian control is a recent development—for example, in Nicaragua (1997), Honduras (1998), and Brazil (1999). Nevertheless, the mere presence of a MOD does not guarantee effective civilian control. Nor, for that matter, does having a civilian minister of defense. Portugal had a MOD that was in reality powerless until the late 1980s, while Nicaragua's remains relatively weak (in comparison with the influence of the armed forces) eight years after its creation. The same has been true of the newly independent states of Eastern and Central Europe, which have had MODs but not democratic civilian control until the last few years. The real question, then, is how do emerging democracies create MODs that have some potential for holding and exercising power?

Why have new (and not so new, in the case of Colombia) democracies only recently created or brought their ministries of defense under formal civilian control? There are two main reasons for these changes. First, these developing states are following the example of other, more established democracies where civilians exercise control over the armed forces in order to maximize military effectiveness in response to political objectives and to enhance efficiency and accountability in the use of resources. This could be termed the "demonstration effect": civilian leaders are increasingly aware that the MOD is currently viewed as an effective and efficient means to institute civilian control of the military. It is widely recognized that the armed forces, which bear the ultimate burden for national defense, rarely if ever acknowledge that they have enough money for equipment, troops, maintenance, or training to perform the functions assigned to them by their civilian political leaders. If the armed forces are left to their own devices, which is most often the situation in authoritarian regimes, they work out deals or understandings among themselves whereby they inflate their requirements to maximize the benefit for all the services. This lack of accountability results in increased costs and the loss of any incentive to improve efficiency. All of these problems are widely recognized, and as new democracies seek to bring their armed forces under control and to cut costs, an effective MOD appears to be the most appropriate institution for these purposes.

Admiral D. Angel Liberal Lucini, who served as first subsecretary of the Spanish Ministry of Defense from its founding in July 1977 to 1983 and subsequently as the first chief of the defense staff (JEMAD)—principal liaison to the minister of defense—between 1984 and 1986, made this point in an unpublished article and reiterated it in an interview with one of the authors.[10] He noted that, prior to 1977, Spain was the only country in NATO's region (which Madrid would join in 1983, reaffirming its membership in a 1986 referendum) without a ministry of defense, and he emphasized the negative effects of the complete independence of the three armed services. The creation of the Spanish MOD, and the definition of its relations with the JEMAD, answered the need for civilian control as well as effectiveness, efficiency, and accountability. An observer of and participant in the establishment of South Africa's MOD writes about the rationale for creating the ministry: "When I asked the Chief of the South African Navy, Vice-Admiral Simpson-Anderson, of his feelings about the establishment of civilian control over the military, he said he welcomed the idea. This was because in Western democracies there were established patterns of civilian control over the military, so South Africa had no choice but to follow suit."[11]

Second, in recognition of the general validity of this point, there is pressure from the more established democracies for the newer democracies to follow these models. This might be termed the "influence effect." Through regional security organizations and arrangements such as NATO and the Partnership for Peace, the presence of U.S. regional "combatant commanders," and the external defense and defense cooperation programs of the United States and European democracies, there is strong encouragement for all countries to establish effective ministries of defense.[12] Although, as noted above, little literature exists on the topic, there is nevertheless a widely held if vague assumption that what has worked elsewhere, in the more established democracies, will also work in the new ones. Consequently, the creation of ministries of defense is on the agenda of international assistance programs that influence democratic civil-military relations. For example, Rudolf Joo, a former Hungarian deputy minister of defense, lists seven societal, institutional, and procedural requirements constituting the democratic model of civilian control of the armed forces. One of the seven requirements is as follows: "the hierarchical responsibility of the military to the government through a civilian organ of public administration—a ministry or department of defence—that is charged, as a general rule, with the direction/supervision of its activity."[13] More recently, in addition to the creation of MODs, the U.S. government is also encouraging countries that receive substantial security assistance to develop national security strategies. In the case of Colombia, the administration of President George W. Bush, as well as congressional language appropriating funds for "Plan Colombia," required development of a Colombian national security strategy as a condition of continued bilateral assistance.

Four Main Purposes of a MOD

After examining existing research and considering extensive firsthand observations in the new democracies attempting to deal with issues of civil-military relations and military effectiveness and efficiency, it becomes apparent that MODs may fulfill four main purposes, although these purposes may not have had much bearing on the ministry's creation in the first place. The four functions are conceptually distinct but, like any social or political phenomena, are functionally intertwined. Previous studies have not linked them together in this manner, but empirical research over a period of at least a decade reveals that these four purposes are the most critical reasons to create a MOD.

The first and most obvious purpose for a MOD is to structure the power relationships between democratically elected civilian leaders and the armed forces command. A MOD is the vehicle whereby the relationships between those who hold the democratically established right to formulate state policy and those who hold a monopoly on the means of violence are institutionalized. How civilians in different countries attain the right to rule, and whether they are in fact able to exercise it, vary tremendously, and the scholarly literature is as ambiguous on this point as it is broad. But once this right has been forged, a critical issue in consolidating democracy is how to bring the armed forces under control.[14] Although a MOD is not only the currently favored but also perhaps the most indispensable institutional mechanism for establishing this control, by itself a MOD is not sufficient to guarantee democratic civilian control of the military[15]—thus the inclusion of the other chapters in this book dealing with other institutions for control.

The second purpose of the defense ministry is to define and allocate responsibilities between and among civilians and military officers. This purpose may seem straightforward in theory, but it most definitely is not in practice. Proof of this lack of simplicity may be seen in the perpetual efforts by the two highly institutionalized democracies of Canada and the United States to sort out these relationships. The creation of the U.S. Department of Defense and the delineation of its responsibilities with regard to the armed services (including the newly created U.S. Air Force in 1947) were extremely complicated and highly political processes, requiring the national security system to be modified or reformed at least twice over the ensuing four decades. The most recent of these reforms, the Defense Reorganization Act of 1986—generally known as the Goldwater-Nichols Act—was equally complicated and political. Indeed, it was virtually imposed by Congress over the resistance of both civilian and military leaders in the Department of Defense and some of the armed services.[16]

It might seem that the difficulty and drama in U.S. civil-military relations could be attributed to the superpower status and global reach of the United States. If this were the case, one should anticipate that relations between civilians and military officers ought to be more tranquil and straightforward in relatively peaceful Canada. Yet, one of the most respected Canadian students of defense issues concludes:

> In Canada, civil-military relations are floundering and uncertain. Recent events have exposed the problem, but they are only the current manifestation of weaknesses long resident in the structure of the defence establishment. . . . The relationship between the government and the defence establishment is troubled because political leaders have failed in their basic responsibility to supervise the armed forces of Canada.[17]

A key factor in the rational definition and allocation of responsibilities is the role a MOD fills as buffer between politics and the armed forces. This role may not initially be obvious, especially for countries that are not accustomed to having elected political figures lead important state institutions. The intent is that a political figure, selected to be defense minister through negotiations within the governing party or coalition of parties, or by presidential appointment, can represent the needs of the armed forces to other political figures, particularly the finance or economics minister, and to the electorate in general. If the armed forces seek to represent their own needs to the public, something they do not need to do under authoritarian regimes, they are assumed prima facie to be subjective and self-serving. Thus, having a civilian as the minister of defense can in fact be beneficial to the armed forces' interests. It clearly is positive for the democracy, since it potentially removes an obstacle to democratic legitimacy: that of having a nonelected organization using its bureaucracy, and quite possibly its monopoly of violence, to influence or even blackmail the political system.[18] The negative implications of the politicization of the armed forces are obvious and range from corrosion of democracy to interstate or intrastate war. In an interview, Alexei Arbatov, vice chairman of the Defense Committee in the Russian State Duma, emphasized to one of the authors the negative aspects of not having such a buffer for both democracy and the armed forces in Russia. He noted that the lack of an empowered civil-military liaison kept the armed forces "in politics" and frustrated every effort at military reform.[19] It should be noted that in Brazil, where the armed forces initially were not enthusiastic about the creation of the civilian-led MOD in 1999, military leaders began to see within two years the advantages of having an outsider promote their interests in the executive and the legislature. High-ranking Brazilian naval officers told one author, for example, that they were pleased because a civilian minister of defense reduced the influence of the army, while representatives from all the services thought that their chances for funding, especially for equipment, were improved by having a respected civilian in charge of the defense ministry.[20]

The absence of a civilian advocate-mediator exacerbates two core causes of the confusion and politicization that arise between democratically elected civilians and military officers. First, as Max Weber recognized in his writings on politics as a vocation, the logic behind it and bureaucracy, including the military, is completely different.[21] In a democracy, politicians often find themselves compelled to make popular, and often unrealistic, promises; there is an understandable tendency for the electoral process to become highly rhetorical. There is also a necessary vagueness to their promises, as their ability to fulfill any pledge is quickly curtailed in the clash with economic and social reality. Military officers in a democracy, by contrast, advance through a largely merit-based, far less subjective promotion system. Furthermore, military leaders expect to be held responsible and accountable for matters of life and death, in which precision and accuracy are fundamental to success.

Second, the armed forces simultaneously are a prominent national patriotic symbol and hold a monopoly on the legal use of violence. This monopoly is really what most distinguishes them as a profession from other professions and as a bureaucracy from other state bureaucracies.[22] Thus, military officers, with symbolic and real power, can offer obvious resources for unscrupulous politicians seeking ways to enhance their positions. To gain support by promoting or retiring officers for largely political reasons, for example, is to disrupt the career progression of the merit-based promotion system, thereby politicizing the officer corps and most likely decreasing the military capability of the armed forces. MODs can help mitigate this danger by institutionalizing processes and mechanisms of civilian oversight and control.

A third purpose in creating a MOD is to maximize the effectiveness of employment of the armed forces. Effectiveness in this case means the capacity to implement policies through the use of armed force. Military bureaucracies are among the slowest to change, because of the time-honored nature of their missions, the entrenched career-promotion structures, and the huge investments and lead time needed to develop new equipment and strategies. This issue of effectiveness may have been of marginal importance to some countries in the past, if either no real threat existed on the borders or the military served to control and intimidate unarmed internal populations. The utility of the armed forces became open to question with the end of the cold war and its superpower alliance relations, the third wave of democratization, and a general lessening of interstate wars. Consequently, in many countries there is wide-ranging debate over not only the future roles and missions of the armed forces but also whether a country needs a military at all.

The question of effectiveness is particularly acute today. In the current environment, where intrastate conflicts far outnumber interstate wars, many countries are embracing peacekeeping and peacemaking as justifications for preserving their armed forces. Successful execution of these missions, which include prominent roles for civilians, particularly in foreign ministries, would be nearly impossible without the involvement of a MOD. Redefining old roles and missions and implementing new ones for the military demand that another, higher-level civilian institution—a MOD—take the lead.[23] Those countries that are most active in peacekeeping not only have had to resolve their interservice rivalries but also have clarified the central functions of civilian leadership. In other words, effectiveness of the armed forces in international peacekeeping puts a premium on an established, active MOD. What holds for peacekeeping, furthermore, will surely hold for counterterrorism since the terrorist attacks of September 11, 2001, the Bali bombings in October 2002, and the bombings in Madrid on March 11, 2004. The U.S. government is seeking cooperation globally for its mobilization against international terrorism, while at the same time emphasizing democratic consolidation. The MOD is the primary means for achieving this wide-ranging and extremely dynamic military and political coordination.

The fourth and last major purpose in creating a MOD is to maximize efficient use of resources (for example, funds, personnel, and equipment) as roles and missions change. Efficiency in this instance means the ability to achieve a goal at the lowest possible cost. In the predemocratic phase, the different branches of the armed forces in many countries enjoyed tremendous independence. Their missions often overlapped, and yet they maintained separate supply and training programs. If they cooperated at all, it was to ensure the greatest amount of resources possible for each separate service. Most often, military budgets were secret, and even if they weren't, ordinary citizens had no mechanism by which to exert influence over allocations. Today the new forces of democratization and globalization demand transparency, and previously acquired privileges and prerogatives are fading away. Popularly elected governments have to respond to the demands of their citizens and can no longer afford the luxury of providing the abundant resources the armed forces once enjoyed.

With globalization, organizations such as the International Monetary Fund, the World Bank, the North Atlantic Treaty Organization (NATO), and the European Union, along with individual states and even individual investors, demand convincing justification for any investment at all in national defense. In the case of the European Union, this pressure is codified in the strict fiscal requirements of membership in the European Monetary Union. Consequently, with defense budgets dropping just about everywhere, the armed forces are under pressure to be as efficient as possible.[24] The best vehicle, or at least the best locus of activity, for this kind of resource and asset management is a MOD. Within the MOD, civilian politicians can implement programs for ensuring budget transparency, act as arbiter, minimize duplication among the services, sell off unnecessary facilities, and negotiate with vendors of equipment and services. The MOD employs lawyers, accountants, and planners to initiate and implement all of these programs and is the best place to concentrate a wide variety of expertise in order to manage effectively and efficiently the defense and security of a nation.

How should a new democracy structure and support military requirements? At a minimum, a country that is serious about national security and defense will have to establish a robust bureaucratic system, presumably led by the MOD, to carry out the following: strategic planning, operational planning, requirements generation and programming, and acquisitions. Most countries have recognized the advantages of integrating planning and resource allocation for national security, but developing formalized, rationalized, and integrated operations is time- and resource-intensive.

Other Tasks

There are other possible purposes for which a MOD would be the best forum. One, for example, is to balance the relative weights of the armed services. In all authoritarian regimes the army was the dominant service, if only because it was the one that maintained internal control. In the transition to civilian control, the other services are particularly eager to have a MOD that can right this imbalance. With the redefinition of roles and missions in support of national interests and a national security strategy, the other services have become more prominent than in the past. Thus one important function of a MOD is to better promote what the Pentagon terms "jointness": the integrated planning and operation of all the armed forces in support of national interests.

It is one thing to create a MOD, however, and quite another to provide it with sufficient legal authority, financial and personnel resources, and power to fulfill these purposes. So far, in fact, very few of the MODs in the new democracies possess these essential requirements. Those of Greece, Portugal, and Spain clearly do. This achievement probably has much to do with their relatively early transition to—or, in the case of Greece, return to—democracy, combined with the normative influences of membership in NATO (after 1983 for Spain) and the European Union. Available literature and recent interviews show that the MODs in Russia, Taiwan, and Thailand clearly do not meet the minimal requirements to function as real executive ministries.[25] Nor, in our experience, do those of Guatemala, Honduras, or Nicaragua. Others, such as those in Argentina, Brazil, Bulgaria, Romania, and South Africa lie somewhere in between. In the case of Colombia, our studies show that organizational constructs and legal frameworks would support a strong MOD, yet in practice the military leadership and the presidency have, until very recently, worked around the ministry rather than through it.

MOD Competencies and External Relations

If a MOD is to fulfill any of the four main tasks outlined above, we have found that it must be empowered with a number of basic competencies. Further, its relations with other agencies must place it in a position of relative authority. To expand on these issues, this section is divided into two main subdivisions: the first reviews the ministry's four key competencies, and the second specifies the four most important relations a functional MOD must manage. These discussions are based on past experiences in established democracies and the lessons being learned in the newer democracies, both positive and negative.

The four key competencies a MOD must master are in the areas of budgets, personnel, acquisitions, and definition of roles and missions. If a MOD does not have power or authority in these areas, it will have little real significance.

Budgets

It is trite but true that the "power of the purse" is the basis of civilian control of the armed forces. In authoritarian regimes, the defense budgets (and probably other budgets as well) were secret. Funds went directly to the armed forces, which enjoyed virtually total autonomy to allocate the funds within the services and other departments.[26] In many countries the system was especially pernicious, as funds for the troops would be allocated to a local commander, with no oversight into how the money was in fact used. Until recently we were still hearing of cases where the commander would use a minimum of funding for the troops' food, clothing, equipment, and training and simply pocket the remainder without fear of punishment.

The challenge lies in how to move from this situation to one where a civilian-controlled MOD assumes responsibility for budget development, resource allocation, and oversight. Based on personal observations, it is a very gradual process in which a MOD and ministry of finance or equivalent body absorb the budget development and execution functions from the general staff and divide the responsibilities between themselves. The ministry of finance makes the general allocations among the ministries, and the MOD then allocates within the defense sectors. This immediately brings up the issue of how these allocations should be made. A rigid programming-planning-budgeting system is probably not the solution, because of the huge requirements for data and technology to make it work, but some kind of system is necessary. At a minimum, the adopted system must guarantee transparency, provide justification for categories and funding levels, and assure accountability.

We have been struck by the fact that in many of the countries we visit there apparently is no direct link between the taxes and resources that citizens turn over to the government and what the government, including the armed forces, does with these resources. Until the population demands accountability, which cannot happen until the government opens itself to citizen input, there can be no transparency throughout the system. All of this requires an active civil society and free and energetic media. In Portugal, Spain, and Argentina, the MODs have in fact assumed control of the budgets within the defense sector, thereby allowing civilians to control the armed forces. According to reports, this also has become the case in South Africa. In Colombia, the MOD's role in budget development and control of the funds provided by the finance ministry remains secondary to that of the military services.

Definition of Roles and Missions

Roles and missions (discussed in Chapter 5), theoretically embedded in a strategy, define the purposes for which the military exists at all. This is particularly obvious in today's strategic environment, which has witnessed the end of cold war bipolarity, the third wave of democratization, accelerating economic and cultural globalization, and the launch of an open-ended global war against terrorism. What are the armed forces to be used for and under what conditions? Clearly, the answer is not what they were intended for during the cold war or under authoritarian regimes. These are issues that are being hashed out everywhere there is sufficient openness and public knowledge for a debate to take place. In a democracy, it should be democratically elected civilian leaders who finally determine national strategy and the functions of the armed forces.[27] This responsibility becomes particularly crucial today with the new emphasis on complex, civilian-oriented peacekeeping missions and risky counterterrorism operations. These missions are of particular interest to civilians, not only with regard to civilian control of the armed forces but also because involvement in either of them is an unwritten but widely understood requirement for membership in the ranks of responsible nations. Thus, it is all the more necessary for civilians to be aware, be in charge, and actually determine national strategy and roles and missions of the armed forces.

Unfortunately, few MODs so far have proved able to develop strategies using the structures, processes, and capabilities available to them. On top of this, general staffs, at least initially, tend to resist adopting clear definitions of roles and responsibilities, believing correctly that they are more likely to lose than gain power in an objective process of definition. Based on recent experience, this appears to be the case in Guatemala and Peru. By contrast, President Carlos Menem overcame much of the authoritarian thrust of Argentine civil-military relations by reorienting the forces and joining the U.S.-led coalition in the 1991 Persian Gulf War. Since that time, the Argentine armed forces have become leaders in international peacekeeping and, as became apparent during the severe economic crisis of 2001–2003, have abandoned their ambitions to rule.

The same general point can be made regarding what are loosely termed "military missions in support of civilian authorities." These broad missions can range from disaster relief—addressing the results of volcanoes, floods, earthquakes, and the like—to riot control, counter–drug operations, and now especially counterterrorism. For obvious reasons, the latter law enforcement–type examples are extremely sensitive issues and are sometimes perceived as a return to the "bad old days." These missions thus require very clear guidance, based on law and exercised through robust structures and processes, to ensure that the military executes the tasks without using them to usurp power. Again, the MOD should be responsible for determining when and how to use the armed forces for these kinds of domestic missions.

Personnel: Professional Staff and Force Management

The issue of armed forces personnel, both officers and enlisted, is more complicated than it might initially appear. If a country's armed forces were founded under the conditions of the cold war and authoritarianism, then their composition and training in the new international order will have to change—not necessarily in terms of larger or smaller numbers but different in scope, function, and complexity. The problem is, it is impossible to know a priori how they should change unless roles and missions are first defined, presumably through national security and national military strategies. Political and career structure considerations also will impinge on these decisions. Civilian and military planners must accept that there are decisions to be made, that the past is not the future, that inertia must not be allowed to rule, and that decisions on personnel and training must be made in the MOD, not only at general staff headquarters. Calling upon its pool of civilian and military experts and the range of information available to it, the MOD can determine force structure by analyzing threats and vulnerabilities based on several factors, including specific scenarios, capabilities, allocations by services, and fiscal caps.

Several fundamental issues pertain to whether a country's military should be based on conscription or should shift over to a smaller all-volunteer professional force (see Edwin Micewski, Chapter 8, and Karen Guttieri, Chapter 9, in this volume). These concerns include, on the one hand, pressure in a democratizing society to abolish conscription and re-allocate some proportion of funds from defense to social areas; and on the other hand, the imperative not to alienate or injure the armed forces by cutting them too far and too quickly. Spain's government, which managed a relatively smooth transition from authoritarian to democratic control, demonstrated a much better understanding of this balance than did the administration in Moscow, which made military reform a political football that resulted in the near-collapse of the Russian armed forces. The professional career structure itself has ramifications for both politics and morale. The number of senior officers, generally colonel and above, optimally depends on the number of troops; thus a reduction in force should, logically, result in fewer senior officers. For reasons of politics and the morale of those retained, however, the upper ranks cannot be reduced quickly and proportionally. Yet failure to do so causes problems of morale in the lower ranks, an appearance of "hollow forces," and the siphoning of scarce resources for salaries and benefits for the higher ranks.

In the contemporary setting, countries may seem to have little reason to use conscription to staff their armed forces. Indeed, as practiced in the United States during the war in Vietnam, and in Colombia more recently, there is much to argue for all-volunteer forces on the basis of equity as well as effectiveness. In some countries, however, concerns about cost, ethnic diversity, and nation building may overwhelm the arguments against conscription. For example, Mozambique's conscription policy is cogently based on the need for national integration following sixteen years of civil war. What becomes clear is many considerations are involved in personnel planning and force structure and that the past is not necessarily a good guide for the future. Given the inherent conservatism of bureaucracies, especially military bureaucracies, these decisions should be made at the more general, higher level of a MOD.

Acquisitions and Facilities

At least two generalizations can be made regarding acquisitions in defense: they are very expensive, and the lead time between procurement and final use can be considerable. It is thus all the more important that an efficient process be put in place to identify and acquire the most appropriate equipment. Appropriateness must be determined by the missions for which the equipment and the forces will be committed, which in turn requires rational strategic and military decision making. The acquisitions process, which can involve enormous amounts of public money, often leads to graft and corruption, so the system must be especially transparent and rigorous. Again, it is difficult to see how the armed forces' bureaucracies alone can achieve the needed levels of openness and robustness. Management of facilities also is an emerging issue, both because of the various requirements that may arise for the different services according to their missions and because armed forces often accumulate installations over the years that may become unnecessary or obsolete. The question becomes how best to sell off or transfer these excess facilities and acquire new ones or to convert old ones to meet new needs. It is easy to imagine the opportunities for graft and corruption when selling off real estate in areas that have appreciated tremendously, while the closing of facilities and subsequent job loss can have major implications for local politics. This activity requires attention at a bureaucratic level above the services command. A MOD controlled by a democratically elected government would be the most logical entity to deal with matters of appropriation and spending in order to avoid the temptation to divert government funds. Good progress apparently has been made in Argentina and Portugal in this area.

These four key competencies obviously are not monopolies of a MOD. A newly formed MOD initially lacks the institutional foundation and expertise to exercise these responsibilities. If the MOD is to fulfill the purposes defined in the section above, however, it not only must create and build on a strong institutional structure but must also be prepared to define relationships with key elements of the domestic political system, the armed forces, and international actors.

Internal and External Relations

A tremendous amount of institutional engineering is required to build the defense ministry, as well as all other basic institutions, of a new democracy. It is essential for the MOD to establish functional relationships with other key agencies and actors as they, too, are developing. At a minimum there are four: the executive, the legislature, the armed forces, and relevant international actors.

The MOD is part of the executive branch of government. Although important differences exist in the structure of relations in presidential versus parliamentary governments, the generalizations made here are meant to apply to both types of democratic political systems, and thus they are fairly generic. The fundamental issue is one of power, as it is in all aspects of civil-military relations. The question that must be answered is whether the MOD as an institution, and the minister of defense as an individual, have a central position in the power structure of a country. Or is the MOD only a facade and the minister without a strong political base? If the MOD is not integrated into the executive cabinet, with clear lines of authority radiating from the president or prime minister, and if the minister of defense is not politically powerful, then the MOD by definition is not a player in the political system. Building a MOD requires establishing new institutions and lines of authority where previously there were nothing. If the MOD and the defense minister are not closely linked to power, then either the armed forces continue to enjoy a great deal of autonomy or some other institution within the executive branch holds the power. Based on direct observation and research, this other institution will most likely be the ministry of finance or its equivalent. While the "power of the purse" may indeed keep the lid on military ambitions, often by starving the services for resources, fiscal policy alone cannot guarantee effectiveness or efficiency.

The ideal situation, at least in a new democracy, is one in which the MOD and its minister are integrated into the governmental power structure and hold the personal confidence of the executive. In this way, the armed forces know they are taken seriously, on the one hand, and they understand, on the other, that they must deal with the MOD and not attempt to avoid its control. The MODs of both Portugal and Spain enjoyed this confidence during the critical period of the early 1980s. In Greece, Prime Minister Andreas Papandreou also held the position of minister of defense. In Nicaragua, by contrast, from the time that President Violeta Chamorro gave up the position of minister of defense in November 1996 until 2002, the MOD was led by several weak political figures, including her son Pedro for two terms.

After the executive, the second crucial relationship for a new MOD will be with the legislature. While there are extremely important differences between a presidential and parliamentary system when it comes to the role of the legislature, several of the points presented here can be applied to either political system.[28] The most important consideration, first of all, is to broaden the interest of legislators and others in matters pertaining to the armed forces, national security, and defense, beyond a typically small group in the executive branch. In most of these countries prior to democratization, few civilians had any interest in or opportunity to deal with the armed forces beyond enlisted service. There was no advantage to such an interest, and it could be very dangerous. By bringing in the legislature, not only are expertise and the means for institutional control improved, but a broader group of politicians will also take an interest in and, it is to be hoped, become experts on issues of oversight and effectiveness. In Portugal, Spain, and Argentina, legislative defense committees were created with some powers of policy and oversight, which encouraged the members to become interested and involved in military issues. Brazil's government also is taking such steps. In Portugal, a member of the legislative defense committees eventually became the minister of defense. This sort of "graduation" is common in the United States, where the three most recent presidents—George H. W. Bush

(1989–1993), William Clinton (1993–2001), and George W. Bush (2001–present)—nominated former members of Congress to be their secretaries of defense.

Third, the MOD obviously will have to work hard to define its relationship with the armed forces, so that elected civilians clearly and unambiguously are in charge. The MOD's counterpart will be some form of joint or general staff comprising the top ranks of the armed forces. In most cases, the MOD will be taking over roles from the joint staff, so it is essential that the competencies of each be clearly defined.

From direct observation, it is apparent that the two primary functions to be clarified concern nominations for the highest military positions (the executive nominates, and the legislature approves) and operational roles. These in turn raise questions that will be critical to the delineation of roles and the distribution of power: How are nominations for senior officers handled? Does the MOD play a central role in handling the candidates and making the nominations, or are nominations made strictly by the general or joint staff? If the MOD takes the lead, it will be able to influence not only the character of the higher officer ranks but also the behavior of those who aspire to higher ranks. This correlation became clear during fieldwork in Spain, as an aspect of asserting civilian control over the armed forces. Spanish officers are very aware that their professional futures depend on their forbearance from political activity.

These are the new rules of the game that must be put in place, tested, and subsequently reaffirmed and institutionalized. The issue here is not simply the power of the president or prime minister to promote or retire officers, which is a first sign of civilian control, but rather the proper management of personnel, including promotion of the best-qualified officers to the highest positions. This prerogative holds clear implications not only for civilian control of the armed forces but also for their morale and capability to accomplish their missions.

The other area of responsibility to be defined, that of operational roles, concerns the division of command responsibility between the MOD and the military staff in both peace and conflict. Ideally, the MOD will have assumed the "support" roles of budgeting, supply, personnel management, training, and the like, and the military staff will be fully responsible for operational roles. We have found that this designation of responsibility is relatively clear-cut in the more advanced new democracies, such as Portugal and Spain, but is much less so in the less established democracies such as Russia, Brazil, and Nicaragua. Colombia's government currently is in the process of working out these roles.

Fourth and finally, MODs must develop good working relationships with the wide number and variety of international actors involved in international defense and security, including civil-military relations. These can include, for example, other countries' MODs, official groups and delegations, governmental organizations such as NATO and the United Nations, international military training and education programs, and nongovernmental organizations such as humanitarian relief and refugee agencies that operate near war zones. The issue here is whether the armed forces, as individual services or through the general staff, should deal directly with them. Again, from observation it seems clear that if the MOD can monopolize its role as initial contact, it will be better able to enhance its influence by mobilizing all the types of resources under ministry control: financial, personnel, training, and loans or grants of equipment. International donors can be an invaluable resource for defense rationalization and development, provided the MOD can create structures and processes for coordinating its relations with them. From our experience, very few MODs are able to do this. In most cases, the services are still in the lead but there is little coordination among them, much less with the MOD. At the other extreme, President Alberto Fujimori of Peru (1990–2000) personally approved every international activity in which military officers were engaged, as a means to assert and maintain his own control. This tactic, while it achieved Fujimori's purposes, did nothing to improve effectiveness or efficiency within the armed forces.

Unless and until at least these four sets of relationships are clarified, the MOD will be unable to fulfill the purposes for which it is created. Yet, defining and managing them demands knowledgeable and qualified personnel, resources a new MOD is unlikely to have. If, however, the executive branch will make the initial commitment, then the MOD can develop infrastructure as it reworks these relationships to its institutional advantage. This has been done in Portugal and Spain, has gone fairly far in Argentina, is just beginning but is on the right track in South Africa and Brazil, and has just begun in Nicaragua, but, sadly, the MOD is regressing in Venezuela.

A MOD will not be born, or reborn, with all of the key competencies and relationships defined, let alone developed. This section has outlined four competencies and four relationships that we have found must be encouraged and finally institutionalized in order for a MOD to be an effective governmental actor. In the more "mature" democracies such as France and the United States, ongoing adjustments, while important, take place at the margins. In the older "new democracies" of Greece, Portugal, and Spain, these eight areas have developed to a reasonable level.[29] Argentina, South Africa, and the new NATO members—the Czech Republic, Hungary, and Poland—are well along. Brazil is just beginning, but the situation is promising, as is the case in El Salvador. Russia remains mired in disorganization, while Honduras and Nicaragua have recently begun to define the issues.[30]

Initial Requirements for Institutional Development

A MOD, like any institution, will grow or decline depending on the terms by which it was founded and the levels of support for or opposition to it within the government. Based on our observations and experience in the United States, Portugal, Spain, and several of the newer democracies, three initial requirements will allow a MOD to begin to take on the kind of institutional life hypothesized throughout this chapter. First, MOD managers must build workable structures and processes, supported by a firm legal status and resources. Second, the MOD must be staffed with informed and responsible professional civilians who can expect some degree of permanence in their positions. Third, the MOD will need a mechanism to incorporate military officers and utilize their professional backgrounds and expertise to support ministry policymaking.

The first concern, creation of structures and processes, is a minimum requirement for any institution. This demands a legal foundation and at least a basic initial definition of what the institution's competencies and relations will be. This definition can be embodied in something akin to an organic law, often following from the constitution, which also defines relationships to other institutions. Even as fundamental a need as facilities can have strong political overtones. In the more successful instances of institutional development that we have observed, the new MOD will be located in the facilities originally inhabited by the services or joint staff, a highly symbolic choice. It has been interesting to observe over the years how the MODs in Portugal, Spain, and Argentina, consigned to a few offices when they first moved into these buildings, have expanded from one floor to another as their responsibilities increased. This currently is happening in Brazil as well. In other countries such as Nicaragua and Peru, however, the small size and marginal location of the facilities make it clear that the MOD is still struggling for ascendance over the armed services. In Honduras in 1999, the new minister of defense actually had to use considerable political capital to wrest the office of the commander of the armed forces, whose position had been abolished, from the recently ensconced vice commander. As a corollary, of course, the MOD must be adequately funded. This includes not only the funds to support the MOD itself, which need not be great, but also the ministry's purview over resources for the armed forces in general. For example, despite its long history as a democracy with civilian defense ministers since 1991, Colombia's MOD does not in fact control these funds; the military staff maintains its monopoly over the allocation of military resources.

Second, the MOD will require a professional civilian staff with some expectation of stability. As democratic control supplants the monopoly of the armed forces in the realms of national defense, civilians will have to hold key positions in the MOD. The dilemma, not surprisingly, is that initially there will be few, if any, civilians who know anything about defense. Therefore, civilians from other ministries, academics, lawyers, accountants, and the like will have to be recruited into the MOD and provided with the means to learn on the job and through training at home and abroad. These training programs are available in the United States, Switzerland, and elsewhere, but each country must be willing to take advantage of them.

One almost insurmountable obstacle to the development of a knowledgeable and dedicated staff is that most new democracies suffer from the noxious combination of an inadequate or nonexistent civil service system and the politicization of most government positions. As a result, there is little prospect for stability in government employment because appointments are at the whim of cronyism and nepotism. Unless these problems are confronted, and at least to some degree resolved, there is little hope that qualified civilians can be attracted or retained.[31] Brazil has an advantage in this regard, as it possesses an objective and well-structured civil service system.

The third requirement, inclusion of both retired and active duty officers in the MOD, is more complicated than it initially might appear. If, as is frequently the case in new democracies, the MOD is staffed with active-duty or retired officers, then there are fewer opportunities or incentives to include civilians. This type of staffing is frequently justified as a stopgap measure but can easily become a permanent "solution" to the problem of informed personnel in the MOD. In Guatemala, for example, as of 2004 the only civilians in the MOD are the janitorial staff. This is the negative side of the involvement of officers, whether active-duty or retired, in the MOD, and it has a profound impact on the ministry's general orientation. After spending their careers in the armed forces of their countries, many of which lack vibrant civil societies and adequate economic options, military officers will continue to identify with the military culture and associate with their peers in the services, thereby weakening the emerging norm of civilian control.

The MOD might include both active-duty and retired officers, so that it might incorporate their professional expertise into the policymaking functions of the ministry. It is essential for the new MOD to strike a balance between military and civilian personnel, so that each can be used to best advantage in fulfilling the ministry's various missions and with the intention that officers will train their civilian counterparts in the issues pertaining to the military. A plausible model would be to assign a military officer as deputy to each senior civilian within the ministry, and a civilian deputy to each senior military officer within the ministry. This system is employed in the U.S. Department of Defense and was explicitly followed in both Portugal and Spain. It apparently also has been adopted in South Africa and Brazil.

Responsibilities for Future Initiatives

Whether there is a MOD or not, whether it possesses scant or abundant resources initially, and the nature of its competencies and relationships will all depend on the initiative of the government's executive branch and possibly the legislature. The southern European democracies, new members of NATO, Argentina, and South Africa have seen their MODs accumulate new competencies and define or redefine their relations with other political institutions and foreign actors. These developments have been made possible through founding statutes, strong leadership early on, and effective bureaucratic dynamics. The MOD itself needs to have a role in initiating and formalizing these new and changing roles, especially in the legal realm. Key types of legislation, from most general to most specific, include changes in the constitution relating to the MOD and the armed forces; an organic law or laws determining the composition of the MOD itself and possibly the general staff; regular legislation pertaining to defense and the armed services; and ongoing policy initiatives of the executive. Some MODs, such as Brazil's, are acquiring these legal prerogatives, whereas others, like Guatemala's, have no power of initiative at all. From our observations, most countries have little awareness of the importance of this power. Again, if the ministry has a role in defining its future legal status, it will be better able to accumulate responsibilities and establish itself as a viable institution in the constellation of powers including the executive, legislature, and armed forces.

In sum, these three initial requirements must be met to increase the chances that the MOD will become capable of fulfilling the purposes for which it has been created. All of them demand adequate resources—political, human, and financial—something in limited supply in any democracy, particularly new ones. If political leaders are not committed to developing the institution of a MOD and providing it with these resources, however, then it is difficult to imagine how democratic civil-military relations can be established or maintained.

Conclusion

This chapter finally is about the politics of the management of defense. In the contemporary process of democratic consolidation, the issues of civil-military relations become less about the likelihood of military coups and more about institutionalizing effective and durable relations between democratically elected civilians and the armed forces. It is about how to manage the difficult relationship between democratic legitimacy and professional military expertise. Based on our observations, most new democracies have similar reasons for creating an effective MOD, and they recognize a common series of responsibilities that must be defined and implemented. These will demand a substantial commitment of human, financial, and political capital. If policymakers are interested in achieving civilian control of the armed forces and maintaining credible defenses, this chapter can serve as an inventory of what is required. It is clear that emerging democracies will be unable to formulate a national security and military strategy without a MOD in place, but policymakers may not be interested in either of these goals. If they are not interested, this chapter allows for assessments of what has not been done. For those who do wish to establish strong civilian control over the armed forces, however, the domestic resources of political capital, energy, funds, and personnel can be supplemented with international programs for training and education.

Notes

1. For an excellent political analysis of the creation of U.S. national security institutions after World War II, see Michael J. Hogan, *A Cross of Iron: Harry S. Truman and the Origins of the National Security State, 1945–1954* (Cambridge: Cambridge University Press, 1998). For an "insider" analysis of how the Defense Department was finally reformed in the 1980s, see James R. Locher III,

Victory on the Potomac: The Goldwater-Nichols Act Unifies the Pentagon (College Station: Texas A&M University Press, 2002).

2. For useful background material, see Martin Edmonds, *Central Organizations of Defense* (Boulder, CO: Westview Press, 1985); and Catherine M. Kelleher, "Defense Organization in Germany: A Twice Told Tale," in *Reorganizing America's Defense: Leadership in War and Peace*, ed. Robert J. Art, Vincent Davis, and Samuel P. Huntington (Washington, DC: Pergamon-Brassey's International Defense Publishers, 1985), 82–107.

3. Both Tom Bruneau and Richard Goetze have worked extensively in this field as researchers, educators in joint professional military education, and technical advisers to countries seeking to develop their MODs.

4. H. H. Gerth and C. Wright Mills, *From Max Weber: Essays in Sociology* (New York: Oxford University Press, 1958), 214.

5. See Sven Steinmo, Kathleen Thelen, and Frank Longstreth, eds., *Structuring Politics: Historical Institutionalism in Comparative Analysis* (Cambridge: Cambridge University Press, 1992), in particular Kathleen Thelen and Sven Steinmo, "Historical Institutionalism in Comparative Politics," 1–32. Also see Peter A. Hall and Rosemary C. R. Taylor, "Political Science and the Three New Institutionalisms," *Political Studies* 44 (1996): 936–957.

6. Data are from Freedom House, http://www.freedomhouse.org/research/freeworld/2003/index.html.

7. For a discussion of the key issues in democratic consolidation, see Philippe C. Schmitter and Terry Lynn Karl, "What Democracy Is . . . and Is Not," in *The Global Resurgence of Democracy*, ed. Larry Diamond and Marc F. Plattner (Baltimore: Johns Hopkins University Press, 1993), 39–52.

8. The most useful examination of these nondemocratic regimes is Juan J. Linz, *Totalitarian and Authoritarian Regimes* (Boulder, CO: Lynne Rienner, 2000).

9. This is of course the obverse of the "democratic peace" approach. See Bruce Russett, *Grasping the Democratic Peace: Principles for a Post–Cold War World* (Princeton, NJ: Princeton University Press, 1993). See also Michael Barletta and Harold Trinkunas, "Regime Type and Regional Security in Latin America: Toward a 'Balance of Identity' Theory," in *Balance of Power: Theory and Practice in the 21st Century*, ed. T. V. Paul, James J. Wirtz, and Michel Fortman (Stanford, CA: Stanford University Press, 2004).

10. The unpublished article is "Evolución de la estructura de la defensa en España desde 1939"; the interview took place in Madrid on February 17, 1993. For an analysis of the role of civil-military relations in Spain, including the creation of the MOD, see Felipe Aguero, *Soldiers, Civilians, and Democracy: Post-Franco Spain in Comparative Perspective* (Baltimore: Johns Hopkins University Press, 1995).

11. Lekoa Solomon Mollo, "Negotiating for Civilian Control: Strategy and Tactics of Umkhonto We Sizwe (MK) in the Democratic Transition of South Africa" (master's thesis, Naval Postgraduate School, Monterey, CA, 2000), 63.

12. Jeff Simon cites four conditions as being necessary to determine whether a state is exerting "effective" democratic oversight and management of the military, one of which specifically includes the MOD. See Jeff Simon, *NATO Enlargement and Central Europe: A Study in Civil-Military Relations* (Washington, DC: National Defense University Press, 1996), 27.

13. Rudolf Joo, "The Democratic Control of Armed Forces: The Experience of Hungary" (Chaillot Paper 23, Institute for Security Studies, WEU, Paris, 1996), 6.

14. One of the most highly respected scholars writing on democratic transitions and consolidations states: "Obviously, the institutional framework of civilian control over the military constitutes the neuralgic point of democratic consolidation." Adam Przeworski, *Democracy and the Market: Political and Economic Reforms in Eastern Europe and Latin America* (Cambridge: Cambridge University Press, 1991), 29.

15. For assessment frameworks to evaluate the status of civil-military relations in different countries, go to the Center for Civil-Military Relations Web site at http://www.ccmr.org.

16. On Goldwater-Nichols, see Locher, *Victory on the Potomac*.

17. Douglas L. Bland, *National Defence Headquarters: Centre for Decision*, study prepared for the Commission of Inquiry into the Deployment of Canadian Forces to Somalia (Ottawa: Minister of Public Works and Government Services, 1997), 47–48.

18. Regarding consolidation, see Juan J. Linz and Alfred Stepan, *Problems of Democratic Transition and Consolidation: Southern Europe, South America, and Post-Communist Europe* (Baltimore: Johns Hopkins University Press, 1996), 5–7.

19. Alexei Arbatov, interview by Bruneau, Naval Postgraduate School, August 29, 2000. For a survey of these issues, see Mikhail Tsypkin, "The Russian Military, Politics, and Security Policy in the 1990s," in *The Russian Armed Forces at the Dawn of the Millennium*, ed. Michael H. Crutcher (Carlisle Barracks, PA: U.S. Army War College, 2000), 23–44.

20. Brazilian officers, interview by Bruneau, Brasília, November 5, 2002.

21. Gerth and Mills, *From Max Weber*, 77–128, 196–239.

22. See S. E. Finer's classic *The Man on Horseback: The Role of the Military in Politics* (London: Pall Mall Press, 1962).

23. In interviews by Bruneau in Portugal and Spain in the early 1990s, military and civilian officials were clear on the need for a strong MOD to redefine the roles and missions of the armed forces.

24. For example, between 1990 and 2000, defense spending as a percentage of GDP dropped from 5.5 percent in the United States to 3.0 percent, and for the other NATO allies it declined from 3.0 percent to 2.0 percent. Data are from "National Responses to 2000 NATO Defense Planning Questionnaire," provided by staff at U.S. Mission to NATO, Brussels.

25. See Michael D. Swaine, *Taiwan's National Security, Defense Policy, and Weapons Procurement Processes* (Santa Monica, CA: Rand, 1999), 17–18. On Thailand, see Ravinder Pal Singh, ed., *China, India, Israel, Japan, South Korea, and Thailand*, vol. 1 of *Arms Procurement Decision Making* (New York: Oxford University Press, 1998), 219.

26. To illustrate how bad this can be, in Angola, for example, the greatest part of defense expenditures are secret but are calculated at 20 percent of GDP, based on International Monetary Fund sources as reported in USAID, *Avaliação estratégica do programa de democracia e governação* (Angola: USAID, 2000), 60–61.

27. According to Arch Barrett, the Goldwater-Nichols Act directed the White House to produce an annual statement on the nation's security strategy. Barrett, interview with Bruneau, Monterey, CA, May 2001. For the last statement from the Clinton administration, see "A National Security Strategy for a Global Age" (Washington, DC: White House, December 2000), i–67. Also see the initial strategy statement of the George W. Bush administration, "The National Security Strategy of the United States of America" (Washington, DC: White House, September 2002). The latter has been followed to date by five other strategy documents dealing with perceived threats to U.S. security.

28. See Kurt Von Mettenheim, ed., *Presidential Institutions and Democratic Politics: Comparing Regional and National Contexts* (Baltimore: Johns Hopkins University Press, 1997).

29. For more on the evolution of these democracies, see Thomas C. Bruneau, P. Nikiforos Diamandouros, Richard Gunther, Arend Liphart, Leonardo Morlino, and Risa A. Brooks, "Democracy, Southern Style," in *Parties, Politics, and Democracy in the New Southern Europe*, ed. P. Nikiforos Diamandouros and Richard Gunther (Baltimore: Johns Hopkins University Press, 2001), 16–82.

30. It is possible in some cases that civilians don't really want to control the military, except in the most general terms. This was the case in Venezuela from 1958 until the mid- to late 1990s. For an analysis of that situation, see Harold Trinkunas, "Crafting Civilian Control in Emerging Democracies: Argentina and Venezuela," *Journal of Interamerican Studies and World Affairs* 42, no. 3 (2000): 77–109.

31. The issue of staffing receives attention in Mollo, "Negotiating for Civilian Control," 68–70.

Part Two Roles and Missions of the Military

Chapter 4
Strategy Formulation and National Defense: Peace, War, and the Past as Prologue

DOUGLAS PORCH

DISPUTES between civilian policymakers and soldiers over issues of defense policymaking offer one of the most potent sources of tension within the decision-making process even of mature democracies. These tensions become especially challenging for democratic stability in wartime. The problems may be magnified for new or emerging democracies, whose decision-making mechanisms are embryonic and untested, and where relations between civilian and military leaders lack the sanctification of precedent and tradition. Ironically, however, the principal strategic theorists devote little time to problems of civil-military relations in general, much less those caused by debates over the size and configuration of the armed forces so that they can best achieve the state's strategic objectives in wartime. The classical strategists—Sun Tzu, Nicolo Machiavelli, Antoine-Henri Jomini, and Carl von Clausewitz—agree (although with different degrees of emphasis) that although wars are fought for political goals, civilians and soldiers should respect their distinct spheres of competence in its direction.[1] In peacetime, as in war, politicians define threats, determine political objectives, set the broad parameters of strategy, build coalitions, and provide resources. The task of soldiers ideally is to argue their case, take the resources allocated to them, and apply force to achieve the political goals as defined by the political leaders. In return, "[the soldier] has the right to expect unambiguous objectives, discretion, and public support," writes American political scientist Eliot Cohen. The soldier must have a voice in "the setting of strategy. . . . He must understand political constraints, but have a free hand" in the operational and tactical direction of war unhampered by political micromanagement.[2]

The reality, of course, is that this seemingly straightforward division of labor between civilian and military functions is seldom respected in practice. One mark of the great wartime political leaders is a healthy interest in the operational, even technological, dimensions of war. At the very least, a familiarity with military capabilities means that any political leader in peacetime is less likely to be bamboozled by military chiefs who employ operational or technological arguments to constrain policy or strategic options or resist military transformation or who suggest questionable "silver bullet" strategies. When Prime Minister Winston Churchill was complimented in November 1943 on the brilliant organization of his Chiefs of Staff system, he lashed out: "Not at all. It leads to weak and faltering decisions—or rather indecisions. Why, you may take the most gallant sailor, the most intrepid airman, or the most audacious soldier, put them at a table together—what do you get? *The sum total of their fears!*" [3]

Despite the objections of classical theorists, political leaders can and do define force structure and even impinge on the operational level of war. Furthermore, strict parameters laid down by civilians in the operational conduct of war is normal and may prove instrumental to the success of the wartime enterprise. The civil-military friction that occurs during the formulation and implementation of policy and strategy is not entirely the result of micromanagement of operations by politicians. Rather, as Eliot Cohen argues, a major source of civil-military friction is poor war management by political leaders tout court. [4]

Nor is it realistic to suppose that a large and cohesive military will recuse itself from debates over the nature of the threat, the purpose and size of the armed forces, or the conduct of foreign and domestic affairs in wartime. Cohen argues that wartime decision making is a product of a civil-military dialogue across permeable frontiers of competence, a "tense and exhausting interaction over matters of detail and not simply the broad outlines of strategy." Because war itself offers a dynamic interaction of adversaries, strategy must be constantly reassessed and adjusted to take account of enemy reactions and evolutions in one's own capabilities. The need to define threats, formulate and reassess strategy, and configure and fund the military offers multiple opportunities for civil-military tension. "Thus," Cohen concludes, "a theory of civil-military relations contains within it a theory of strategy." [5] This chapter seeks to identify the principal sources of conflict that arise between civilians and soldiers during the "tense and exhausting dialogue" that occurs in the process of policy formulation, net assessment, and matching strategy to policy in the operational conduct of war. The lessons derived here apply not only in wartime, when they are at their most serious because the stakes are highest, but also on a regular and continuing basis in democratic civil-military relations.

Matching Means to Ends: Four Tests

Few would argue with Clausewitz's celebrated dictum that "War is not a mere act of policy but a true political instrument, a continuation of political activity by other means. . . . The political object is the goal, war is the means of reaching it, and means can never be considered in isolation from their purpose."[6] But unanimity on political goals, or on the means of achieving them, is rarely achieved and offers opportunity for serious disagreement, both among civilians and between civilians and soldiers. To be successful, that policy must pass at least four tests: it must take vital interests into consideration; it must have the support of the population; it must be achievable within a reasonable cost; and, finally, it must be clear. The answers to these policy questions will influence the sizing, budgeting, and procurement phase of force planning and will have much to do with establishing good civil-military relations.

What Are We Fighting For?

The Weinberger-Powell Doctrine was devised initially in 1984 by U.S. secretary of defense Casper Weinberger and later refined by General Colin Powell, chairman of the Joint Chiefs of Staff. Their object was to avoid a recurrence of the American defeat in Vietnam through the application of a set of conditions to assess the appropriateness of engaging in a military conflict and to measure the chances of success. Some in the George W. Bush administration argue that Weinberger-Powell is a relic of the cold war made obsolete by the absence of a "peer competitor," by "military transformation" that has given the U.S. military an untouchable technological lead over its adversaries, and by the requirement to take "preemptive," unilateral action against terrorist adversaries. This reasoning is called the "blitzkrieg fallacy" by British historian Michael Howard, the assumption that winning is composed of the accumulation of successful battles.[7] It is a reasoning that led straight to the Iraq War of 2003 and points up the continued relevance of Weinberger-Powell as a starting point for successful civil-military relations.

The doctrine's first proviso is that war should be undertaken only when it serves "the vital interests of the United States or its allies." But politicians may fail to reach a consensus on what actually constitutes vital national interests or whether "secondary" interests, including the defense of an ally, are worth the sacrifices of war. Civilians and soldiers may line up on opposite sides of a debate about vital national or allied interests.

Threats that seem to politicians to be remote or of low priority or that may require unpopular public sacrifice to counter, may conspire to keep generals and admirals awake at night. Conversely, politicians may communicate their disputes to the armed forces, which in turn can become factionalized along party, or service, lines. Churchill instinctively grasped the strategic benefits of fighting in the Mediterranean from 1940, when many of his service chiefs wanted to husband assets in Britain against the distant possibility of a German invasion. The conviction of many American soldiers that Franklin Roosevelt's 1942 decision to commit troops to the Mediterranean obliged them to defend the interests of the British Empire rather than those of the United States made for rocky Anglo-American relations in that theater. Opponents of American military intervention in Korea in 1950 or Vietnam in 1965 argued that the survival of neither country as a noncommunist state was worth the bones of an American soldier.[8] In both of those wars, the president and his generals clashed over expanding the parameters of the conflict, a clash that in Korea cost General Douglas MacArthur his job.

Even if consensus exists over vital interests, debate may turn on whether diplomatic, economic, or military means, or some combination of all three, offers the best way to counter the threat to national interests. In that case, the least forceful option may be all that a nation or an alliance can agree upon. Sanctions are a popular alternative to force, especially when allies are divided over the degree of the threat. Military force may also prove difficult to apply when the consequences of an aggressive strategy appear to carry great risks. The debate that raged within the United States and between Washington and its allies in 2002–2003 over whether containment or confrontation offered the most appropriate response to Iraqi president Saddam Hussein's alleged quest for weapons of mass destruction hinged on one's assessment of the degree of threat represented by the Iraqi dictator, and the risks versus rewards of either strategy.

Means to the End

Democracies debate in the open the suitability of the policy or the viability of strategies to achieve that policy. Soldiers may take away from this debate the impression that popular support for military action is lacking. The Weinberger-Powell Doctrine insists in its fifth condition that "before troops are committed, there must be a reasonable assurance of support from American public opinion." This condition corresponds to a perception widespread in the post-Vietnam U.S. military that the political leaders committed them to a war that had no deep support in the population. The political leadership is tasked to "sell" the war to its population and its allies. To do this, the government must make the case that war advances the state's vital interests, that all other options short of war have been exhausted, and that the conflict is being fought in harmony with the principles and expectations of the citizens. Without a firm commitment of the population, the "moral factors" that Clausewitz believed to be the essential underpinnings to sustain combat—motivation, dedication, spirit of sacrifice—will be absent. Populations will weary of wartime sacrifice, allies will defect, and soldiers will succumb to a sense of betrayal, the feeling that they have been "stabbed in the back" by a feckless government, an ungrateful people, or a factious alliance. If the Vietnam War could roil the politics of an established democracy like the United States, imagine the damage that a contentious military policy or poor strategic choices may inflict on the fragile legitimacy of a new democracy.

Whereas the government's task is to lay a solid political, economic, and moral framework for defense policy, soldiers have the responsibility to choose military strategies, force structures, and operational and tactical methods that deliver timely success at reasonable costs. Civil-military friction occurs when the policy goals may be too vague to allow soldiers to formulate a clear military strategy to achieve them. The policy may also be beyond available military means to achieve. This was the case in World War I, where vague political goals combined with technological, operational, and tactical constraints to condemn belligerent nations to a grinding war of attrition that did serious harm to civil-military relations. The horrific losses sustained by Europe's armies in that war cast doubt on traditional values such as duty, honor, and patriotism that sustain military organizations in wartime. Postwar novels like Erich Maria Remarque's *All Quiet on the Western Front*, Robert Graves's *Good-bye to All That*, and Ernest Hemingway's *Farewell to Arms* reflected the popular view that the war had been a terrible waste, and they contributed to a general distrust of authority that infected the postwar generation.[9]

French soldiers opposed going to war in 1936 and 1938, after French public opinion evinced a reluctance to fight to secure the Rhineland or Czechoslovakia. The consequence for French politicians of their failure to confront the Nazi threat was the collapse of the legitimacy of the Third Republic. The French people blamed their stunning defeat in 1940 "on the French system of parliamentary government . . . on the rank and file of the fighting services, on the English, on the fifth column—in short, on any and everybody but themselves," wrote French historian Marc Bloch, who served as a reserve staff officer in 1940. This filament of alibis ob-scured, in their own minds, the appalling strategic and intelligence lapses that permitted the German breakthrough in the Ardennes. It is often easier to assume that sweeping events emerge from grand causes, rather than to identify the miscalculations that might have been remedied by better operational choices and more-careful management. For this rea-son, the popular verdict on France's defeat discounted the technical and tactical shortcoming built into the peacetime system that precluded a suc-cessful French recovery from German strategic surprise. "Whatever the deep-seated causes of the disaster may have been, the immediate occasion was the utter incompetence of the High Command," Bloch concluded.[10] French soldiers, however, spun the defeat into an indictment of the lack of resolve of the French people and the inability of the French republic to guarantee the security of France.

Likewise, the belief that America's retreat from Vietnam can be laid at the feet of a vocal antiwar movement that undermined U.S. morale and sent politicians scurrying for political cover offered comfort to both civil-ian and military proponents of a "stab-in-the-back" explanation of Amer-ica's defeat.[11] But a more cogent question to ask is, how did a military force configured to operate in Europe against the Soviet Army plan to apply force against a tenacious but low-tech enemy in the jungles of Indochina to achieve the objective of an independent, noncommunist South Viet-nam? The failure of politicians to ask hard questions of their soldiers, and of soldiers to adapt their forces to the requirements of a new theater, laid waste to U.S. civil-military relations for practically two decades.

Reasonable Cost for a Clear Benefit

The third precondition of successful policy is that it must be achiev-able within a cost deemed reasonable by the population. If the value of the objective is high, then the population is willing to make consider-able sacrifices. Few doubted in 1914 that the stakes of World War I were huge—national cultures as well as social ideals seemed to be on the line. The war "was to be, in a sense, the great moral achievement of the European middle classes."[12] Most, surveying the wreckage of that war after 1918, concluded that the price paid had been exorbitant and that Europe would have been much better off had the war never been fought. Few Americans doubted in World War II that the world position and fu-ture prosperity of the United States were threatened by the Axis. In any case, Japan's successful surprise attack on Pearl Harbor took the option of neutrality off the table and jolted Americans into making great sacrifices for victory.

When the value of the objective is low or when the threat is less apparent, the political leadership may have difficulty making a convincing case for war. In that case, the government must seek a rapid conclusion by the application of overwhelming force. Or it must keep the level of military commitment low enough that it does not impinge on other programs or national priorities. The strategic counter by the enemy is to raise the costs either through escalation or attrition. This can provoke a crisis in civil-military relations, as occurred in the United States during the Vietnam War, when the willingness of the Vietnamese revolutionaries to achieve national unity under a communist government far exceeded the dedication of Americans and South Vietnamese to an independent, non-communist South Vietnam. Although more powerful than its opponent militarily and economically, Washington discovered that an open-ended commitment to fight a distant war for a low-value political objective gradually exhausted the patience of its population. The growth of antiwar demonstrations and of evasion of military service, as well as the incorporation of increasingly unmotivated conscripts, left the U.S. military with the conviction that it had been forced unfairly to bear the brunt of an unpopular policy.

Nonetheless, generals also have a responsibility to select military strategies that deliver incremental success leading to ultimate victory at a reasonable cost. Even if support for the goals of the war are high, if operational and tactical methods produce debilitating casualties and showcase more than ordinary incompetence or insensitivity toward the fate of the troops, popular support for a war may be exhausted short of victory. American forces enjoyed widespread popular support in the early years of the Vietnam War. American commander General William Westmoreland's strategy of big sweeps and massive firepower was designed to keep down U.S. casualties and hence contain the war's political costs. It also offered "body counts" of communist casualties as the measure of progress toward victory. This strategy, however, inflicted heavy collateral damage that undermined civilian support for the war both in Vietnam and in the United States and triggered debates among civilians and soldiers over the advisability of adopting less destructive pacification strategies. The 1968 Tet Offensive, though extremely costly to the communists, showcased an insurgency that had much life left in it, discredited the "body count" measure of success, and convinced many in Washington that the war was unwinnable.[13] Tet accelerated the erosion of American determination to

see through to victory a war whose costs seemed increasingly disproportionate to the stake of U.S. national interests.

Emerging democracies may face choices that are less stark but nonetheless proportionate to their limited resources or brittle legitimacy. Soldiers
and politicians may split over the costs of victory and the strategies required to achieve them. Colombian president Andrés Pastrana's decision
in 1998 to open negotiations with the revolutionary movement FARC,
and even to concede to the guerrillas safe havens within the country, left
Colombian soldiers, who favored a more muscular approach, gape-jawed
with disbelief. Politicians may prove reluctant to increase the size and
influence of the military, even though the country faces a dire emergency.
One reason that Pastrana may have adopted a conciliatory approach toward Colombia's internal insurgency was that the government and the
country were clearly unwilling, or unable, to commit the major military
resources required to win the armed conflict with the Colombian insurgencies. In some cases, politicians may seek to restructure the military to
curtail its political influence. The military may resist new roles and missions, bridle at reduced funding streams, resent a reduction in prestige,
rail against political influence in promotion decisions, and oppose an obligation to display democratic transparency and accountability.

When Do We Know We Won?

Soldiers desire clear and unambiguous policy objectives from political
leaders. But a war's goals may remain unclear at the war's outset. Decisions made in 1914 are often viewed, correctly, as the quintessential example of policy-strategy mismatch, when Europe slithered into war without clear goals and consequently with confused and directionless military
strategies. The vagueness of political objectives tempts the military to
set its own strategies that, in turn, affect the political dimensions of a
war. For instance, Germany's main purpose in 1914 was to support its
Austro-Hungarian ally, whose major enemies were Serbia and Russia. The
Schlieffen Plan, drawn up by the German general staff before 1914 in the
absence of political guidance, however, virtually guaranteed a wider war
by attacking France through Belgium, whose sovereignty was considered
a traditional interest of Great Britain. Meanwhile, Vienna was left virtually on its own to deal with Russia.

When political leaders have not settled in their own minds what they
wish to achieve, they may react to the battlefield situation rather than
set clear parameters and hold their military leaders to them. When this

happens, strong-willed soldiers may set policy agendas of their own, as did Douglas MacArthur in Korea. He agreed neither with U.S. president Harry Truman's "Europe first" policy nor with the limited goal of defending South Korea against the North. He remained indifferent to the prospect of Chinese entry into the war, and so he surged north of the 38th parallel toward the Chinese border with the goal of unifying Korea, brushing aside warnings from the Joint Chiefs of Staff that he had exceeded his mandate.[14]

In some cases, policy goals may have been obscured or left unstated to mollify or manipulate popular or alliance opinion, leaving military leaders confused or with a great deal of leeway to impose their own agendas. Despite Lyndon Johnson's public commitment to an independent, noncommunist South Vietnam, only 29 percent of American generals in Vietnam found U.S. goals there "clear and understandable."[15] This confusion occurred in part because Johnson often reiterated his political goals in the process of launching a peace initiative whose purpose was to assuage antiwar opposition both at home and abroad.[16] General Phillip Davidson, Westmoreland's intelligence chief, complained not only that the absence of clear policy goals left soldiers directionless in their attempts to formulate a coherent strategy but also that Johnson's restrictions placed U.S. forces in a defensive posture that left the strategic initiative to the enemy.[17]

The true alliance objective in the 1991 Gulf War—a free Kuwait, or "regime change" in Iraq—also was fudged. If the goal was to free Kuwait, then the alliance was perhaps justified in pulling its punches short of the gates of Baghdad. Regime change would have required the capture of Saddam Hussein, the destruction of his Republican Guard, and help for the Kurdish and Shi'a uprisings deliberately incited by President George H. W. Bush. The ambivalence of the Bush administration toward its war goals in Iraq, and tensions between "stated" and "unstated" goals, virtually ceded to the military the decision on when to end the war. The chairman of the Joint Chiefs of Staff, General Colin Powell, convinced the American president to cease fire after barely a hundred hours of combat, leaving Saddam in office and his military free to crush the rebellions.[18]

As a war is prolonged, goals also can escalate. Sunk costs can radicalize populations and incite them to demand concessions commensurate with the sacrifices they are forced to endure. This may hamstring political leaders who conclude that a continuation of the conflict will bring victory no closer, but who are powerless to stop it because popular pressure has inflated the goals beyond their capacity to achieve them. Japanese leaders, aware that they had exhausted their gold reserves and bled their army white in Manchuria, confronted popular outrage in 1905 when they made a soft peace with Russia.[19] Select European leaders in all combatant nations in World War I understood by 1916 that the conflict had lost any political rationale. But halting it was beyond their capacity because no equitable settlement could be reached that would convince the populations that their sacrifices had not been in vain. The result in Germany was a debate between those who believed that the "rewards" of sacrifice should be a democratization of the rigid political system, and conservatives who inflated the initial push for territorial acquisition into a goal of German hegemony in Europe. Chancellor Theobald von Bethmann-Hollweg's inability to mediate between these conflicting visions led to his downfall. Conservatives rallied behind the general staff to demand a "Ludendorff peace," a strategy that led to an increasing militarization of policy, as the government put its faith in military victory—including the unrestricted U-boat campaign against shipping that tilted the United States into the war—to solve its political dilemmas.[20]

The dynamics of popular and alliance politics may cause political leaders to stray into areas that soldiers consider their traditional preserve. Maintaining the moral high ground in policy issues is essential to domestic and alliance cohesion. For this reason, politicians may intervene to prevent the targeting of civilians or invasion of territories, if they fear those acts might undermine support for the wartime enterprise. U.S. Air Force leaders, basing their bombing theories on World War II precedents, favored a massive bombing campaign of North Vietnam, on the assumption such an assault would cause the enemy's social fabric to unravel. Johnson, however, vetoed this strategic option as well as others like an invasion of the North, because it could escalate the goals and hence the costs of the war. Indeed, so concerned was the American president to avoid civilian casualties that Air Force generals complained of civilian "micromanagement" of bombing campaigns by politicians keen not to undermine popular support for military action, even if the trade-off was a curtailment of military pressure on the enemy.[21]

Likewise, politicians may order operations whose strategic objectives have a political, rather than a military, rationale. Lincoln directed military resources toward the capture of Atlanta in the summer of 1864 because a major victory against the Confederacy was vital to his reelection bid. Churchill ordered his Middle East commander, General Archibald Wavell, to launch a doomed operation to support Greece in the spring of 1941 because he was keen to contrast his willingness to support allies with that of his predecessor Neville Chamberlain, who had allowed Poland to be overrun without deigning to intervene. Likewise, in the summer of 1942, Roosevelt ignored the objections of Chief of Staff George Marshall that the Mediterranean was a dead-end theater, ordering the invasion of French North Africa, Operation Torch, for November. The American president sought to strengthen the position of his British ally Churchill, reinforce his "Europe first" strategy, and subvert Marshall's plans for a 1943 invasion of northeastern Europe, which in his view would probably shatter the Alliance, cost the Allies the war, and have severe repercussions for the future of American democracy.

Net Assessment

Sun Tzu's celebrated dictum—"Know your enemy and know yourself; in a hundred battles you will never be in peril"—is an invitation to carry out an inventory of one's own capabilities and those of allies, adversaries, and the allies of adversaries as a prerequisite to successful strategy formulation. "When you are ignorant of the enemy but know yourself, your chances of winning or losing are equal," Sun Tzu continues. "If ignorant of both your enemy and yourself you are certain in every battle to be in peril."[22] As in policy formulation, the scope for civil-military friction in the net assessment process is practically infinite. One group may overestimate a nation's strengths, believing, like Hitler, that will, determination, even bluff, can carry the day in the face of an alliance that had greater residual power in the long run. Indeed, Hitler's refusal to acknowledge Germany's long-term strategic weaknesses caused him, and his generals, to emphasize operational solutions to strategic problems. "Given human nature and the problems of perception, ethnocentrism, and wishful thinking, to name but a few," writes Michael Handel, "it is impossible to understand the enemy fully. Often nations are unaware of their own weaknesses and limitations, let alone those of their adversaries."[23]

As Handel suggests, the problems of miscalculation are more likely to relate to psychological and cultural factors than to poor intelligence. Even good intelligence can be filtered, distorted, or misinterpreted to fit the preconceptions, and thus support the desired outcomes, of the "consumers" and "decision makers." Ethnocentric assessments may transpose onto the enemy subliminal fears of one's own vulnerabilities. Aggressors may calculate that the enemy is weak, divided, or lacking in toughness or capability because this mirrors fears of their own inadequacies. The Japanese were encouraged by their narrow victory over Russia in 1905 to emphasize the cultivation of the military spirit and Bushido—the way of the warrior—to compensate for their relative material inferiority.[24] Fascist and militarist regimes in World War II tended to deemphasize material factors in the belief that the racial purity, moral preparation, unity, and discipline of their populations would give them the edge over wealthy but soft, ethnically diverse industrial democracies. Using these calculations, Hitler and Mussolini rode roughshod over the objections of their generals and admirals, who were more used to calculating men, tanks, and guns and assessing operational potential than attempting to calculate the probabilities of victory on the basis of "moral factors."

Quick victory strategies anchored in "military transformation" may betray military pessimism and insecurity over shallow popular and political support for war. For instance, the transposition of the operational methods of the blitzkrieg into a strategy to conquer Europe from the Atlantic to the Caucasus and beyond bore witness to a deep cultural pessimism among German soldiers, and by Hitler, who blamed Germany's 1918 defeat on a "stab in the back" by a war-weary population influenced by communist propaganda. The Japanese military's inclination to view foreign policy as a sequence of "problems" whose rectification required aggressive military solutions ultimately propelled Japan into desperate overextension, which in turn created a backlash of antimilitarism.[25]

Strategy Formulation

Strategy must achieve the policy within the limitations calculated in the net assessment—in other words, it must match ends to means. To do this, two questions must be answered. First, are the policy goals limited or unlimited? In other words, does one seek merely to modify behavior of the adversary or gain some relatively minor concession, like the abandonment of an aggressive policy, the cession of a territory, or the breakup of an alliance? Or, to accomplish the goal, must one seek the complete overthrow of the enemy, the occupation of its capital, and the imposition of a victor's peace—in short, unconditional surrender? The limited or unlimited nature of the goal, combined with the calculation of resources compared with those available to the enemy, will determine the level of effort required, that is, the means that one must devote to the conflict. The second question strategists must answer is whether they are able to designate targets likely to induce enemy compliance, while at the same time protecting their own vulnerabilities from enemy attack. Adjusting the relationship between force and politics in the application of strategy offers ample scope for civil-military discordance. It also highlights the synergistic relationship among the strategic, operational, and tactical levels of war that must complement, rather than undermine, each other.

With the demise of its major ally and protector the Soviet Union, Mongolia determined that its army, composed of heavily armored units, could no longer guarantee its security. China may continue to constitute a distant threat, but the best way to guarantee Mongolia's security, in the view of Mongolia's new democracy, is to build credibility within the international community by engaging in peacekeeping operations. Neoconservatives in the Pentagon, concerned about American vulnerability to terrorist attacks, have favored forces tailored for speedy, technologically driven operations to carry out "preemptive" interventions. Whatever the advantage these forces have shown on the battlefield—and they are significant—the focus on operations at the expense of strategy clearly blinded them to the political, administrative, and security challenges of occupying and pacifying Iraq.

The Danger of Inefficiencies

Adjusting force levels to achieve the goals of policy can give rise to several problems. The first problem may occur when military inefficiencies compromise the strategy. This happens because the strategic objective is simply too vast for the military to achieve. Even the Wehrmacht, the premier military force of its day, proved unable to achieve Hitler's vision of a European empire stretching from the Atlantic to the Caucasus and beyond. Saddam Hussein ordered his forces to attack Khafji, Kuwait, on January 29, 1991, based on a faulty net assessment that American resolve would waver when his forces inflicted heavy casualties on U.S. forces. Unfortunately for the Iraqi leader, his army, poorly prepared to deal with superior U.S. tactics and technology, proved more adept at taking casualties than inflicting them.[26]

Military organizations may lack the flexibility to adjust to operational and tactical adaptations of the enemy or may fail to integrate available technology or support activities—intelligence, supply, communications—into its operational concepts. One can argue, for instance, that the Anglo-French strategy in 1940 was sound: defeat the initial German onslaught, ensure a strategic stalemate in the short term, and use their external lines of communication to the United States to build up their forces and alliances until, eventually, they would be strong enough to take the offensive against the European Axis. In short, make time work for the Allies.

Unfortunately, the Germans were able to turn strategic surprise into decisive defeat of France because Anglo-French forces and their leaders lacked the intellectual, organizational, and technological framework that would have allowed them to adapt to joint and combined-arms maneuver warfare. Italian military inefficiencies actually encouraged Hitler to rescue his beleaguered ally in the Mediterranean, upsetting Mussolini's goal of achieving parity with Germany in the Axis through Mediterranean conquests. Likewise, a military leader whose operational shortcomings and ill-considered tactics kill too many soldiers, as in World War I, or sacrifice planes, ships, and men to no obvious benefit, as did Italian commanders between 1940 and 1943, risks demoralizing his force and encouraging war weariness in his population. The temptation of the political leader who witnesses operational failure is to intervene on the operational level, much as did Hitler, who was fond of sending "no withdrawal" orders to his generals. Lyndon Johnson also raised the ire of soldiers by restricting bombing targets in North Vietnam.

Clausewitz insisted that it is not the role of the political leader to "determine the posting of the guards or the employment of patrols," although he did concede "that a certain grasp of military affairs is vital for those in charge of general policy."[27] But political leaders may grow impatient when, in their view, routine, bureaucratic inertia, or a reluctance on the part of military chiefs to adapt new technologies impedes the ability of a military organization to achieve goals rapidly and at an acceptable cost. In this case, the political leader may intervene to force the pace of reform, which can lead to friction. It is also fair to note that technologies, including pervasive media, that bring increasing scrutiny to the front also tempt political leaders to interfere in the "posting of the guards" for fear that a televised military encounter might influence public support for the war. Senior generals who stand closer to the centers of decision making may be more sensitive to the political repercussions of strategic choices than are field commanders. For instance, during the 1991 Gulf War, Colin Powell was accused of micromanaging General Norman Schwarzkopf's campaign to hunt Scud missiles and designate air targets in Baghdad.[28] At the very least, the duty of the political leader frustrated by military inability to operate efficiently or achieve the strategy at a reasonable cost is to search high and low for a general or admiral more capable of achieving the strategy and to monitor his progress. Abraham Lincoln, Winston Churchill, and Harry Truman were perfectly willing to fire generals until they struck upon men capable of delivering victory. Leaders of new democracies may be playing political roulette when they replace well-connected generals for underperformance. The political leader who, like Czar Nicholas II, assumes the direction of armies himself after his generals fail, however, risks transferring the burden of defeat onto his own shoulders.

Victory at What Cost?

A second point of civil-military tension may occur when a strategy that is militarily feasible is proscribed by the political leaders because it is politically unacceptable. Harsh measures toward civilians may be seen as the best way to break resistance. A war against populations who support the enemy sometimes formed the basis for counterinsurgency strategies. But such strategies may stiffen resistance, discredit the war at home, and make reconciliation of a defeated enemy more difficult. Similar consequences may flow from strategic bombing campaigns that target civilians. Military leaders may argue that bombing offers a way to disrupt an enemy's economy, demoralize its population, and break its will to continue. Since the end of World War II at least, inflicting widespread collateral damage that includes the deaths of noncombatants nevertheless is not only contrary to international law but also bound to produce sympathy for the enemy in the court of world opinion, while it undermines support for the war in one's own population as well as in those of allies. It also may stiffen the enemy's will to resist, escalate the war beyond the level desired by the political leadership, and encourage outside support for the enemy.

The targeting of civilians also complicates postconflict reconstruction, which in turn can upset delicate ends/means calculations. Considerations of this sort required political leaders to reign in bombing campaigns during the Korean and Vietnam wars and in Kosovo. President Johnson's interdiction against the bombing of China, of Hanoi, or dams that would have wrecked North Vietnamese agriculture and forced many Vietnamese from their homes may, on the one hand, have produced complaints of civilian "micromanagement" of operations by military chiefs. On the other hand, television images of Vietnamese civilians killed by U.S. air strikes stoked the antiwar movement that helped persuade Lyndon Johnson not to stand for reelection. The destruction by an American laser-guided bomb of the Al Firdos bunker in Baghdad, where hundreds of Iraqi civilians had sought refuge, caused President George H. W. Bush to suspend the bombing of Baghdad.[29]

General Wesley Clark remembered that admonitions to limit civilian casualties in the air war to liberate Kosovo became "the most pressing drumbeat of the campaign."[30] Unscrupulous adversaries like Serbian president Slobodan Milosevic have exploited this reluctance to inflict civilian casualties by infiltrating their tanks into population centers and then publicizing the civilian casualties when they are bombed. Saddam Hussein threatened to take a stand in Baghdad at the outset of the second Gulf campaign in 2003, which he hoped would force U.S. ground troops to engage in urban warfare to draw him out. This promised to create significant civilian casualties, as in Mogadishu in 1993 when thousands of Somalis were estimated to have died in urban combat with U.S. Special Forces. One operational counter to this strategy is laser-guided munitions and lighter weapons, often handheld, which can destroy an enemy emplacement while minimizing collateral damage. The downside of the technological counter is that public opinion tends to be less tolerant of mistakes made by "professionals" with the latest technology. The bombing of the Al Firdos bunker in Baghdad and the Chinese embassy in Belgrade demonstrated that even precision technology, when guided by poor intelligence, can cause negative political fallout. One consequence may be that commanders become cautious, reluctant to call in strikes that will produce unacceptable collateral damage, and hence place their own troops at risk. This tendency to pull one's punches may cause vital targets to be spared and prolong conflicts, further jeopardizing popular and alliance support.

Restraints and Reassessment

Political leaders may place other constraints on military operations that a commander believes raise the costs of victory or even jeopardize his ability to win. For instance, the desire to limit casualties for political reasons could pressure a commander to make a disproportionate use of allied forces, defensive strategies, or technological substitutes. French commanders after 1940 maintained that the political desire to avoid a repeat of the invasion and occupation of northeastern France in 1914–1918 led to the costly and ultimately pointless construction of the Maginot Line. American generals forbidden by political leaders to go north of the 38th parallel in Korea or invade North Vietnam complained that an important strategic option had been denied them.

The continuous reassessment of political and military objectives "to keep cause and response in synchronization" forms the fourth admonition of the Weinberger-Powell Doctrine. Although this seems obvious, given the interactive nature of war, reassessment may in fact prove extremely difficult to accomplish. In the first place, a mechanism for reviewing the "synchronization" of policy and strategy might not exist, especially in new democracies with unformed political institutions, including those for defense decision making. Or the process of review may prove so cumbersome and involve so many risks that political and military leaders hesitate to undertake it. Politicians, having crafted a policy and staked their reputations on it, may be unable to alter the policy without sacrificing their credibility, as happened in Vietnam. Political leaders might make so many concessions and compromises to assemble a coalition to support the policy that any amendment or alterations would crumble the consensus upon which the policy rests. "Unconditional surrender" of the Axis powers was adopted at the January 1943 Casablanca Conference as a way to keep the Alliance together. Any amendment of that policy vis-à-vis Germany would have jeopardized public support for the war and threatened the cohesion of the Alliance.

Likewise, a military, or at least a portion of the military, may have a vested interest in the policy, based on loyalty to fallen comrades or arguments that to abandon the field will subject those who supported its cause to retribution. Such interest may reach the point that the military is willing to challenge the legitimacy of the state. This was the case of French colonial forces in Algeria, who, backed by a significant settler community of European origins, balked at what they saw as the Fourth Republic's tepid support of French Algeria—to the point that they threatened to plunge France into civil war. French president Charles de Gaulle's retreat from Algeria set off a mutiny among elite units of the forces. On the other side of the coin, the unwillingness of Portuguese prime minister Marcello Caetano to negotiate independence for Portugal's colonies, especially for Guinea-Bissau, triggered a 1974 coup d'état led by officers unwilling to bear the burden of what they saw as unwinnable wars.[31]

Military leaders may prove reluctant to revise a strategy because they lack the imagination, they are paralyzed by interservice rivalries, or their organizations lack the ability, short of root and branch reforms, to come up with innovative proposals. They may also complain that strategic options are limited by political constraints, the requirement to choose among unattractive alternatives, or competing defense priorities. For instance, the U.S. Joint Chiefs proved remarkably incapable of suggesting strategic alternatives in Vietnam beyond intensified bombing of the North.[32] They saw no reason to reconfigure an organization crafted for combat against the Red Army into a light infantry model suited to counterinsurgency, simply to fight a peripheral campaign in the jungles of Vietnam.[33]

When Winning May Not Be Everything

War termination can be a source of bitter dispute between political and military leaders. Ideally, one should cease hostilities when one has achieved the political goal. When that goal is "unconditional surrender" of the enemy, and one has the power to achieve that goal, as did the Allies in World War II, then the problem is resolved to a point, at the price of jeopardizing flexibility in negotiations of a surrender short of unconditional, as was the case with Italy in 1943. In limited wars, however, the question of when one has achieved one's objectives may be far more fluid. "Victory fever" may tempt a commander to exceed his original objective and pursue a revised goal, much as in the autumn of 1950 when General MacArthur altered the U.S. goal from the defense of South Korea to reunification of the Korean peninsula. In the process, he changed the U.S. policy objective, if only temporarily, from "containment" to "rollback." Likewise, no matter how elusive the prospect of victory, "sunk costs" in blood and treasure may oblige a nation to continue so long as it retains the ability to do so, in the hope of the payoff of victory. Politicians may want to continue even when their people no longer have the heart for the war, as did Alexander Kerensky in Russia in 1917 and Italy and Germany in World War II. Mao was ready to end the Korean War by 1951 but could find no face-saving way to do so, until he had accumulated "symbols of victory" to obscure his defeats.[34] Finally, small nations may find that their ability to opt out of a conflict is blocked by larger allies, as was the case of Hungary and Romania in World War II.

How to terminate a war short of total victory is also problematic. One can stop fighting and negotiate, as in 1918 or in the Franco-Prussian War of 1870–1871. One risk of this strategy is that it will be taken as a sign of weakness by the enemy and as an invitation to press the advantage. Another is that generals will complain that the political leader has allowed the enemy to recuperate while their own forces lose momentum. Ludendorff's request for an armistice in October 1918, calculated to buy time for his hard-pressed troops, actually backfired as the sudden release of pressure after four years of war triggered a complete breakdown of morale and discipline in the German army and the flight of the kaiser to Holland. Unfazed by his miscalculation, the German commander successfully shifted the blame for defeat in the popular imagination to the Weimar Republic. Bombing pauses in Vietnam—calculated to jump-start negotiations and demonstrate to U.S. and world opinion that Washington sought an end to the conflict—were used by the North as breathing space to shore up its defenses. What many consider the premature cease-fire in the 1991 Gulf War allowed Saddam Hussein to use his military to quell internal rebellion.

One can also fight while negotiating. In Korea and Vietnam, each side tried to use battlefield success as leverage at the peace table. This strategy is very stressful for soldiers, who fear that they are asked to make sacrifices and take casualties for objectives that may be negotiated away at the peace table. Thus, the trade-offs between the political risks and military costs of war termination strategies are certain to exacerbate tensions between statesmen and soldiers.

Conclusion

The "tense and exhausting dialogue" between civilian leaders and soldiers is hardly an aberration. It becomes a normal condition of the bureaucratic struggle in every state that must weigh threats to its sovereignty, consider its obligations to the international environment, and set defense needs alongside other budgetary priorities. But an endemic feature of civil-military relations in peacetime becomes, in wartime, a special challenge to new democracies. No hard-and-fast rules govern the interaction of civilian and military concerns. Nor should they, for each war combines unique factors, each nation is the heir of its own traditions of civil-military relations, and each leadership combination of personalities is a product of its own dynamic. What is more important is that political leaders set clear objectives that support national interests, ones likely to find broad-based popular support that is able to withstand the inevitable setbacks in war. For their part, soldiers must clearly explain their capabilities and coordinate them toward achieving the strategic objective at a reasonable cost. A mechanism for reassessing strategy must exist. Only then can civil-military interaction in wartime become a creative dynamic rather than a dysfunctional relationship that paralyzes strategic choice and courts defeat.

Notes

1. Michael I. Handel, *Masters of War: Classical Strategic Thought* (London: Frank Cass, 2001), 71–75.
2. Eliot A. Cohen, "The Unequal Dialogue: The Theory and Reality of Civil-Military Relations and the Use of Force," in *Soldiers and Civilians: The Civil-Military Gap and American National Security*, ed. Peter D. Feaver and Richard H. Kohn (Cambridge, Mass.: MIT Press, 2001), 432.

3. Harold Macmillan, *War Diaries: Politics and War in the Mediterranean, 1943–1945* (New York: St. Martin's Press 1984), 295.

4. Cohen, "The Unequal Dialogue," 432–433.

5. Ibid. Cohen develops these ideas further in *Supreme Command: Soldiers, Statesmen, and Leadership in Wartime* (New York: Free Press, 2002), 453.

6. Carl von Clausewitz, *On War*, ed. and trans. Sir Michael Howard and Peter Paret (Princeton, NJ: Princeton University Press, 1984), 86–87.

7. Michael Howard, "The Forgotten Dimensions of Strategy," in *The Causes of Wars and Other Essays* (Cambridge, MA.: Harvard University Press, 1984), 106–109.

8. William Stueck, *The Korean War: An International History* (Princeton, NJ: Princeton University Press, 1995), 320–322.

9. Modris Eksteins, "Memory and the Great War," in *The Oxford Illustrated History of the First World War*, ed. Hew Strachan (Oxford: Oxford University Press, 1998), 308, 313.

10. Marc Bloch, *Strange Defeat: A Statement of Evidence Written in 1940* (New York: W. W. Norton and Co., 1968), 25.

11. Eric M. Bergerud, *The Dynamics of Defeat: The Vietnam War in Hau Nghia Province* (Boulder, CO: Westview Press, 1991), 323–325.

12. Eksteins, "Memory and the Great War," 306.

13. William J. Duiker, *The Communist Road to Power in Vietnam* (Boulder, CO: Westview Press, 1981), 247–248, 267, 270.

14. Stueck, *The Korean War*, 75–76.

15. Douglas Kinnard, *The War Managers* (Hanover, NH: University Press of New England, 1977), 24.

16. George C. Herring, *America's Longest War: The United States and Vietnam, 1950–1975* (New York: McGraw Hill, 1986), 135.

17. Phillip B. Davidson, *Vietnam at War: The History, 1946–1973* (Novato, CA: Presidio Press, 1989), 529–530.

18. Michael R. Gordon and General Bernard E. Trainor, *The Generals' War: The Inside Story of the Conflict in the Gulf* (New York: Little, Brown, 1995), 416, 435, 443, 450, 456, 477.

19. J. N. Westwood, *Russia against Japan, 1904–1905: A New Look at the Russo-Japanese War* (London: Macmillan, 1986), 163.

20. Roger Chickering, *Imperial Germany and the Great War, 1914–1918* (Cambridge, England: Cambridge University Press, 1998), 161.

21. Robert A. Pape, "Coercive Air Power in the Vietnam War," *International Security* 15, no. 2 (1990): 115.

22. Sun Tzu, *The Art of War* (New York: Oxford University Press, 1971), 84.

23. Handel, *Masters of War*, 238.

24. Meirion Harries and Susie Harries, *Soldiers of the Sun: The Rise and Fall of the Imperial Japanese Army* (New York: Random House, 1992), 101–102.

25. Peter Duus, ed., *The Twentieth Century*, vol. 6 of *The Cambridge History of Japan* (Cambridge: Cambridge University Press, 1988), 220, 223.

26. Gordon and Trainor, *The Generals' War*, 269–271, 287–288.

27. Clausewitz, *On War*, 606, 608.

28. Peter J. Roman and David W. Tarr, "Military Professionalism and Policymaking: Is There a Civil-Military Gap at the Top? Does It Matter?" in Feaver and Kohn, *Soldiers and Civilians*, 417.

29. Gordon and Trainor, *The Generals' War*, 324–326.

30. General Wesley K. Clark, *Waging Modern War: Bosnia, Kosovo, and the Future of Combat* (New York: Public Affairs Press, 2001), 434.

31. Douglas Porch, "Colonies and Coups: Portugal's Colonial Wars," in *The Portuguese Armed Forces and the Revolution* (London: Croom Helm, 1977), 28–60.

32. Cohen, "Unequal Dialogue," 439.

33. Andrew F. Krepinevich Jr., *The Army in Vietnam* (Baltimore: Johns Hopkins University Press, 1986), 271.

34. Stueck, *The Korean War*, 223–234.

Chapter 5
The Spectrum of Roles and Missions of the Armed Forces

PAUL SHEMELLA

BEFORE governments can decide how to structure the organs of national security, they are obliged to decide whether to have armed forces at all. If a nation resolves to have armed forces, the very next step should be to determine what such forces should do in their role as protector of the state. All governments, and particularly democratic governments, face the challenge of how to distribute limited resources for a wide variety of public purposes. Without a clear understanding of what armed forces are expected to do, any distribution of resources will be unbalanced, unfair, and perhaps catastrophic. The difficulty of achieving such an understanding is often underestimated, illustrating, perhaps ironically, Carl von Clausewitz's dictum that everything in war is simple, but that the simplest thing is very difficult.

Clearly defined military roles and missions are fundamental to the structuring of any state's defense establishment and to decision making about the use of armed force. On a global level, the way in which particular countries are seen (or wish to be seen) internationally reflects the choices they make with regard to the employment of their military.

If we imagine these efforts in architectural terms, decisions about roles and missions constitute the steel that supports and shapes the national security building. This chapter will examine the issues surrounding roles and missions for democratic systems generally, rather than focus on the "older," established democracies. It will draw examples from the experiences of many countries that are attempting to develop effective civil-military decision-making processes for national defense.

Defining Roles and Missions

What exactly are roles and missions? Despite the almost universal application of these terms, there is no consensus on what they mean. U.S. policymakers generally speak of roles and missions with great certainty but seldom attempt to distinguish between the two concepts. Explaining the Pentagon's 1993 report on roles and missions to journalists, Lieutenant General Edwin Leland (former Joint Staff director of Strategic Plans and Policy) defined a role as "a broad and enduring purpose" provided by the Congress to each branch of the armed services. He went on to say that missions (specific tasks that clearly indicate an action to be taken) are given to operational commanders, to be undertaken with forces provided by the services.[1]

This characterization offers a good starting point to begin discussing roles and missions with officials of other governments as they attempt to design the institutions to guide their defense thinking. It will not matter if those officials call them "missions and tasks" or "roles and functions," as long as everyone can agree that there are two categories to describe and that they are different from one another. If the United States is to assist other governments with defense planning, policymakers must be able to draw on a common framework for describing roles and missions— what they are and how they work. This framework must be conceptual enough to allow different governments to interpret the issues raised by roles and missions according to their own operational and bureaucratic circumstances, yet it must be concrete enough to have practical value.

Defining something often forces one to distinguish it from something else. Because roles and missions in the U.S. system are given separately to two standing organizations, distinguishing between them is sometimes difficult. U.S. "combatant commanders" employ military forces, provided to them by the services (which have more or less fixed roles), within specific areas of responsibility. American military personnel do not really have to think about whether something is a role or a mission and often use the terms interchangeably.

In most other countries, however, the distinction between roles and missions is critical. The armed forces of the Dominican Republic, for example, are given roles through an "organic law" that aggregates military statutes into one document (the equivalent of U.S. Title 10). The law, which charges each of the three services to "protect the public order" in their respective media of operation, obliges all Dominican military units to be trained, manned, and equipped for riot control and refugee apprehension. What could have been a specific task (a mission) has become, through law, a "broad and enduring purpose" (a role) for three military organizations.[2]

At the policy level, the defense decision-making process should be driven by the concept of roles. Concentrating on missions (which come and go under an infinite variety of circumstances) instead of roles (which seldom change) can lead to ad hoc decisions in every aspect of defense decision making. At the operational level, this lack of focus can be debilitating to military organizations that need a steady stream of resources and guidance to develop real capabilities. If they are to prevail in the most extreme circumstances, military forces must concentrate on doing a few things well. By concentrating on roles, civilian leaders can keep military planners from having to take on too many missions.

Distinguishing between roles and missions leaves us with the challenge of determining which roles and missions are generally appropriate for military forces and which are not. This second act of distinction is more important than the first. There are many reasons for governments to assign roles and missions to military forces. What appears inappropriate to one government can be quite legitimate to another. The best example might be the use of military forces by developing countries to undertake large public works projects.

The participation of military forces in the national economy can even be viewed as a national security priority for some countries. Managing the national economy and extending government services to all citizens can demand the involvement of military organizations. The U.S. Army, for example, had a considerable role in settling the American West and building infrastructure during the nineteenth century. Civilian and military leaders must therefore define the national interest in the broadest possible terms, with domestic as well as external roles and missions in mind, using armed forces to accomplish what new democracies need at home to survive as nation-states.

The third act of distinction necessary to gain a thorough understanding of roles and missions is perhaps the most critical of all: the identification of roles and missions appropriate for the armed forces versus the police. The inability to make this distinction clear enough, and to define the conditions under which those forces should work together, has often led governments to military and political failure. The classic and preferred role for armed forces is to defend a nation from external attack; the only role for the police is to enforce laws. Each government defines these roles according to its own historical and cultural circumstances, but every government must decide how to manage the often indistinct area where they come together.

Macro and Micro Roles

Before proceeding, it is important to note that roles operate at two different levels. The greater portion of this chapter focuses on roles given to the armed forces collectively, and relative to nonmilitary instruments of government power. This set could be called macro roles. At the next level down, individual services also have operational roles assigned to them. These could be called micro roles. Macro roles operate at the policy level, where governments decide how military forces will be used generally in domestic and foreign affairs. Micro roles determine how national security organizations will be used relative to one another, and which types of forces are appropriate for such uses. Tables 5.1 and 5.2 list some of the primary macro and micro roles for the armed forces, but these lists are by no means exhaustive.

Every government brings unique historical, geographical, and cultural baggage to the defense decision-making table. Roles assigned to military forces reflect that baggage, and the missions that support them reflect the characteristics of the roles themselves. Although the most important role for armed forces is to defend against external threats, many other roles are available to government officials and their citizens. It is they who determine how military forces are to be employed. In so doing, nations "brand" themselves, according to the ways they use armed forces at home and abroad.

Macro Roles That Define National Reputation

Establishing a reputation for one's country should result from a public debate, punctuated by decisions that guide the funding, structuring, preparation, and employment of military forces. A country's brand is both the result and the function of what was described above as macro roles. Many governments go beyond merely assigning macro roles to their military forces; they actively "market" their countries to the rest of the world through branding. Table 5.1 lists five separate macro roles available to national governments that wish to use their military forces for a broad and continuing purpose (most use them for more than one), and it illustrates each type with five examples. Countries are listed under each rubric according to the preponderance of one macro role over others. These characterizations can change over time, according to political circumstances at home and abroad. They are also debatable (and that is part of their utility). The art of defense decision making is, in essence,

TABLE 5.1. MACRO ROLES FOR ARMED FORCES

War Fighter	Defender	Peacekeeper	Fire Fighter	Police Officer
United States	Japan	Canada	Peru	Indonesia
Russia	Taiwan	Sweden	Botswana	Honduras
Britain	Jordan	Argentina	Mexico	Albania
China	South Korea	Bangladesh	Georgia	Togo
France	Kuwait	Mongolia	Brazil	Bolivia

sensing the need for macro role changes and creating the conditions for successfully using armed forces in the most appropriate ways.

If fighting wars is the most important role for armed forces, it is also, in most of the world most of the time, the least likely. National reputations are acquired through frequent exercise of the most abundant capabilities for which a government's leadership has the political will. It is useful to categorize countries based upon the roles their armed forces are most likely to perform. Countries with similar macro roles for their armed forces can more easily develop interoperable doctrine, facilitating the management of alliance or coalition operations. Understanding the choices available and considering the example of other countries can motivate governments to change the ways they use armed forces over time.

War fighter countries maintain large armed forces, capable of waging offensive war. The governments of war fighter countries have the political will to use their military power for settling international disputes alone or in coalition with others. It is no surprise that the five countries on this list are the five nuclear-armed permanent members of the United Nations Security Council. Some of these countries use military forces in all five macro roles, but their governments choose to brand them as war fighters first.[3]

Defenders are countries whose military forces are presumed to exist primarily for response to an armed attack from within the region. These countries are constrained by poor strategic circumstances (Taiwan), legal proscriptions (Japan), or unusual political situations (South Korea) from preparing military forces for offensive operations. Defender countries maintain the capability to fight wars but not to start them.[4] Some involve their armed forces in other macro roles, but their militaries do not participate in them enough to brand their nations as anything other than defenders.

Peacekeeper countries are specialists in peace support operations and regard peace operations as the most important macro role their military forces perform. Peacekeeping as a macro role has grown in popularity for both global and domestic political reasons. It enables governments to gain international prestige (often at minimal cost) and to develop more-professional armed forces, which remain focused beyond the nation's borders.

The "fire fighters" are countries whose armed forces are used for a variety of domestic purposes but do not regularly perform regular law enforcement (as opposed to counter–drug enforcement, for example). These military forces are involved primarily in the development of a nation's infrastructure and in crisis management. The fire fighters have military forces with significant roles in the national economy and a wide spectrum of nontraditional missions. These countries are blessed with no immediate external threats and can thus avoid becoming war fighters or defenders. Like real fire fighters, the military forces of these countries are used in missions for which no other organizations are available. In some cases, they will be obliged to fight insurgencies or even civil wars. Armed forces in fire fighter countries seem to be either underemployed or taxed beyond their means, often being thrown between the two extremes.

The "police officers" are countries whose militaries perform law enforcement as their primary role. Regular police officers in these countries are weak, and the use of the military in their place only makes them weaker. When armed forces are used in this way, it is very difficult for them to do anything else. Police officers are among the most unstable countries in the world; their governments tend to remain convinced that a shift of military forces away from law enforcement would create even more instability. Fire fighters distinguish themselves from police officers in the way they use armed forces to fight internal conflict. In the former, military and police forces work in tandem, cooperating to one degree or another; in the latter, military forces *replace* law enforcement organizations altogether.

In an ideal world, then, all countries would converge at the center of the table and become peacekeepers, leaving nothing to do at either end. The existing peacekeeper countries actively choose to place themselves at the center, while others, such as Bolivia, aspire to move to the center but, because of domestic circumstances, cannot. Understanding this horizontal mobility, which operates in both directions, is an essential element of strategic planning for any government. But all macro roles are important to the governments that choose them. Those choices determine how micro roles and the missions to support them will be decided and funded. In sum, macro roles help governments create a vision, micro roles determine which military forces will be used to achieve that vision, and missions are the vehicle by which they do it.

No discussion of this nature would be complete without mentioning the most basic of all roles for armed forces—that of giving the country a sense of national identity. With many countries following the current U.S. lead in adopting professional armies, this role has been forgotten in large parts of the world. One place it has not been forgotten is Afghanistan, where a spokesman for the newly formed Afghan army recently stated this role better than anyone else: "We can give assurance to the Afghan people and the people of the world that Afghans can make their country united . . . and we in the Army are going to prove it."[5]

As the United States and its imitators move their armed forces farther away from conscription, it is helpful to remember the potential consequences of separating the armed forces from the people they serve. Once called the "Great Divorce," such a bifurcation of society can lead to a lack of both expertise and interest in defense issues within the civilian sector, which percolates up through the political structure so that elected leaders eventually lose touch with the realities of the military concerns.[6]

Micro Roles

The concept of micro roles requires a different construct. Table 5.2 plots the traditional military services, a coast guard, and a police force against the macro roles listed in Table 5.1. When we examine the most basic micro roles for each organization in each of the five types of countries, we can see a pattern emerging. Armies, navies, and air forces follow traditional paths in war fighter and defender countries but diverge from these norms in peacekeeper, fire fighter, and police officer countries. The roles for coast guards are traditional in all five, in the sense that these services discharge both military and law enforcement responsibilities. Police officers fill traditional roles in three of the five and depart from the norm in the other two.

In peacekeeper countries, the police also provide law enforcement personnel and training to peace support operations outside their own country. This micro role does not predominate over their traditional role of law enforcement at home, but it does force those governments to treat their deploying police more like military personnel. This transformation turns a micro role into a macro role and distinguishes peacekeeper

TABLE 5.2. MICRO ROLES FOR ARMED FORCES AND LAW ENFORCEMENT

Macro Role	Army	Navy	Air Force	Coast Guard	Police Force
War Fighter	Ground component in joint warfare	Maritime component in joint warfare	Air component in joint warfare	Augments navy for combat operations	Enforces the law at home
Defender	Ground component in joint warfare	Maritime component in joint warfare	Air component in joint warfare	Augments navy for combat operations	Enforces the law at home
Peacekeeper	Conducts peace support operations (PSOs) ashore	Conducts PSOs in coastal and riverine areas	Provides logistic support to ground troops	Conducts maritime law enforcement at home	Trains indigenous police during PSOs
Fire Fighter	Conducts military support to civilian authorities (MSCA)	Conducts MSCA in coastal and riverine areas	Provides air service to remote areas	Conducts maritime law enforcement	Enforces the law at home
Police Officer	Enforces the law in rural areas and cities	Enforces the law in coastal and riverine areas	Provides logistic support to ground forces	Conducts maritime law enforcement	Augments the army in law enforcement

countries from all the others. In police officer countries, by contrast, domestic law enforcement bodies are supplanted by the army. Such a practice forces the police into a de facto subordinate role, owing to the superior numbers, organization, and weaponry of most armies. Honduras provides an excellent example of this kind of military domination of traditional policing roles.

Furthermore, the Honduran Army, in addition to its role of defending the national territory, operates one of the largest banks in the country. Bolivia's navy transports cargo; Indonesian soldiers act as constabulary forces in most of the country; Botswana's military is heavily involved in controlling poachers in the country's game reserves; and Peruvian military personnel guard and transport ballots during elections. These are not temporary nontraditional missions that come up only now and again; they are assigned micro roles that regularly compete for the professional attention of military personnel. Although all military roles beyond traditional national defense reduce the combat effectiveness of the armed forces, nontraditional micro roles have some offsetting social and economic benefits as well. The Honduran Army bank collects and invests retirement funds in the absence of government financing. The Bolivian Navy already operates a fleet of barges and needs the additional revenue they bring in that cannot be supplied by the national budget. Indonesia is a vast, multiethnic archipelago of some seventeen thousand islands, where public order is most readily maintained by military forces. Botswana considers its game parks to be a national security asset, and therefore the military's role in policing them is a legitimate component of national security. Peru's leaders have decided that only military personnel can guarantee the right of all citizens to vote, even though soldiers have lost their own as a consequence.

It is the extent to which roles endure, not the roles themselves, that largely determines whether military forces and societies will be better off. If military roles change frequently, the military cannot focus its resources, training, and planning efficiently, and society must pay a higher cost for defense. If missions change frequently, military forces retain the flexibility needed to return to their proper roles once the missions are accomplished. Temporary missions thus support permanent roles, or if missions deviate from that support, they disappear quickly enough to avoid a loss of attention to what is most important in the long term. Civilian officials and military officers must continuously review roles and missions to ensure that this connectivity is firmly rooted and sustained.

In the end, all military and police forces are "fire fighters," serving the needs of the nation as deemed necessary by political leaders. The extent to which military forces are used in this role and the duration of that usage are what distinguishes military and police forces from each other, and the fire fighter countries from all the others.

The Role of Roles and Missions

Assigning roles and missions to military forces is both a starting point and a product of the civil-military decision-making process. The clarification and revalidation of roles and missions forces approximation of civilian officials to military leaders in a continuing debate over the most basic question: Why do we have armed forces, and what do we want them to do? Such a debate, conducted in the public eye, is a precondition for genuine democratic civil-military relations. Transparency will ensure that society at large—its individuals, groups, and institutions—is continuously aware of exactly what the government is doing to protect it and how much of the national treasure is being applied to that effort.

The fundamental nature of roles and missions in the defense decision-making process can be best understood by examining each manifestation of that process from the perspective of roles and missions. Considerations about roles and missions are a common denominator in the defense decision-making process and link the following activities together.

Strategy Formulation

The national security of any country is defined and understood through a process of strategic planning. That planning normally yields two products, one comprehensive (what the United States calls national security strategy) and the other focused (national military strategy). The former leans heavily toward policy considerations, suggesting roles, whereas the latter tends toward operations, suggesting missions. Strategic planning thus constitutes the linkage between policy and operations and forms the basis for distinguishing between roles and missions.[7]

Strategy itself can be seen as a hierarchy of considerations, from the highest political level all the way down to the technical. The vertical dimension of strategy is complemented by a horizontal one that acts within each level as what Edward Luttwak calls "the dynamic contention of opposed wills."[8] This multilayered struggle drives opposing leaders to assign new roles and missions to military forces while producing new technologies that make possible still newer ones. Strategy formulation is thus the major source of decisions about roles and missions.

Acquisition

The extent to which governments control the integration of technology issues into their defense decision-making processes will determine to a large degree whether or not their forces remain relevant. Governments also are resource constrained, however, and it is not always possible for militaries to buy the technology they desire. Acquisition decisions—determining what to put in and what to leave out—thus cannot be divorced from strategy formulation. Does strategy drive technology, or is strategy itself driven by technology? The answer today is that, more than ever, strategy and technology drive each other. The wars we fight are, to some degree, determined by on-the-shelf technology.[9] A streamlined acquisition process, balanced among the armed services, ensures that strategy keeps pace with that technology. If technology is permitted to outpace strategy by too wide a margin, defense organizations are left with expensive gadgets that may or may not assist them in achieving the actual goals assigned them by political leaders. Determining service roles within the acquisition process therefore is just as important as defining operational roles.

Defense Restructuring

Defense establishments are, of necessity, dynamic organizations. To remain relevant and effective, they must continually change in response to domestic and international stimuli. Change is thus a theme that runs through all defense decision-making processes, rendering them even more challenging. Decision makers, attempting to deal with the complexity of restructuring, seek some mechanism for injecting order into the system. Placing roles-and-missions considerations at the heart of the process can provide a framework for imposing that order.

The careful consideration of roles cannot be separated from force structure, acquisition, intelligence architecture, and an array of subordinate issues. An example of the influence of roles on force structure is the formation of the U.S. Central Command, which came about as a direct response to President Jimmy Carter's declaration that the United States would use military force if necessary to protect its interests in the Persian Gulf region. Central Command began as a joint task force but quickly evolved into a permanent command structure ready to assume specific missions for defense of the region. Roles also are reflected in the formation of a new Colombian Army brigade for protecting critical petroleum infrastructure; this new task constitutes a "broad and enduring purpose" that does not seem likely to go away. In each case, military roles were changed or added through deliberate political decisions.

The size and capabilities of the military force will also determine the cost of the force in both current and future terms. In the absence of cost constraints, and given the tendency of military leaders always to want more, limiting roles at the front end of the restructuring process can be an effective way for civilian leaders to control the bottom line. If the restructuring process does not begin with roles, costs often escalate. There are human costs as well, measured in terms of time away from home and individual fatigue. With each new role, military units become eligible for a host of additional missions, some of which can endure for years. As most military personnel know, once a new role emerges, it never goes away.

Duplication of roles among services can waste funds. Indeed, roles should be used to distinguish one service from another. Additionally, the assignment of questionable roles can degrade military readiness. On the one hand, if military personnel find themselves consistently performing nonmilitary missions, they can become disaffected. On the other hand, too few roles—or none at all—can result in confusion or the misemployment of military forces.

Combating Terrorism

Two questions must be considered when thinking about military roles in combating terrorism. The first is whether countering terrorism should be a role or a mission; the second is whether it should be a military or a police responsibility. To answer the first question, governments must examine the threat from terrorism and decide whether or not a sustained counterterrorism effort will be required. If terrorism begins to threaten national security and promises to continue, decision makers will need to assign certain military forces the role of dealing with it.

If the threat is minor or intermittent, military forces may acquire a collateral capability of countering terrorism, but only through a series of potential missions. This distinction is not trivial. A combat commander whose role is to counter terrorism will look and act differently from one who is merely tasked with supporting others when the need arises. A "broad and continuing purpose" to combat terrorism produces a force structure that must be trained, manned, and equipped to be capable of conducting specific counterterrorism missions as they emerge.

Determining whether to use police or military forces can be difficult, especially when distinctions among types of terrorism become blurred.[10]

For countries with weak police forces, and especially those where the terrorist threat resides at home, police-military role clarification can be particularly challenging. Even Great Britain, with a strong police sector, found it necessary to introduce military forces into Northern Ireland in order to quell terrorist violence. Thirty years later those forces are still there, with no reliable date for their withdrawal.[11]

Governments facing a terrorist threat overseas must almost always rely on foreign police and military forces to resolve terrorism directed at their citizens and interests. In cases where foreign governments have robust counterterrorism capabilities, tactical resolution is fairly straightforward; in cases where local forces are less capable of resolving a terrorist situation, the crisis becomes a negotiation over whose forces should be used and how they should be used.[12] Domestic terrorism thus breeds roles-and-missions problems at home, while international terrorism raises the same issues between governments.

Peacekeeping

Governments wishing to contribute military forces to peace support operations must first determine whether they have enough resources to dedicate them to peacekeeping as a role. The assignment of a peacekeeping role to military forces implies—indeed ensures—that military assets will be dedicated to peace support operations on a continuing basis. It also implies, though it does not ensure, that governments will provide peacekeeping forces with the personnel, training, and equipment they need to succeed in the field.

There are three basic groups of peacekeeping forces in the world today. The first could be called the heavyweights. This group includes the United States, Great Britain, France, and Russia. These countries alone possess military forces that can be introduced into theaters of conflict to "freeze" the combatants in place. Other countries may have the capability to stop certain local conflicts, but only the heavyweights can do it worldwide on short notice. These countries do not maintain dedicated peacekeeping forces and do not view peace support operations as a role. The military forces from these nations take on peacekeeping *missions* when their governments decide that political circumstances require them.

The second group of nations that engage in peace support operations could be called the specialists. These countries have designated a certain portion of their military force structure to conduct peace support operations and have assigned that role to them. The governments, and even the societies, of these nations regard peacekeeping as a politically acceptable form of military intervention; for some, peacekeeping has become a noble calling. These forces also distinguish themselves by aspiring to develop and maintain the capability to *command* regional or global peace support operations. The list of specialist countries includes Canada, Argentina, Sweden, and Germany, with many others building the capacity to field such forces.[13]

The third group of peacekeeping nations might be designated the rank and file. The military forces provided by these nations are less capable but still essential elements of regional and global peacekeeping coalitions. The number of nations belonging to this group has increased significantly in recent years and continues to grow. Peacekeeping duties permit governments to assign legitimate external roles to military forces that might otherwise remain at home, complicating the division of labor among other public institutions and themselves. Peace support operations also give military personnel a set of missions for which they can develop professional skills and a sense of pride. The societies and governments they represent often share that pride.

Military Support to Civilian Authorities

Virtually all governments require their armed forces to help them manage natural disasters and rescue accident victims. Many require military personnel to maintain or restore public order. Some require them to engage in construction projects, guard prisons, carry ballots, teach the young, administer medical services, and a wide variety of other duties. The key question for governments is not whether to use military forces at home but whether to assign each duty as a role or a mission. If military support to civilian authorities becomes systematic, it should make the transition from being a mission to being a role. Such a transition is manageable, but only if it results from a deliberate process of decision. A nation whose armed forces perform this role distinguishes itself from other nations in ways we will examine later.

The advent of insurgency, drug trafficking, and terrorism places enormous pressure on governments to use military forces for new missions and, perhaps, new roles. The addition of so-called superterrorism has increased that pressure and forced governments to focus on blending military capabilities with civilian efforts to protect their societies. The distinction between civilian and military, as well as the difference between domestic and international, is being eroded by these trends, forcing governments to take interagency and multinational approaches to all decisions. The roles and missions of military forces are thus more dynamic than ever.[14]

Two Menus of Missions

The final distinction needed for this analysis is that between traditional and nontraditional missions. Unlike previous types of distinction, this one comes from the field, where military missions are performed. Missions can be synchronized more easily with the roles they support from such a perspective. If the top-down view does not accord with what actually is taking place, decision makers should be motivated to reevaluate the roles they assign to their armed forces. The chain of command must therefore support a feedback mechanism that continuously compares roles with missions.

The evolution from traditional to nontraditional missions has accelerated in the wake of the cold war. The strategic nuclear standoff has been replaced by "complex contingencies" that require military personnel to be able to change the way they act and think, perhaps several times in a career. Peacekeeping responsibilities best exemplify this trend. As several secretaries general of the United Nations have noted, "Peacekeeping is not a job for soldiers, but only soldiers can do it."[15] Military personnel involved in such operations find themselves negotiating with civilians to resolve domestic disputes, staffing checkpoints, delivering food, and managing refugees. Specialist and, to some degree, rank-and-file peacekeepers are able to focus their preparations on such nontraditional missions; the heavyweights often are not. Military personnel who must perform both traditional and nontraditional missions risk becoming less capable at both. The United States has incorporated ideas from the "low-intensity conflict" debate of the 1980s and substituted the term "operations other than war" to describe these operations. Field personnel have wondered ever since whether performing these missions will make them something other than warriors. The differences between traditional and nontraditional missions, detailed in Table 5.3, are significant and qualitative and must be considered by civilian leaders charged with assigning roles, and their attendant missions, to the armed forces.[16]

The shift in emphasis from external to internal security functions is more pronounced in less developed countries, but combating terrorism has accelerated the transition in the developed countries. When citizens are attacked by organized, heavily armed groups of criminals, governments

TABLE 5.3. MISSION CHARACTERISTICS

Traditional	*Nontraditional*
External security functions	Internal security functions
Lethal force	Nonlethal force
High-profile, large-unit operations	Low-profile, small-unit operations
Nonpermissive environment	Permissive environment
Heavily armed	Lightly armed
National control	Local control
Little civil-military interaction	High civil-military interaction
Centralized command and control	Diffuse command and control
Warrior mentality	Law enforcement mentality

often have no choice but to involve military forces. As military forces assume these missions, whether in support of or as a replacement for law enforcement, they also shift to a bias for nonlethal force. Even the fight against terrorism, when waged in cities and villages at home, places extra responsibility on military personnel to use caution they would not use on a more conventional battlefield.

Traditional military operations are high-profile, large-unit affairs, conducted by heavily armed combatants in an environment where everyone is a target. Nontraditional missions bring soldiers into situations where those they are targeting are mixed with those they are protecting. Although this is not a completely new development for military forces, it is the case for an increasing number of missions. Such operations, especially overseas, often are conducted under local control that tends to be decentralized and generally more confusing to soldiers accustomed to clear lines of command.

There is little civil-military interaction in traditional missions, but recent trends have brought military forces into closer and more frequent contact with civilians. In some nontraditional missions such as peacekeeping and humanitarian assistance, the civilians themselves are the mission. In these cases, a warrior mentality is not what is needed to achieve success. Military personnel trained as warriors find themselves trying instead to understand and adapt to a law enforcement mentality. This transformation places fighters at great risk, requiring them to conduct missions in dangerous places without overwhelming force to protect themselves.

Roles, Missions, and Civil-Military Relations

Michael Desch and others have argued that countries confronting a clear external threat tend to have stronger civilian control and better civil-military relations than those that do not. The exception to this rule of thumb appears to be when a country faces such an overwhelming external threat that its military forces gather too much political power, whether from a sincere effort to defend the state or in a cynical ploy to use the threat as cover for taking control.[17]

The aggregation of political power to military institutions can create a sixth national brand: the "troublemaker." Troublemaker countries tend to have the poorest civil-military relations, often becoming regional or global rogue states. Institutional mechanisms for democratic civilian control of the armed forces are an indispensable tool that governments use to avoid falling into the troublemaker category.[18] Toward that end, civilian leaders, with professional military advice, must ensure that the roles and missions of their armed forces remain legitimate and, wherever possible, externally focused. Few things are more dangerous to a democracy than military forces with roles either self-assigned or sloppily assigned by civilian leaders.[19] Military officers quantify risk; civilians must judge it. Otherwise, armed forces might waste public resources or blunder into unwise military engagements.

Lack of a clear external threat removes the most important basis for maintaining armed forces but does not necessarily render them unjustified. All nations require a means of exercising sovereignty, whether they have belligerent neighbors or not. Neighbors tend to treat another nation's sovereignty with more respect if that nation can field a credible defense, regardless of whether the neighbors harbor aggressive designs. National governments must evaluate each other, then, in terms of how they use military forces. Members of society, on the other hand, regard their own governments according to how they employ military forces in roles and missions other than war fighting. Civilian control issues thus become even more challenging in the domestic context.

The countries listed in Table 5.1 illustrate this analytical relationship. The war fighters and defenders tend to sustain public support for armed forces because the need for them is palpable. The peacekeepers also tend to have strong public support, especially if military forces are deployed abroad with regularity. Difficult civil-military relations become common in those countries designated fire fighters and police officers, especially if their leaders do not understand the three distinctive dimensions or conceptualizations of security: national, public, and citizen.

National security is a matter of safeguarding the state's sovereignty over its territory and population. Public security is the ability of a government to maintain the civil order necessary for the execution of basic functions such as commerce, transportation, and communication. Citizen security has to do with the capacity of individuals and groups to exercise the political, economic, civil, and human rights that make them citizens. These dimensions of security are interrelated. States must maintain public order if citizens are to exercise their individual rights, unless or until the exercise of such rights diminishes public security. In some cases, the erosion of public security becomes serious enough to diminish national security, as in the event of armed insurgency or terrorist violence. Governments typically respond by suspending or reducing certain individual rights, thereby diminishing citizen security.[20]

Military forces usually are dedicated to the preservation of national security, while police forces and justice systems are used to safeguard public and citizen security. In cases where military force is needed to prevent deteriorating public and citizen security from placing national security at risk, governments must exercise care in distributing roles and missions to both military and police organizations. Such decisions are relatively easy during crises; it is the routine, long-term sharing of roles and missions that can cause both institutions to lose focus and become weak. Another consequence of the blurring of these distinctions is the loss of public confidence in military forces. The performance of armed forces, like all government functions, is measured by the legitimacy they derive from the citizens they serve. Such legitimacy is the very basis for healthy civil-military relations.

Joseph S. Nye has described the "liberal tradition" of civil-military relations as a two-way understanding between military officers and civilian officials. In this construct it is the responsibility of military officers to subordinate themselves to the rule of law and refrain from participating in partisan politics. The civilian end of the bargain is simple in theory but not altogether easy to implement. Civilian officials, according to Nye, must recognize that armed forces are legitimate tools of democratic states; they must educate themselves on defense issues; and they must support and provide funds for properly developed military roles and missions.[21]

Conclusion

Roles and missions for armed forces are the fundamental component of defense decision making. The inability to distinguish between them can lead to waste or, worse, inadequate and ineffective national defense. Defense establishments all over the world have been plagued by an institutional failure to consider seriously the issues raised by roles and missions, even as responsible officials lament the intractability of their problems. Without a set of roles that are balanced with their requisite resources, military forces will never be capable of conducting successful missions. If national security officials want to be diligent in discharging their responsibilities, they must consider roles and missions to be the beginning of a cyclic process of defense decision making.

Only the wisdom of governments and their societies can ensure that armed forces remain focused on properly developed roles and missions. Adherence to these precepts can help governments maintain armed forces that contribute to solving problems at home and abroad rather than causing them.

Notes

1. General Colin Powell and Lieutenant General Edwin S. Leland, "1993 Report on the Roles, Missions, and Functions of the Armed Forces" (transcript of news briefing, February 12, 1993), available from Federation of American Scientists at http://www.fas.org/man/docs/corm93/brief.htm.

2. *Ley Orgánica de las Fuerzas Armadas de la República Dominicana*, vol. 1—1996, chap. 1.

3. Although the U.S. military has taken on the new role of homeland defense in response to the September 11, 2001, terrorist attacks, for example, the United States remains indisputably the world's premier war-fighting nation.

4. The most glaring exception to this is Israel's "offensive defense," now apparently emulated by the George W. Bush administration in its comprehensive strategy to combat terrorism.

5. Scott Baldauf, "Afghan Army Gets Ahead by Getting Along," *Christian Science Monitor*, February 11, 2003.

6. U.S. congressman Charles B. Rangel has moved to bring back the draft, in part as a way to make citizens more aware of how their government proposes to use military forces and to involve them more deeply in the decision-making process. The term "Great Divorce" comes from Arthur Hadley, *The Straw Giant* (New York: Random House, 1986), 274.

7. See Richard K. Betts, "The Trouble with Strategy: Bridging Policy and Operations," *Joint Forces Quarterly* (Winter 2001–2002).

8. See Edward N. Luttwak, *Strategy: The Logic of War and Peace* (Cambridge, MA: Belknap Press of Harvard University Press, 1987), 69. Luttwak's discussion regarding the paradoxical logic of strategy is particularly useful for analyzing today's menu of wars.

9. See Nicholas Thompson, review of *War in a Time of Peace*, by David Halberstam, *Washington Monthly* (September 2001): 41. Thompson argues that military leaders understand that the technology we choose to fight wars helps us choose the wars we fight.

10. For the differences between terrorism and insurgency, see Ariel Merari, "Terrorism as a Strategy of Insurgency," *Terrorism and Political Violence* 5, no. 4 (1993): 213–251.

11. Regarding the consequences of using military forces domestically, see María José Moyano Rasmussen, "The Military Role in Internal Defense and Security: Some Problems" (CCMR Occasional Paper 6, Center for Civil-Military Relations, Monterey, CA, October 1999), http://www.ccmr.org/public/home.cfm.

12. For a description of the U.S. response to the hijacking of the cruise ship *Achille Lauro*, for example, see "Getting Even," *Newsweek*, October 21, 1985, 21–32.

13. The Center for Civil-Military Relations (CCMR) offers a series of courses known as the Enhanced International Peacekeeping Capabilities program. This is part of a U.S. government effort to build the capacity of foreign governments to train and deploy peacekeeping forces around the world. CCMR's program, conducted with personnel from specialist countries such as Canada and Sweden, aims to enable rank-and-file countries to assume and sustain this macro role.

14. See John Arquilla, David Ronfeldt, and Michele Zanini, "Networks, Netwar, and Information-Age Terrorism," in *Countering the New Terrorism*, ed. Ian O. Lesser, Bruce Hoffman, John Arquilla, David F. Ronfeldt, Michele Zanini, and Brian Michael Jenkins (Santa Monica, CA: Rand, 1999), 54.

15. This comment is usually traced to Dag Hammarskjöld, but all subsequent secretaries general appear to have restated it.

16. Drawn from Barry Crane and Paul Shemella, "Between Peace and War: Comprehending Low Intensity Conflict" (National Security Program Discussion Paper, ser. 88-02, John F. Kennedy School of Government, Harvard University, Cambridge, MA, 1988).

17. See Michael C. Desch, "Structural Theory of Civil-Military Relations," in *Civilian Control of the Military: The Changing Security Environment* (Baltimore: Johns Hopkins University Press, 1999), 11–17.

18. Examples of troublemaker countries include North Korea and Burma. Nigeria, a potential troublemaker, appears to be improving its civil-military relations through democratic reforms and peacekeeping deployments, while Turkey, which has hovered near this category, is now making steady progress on limiting the political influence of the armed forces.

19. See Charles Dunlap, "The Origins of the American Military Coup of 2012," National War College Paper (1992; reprinted in *Parameters* [Winter 1992–1993]); and the sequel, "Melancholy Reunion" (Institute for National Security Studies Occasional Paper, U.S. Air Force Academy, Colorado Springs, 1996).

20. See A. Douglas Kincaid, "Demilitarization and Security in El Salvador and Guatemala: Convergences of Success and Crisis," *Journal of Interamerican Studies and World Affairs* (Winter 2000): 2.

21. From the edited text of a speech given by Joseph S. Nye Jr., "Epilogue: The Liberal Tradition," in *Civil-Military Relations and Democracy*, ed. Larry Diamond and Marc F. Plattner (Baltimore: Johns Hopkins University Press, 1996), 152–153.

Part Three Issues in Civilian Control of the Military

Chapter 6
Reforming Intelligence:
The Challenge of Control in New Democracies

THOMAS C. BRUNEAU AND KENNETH R. DOMBROSKI

WITHIN the realm of civilian control of the armed forces as a subset of civil-military relations, probably the most problematic issue in new democracies is control of the intelligence services. The problems around this issue are due not only to the legacies of prior nondemocratic regimes, in which the intelligence or security apparatus was a key element of control and in which human rights abuses often were allowed, but also to the inherent tension everywhere between intelligence and democracy. Democracy requires accountability of the governors to the governed, as well as transparency. Intelligence services, by contrast, must operate in secret to be effective, thus violating to some degree both accountability and transparency. Whereas well-established democracies have developed institutions to deal with this dilemma, new democracies are still in the process of abolishing remnants from the past and creating new ones.

Democratic control of intelligence services is clearly an issue in civil-military relations, although to the best of our knowledge, only Alfred Stepan has treated it from this perspective.[1] It is a civil-military issue for two main reasons. First, in most authoritarian regimes, including those in the former Soviet Bloc, the intelligence services were militarized. This is the legacy from which these authoritarian regimes are redefining and restructuring themselves. Second, even in those countries where civilian-led intelligence services are being established, the military services continue to have their own, normally separate, intelligence organizations.[2]

Any discussion of control and intelligence is challenging for several reasons. First, the terms and concepts associated with intelligence are ambiguous and frequently controversial. Second, much about intelligence—collection, analysis, and dissemination—is secret; knowledge is power, and those who hold it want to keep it to themselves. Intelligence professionals are a special club even within their own military or civilian organizations, and they deliberately minimize the knowledge that outsiders have about them and their activities. Third, relatively little has been written about intelligence and democratization. What good material exists usually pertains to the established democracies such as Canada, Great Britain, France, and the United States. This chapter describes the structures and processes involved in the intelligence function; analyzes the civil-military challenges of democratic control over intelligence organizations, particularly in new democracies; and highlights the importance of intelligence as a profession in these countries.

As will be shown in this chapter, a small but notable number of countries have undertaken to reform their intelligence systems and, in doing so, have generated a public debate over the functions and responsibilities of intelligence services in a democracy. The body of useful literature that addresses these concerns is very limited but recently has begun to grow.[3] Consequently, the authors wrote this chapter with the intention to demythologize intelligence in new democracies by providing an introduction to some of the key issues involved in the institutions of intelligence activities. This chapter bridges three areas that are usually examined separately: democratization, civil-military relations, and intelligence studies. Those who research and write on democracy apparently are either unaware of the centrality—or unwilling to deal with the implications—of intelligence services in democratic consolidation. Students of civil-military relations have focused overwhelmingly on the operators rather than intelligence professionals. And those who are experts on intelligence have not dealt directly with the military nor with the different forms a government can take, at least not in terms of the impact of intelligence activities on democratic consolidation.

The Meaning of Intelligence

Intelligence organizations perform essential functions in a democracy, and arguably the most important function is informing the government of what it needs to know about external and internal threats. The scope and diversity of intelligence activities contribute to understandable disagreement about the meaning of "intelligence."[4] As Mark Lowenthal points out, the term can have at least three meanings. It can be seen as a process, that is, the means by which governments request, collect, analyze, and disseminate certain types of required information, and the rubric by which covert operations are planned and executed. "Intelligence" also comprises the products of these gathering, analysis, and covert activities. Finally, "intelligence" can refer to the organization, that is, those agencies that carry out its functions.[5] Process—the gathering and using of information for some purpose—is the most salient of the three definitions for this discussion. Given that processes vary, as do the sources and ultimate uses of information, much about them is of necessity vague. Those who become familiar with intelligence processes and their limitations are more likely to understand that not everything is knowable, let alone known.

Most discussions within the intelligence community center on tradecraft—the "how-to" of sources, methods, and analysis—rather than on "what is." The intelligence community's obscure, exclusive character is cultivated intentionally, to prevent information from reaching unintended eyes. Intelligence officers are trained to collect information and sequester it, except from those very few of their superiors with a "need to know." Given this chapter's focus on the functions of intelligence in new democracies, we must adopt a broad definition of intelligence in order to convey the scope of what it can include.[6] Glenn P. Hastedt, in his book *Controlling Intelligence*, states succinctly: "The four elements of intelligence are clandestine collection, analysis and estimates, covert action, and counterintelligence."[7] Loch Johnson describes the interrelationship between these four functions, which is the focus of this section:

> Intelligence commonly encompasses two broad meanings. First, the secret agencies acquire and interpret information about threats and opportunities that confront the nation, in an imperfect attempt to reduce the gaps and ambiguities that plague open sources of knowledge about the world. A nation especially seeks secret information to help it prevail in times of war, with as few casualties as possible. Second, based on information derived from denied and open sources, policymakers call upon their intelligence agencies to shield the nation against harm (counterintelligence) while advancing its interests through the secret manipulation of foreign events and personalities (covert action). Intelligence thus involves both information and response.[8]

Most authors on the subject agree on the general functions of intelligence and incorporate them in their models of intelligence systems.[9] Although these functions are common to most intelligence organizations, however, the ways in which they are distributed within the organization differ from state to state.

For our purpose here, intelligence is understood to consist of the four functions described by Hastedt: collection, analysis, counterintelligence, and covert action. Although the term also refers both to the organization that collects the information and the information collected, the information itself is not the defining characteristic. The key characteristics are that these functions are *centered in and intended for the state* and that they are *secret*. We will briefly examine each of them individually, but it is important to remember that they operate most effectively as parts of a process, in close conjunction with one another. As Roy Godson points out succinctly in the introduction to his book *Intelligence and Policy:*

> It is difficult to imagine an effective system for collecting intelligence without the analysis that provides effective guidance or "tasking" to collectors. Counterintelligence is necessary to protect collectors from becoming known, neutralized, and exploited by hostile intelligence services. Similarly, a successful program of covert action must be grounded in effective collection, analysis, and counterintelligence. All of this is to say that the nature of intelligence is such that the several elements of intelligence are parts of a single unified system, whose success depends on all parts working effectively. In short, it must be a "full-service" intelligence system.[10]

Collection

Intelligence organizations collect information. The questions and controversies that often surround this activity concern the kinds of information they collect and the means they use to collect it. At a minimum, they use what today are termed "open sources," which include periodicals, the Internet and the World Wide Web, and seminars and conferences—any information available to the public. There is an ongoing debate regarding the relative value of open sources versus classified sources, since so much information on so many topics is readily available nowadays through the public media.[11] Collectors of intelligence further distinguish between human intelligence (HUMINT) and various types of scientific and technical intelligence: signal intelligence (SIGINT, from intercepts in electronic communications, radar, and telemetry), imagery intelligence (IMINT, including air, satellite, and ground imagery), and measurement and signatures intelligence (MASINT, which is technically derived intelligence data other than imagery and SIGINT). HUMINT is information collected directly by people, including that provided by ambassadors or defense attachés as part of their normal reporting routines, information obtained at public and social events, and information garnered clandestinely through operatives who read others' mail and purloined documents. HUMINT is the traditional espionage, carried out mainly by agents operating in another country to provide information to their case officers, who then forward it to their home agencies.

Analysis

Raw intelligence data are not much good without analysis. Analysis, or the anticipation of analysis, also shapes collection requirements. The difficulty at this stage lies not only in the need to process gigantic quantities of data, but even more in determining what conclusions to derive from the information. Production is only the first step; the intelligence must then be marketed. Analysis, in short, is not a simple technical issue but includes a choice of methods, as well as the perceptions and political preferences of both the providers and the "customers." Much of the analytical literature on intelligence activities focuses precisely on whether, and to what extent, leaders use the information provided to them by their intelligence organizations.[12] For our purposes of definition, then, analysis includes marketing the product to the decision maker.

From a national security point of view, timely and accurate intelligence can be a powerful tool and a force multiplier. Every strategic plan is based on assumptions. Such assumptions, particularly those concerning the capabilities and intentions of a potential adversary, must be based on well-thought-out intelligence estimates. The process of creating reliable, accurate strategic intelligence, however, is dynamic. This process, often referred to as the intelligence cycle, begins when the policymaker and his or her planning staff—in the United States, this is the president and his National Security Council (NSC) staff—express a need for intelligence information to help them make a national security–related policy decision. Intelligence managers—in our example, the Central Intelligence Agency (CIA) at the national level—convert these requests into information collection plans. The raw data are gathered by various intelligence methods and then processed, exploited, and given to analysts for integration, evaluation, and examination, which results in finished intelligence products (written reports or oral briefings, for example). These products are disseminated to the consumers (here the president and strategic planners of the NSC), who may then ask the intelligence managers to provide additional or more-focused information.

Counterintelligence

At its most basic level, the purpose of counterintelligence is to protect the state and its secrets from other states or organizations. Seemingly clear and straightforward in these terms, in fact it becomes—in the words of James Angleton, the longtime, often controversial head of counterintelligence at the CIA—"'the wilderness of mirrors,' where defectors are false, lies are truth, truth lies, and the reflections leave you dazzled and confused."[13] Abram N. Shulsky defines the scope of issues involved:

> In its most general terms, counterintelligence refers to information collected and analyzed, and activities undertaken, to protect a nation (including its own intelligence-related activities) against the actions of hostile intelligence services. Under this definition, the scope of counterintelligence is as broad as the scope of intelligence itself, since all manners of hostile intelligence activities must be defended against.[14]

Shulsky, like most American authors on the subject of intelligence, associates counterintelligence primarily with countering foreign threats. In common usage, the term "counterintelligence" also is applied to those intelligence activities aimed at countering internal threats. British and Commonwealth scholars, however, prefer to use the term "security intelligence" to describe intelligence functions aimed at countering domestic threats. Peter Gill defines security intelligence as "the state's gathering of information about and attempts to counter perceived threats to its security deriving from espionage, sabotage, foreign-influenced activities, political violence, and subversion."[15]

Memoir accounts by retired intelligence professionals, as well as books by students of intelligence, indicate that counterintelligence and security intelligence activities have the greatest negative implications for democracy because of their covert surveillance of the citizenry.[16] The implications for democracy are much more severe in new democracies where, as we will demonstrate in the next section, counterintelligence and security intelligence were the principal functions of intelligence services under the old regimes. The intelligence service sought to root out real and imagined enemies of the state, often resulting in yet more opposition, thus leading to a spiral of distrust and violence. If even in established democracies a certain amount of paranoia is inherent in counterintelligence and security intelligence—as in "there is an enemy at work here and we must root him out"—then in less institutionalized and nondemocratic

Third World countries this attitude routinely resulted in extreme violations of human rights and impunity for the intelligence agents.[17]

Covert Actions

Covert actions, or "special political actions" in Great Britain and "active measures" in the former Soviet Union, are activities intended to influence another state by means that are not identified with the state behind the actions.

Covert action is not, per se, part of the intelligence process. Intelligence, considered as a product, supports operations, whether they are overt or covert. That covert action has become identified as an intelligence function is an organizational choice. Governments choose where to place this function; some prefer it to be a military responsibility, and others such as the United States have placed it in a civilian intelligence organization. Where governments decide to place this function can have profound and long-lasting second-order effects on the intelligence organization. Arguably, by placing the covert action function in what was originally intended to be a national intelligence analysis organization, the U.S. government in 1947 shaped the dominant intelligence culture of the CIA for more than a generation. In addition, by placing the covert action function in the same agency responsible for national intelligence analysis, the U.S. government created an internal agency conflict of interests that persists to this day.

There are several categories of covert action, ranging from propaganda to paramilitary operations. Mark Lowenthal categorizes them in terms of level of violence and degree of plausible deniability. The first level, propaganda, includes the use of the media in another country to convey a certain message. It is categorized as the least violent means of covert action with the highest degree of plausible deniability. The second level is political activity, which includes funding or other support to government leaders, political parties, unions, religious groups, armed forces, and the like in another country, to induce them to follow a certain course of action. Closely linked to this level is economic activity, in which governments use economic weapons, such as destroying crops, influencing markets, and circulating counterfeit currency, to destabilize a regime. The final two levels involve much higher degrees of violence and usually provide a lesser degree of plausible deniability. The overthrow of governments by coups, usually through surrogates, is a more violent method of regime change that has a lower degree of plausible deniability.

Paramilitary operations are inherently the most violent covert actions, and consequently they offer the lowest likelihood of plausible deniability for the government involved. This ultimate level involves the use of force, usually by means of indigenous armed elements, to launch a direct attack on the government of another state (such as the U.S.-backed Contra insurgency in Nicaragua during the 1980s).[18] Paramilitary operations can range from smaller actions, like assassination or the arming and training of a small contingent of dissident tribal groups, to actions as large as the 1961 Bay of Pigs invasion of Cuba. The larger the paramilitary operation, the less likely it is to provide the cover of plausible deniability for the sponsoring state. Richard Bissell, an American covert operations insider, has crafted a straightforward rationale for covert action:

> It becomes overwhelmingly obvious that we are deeply concerned with the internal affairs of other nations and that, insofar as we make any effort to encourage the evolution of the world community in accord with our values, we will be endeavoring purposefully to influence these affairs. The argument then turns out to be not about whether to influence the internal affairs of others, but about how. Open diplomacy, however, has its limitations as a policy tool. There are times when a great power can best attain its objectives by acting in total secrecy. On certain occasions, however, a great power may seek to influence the internal affairs of another nation without its knowledge or without the knowledge of the international community. These circumstances require covert action.[19]

Obviously, not every country has robust capabilities in all four intelligence functions, but the fact that some nations do have these capabilities means that this is the global framework within which intelligence must be understood. Intelligence is created to defend the state from potential enemies, other states, and nonstate actors, taking into consideration the instruments that these others have available. All countries are aware to some degree of the intelligence capabilities of other countries and are aware that they themselves will be involved in, or even the target of, data collection and covert action.

Security Intelligence and the Counterintelligence State

In virtually all authoritarian regimes (including the former Soviet bloc), the intelligence apparatus was a key means for maintaining power. In those countries with military regimes, the intelligence services came under direct military control. In others, with communist or socialist governments, the intelligence apparatus was a mix of military and civilian services. In both, however, the problems of reform are similar.

As Kieran Williams and Dennis Deletant point out in their study of intelligence services in three postcommunist states of central Europe, these governments are very new and somewhat formal democracies grafted onto societies that still suffer from a lack of trust in state institutions in general and intelligence organizations in particular. Reform in the intelligence sector has been difficult because of this pervasive public distrust of institutions, as well as the common problem of politicization of the bureaucracy and the consequent lack of a corporate culture or tradition of public service. In addition, postcommunist states in Europe, long dominated by the Soviet Union, have little experience in external threat assessment and prioritizing their national security needs.[20] Our research indicates that these impediments to intelligence sector reform are not unique to postcommunist European nations, however, but are, with varying degrees of significance, fairly common to most new democracies emerging from an authoritarian past. The main challenge is to transform the institutions—including "formal or informal procedures, routines, norms, and conventions"—that were central to an authoritarian regime into those that can support a democratic regime and operate under the control of civilians.[21] In this regard the challenge is similar to the more general challenge of establishing democratic civil-military relations, but it is even more complicated.

In established, modern democracies such as the United States and Great Britain, national intelligence organizations exist for one primary purpose: to inform and support foreign policy decision makers. Their most essential role is to determine the capabilities and intentions of a nation's adversaries and to warn of potential threats. In virtually all these organizations, particularly those military intelligence services dealing with strategic issues, the lion's share of people and assets are focused on capability and threat assessment to support the development of plans and to identify emerging issues that affect long-term planning and the strategic environment. Counterintelligence is a purely secondary mission in these services, whether military or civilian. Domestic security intelligence is primarily a "high policing" function, and, in most modern democracies, it is assigned to a separate civilian agency such as the U.S. Federal Bureau of Investigation (FBI) or the Security Service (MI5) in the United Kingdom.

This was not the case in authoritarian regimes, where the boundaries and functions of military intelligence and police organizations overlapped or became indistinguishable from each other. Because these authoritarian regimes were based on something other than democratic legitimacy exercised through free elections, they had to rely on security organizations to identify domestic opponents, neutralize opposition to the government, and seek through a variety of means, including control over news media, to generate at least domestic apathy. In most cases, intelligence organizations provided these services. Precisely because of this heavy reliance and its centrality to power, the intelligence apparatus in most nondemocratic states grew in size and influence, with the result that it was largely autonomous even within authoritarian regimes.[22] In these countries, intelligence meant mainly counterintelligence or security intelligence.[23] That is, its purpose was to protect the state and its secrets from outsiders, which meant anyone outside the central core of power. And, as almost anything could be defined as a matter of state security, the scope of that which had to be controlled was immense. While in most instances the intelligence service rhetorically linked internal opposition to putative foreign enemies, the overwhelming focus of the intelligence service in most countries was on domestic opposition, not other states.[24]

In general, these security intelligence services functioned more as "political police" than domestic intelligence bureaus familiar to the older democracies. As they accrued influence over time, the security intelligence organizations acquired greater autonomy from the civilian policy-making process, and they increasingly became insulated from legislative or judicial scrutiny. They tended to be responsive only to the regimes in power, and they derived their own powers and responsibilities directly from executive authority rather than through legal mandates. They inevitably gathered political intelligence on tremendous numbers of people, usually unrelated to specific criminal offenses. These security intelligence organizations were the means with which authoritarian regimes conducted aggressive countering operations against political opposition. In some cases, such as South Africa under President F. W. de Klerk, the militarized intelligence services resembled what W. W. Keller and Peter Gill have called the "independent security state." This extreme form of security intelligence organization is characterized by an almost total lack of external controls on intelligence activities. It differs from the political police in that the security intelligence organization determines its own agenda and goals, which may not coincide with those of the ruling elite. Its funding and policies remain hidden from the rest of the policymaking process, and the organization itself selects the targets for its information gathering and countering activities.[25]

Typically, authoritarian regimes are at best formal democracies. If the ruling elite preserves a facade of democratic institutions, the persistence of political conflict allows them to resort to emergency powers at will. Often in such situations, the regime's legitimacy is at stake, civil rights are restricted, political conflict becomes militarized, and the security intelligence services, often closely linked to or controlled by the military, are granted exceptional powers. Most authoritarian regimes rely on militarized political police for their security intelligence needs and for protection from internal threats.

Taken to its extreme form, an authoritarian regime may become so preoccupied with threats to its political power, both real and perceived, that it devolves into a totalitarian state where the military and security intelligence structures dominate political activity, opposition is outlawed, and the ruling regime retains power over its populace by extralegal means, typically intimidation and terror. As the ruling elites become increasingly paranoid about internal threats, they tend to cede more power to the military and security intelligence apparatus, leading to the eventual emergence of an independent security state.[26]

Obviously, an independent security state is totally incompatible with the nature of a modern democracy. Policymakers in a democracy must balance security needs with social welfare expectations by seeing to it that the military, the police, and the security intelligence organizations are subject to civilian control and oversight. The government itself is accountable to the institutions of a democracy. Consolidated democracies are likely to have as their main intelligence arm a civilian domestic intelligence agency that comes under tight democratic control. However, if a government becomes preoccupied with perceived internal threats (terrorism or insurgency, for example), it tends to emphasize national security matters over social welfare policies, thus creating the preconditions for the emergence of a more autonomous and less accountable security intelligence apparatus to protect the state. Emerging democracies, where the institutions of democracy are new and still primarily procedural, are particularly vulnerable to this type of devolution.

The Challenge of Democratic Consolidation

"Consolidation" is a familiar concept in comparative politics, and it is useful because it reflects the idea that a new regime's structures and processes are becoming stable. That is, a democratic regime is consolidated when the elites and the masses accept it as "the only game in town" and support its institutions.[27] This acceptance is no easy task, especially if one considers the basic characteristics that a regime must have in order to be termed democratic. The following is a brief standard definition of contemporary democracy: "Modern political democracy is a system of governance in which rulers are held accountable for their actions in the public realm by citizens, acting indirectly through the competition and cooperation of their elected representatives."[28]

For accountability to function, procedural minimal conditions are necessary. As more countries began to consolidate their new democracies, it became apparent that some, such as Iran, Pakistan, and Turkey, did not seem to empower the necessary institutions fully. Scholars identified a further defining characteristic of real, functioning democracy, which is that no unelected body has authority over the popularly elected officials. In all three of the countries noted above, the supervisory or monitoring role has been assumed by an unrepresentative body, such as a national security council or a council of guardians, that has the power to veto legislation passed by the democratically elected legislature and executive. It should be noted that in Portugal at the beginning of the "third wave of democratization," the Portuguese constitution of 1976 empowered precisely such a body in the form of the Revolutionary Council. Portugal became fully democratic only with the constitutional revision of 1982, which eliminated this body and distributed its powers among the democratically derived sectors of government.

Elected leaders in new democracies face major challenges both in the institutional lack of recent experience with democracy and in the inability of a wary population to value these new political structures and processes.[29] Furthermore, the governments in most cases are confronting dire economic problems, often accompanied by social disruption. Overall, democracy is a very demanding political system both for elites and for average citizens, and new democracies are highly tentative. The issue for these leaders is how to develop trust and transparency while struggling with the legacies of the authoritarian regime.

The former regime's intelligence apparatus is very unlikely to have come under democratic government control, but instead either retains power over civilian officials or operates on its own agenda. This was clearly the case in Peru under President Alberto Fujimori and in South Africa during periods of the de Klerk presidency. We expect that this remains an issue in a great many countries. If the elected government does not control the intelligence structures, it is by definition not a consolidated democracy, since democratic consolidation requires both the institutions and the culture of democracy. Legitimacy is central to the culture of democracy. If a government is monitored—or blackmailed—by the intelligence service, then the elected leaders' claim to democratic legitimacy will be suspect, and the citizens' trust in the institutions of democracy will be damaged. Democratic consolidation is a huge challenge in the best of circumstances. Any handicap, especially one as critical as lack of legitimacy, is an impediment difficult to overcome.

Intelligence and Democracy

All countries have an intelligence apparatus of some scope and capability. The question for new democracies is, what kind of intelligence structure do they need and how can it be controlled? While the challenge is especially cogent in the new democracies, democratic control of intelligence is a subject of intense debate everywhere for at least four reasons. First, as Pat Holt states, "Secrecy is the enemy of democracy," because secrecy encourages abuse.[30] If there is secrecy, how can there be accountability, the operative mechanism of democracy, especially when both the purveyors and the end users of secret information mutually benefit from the exclusion of oversight? Because intelligence organizations operate in secrecy, they largely avoid the checks and balances on which democracy is based. Second, intelligence agencies collect and analyze information, and information means power. High-level officials in intelligence organizations can leverage access to information to promote agendas and purposes of their own, including to benefit their "friends" in government, meaning those who will protect the organization's prerogatives. Gill uses the metaphor of the "Gore-Tex" state to illustrate a high degree of domestic penetration by the security intelligence services. Information flows in one direction only: to the intelligence services, but not from them to state and society.[31] Intelligence structures may be autonomous from state control and, through the use of information that others do not have, even determine state policy.

Third, intelligence organizations routinely break laws abroad. Although spying is illegal everywhere, intelligence officers regularly provide undeclared funds to foreign nationals to act as agents and propagandists, tap phones, steal documents, and the like, all of which are outside the law. In most such cases, operatives do not admit who they are or for whom they work. In such a culture, in which people are paid to operate outside the law with impunity, there may be a problem in making the distinction between breaking laws abroad and not breaking them at home.

Fourth, intelligence officials can always invoke self-justification that their work is critical to the defense of the nation. In the words of former intelligence officer Peter Wright, "[Intelligence] is a constant war, and you face a constantly shifting target."[32] It is up to the intelligence organizations to root out spies, domestic and foreign, that are threats to the nation. Their members may easily develop the perception that they know better than anyone else what is going on out there and how dangerous the threat really is. Their knowing things that others do not, combined with their de facto license to operate outside society's rules, may easily lead intelligence officials to develop a condescending, even adversarial attitude toward anyone who is not initiated into the club.

Critical Issues in Reforming Intelligence Services

In view of the difficulty that states everywhere have in trying to control intelligence, and considering the dangerous institutional legacy of intelligence services in most new democracies, what are the choices to be made concerning different options for democratic control, and what are the implications of those options? This section lists the most important institutional choices and evaluates their likely impacts on democratic governance.

To comprehend the relationship between states and their intelligence services, several critical issues should be addressed. These are all within a framework of New Institutionalism in that the decisions reflect the configuration of power at a particular time, and their impact will reverberate long into the future, with positive or negative implications for democratic consolidation. First we deal with less well-known or recognized institutional decisions and then turn to the more familiar and explicit mechanisms of control.

Basic Decisions Regarding Intelligence Services

Initially, democracies must establish a clear and comprehensive legal framework for intelligence activities, as is required for the armed forces in general. Intelligence is "slippery," and if the legal framework is not clear and explicit, intelligence agencies will be much more difficult to bring under democratic control. As is the case in civil-military relations in general, a legal mandate for intelligence activities is a necessary, but by itself not sufficient, condition for democratic control.[33]

There are three fundamental decisions and several secondary decisions that can be made regarding the establishment of civilian control over intelligence operations. These choices should be stipulated within a clear and explicit legal framework adopted by the government's legislative body. The first choice is to determine which of the four intelligence functions will be implemented and how much of the country's resources will be allocated to them. The initial part of the question can be answered only by assessing the global and regional situation, alliances, recent history, and capabilities. The latter part—how much is intelligence worth?—is a political decision. Obviously it is worth a great deal if it provides the nation with the means to maintain its independence in the face of a hostile neighbor. Intelligence also can be valuable in lieu of maintaining large military forces, by allowing a country to focus its capabilities on the most serious threats and thereby minimize redundancy and higher operational costs. But can the mere fact of having a certain level of intelligence capability serve to deter hostile intentions and actions? Much depends on the government's relationship with other, more powerful countries that may be willing to share intelligence with it under certain circumstances. These choices optimally would be integrated into an overall institutional framework for defense decision making, based on an assessment of what the nation requires and how much it is willing to pay for it. This is, of course, an abiding issue in all civil-military relations.

The empirical evidence clearly shows that the top level of the executive branch of government (the president or prime minister and relevant cabinet ministers) must take responsibility for making these decisions and seeing that they are in synchrony with the rest of the defense apparatus. This raises the issue of how to structure the bureaucratic organization that manages or integrates the intelligence functions. In the United States, the director of Central Intelligence provides the integrated intelligence product, but it is the National Security Council that must coordinate national policy.[34] In Brazil after the most recent reforms, the Secretariat of Institutional Security has responsibility for that coordination, working directly under the president. And since South Africa instituted its reforms in the mid-1990s, the National Intelligence Co-ordinating Committee reports directly to the president and the cabinet on intelligence matters.

The second critical choice facing a new democratic government concerns the balance between civilian and military involvement in intelligence, in terms of both production (collection and analysis) and consumption. In most authoritarian countries, the military had a monopoly on intelligence as producer and end user. During democratic consolidation, leaders must decide whether military intelligence should be replaced in whole or in part by new civilian organizations. One alternative is to give the military responsibilities only for military intelligence and to have civilians assume responsibility for strategic intelligence and counterintelligence. The question of who will have access to the final "goods" is as important as that of collection. To whom will the intelligence product be distributed? Will access be limited to the president of the country, his director for intelligence, members of the cabinet, or the military? Should members of the legislature or anyone else be in the loop? Access to intelligence information, and the form in which it is made available—such as open or classified, written reports or oral briefings—have great implications for the potential power of those who receive it.

A subtheme of this balance between civilian and military institutions is the issue of domestic and foreign intelligence. Does the same organization have responsibility for internal surveillance, which is mainly security intelligence, and for external operations? Should these functions be fused, and if they are, what controls need to be in place so that operations and products are not used for political purposes? In most democracies the internal and external functions are separate. For example, the FBI handles counterintelligence and security intelligence within the United States, while the CIA has responsibility for intelligence gathering and counterintelligence outside the country. In most European democracies, the functions are divided between security (domestic) intelligence and foreign intelligence, with the organizations doing their tasks wherever necessary, at home or abroad. This division has not been much of an issue in most of the new democracies because the operations they inherited were focused internally for the most part. It should be noted that domestic intelligence is cheap in comparison with foreign intelligence, and most countries cannot afford to support the latter professionally on a large scale.

The third choice that new democracies face concerns the relationship between intelligence and policy, a choice that logically also involves the matter of coordination among the intelligence organizations. At issue is whether all intelligence activities should be formally coordinated by a director of central intelligence, as in the United States, but kept separate from the policymaking branch (by excluding the director from the president's cabinet). Alternatively, should they be placed in separate ministries, as with MI5 and MI6 in Great Britain, and rely on more-collegial coordinating procedures? These issues reflect an ongoing debate about the implications for objective intelligence analysis when it is closely linked to policy versus the supposed loss of efficiency by having intelligence that is not linked. How different democracies handle this issue varies greatly.[35]

The answer depends in large part on the political traditions and structures of the country, but the underlying issue of policy-relevant, but not policy-driven, intelligence must be assessed. Critics of covert action in the United States claim that such operations blur the distinction between intelligence and policy within the CIA. Rather than simply providing objective intelligence, the agency develops the policy, carries it out, and largely evaluates its success. Hastedt, who has written one of the few books on controlling intelligence, makes his position explicit on this issue: "The purpose of intelligence is to inform and warn policy-makers. The choice of what to do lies with the policy-maker. If intelligence is brought into too close a contact with policy making it runs the risk of being corrupted."[36] In the new democracies, it is too early to determine how decision makers are dealing with this issue, since they are still in the process of defining and implementing structures and processes in the (often newly created) ministries of defense and intelligence organizations.[37]

All three of these institutional decisions hold significant implications for democratic control over intelligence. The first choice, about which intelligence functions to fund, will have an obvious impact, especially on the scope of counterintelligence operations. Second, the decision whether to locate intelligence functions in civilian structures or in military ones will directly affect civilian control over the armed forces, as well as civilian control over intelligence. Third, close links with policymaking can make intelligence less a function of information gathering and analysis and more a tool used by political leaders to retain power. In the cases with which our research is most familiar—Argentina, Brazil, Guatemala, Romania, South Africa, and South Korea—the evidence suggests that they are dealing well with the first two decisions, but resolution of the third remains challenging.

Explicit Mechanisms of Control over Intelligence

A common mechanism to control intelligence is to separate it into different agencies in order to prevent any single entity from having a monopoly on its production or use. This is the model in the United States. A possible arrangement could be to have separate intelligence organizations for each of the armed services and the police, as well as separate structures for domestic and foreign intelligence. This proliferation of organizations might not be the most efficient system, since the different agencies tend to battle among themselves over territory and access to decision makers, but it eliminates the chances of monopoly by any single organization or individual and creates opportunities for more-democratic control. Most countries that are seeking to reform their intelligence structures have moved in this direction. In South Africa, South Korea, Argentina, Brazil, and Guatemala, the governments have created civilian intelligence services—two each in the case of Brazil and Guatemala—to complement (or compete with?) their military counterparts. Romania is an extreme case, however, having created so many smaller, competing, and often redundant intelligence organizations that achieving effectiveness has become difficult.

A second mechanism for democratic control is external oversight. Does anyone have oversight over intelligence, or does the apparatus alone have responsibility for monitoring its own performance? The latter option is extremely dangerous to democracy. In the United States, oversight has expanded over time, so that now not only do the intelligence agencies have inspector generals, but the executive branch and the two houses of Congress also maintain oversight bodies.[38] Although formal oversight remains very limited in Great Britain, democratic institutions are sufficiently hallowed as to guarantee a high level of accountability. If intelligence is to be under democratic civilian control in countries that are seeking to consolidate their democracies, it is clear that the governments must institutionalize oversight.

As Marina Caparini notes, executive oversight generally concerns itself with issues of efficacy—whether the intelligence services are functioning efficiently and carrying out their assigned tasks. Judicial oversight usually involves issues of propriety and legality. Legislators monitor both the efficacy and the propriety of intelligence activities, and most new democracies emphasize this legislative oversight function. Argentina and Brazil now have legislative oversight, but Guatemala does not. Whether these mechanisms in fact work or not, however, depends on the composition of the oversight committee and the quantity and quality of its staff. Public oversight, mainly a function of the media, usually focuses on issues regarding the propriety of intelligence activities.[39]

Access to the Product

Since knowledge equals power, it is important to specify who may see the intelligence and in what form. Are those who "need to know" limited only to the military, or do civilians in the executive also have access? What about the legislature? The question of access is a critical one in many countries, because democratic elections make it possible for former opposition elements, even guerrillas, to be elected to executive and legislative offices. Countries must establish criteria and processes for sharing intelligence with elected officials that will permit informed decision making without increasing the likelihood that privileged information will be misused for political purposes.[40] Basic issues, such as whether any or all officials "need to know" even before operations such as covert actions take place, concern not just the immediate distribution of intelligence (which here extends to covert actions as well) but also the general availability of information after a certain period of time. The possibility of wider distribution holds implications for democratic control of operations. If the intelligence agencies know that in the future their files will be open for public scrutiny, they are logically more likely to keep a rein on the behavior of their members.

A dilemma is inherent in the issue of control, and that is the trade-off between democratic control over intelligence and the effectiveness of the intelligence apparatus in doing its job to defend the nation. This dilemma can be reduced conceptually to the tension between accountability, which requires transparency, and the intelligence function, which requires secrecy. For example, does legislative oversight result in secrets being leaked and agents being uncovered? Democracies wrestle constantly with this dilemma, which has no easy or sure solution. When discussing legislative oversight in other countries, the issue of the reliability or sense of responsibility of legislators always comes up. It is very difficult to make a priori judgments on this issue, but it should be noted that since legislative oversight was imposed in the United States in the 1970s, there have been far fewer cases of members of Congress or their staffs releasing classified information than of leaks from the executive branch. More than whether to legislate oversight, new democracies must realize the need to grapple with the questions of how and by whom oversight should be implemented.

One basic problem, paradoxically, is that democratically elected civilians may not in fact be interested in controlling the intelligence apparatus in new democracies. In virtually all of these countries, the use of elections to determine leadership is a new and relatively fragile means of determining who has power. Even in older democracies, leaders often prefer "plausible deniability"—the right to claim innocence by ignorance—rather than access to the information required to control a potentially controversial or dangerous organization or operation. Except in a crisis, most politicians in democratic states find little to gain by serving on intelligence oversight committees or involving themselves in routine intelligence sector activities that, by their nature, will have little public recognition and therefore accrue little political capital. The sad fact is that intelligence sector reforms usually occur only when a major scandal is revealed, thus forcing politicians to respond to public outcries that they "do something."[41] Logically, this situation would be even more prevalent in newer democracies for at least three reasons. First, politicians may be afraid of antagonizing the intelligence apparatus through efforts to control it, because the intelligence organization might have some embarrassing information on them hidden away. Second, they may be afraid because the intelligence organization in the past engaged in arbitrary and violent actions, and the politicians are not sure that the organization will not revert to such tactics. Third, there are probably no votes to be won in attempting to control an organization that most people either don't know about or want to ignore.

Intelligence as a Profession

A fundamental institutional decision in both controlling and achieving effective intelligence capability concerns the recruitment, education and training, management, and separation or retirement of intelligence professionals. External control mechanisms, while a necessary condition for democratic control, can be subverted by the intelligence agencies. This was obvious in Brazil, where continued abuses resulted in the abolition of the National Intelligence Service (SNI) in 1990 by President Fernando Collor de Melo. Of course in Brazil, as in Peru in 2004, abolition of the main intelligence agency did little for effectiveness. The challenge is control combined with effectiveness. The focus on intelligence as a profession is particularly apt since its members, more than any other type of specialist, are constrained more by professional norms than outside controls (such as oversight), even in a democracy.[42] Whereas the armed forces are regulated by budgets, promotions, and a myriad of civilian control mechanisms, intelligence professionals are controlled only in the last analysis, if that, by the external structures and processes noted above. They are granted impunity to break laws abroad and have tremendous leeway to bend laws within their own country and organization. They operate secretly outside the system of checks and balances, they are ensconced in a bureaucracy with other like-minded officers and develop a closed-club mentality, and they are very suspicious of outsiders, including at times their own superiors. In new democracies, where accountability is minimal in any case, the impunity of the intelligence services from the consequences of their actions is a given.

Professions are clearly considered an institution within the New Institutionalism framework. Like most professions, intelligence can be defined in terms of the three criteria of expertise, corporateness, and responsibility.[43] The first criterion, expertise, encompasses the four intelligence functions of collection, analysis, counterintelligence, and covert action. While the range of what intelligence professionals do is extremely broad, what unifies them, or defines them as intelligence professionals, is secrecy. (The military profession also has elements of secrecy, but these pertain mainly to intelligence.) With regard to covert actions, prominent American intelligence specialist Richard M. Bissell Jr. emphasizes both the diversity of intelligence operatives and the secrecy that is their defining characteristic:

> The professional competence of a clandestine service consists of, and is measured by, its ability to carry out operations secretly (or deniably), much as lawyers' competence consists in their ability to win cases, and doctors' in their ability to prevent or treat illness. The clandestine service may number among its members brilliant journalists, able warriors, and superior political analysts, but the professional skill for which, presumably, they are hired is the ability to organize and conduct operations covertly. This is a rather specialized skill not widely found outside of intelligence and internal security services.[44]

Second, an intelligence service's corporateness lies in its access to classified systems, documents, information, sources, and operations. Clearances are the control mechanism for entry into and continued membership in the profession. There are few hard-and-fast educational requirements for intelligence professionals or even among different intelligence organizations within one country, and little defines their corporate identity beyond their access to classified information.[45] The security clearances and the classified nature of the profession reinforce a deliberate culture of identification as a member of a unique, even elite club. It may also breed a dangerous level of arrogance, including a sense of impunity—if nobody else knows what is really going on, then how can outsiders control those who do? Furthermore, how can those same outsiders presume to judge the value of the product, or the effectiveness of operations, when they don't have access to all the information?

Third, the responsibility of the intelligence professional is to serve in defense of the democratic state. But if we consider the first two criteria of expertise in secret matters and a corporate culture based on security clearances, we are led inexorably to the view of intelligence as a profession that largely governs itself according to its own definition of responsibility. In new democracies this is doubly dangerous, not only because the previous regime was not accountable to the general population but also because intelligence officers may not even have been responsible to the small group controlling the state. This legacy begs the questions of who should know what and who is in control. An institutionalized ethos of responsibility is extremely important to democracy, and even in stable democracies enough incidents of wrongdoing come to light to cause concern that intelligence officers may not be serving the state. Or, rather, the concern is that they are serving it according to their limited organizational terms and not according to the terms of the democratically elected leaders. In new democracies this situation is all the more difficult and destabilizing because the intelligence community has no tradition of responsibility to the democratic state, so the process of building professionalism, as we have defined it here, will be problematic at best.

To Change a Profession

One of the greatest obstacles to change is the tendency of governments to recruit retired military personnel into civilian intelligence positions. These former officers may have taken off their uniforms, but their attitudes and loyalties tend to remain what they were during their military careers. If new personnel cannot be found, the question becomes whether retired military officers will be able—and willing—to shift their ethic of responsibility from their former organization to the state. In most countries, including the older democracies, little explicit attention is paid to promoting this ethic of service to the state within the intelligence community.[46] In the older democracies there is less need to promote the ethic, as it is a generally embraced societal norm and the rule of law generally prevails. In the newer democracies, however, the need is clear and goes along with the need for an open debate on intelligence and with the active recruitment of civilians into the field.[47] It has been recognized in several countries, including Brazil and Romania, that major efforts must be taken in the new democracies to promote and inculcate a sense of professional responsibility by making intelligence officers and agencies answerable to the state via its democratically elected leaders. This can be accomplished only by committing serious attention and resources to recruitment and training and by obligating the services to remain involved in the larger polity and society. The specific elements of this prescription have to be defined separately for each nation.

A practical problem in reforming intelligence activities involves the organizational dynamics of transforming a bureaucracy. One of the most persistent arguments against reforming intelligence agencies is that the transformation process will leave the nation vulnerable to both internal and external threats. In most organizations, a radical transformation process will inherently involve a period of declining organizational task efficiency. One goal during the transformation process is to limit this decline while minimizing the time it takes for the organization to recover. As a high-level South African official described it, a dilemma arises when the organizational level of efficiency reaches a lower plateau and seems to stagnate rather than improve to the level of the old organization. A common reaction to this problem is to attempt to reorganize further in order to improve efficiency (or as one longtime intelligence officer suggested, to increase managerial control over the organization). The result usually is another decline in organizational task efficiency as the agency struggles to adapt to these new changes. The problem can become systemic if the agency's leadership does not recognize it and does not allow the organization sufficient time to adapt and gradually recover efficiency (Figure 6.1).

The first critical point of divergence occurs at the new organizational level of efficiency *(C)*. Management expects to see improvements in efficiency along a gradual slope toward a desired level *(X)*, when instead the organization seems stuck at the lower efficiency. When improvement does not occur in the expected timely manner, there is a tendency to reorganize *(D)*, thus leading to another decline in efficiency (slope *D–E*) and another reorganization *(E)*. Obviously, this can become a self-defeating process for a consolidating democracy that is attempting to transform its intelligence apparatus into a more democratically accountable, yet efficient organization.[48]

Political leaders must recognize that any reorganization will have a cost in terms of organizational efficiency, at least in the short run. The transformation of intelligence agencies is a long-term process. The initial design of the bureaucratic structure and responsibilities is critical and likely to affect organizational relationships and the professional culture of its members for years to come. Whereas a bureaucratic structure can be created in a relatively short span of time, changing a professional culture takes years. New intelligence officers, professionally dedicated to working

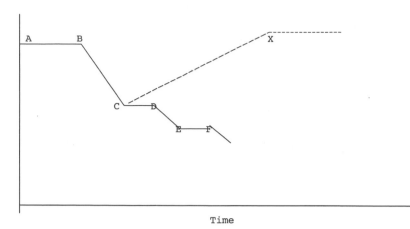

FIGURE 6.1. Problems in organizational transformation efficiency. *A*, operating level of efficiency of old organization; *B*, transformation point; *C*, new organization level of efficiency; *D*, reorganization point; *E*, reorganization level of efficiency; *F*, reorganization point; *X*, desired level of efficiency after transformation. (Concept based on participant discussions during the Center for Civil-Military Relations Executive Seminar, June 12, 2002, Monterey, California.)

within a democratic system, may have to cope with a decade or longer of service before progressing up the ranks where they can make significant impacts on the intelligence culture of their organization.

Conclusion

All nations engage in intelligence activities on some scale. Most leaders believe their countries must do so because others do, and no government can afford to be ignorant of what is going on inside and outside its territory. Furthermore, leaders must be prepared, if necessary, to counter other states' efforts to influence developments in their country. After the terrorist attacks of September 11, 2001, and subsequent attacks in Bali, Spain, Russia, and other locations, there has been renewed emphasis on the need for effective and efficient intelligence services, along with greater attention to nonstate actors. In most of the world, however, the legacy of intelligence services that supported authoritarian regimes has been detrimental to democracy. In the midst of today's challenges to democratic consolidation, efforts to ensure democratic control over intelligence are both necessary and extremely difficult. Without decisive action by governments of emerging democracies, the legacy of the intelligence

organizations they inherited will remain an obstacle to democratic consolidation. Those countries that want to begin exerting democratic civilian control over the intelligence apparatus may undertake several tasks.
These tasks are similar to those of asserting civilian control over the
military in general but are riskier and more demanding because of the
requirement for secrecy and the penetration of state and society in line
with the counterintelligence function.

The first task is to motivate civilians to learn about intelligence so
they can control it. That is, government officials need to demystify intelligence so that, under civilian control, it can both be effective and serve
to defend the nation. In countries that had authoritarian regimes, intelligence often was monopolized by the military. These countries will be
unable to control intelligence unless the elected leaders prepare civilians
to learn enough both to understand what intelligence is all about and
to achieve some degree of cooperation, if not respect, from the intelligence professionals. The government's commitment to reform need
also create openings for civilian employment in intelligence. As in civil-
military relations in general, civilians will have no motivation to come
forward unless they can anticipate viable careers in the field. They can
then begin to learn about intelligence by reading about the experiences
of different countries and taking advantage of cooperative training arrangements in intelligence offered by other governments such as that of
the United States.

The second, broader task is to encourage a political culture that supports the legitimate role of intelligence in a democracy but does not allow
it to run rampant. James A. Schlesinger noted that "to preserve secrecy,
especially in a democracy, security must be part of an accepted pattern
of behavior outside of government and inside."[49] The responsibility for
making the system work must go in both directions: from the intelligence
community to those democratically elected civilians who maintain oversight, in order to provide complete information as and when directed;
and from civilian officials to the intelligence community and society in
general, in order to preclude the unauthorized release of classified information for personal or political reasons. This culture can be encouraged,
as with democratic civil-military relations in general, by fostering a public debate that will break through the residual apathy or fear within the
population regarding intelligence. In some older democracies, including Canada, France, Great Britain, and the United States, this debate
is stimulated by nongovernmental organizations (NGOs) and the media
fairly regularly and is periodically dramatized by intelligence fiascoes that

become public. The commitment of elected politicians to establish a policy on intelligence can act as a salutary catalyst to this society-wide debate.[50]

The public discussion of the role of intelligence in democracy serves a number of important functions. Demythologizing intelligence allows outsiders to assess more realistically its necessity and value for a country, creates legitimate employment for civilians who want to become intelligence specialists, and puts pressure on the government to make its functions more transparent. Several international NGOs (the Federation of American Scientists and the Geneva Centre for the Democratic Control of Armed Forces, for example) are very willing to assist other countries in generating this debate.[51]

In many countries, however, there is virtually no public recognition of the need for reform in intelligence organizations. Like other aspects of civil-military relations, change will require continual efforts by civilians and intelligence professionals to achieve the most appropriate balance of efficiency and transparency for their countries. A small but significant group of countries has undertaken to reform their intelligence systems and to foster a healthy public debate over their future. International assistance is available for these pursuits, as well as a limited but rapidly increasing body of useful literature.

Notes

1. Alfred Stepan, "The Brazilian Intelligence System in Comparative Perspective," chap. 2 in *Rethinking Military Politics: Brazil and the Southern Cone* (Princeton, NJ: Princeton University Press, 1988), 13–29. The similarity between intelligence and civil-military relations is touched upon in Uri Bar-Joseph, *Intelligence Intervention in the Politics of Democratic States: The United States, Israel, and Britain* (University Park: Pennsylvania State University Press, 1995). Bar-Joseph, however, deals only with established democracies and not with the particular problems that arise in new democracies.

2. In the United States, before the Central Intelligence Agency (CIA) was created in 1947, most intelligence activity was carried out by the military departments. Today, by far the greatest part of the intelligence budget—perhaps up to 90 percent—and other resources are still within the Department of Defense, which includes not only the military services but also the Defense Intelligence Agency (DIA), the National Security Agency (NSA), the National Reconnaissance Office (NRO), and the National Geospatial-Intelligence Agency (NGA). For a case study of the demilitarization of intelligence, see A. Giménez-Salinas, "The Spanish Intelligence Services," in *Democracy, Law,*

and Security: Internal Security Services in Contemporary Europe, ed. J.-P. Brodeur, P. Gill, and D. Töllborg (Aldershot, UK: Ashgate, 2003).

3. See Peter Gill, *Policing Politics: Security Intelligence and the Liberal Democratic State* (London: Frank Cass, 1994); Michael Herman, *Intelligence Power in Peace and War* (Cambridge: Cambridge University Press, 1996); Pat M. Holt, *Secret Intelligence and Public Policy: A Dilemma of Democracy* (Washington: CQ Press, 1995); Mark M. Lowenthal, *Intelligence: From Secrets to Policy*, 2nd ed. (Washington: CQ Press, 2003); and Kieran Williams and Dennis Deletant, *Security Intelligence Services in New Democracies: The Czech Republic, Slovakia, and Romania* (London: Palgrave, 2001). In addition, shorter academic studies include Thomas C. Bruneau's article on which this chapter is based, "Controlling Intelligence in New Democracies," *International Journal of Intelligence and Counterintelligence* 14, no. 3 (2001): 323–341; Philip B. Heymann, "Controlling Intelligence Agencies" (Working Paper Series on Internal Security Reform, Project on Justice in Times of Transition, Kennedy School of Government, Harvard University, Cambridge, MA, 2001), http://www.ksg. harvard.edu/justiceproject/workingpapers.htm; Jonathan Moran, "The Role of Security Services in Democratization: An Analysis of South Korea's Agency for National Security Planning," *Intelligence and National Security* 13, no. 4 (1998): 1–32; and K. G. Robertson, "Recent Reform of Intelligence in the UK: Democratization or Risk Management?" *Intelligence and National Security* 13, no. 2 (1998), 144–158.

4. See Glenn Hastedt, "Controlling Intelligence: Defining the Problem," in *Controlling Intelligence*, ed. Glenn Hastedt (London: Frank Cass, 1991), 6–8.

5. Lowenthal, *Intelligence*, 9.

6. For example, in its unclassified *A Consumer's Guide to Intelligence*, the CIA describes only sources and analysis, not discussion of the more controversial intelligence functions of counterintelligence and covert action. These, by contrast, are the focus of books in the more common memoir and exposé categories of the literature on intelligence. *A Consumer's Guide to Intelligence*, PAS 95-00010 (Washington, DC: CIA Public Affairs Staff, 1995).

7. Hastedt, "Controlling Intelligence: Defining the Problem," 6.

8. Loch K. Johnson, *Secret Agencies: U.S. Intelligence in a Hostile World* (New Haven, CT: Yale University Press, 1996), 119.

9. See, for example, Lowenthal, *Intelligence*, 25–53, particularly the explanation of what he terms the "multilayered" intelligence process; and Herman, *Intelligence Power*, 29–35.

10. Roy F. Godson, "Intelligence and Policy: An Introduction," in *Intelligence Requirements for the 1980s: Intelligence and Policy*, ed. Roy Godson (Lexington, MA: Lexington Books, 1986), 2. For more details, see CIA, *Consumer's Guide*; Lowenthal, *Intelligence*, chaps. 4–8; Herman, *Intelligence Power*; Holt, *Secret*

Intelligence, chaps. 3–7; Roy F. Godson, *Dirty Tricks or Trump Cards: American Counterintelligence and Covert Action* (Washington, DC: Pergamon-Brassey's International Defense Publishers, 1995); Walter Laqueur, *The Uses and Limits of Intelligence* (New Brunswick, NJ: Transaction Publishers, 1995); and Gregory F. Treverton, *Covert Action: The Limits of Intervention in the Postwar World* (New York: Basic Books, 1987).

11. For examples of open-source intelligence analyses, see Jane's Information Group, http://www.janes.com; and Strategic Forecasts, http://www.stratfor.com.

12. See for example, Michael I. Handel, ed., *Leaders and Intelligence* (London: Frank Cass, 1989); Christopher Andrew, *For the President's Eyes Only: Secret Intelligence and the American Presidency from Washington to Bush* (New York: Harper Collins, 1995); and Christopher Andrew and Vasili Mitrokhin, *The Sword and the Shield: The Mitrokhin Archive and the Secret History of the KGB* (New York: Basic Books, 1999). For a short and useful discussion of the production and consumption of intelligence, see Mark M. Lowenthal, "Tribal Tongues: Intelligence Consumers, Intelligence Producers," *Washington Quarterly* (Winter 1992): 157–168.

13. Peter Wright, with Paul Greengrass, *Spycatcher: The Candid Autobiography of a Senior Intelligence Officer* (New York: Viking, 1987), 305. Wright was a high-level official in MI5, the British Security Service, for two decades that included the height of the cold war.

14. Abram N. Shulsky (revised by Gary J. Schmitt), *Silent Warfare: Understanding the World of Intelligence* (Washington: Pergamon-Brassey's International Defense Publishers, 1993), 111.

15. Gill, *Policing Politics*, 6–7.

16. Shulsky, *Silent Warfare*, 163. For the implications of this surveillance for British citizens, see Wright, *Spycatcher*.

17. For an analysis of what he terms "state and security intelligence," see Gill, *Policing Politics*. The following quote from the Doolittle Report, presented to President Eisenhower in 1954, conveys the national mood in which U.S. intelligence fought the cold war: "It is now clear that we are facing an implacable enemy [the USSR] whose avowed objective is world domination by whatever means and at whatever cost. There are no rules in such a game. Hitherto acceptable norms of human conduct do not apply. If the U.S. is to survive, long-standing American concepts of 'fair play' must be reconsidered. We must develop effective espionage and counter-espionage services. We must learn to subvert, sabotage and destroy our enemies by more clear, more sophisticated and more effective methods than those used against us. It may become necessary that the American people will be made acquainted with, understand and support this fundamentally repugnant philosophy." Quoted

in Johnson, *Secret Agencies*, 138. The concept of the "national security state," used throughout Latin America, conveyed this same paranoia and helps explain the present negative reaction to the term "national security" in countries such as Guatemala, Argentina, and Brazil.

18. Lowenthal, *Intelligence*, 129–131.

19. Richard M. Bissell Jr., with Jonathan E. Lewis and Frances T. Pudlo, *Reflections of a Cold Warrior: From Yalta to the Bay of Pigs* (New Haven, CT: Yale University Press, 1996), 216.

20. Williams and Deletant, *Security Intelligence Services*, 17–20.

21. Peter A. Hall and Rosemary C. R. Taylor, "Political Science and the Three New Institutionalisms," *Political Studies* 44 (1996): 938.

22. Stepan, "The Brazilian Intelligence System," 19–20. Stepan compares the prerogatives of the Brazilian National Intelligence Service (SNI) with the intelligence organizations in several established democracies.

23. To reiterate the important point of terminology, British and Commonwealth scholars prefer the term "security intelligence" to describe domestic intelligence activities aimed at countering internal threats, usually political crimes. Counterintelligence is usually associated with foreign intelligence threats. See Gill, *Policing Politics*, 6–7; and Williams and Deletant, *Security Intelligence Services*, 1–5.

24. Soviet and Russian scholars coined the term "counterintelligence state" to capture its pervasiveness. Michael Waller defines it as follows: "The counterintelligence state is characterized by the presence of a large, elite force acting as the watchdog of a security defined so broadly and arbitrarily that the state must maintain an enormous vigilance and enforcement apparatus far out of proportion to the needs of a real democracy, even one as unstable as that of Russia. This apparatus is not accountable to the public and enjoys immense police powers with few checks against it. The powers are not designed to protect the rights of the individual, despite rhetoric to the contrary, but to protect the privileges of the ruling class and the chekist [secret police] organs themselves." J. Michael Waller, *Secret Empire: The KGB in Russia Today* (Boulder, CO: Westview Press, 1994), 13. See also John J. Dziak, *Chekisty: A History of the KGB* (Lexington, MA: Lexington Books, 1988).

25. W. W. Keller, *The Liberals and J. Edgar Hoover: Rise and Fall of a Domestic Intelligence State* (Princeton, NJ: Princeton University Press, 1989); Gill, *Policing Politics*, 60–61.

26. For a detailed study on different types of nondemocratic regimes, see Juan J. Linz, *Totalitarian and Authoritarian Regimes* (Boulder, CO: Lynne Rienner, 2000).

27. See, for example, John Higley and Richard Gunther, eds., *Elites and Democratic Consolidation in Latin America and Southern Europe* (Cambridge: Cambridge University Press, 1992), 3–4; and Juan J. Linz and Alfred Stepan, *Problems of Democratic Transition and Consolidation: Southern Europe, South America, and Post-Communist Europe* (Baltimore: Johns Hopkins University Press, 1996), 5–6.

28. Philippe C. Schmitter and Terry Lynn Karl, "What Democracy Is . . . and Is Not," in *The Global Resurgence of Democracy*, ed. Larry Diamond and Marc F. Plattner (Baltimore: Johns Hopkins University Press, 1993), 40.

29. For excellent insights into some of the key elements of democratic consolidation, see the figure "A Heuristic Model of the Factors Influencing the Type/Extent of Democratic Consolidation" in Philippe C. Schmitter, "The Consolidation of Political Democracies: Processes, Rhythms, Sequences, and Types," in *Transitions to Democracy*, ed. Geoffrey Pridham (Aldershot: Dartmouth, 1995), 564.

30. Holt, *Secret Intelligence*, 3.

31. Gill, *Policing Politics*, 79–82. Gore-Tex is a fabric that allows moisture to move in only one direction.

32. Wright, *Spycatcher*, 169.

33. In Argentina, for example, long after the collapse of the military dictatorship in 1983, the intelligence law remained a secret leftover from the old regime for almost another twenty years. Despite the obvious need for new laws, the Argentine Congress was unable to pass a new legal framework for intelligence until 2001. Another, more encouraging example is South Africa, where the government initiated legislative reform of the intelligence apparatus soon after the transition to majority rule in 1994. This involved three major bills in Parliament, which together clearly defined and restructured the intelligence system. See Shaun McCarthy, "South Africa's Intelligence Reformation," *International Journal of Intelligence and Counterintelligence* 9, no. 1 (1996): 63–71. Brazil, like Argentina, took considerably longer to institute reforms after the transition to civilian government in 1985. It finally created the Brazilian Intelligence Agency (ABIN) in 1999 to replace the authoritarian regime's National Intelligence Service. Even so, it was not until September 2002 that President Fernando Henrique Cardoso decreed into being the Brazilian Intelligence System, of which the ABIN was named the "central organ." The Brazilian Congress did play a key role in the final creation of ABIN, and the legislation provides a clear legal basis for civilian control of Brazil's intelligence organs. In Chile the reform legislation was completed in late 2004.

34. On this topic, and in line with our approach in this book, see Amy B. Zegart, *Flawed by Design: The Evolution of the CIA, JCS, and NSC* (Stanford, CA: Stanford University Press, 1999). The relations in the U.S. are changing with intelligence reforms in 2004–2005.

35. The main options are nicely summarized in Johnson, *Secret Agencies*, 129–131. It should be noted that the director of Central Intelligence may not in fact be able to coordinate all intelligence, because he does not control the budgets for the larger and more expensive collection and analysis assets in the National Security Agency, part of the Department of Defense. This issue obviously has been the focus of great debate in the United States since the disaster of September 11, 2001, and especially in the fall of 2004 when Congress debated new structures and processes.

36. Hastedt, "Controlling Intelligence: Defining the Problem," 10. For the comments on covert action, see Admiral Stansfield Turner, *Secrecy and Democracy: The CIA in Transition* (Boston: Houghton Mifflin, 1985), 174.

37. Argentina is among the furthest along in this area, but it took until December 21, 2001, to pass its law that regulates intelligence. This followed almost twenty years of debate. In Brazil, although the head of the Secretariat of Institutional Security, located in the office of the president, ostensibly is responsible for advising and coordinating policy, it is unclear how far his responsibility extends within the military services and the Federal Police.

38. See Turner, *Secrecy and Democracy*, esp. 132, 269–271. For background and details on congressional oversight, see L. Britt Snider, *Sharing Secrets with Lawmakers: Congress as a User of Intelligence* (Washington, DC: Center for the Study of Intelligence, 1997).

39. See Marina Caparini, "Challenges of Control and Oversight of Intelligence Services in a Liberal Democracy" (paper presented at the workshop "Democratic and Parliamentary Oversight of Intelligence Services," Geneva Centre for the Democratic Control of Armed Forces [DCAF], Geneva, October 3–5, 2002), 8–9, http://www.dcaf.ch/news/Intelligence%20Oversight_051002/ws_papers/caparini.pdf.

40. This issue is particularly interesting in Brazil, given that the president of the legislature's Mixed Commission of Control of Intelligence Activities, Deputy Aldo Rebelo, is a member of the Communist Party of Brazil and led a clandestine existence during the previous military regime. From our information, it appears that Brazil is developing protocols that will allow officials such as Rebelo access to intelligence. Rebelo is now the leader of the government party in the lower house, the Câmara.

41. The most famous recent instance of this before the September 11 attacks was the Iran-Contra scandal during the Reagan administration. See, for example, Andrew, *For the President's Eyes Only*, 478–493.

42. Hastedt argues persuasively that formal, legalistic controls have limited value in controlling intelligence and that informal norms and values are extremely important. His study, however, is limited to the directors of U.S. Central Intelligence. See Glenn Hastedt, ed., "Controlling Intelligence:

The Values of Intelligence Professionals" (London: Frank Cass, 1991), 97–112.

43. The classic work on the military as a profession is Samuel P. Huntington, *The Soldier and the State: The Theory and Politics of Civil-Military Relations* (Cambridge, MA: Harvard University Press, 1957). The most useful additions and critiques include Bengt Abrahamsson, *Military Professionalization and Political Power* (Beverly Hills, CA: Sage Publications, 1972); Peter D. Feaver, "The Civil-Military Problematique: Huntington, Janowitz, and the Question of Civilian Control," *Armed Forces and Society* 23, no. 2 (1996): 149–177; and Samuel E. Finer, *The Man on Horseback: The Role of the Military in Politics* (New York: Praeger, 1962).

44. Bissell et al., *Reflections of a Cold Warrior*, 216.

45. Bar-Joseph, noting the absence of formal educational requirements, comes to the untenable conclusion that intelligence should not be considered a profession. Bar-Joseph, *Intelligence Intervention*, 49.

46. This is precisely what Hastedt advocates: "Only by seeking to structure how intelligence professionals see their job can one hope to prevent abuses from occurring in the first place or ensure responsiveness." Hastedt, "Controlling Intelligence: Defining the Problem," 14.

47. The other side of the recruitment coin is retirement. Governments must ensure that their intelligence organizations offer stable career progression based on merit, including provisions for a decent retirement after service. This ensures loyalty and gives officers incentive not to stay on past their usefulness or, worse, to turn to illegal activities, since their skills are not easily transferable to other occupations.

48. Russia's consolidation of its security intelligence services into the Federal Security Service (FSB) is an alarming example of this phenomenon, although we suspect this reorganization was motivated more by issues of control than efficiency. See "Russia's Putin Announces Gov't Shakeup," *Guardian*, March 11, 2003.

49. Quoted in Adda Bozeman, "Political Intelligence in Non-Western Societies: Suggestions for Comparative Research," in *Comparing Foreign Intelligence: The U.S., the USSR, the UK, and the Third World*, ed. Roy Godson (Washington, DC: Pergamon-Brassey's International Defense Publishers, 1988), 133.

50. Such a discussion has been initiated in a few of the newer democracies. In Argentina the debate was started by a small number of civilians who realized that democratic consolidation requires civilian control over intelligence. See, for example, José Manuel Ugarte, *Legislación de inteligencia: Legitimidad y eficacia* (Guatemala City: WOLA [Washington Office on Latin America], 2000). In November 2002 the Brazilian Congress held an open two-day conference

entitled "Intelligence in Brazil and Its Contribution to Sovereignty and Democracy," which attracted three hundred attendees, including coauthor Bruneau, and received extensive media coverage. The results of the conference were published in *Congresso Nacional Seminário: Atividades de Inteligência no Brasil: Contribuições para a Soberania ea Democracia* (Brasília: Gráfica-Abin, 2003).

51. See the Federation of American Scientists online periodical *Intelligence Resource Program*, http://www.fas.org/irp/.

Chapter 7
Defense Budgets, Democratic Civilian Control, and Effective Governance

JEANNE KINNEY GIRALDO

S TUDENTS of civil-military relations have long stressed the centrality of the defense budget for democratic control of the military and effective governance. It is taken as axiomatic that "money talks" and that the power of the purse provides civilians with a key lever of control over the military: government and legislative preferences are more likely to be taken into account when they are backed by the provision or withholding of resources. In addition, it is generally agreed that "excessive" military spending can undermine effective governance by bankrupting the state or detracting from the government's ability to meet its social and economic goals. For these reasons, politicians in new democracies and international observers have long placed great weight on the need to assert control over absolute levels of defense spending. More recently, the focus among academics and international organizations has shifted from levels of defense spending to the transparency and effectiveness of the decision-making process, or, in terms of this book, the institutions that shape defense budgets. At the same time, there has been a much less uniform shift among politicians in consolidating democracies to move beyond their initial successes in reducing defense spending and to strengthen the procedures and institutions particular to the defense budget process—in particular, linking budget decisions to debates over national security policy.

This chapter begins by describing the consensus that has emerged within academic and policy circles on the importance of institutionalizing the budget process for the defense sector in a way that conforms to the principles of effective democratic governance such as transparency, accountability, and policy orientation. It then reviews the four stages of the budget process: (1) the formulation of the budget by the executive; (2) its enactment into law by the legislature; (3) the disbursement and spending of the funds; and (4) an evaluation of the efficiency and effectiveness with which the money was spent. It identifies the key actors who are involved at each stage and describes the general principles that the budget process should respect in a democracy, while acknowledging the diversity of practices among established democracies.

This chapter highlights the challenges that consolidating democracies have faced at each stage as they sought to create an institutionalized, transparent, and efficient budget process controlled by civilians. Many countries have had a surprising amount of success in establishing control over absolute levels of defense spending, but this success has usually been offset by their failure to control the allocation of resources within the defense sector. Importantly, the executive branch in many consolidating democracies has failed to take the lead in devising national security policies that should inform decisions about the level and distribution of the defense budget. Finally, the chapter turns its attention from the formal defense budget to the practice of off-budget defense expenditures, common in a large number of consolidating democracies. The ability of civilians to gain control over levels of spending in the formal defense budget has generally not been matched in off-budget expenditures, despite the negative impact of this practice on many national policy goals, and the chapter offers some hypotheses as to why this might be the case.

Convergence on a Process-Oriented Approach: A Focus on Institutions

Over the years, defense budgets have been the subject of much scrutiny, but until recently the focus had been almost entirely on the level of defense spending: academics devised statistical models that attempt to explain it, and international organizations administered surveys and compiled databases to try to monitor it. With the end of the cold war, talk of a "peace dividend" and a wave of transitions away from authoritarian regimes (many of them led by the military) put defense budgets on the political agenda and held out the prospect of a decline in military spending. The spotlight on aggregate levels of defense spending shone still brighter after 1989 as the International Monetary Fund and the World Bank began to speak out publicly about the difficulties that "excessive" military expenditure posed for the economies of developing countries. In response, the international development community began to set upper limits on military expenditure as a condition of aid.

This focus on expenditure levels was heavily criticized at donor meetings in the late 1990s on a number of grounds. First, it was not clear how donors could define the "appropriate" level of defense spending. A rule setting a uniform upper limit for diverse countries facing different threat and resource levels was destined to be too generous with some countries and too stringent with others. Second, the data on the amount needed to enforce an upper limit were either lacking or unreliable for many countries. In fact, the rule itself had the perverse effect of increasing the unreliability of data as states now had greater incentives to underreport or misreport their spending or to rely more heavily on off-budget expenditures (a practice that is discussed later in the chapter).[1] Third, the approach ignored the fact that most states lacked the procedures for determining "appropriate" levels of spending and the capacity to carry out the budget cuts and to force the restructuring necessary to reach those levels.

This critique resulted in advocacy of a new approach within the donor community, one that focused more on the decision-making process that leads to defense expenditures than on the spending levels themselves. As two advocates of this approach noted: "While data collection and dissemination can be an empowering force for change, the priority for donors should be to help countries address the underlying governance problems that reduce transparency within the defence sector."[2] The same principles of good governance that apply to budgeting in other policy sectors would also be applied to the defense budget. The new approach would focus on defining the main elements of an efficient, effective, and democratic policy process and strengthening the institutions that play key roles in the process, including the ministry of defense, legislature, auditors, and civil society. Despite this new focus, however, the donor community's long-standing concern with absolute spending levels and with compiling accurate information on defense expenditures persists and may strengthen the hand of internal actors concerned with increasing the transparency of an institutionalized budget process.

This shift in thinking was reinforced by trends in the international financial institutions and regional security organizations and among students of civil-military relations. By the end of the 1990s, the promotion of good governance principles was a firmly established practice within the World Bank and the development community more generally; it therefore was not much of a leap to argue that these principles should apply to the defense sector as well. This conviction was reinforced by the increasing realization that spending on security was not necessarily "unproductive" but rather was essential if sustainable economic development were to take place. Under such circumstances, the effective governance of the security sector assumed new importance. Also in the 1990s, regional organizations such as the Organization of American States and the European Union highlighted the transparency of defense budget planning as a component of confidence-building measures designed to reduce regional tensions.[3]

At the same time, the civil-military relations community began to focus on the institutions needed for effective democratic governance of the defense sector, as countries successfully transitioned to democracy and the threat of military coups receded in importance. For scholars and politicians traditionally concerned with the prospect of a coup, a litmus test of civilian control of the military was the ability to cut the defense budget without negative repercussions. As many new democracies passed this initial test, observers began to consider how civilians should address new items on the agenda, such as the restructuring of defense sectors to deal with new threats, operating with a reduced budget, or both at once. Under these circumstances, principles of effective democratic governance came to the fore.[4]

Within this new framework, it is possible to identify an "ideal type" procedure against which to compare those that already exist in defense sectors. Fiscally, the process by which budget decisions are made should be structured so that defense spending does not "break the bank" by exceeding the government's capacity to pay. Sectorally, defense should compete with other government ministries so that the final overall budget is a monetary expression of the priorities of the nation—its choices between "guns and butter." Within the defense sector, civilians should shape the allocation of resources for training, personnel, and equipment in a way that reflects the roles and missions assigned to the armed forces through national security planning. The key institutions of democratic civilian control of the military, including the ministry of defense, the legislature, auditing agencies, and organizations in civil society, should play a central role in the regularized process.

The ongoing budget cycle, with planning for the next year beginning soon after the current year's budget is approved, can contribute to civilian control over the military and effective policymaking in a number of ways. Ideally, it encourages a yearly debate on defense policy and forces governments to make hard choices that might otherwise be postponed. It also can provide a key venue for legislative control of the defense sector. The writing of laws that affect the defense sector and the military is a periodic event, but the need for the legislature to approve and review expenditures is a perennial source of influence. To the extent that a public debate over the defense budget occurs, a measure of control and participation by the civilian population is introduced into a policy arena that is often otherwise closed. The following sections evaluate the extent to which the defense budget process in consolidating democracies conforms to the ideal type.

Stage One: Budget Formulation

Formulation of the budget usually takes place within the government's executive branch and requires two sets of decisions: one about the distribution of funds between sectors (defense, transportation, or health, for instance), and another about resource allocation within sectors. In most countries, the "center"—some combination of the ministry of finance (MOF), the head of the government, and the cabinet of ministers—is responsible for the first decision, which should reflect macroeconomic constraints on spending as well as the policy priorities of the government of the day.[5] The second decision, about the allocation of resources within a sector, is the responsibility of the relevant ministries (in this case, the ministry of defense). To make this decision, the minister is guided by input from subordinate service agencies (here the armed forces) and the government's policy agenda for the sector, as laid out in such instruments as national security strategies or white papers.

Neither decision can be made in isolation from the other. The minister of finance will not be able to distribute resources between sectors unless he or she has some sense of the needs of each sector. Similarly, the sectoral minister, for whom needs always exceed limited resources, will not be able to make the hard choices about spending unless the MOF offers some realistic estimate of the amount of money that will be devoted to the sector. As a result, the writing of the budget is usually an iterative process, in which the center consults ministries about their spending needs and sets spending ceilings, ministries submit detailed spending requests based on these numbers, and then the center reevaluates the initial ceilings based on these requests, in order to determine whether to reallocate funds.[6] The head of government or the cabinet typically arbitrates any disputes between spending ministries and the MOF, either formally or informally. The ministries are then expected to modify their spending estimates to match the revised ceilings set by the center. The final figures from each ministry are compiled into a draft budget bill that is then sent to the legislature for approval.

The formulation of the budget is clearly dominated by the executive and tends to be the most closed part of the process. In a number of countries, however, the legislature has some involvement at this stage. In the United States, for example, congressional leaders play a key role in setting initial spending limits. The executive also must take legislative preferences into account when formulating the budget, given Congress's broad powers to rewrite any executive proposal. In Germany, ministries work closely with their respective committee in the Bundestag during budget formulation. In South Africa, a special budget working group brings together representatives from the Department of State Expenditure (accountable to the MOF), the Department of Defense, and the parliamentary defense committee.[7] The executive may also be influenced at this stage by whatever political or societal debate has taken place on national security policy.

Assessing Control over Defense Spending in Consolidating Democracies

Many consolidating democracies have generally weak systems of fiscal management, the problems of which can be exacerbated further by inflation and a lack of state resources. In these cases, the defense budget is just one of many budgets outside the control of the central government (although the military may be in a position to abuse the system even more than other state ministries). This seems to be the case in many African countries and in the countries of the former Soviet Union. By contrast, in a majority of consolidating democracies in Latin America and Central and Eastern Europe, civilian elites have demonstrated a surprising ability to rein in defense spending as part of their overall campaigns of fiscal reform. The ability to do so has contributed to macroeconomic stability and allowed governments to free up resources to spend on other economic and social priorities. Despite the importance of this accomplishment, observers are concerned that civilians have abdicated their responsibility to provide for national security when setting spending levels and have permitted excessive military autonomy in deciding how resources are allocated within the defense sector.

In many countries, observers note that cuts in defense spending have been made based solely on fiscal criteria in disregard of national security needs. In the case of Argentina, for example, David Pion-Berlin explains:

> National security considerations and fiscal considerations are largely divorced from one another, with the latter taking precedence. That means that the military is left "out of the loop." The flow of budgetary decisions does not involve a constant mix of defense and fiscal strategists. It is only after the budget is assembled and approved that the military moves to center stage, with planners and programmers figuring out how to spend the scant funds delivered to them. Economists within the secretariat of finance are not obligated to consult with defense experts on how the size of the budget would impact national security objectives.[8]

In addition, there has been little civilian control over the allocation of resources within the defense sector. For example, Consuelo Cruz and Rut Diamint point out that in Latin America "elected officials, in the main, favor streamlining military establishments; but after making resource allocations, they leave the armed forces to their own devices."[9] There are some indications of comparable military autonomy in the consolidating democracies of Central and Eastern Europe as well. Even in countries in which civilians have made the most gains in asserting control over the military (e.g., Poland, the Czech Republic, and Hungary), the political leadership has made little progress in "break[ing] the senior military's tight grip on determining its own requirements."[10] As in Latin America, the general trend in the region might be characterized as "we know what we spent, but not why we spent it."[11] In the absence of guidance from civilians, the allocation of resources within the defense sector may be the product of inertia and a power struggle among the services pursuing their narrow corporate interests, largely bereft of strategic considerations on how best to promote national security.[12]

Explaining the Pattern: Incentives to Cut But Not Shape the Defense Budget

In many democratizing countries, civilians assumed control of the government at a time of severe economic crisis and faced pressure from international lending institutions such as the World Bank and the International Monetary Fund to put their fiscal houses in order. In addition to reducing spending across the board, democratically elected officials often had incentives to cut the defense budget in particular. In all cases, democracy brought with it compelling demands for increased social spending, which, in the context of fiscal restraints, could be met only by cutting the budget of less electorally important sectors, such as defense. In many Latin American cases, defense budgets were bloated after years of authoritarian rule and, often, internal conflict, during which the military frequently operated with great autonomy. The perceived need to rein in defense spending and military autonomy often animated budget cuts. In Central and Eastern Europe, where militaries had often been subject to civilian control under communist regimes, the end of the cold war provided an initial justification for new democracies to reduce defense spending and devote attention to other pressing concerns.[13]

Although these factors help explain government's ability to cut spending, they do not explain the failure of civilians to assess the impact of budget cuts on security goals and to assert control over the allocation of resources within the defense sector. The most obvious culprit is the lack of a strong civilian ministry of defense, able to challenge the finance minister in intragovernmental debates or guide military input into the budget process. In some consolidating democracies, the minister of defense was a military officer; in others a civilian held the post, but key decision-making positions within the ministry were still largely controlled by the military. This contrasted sharply with the general strengthening in many countries of the ministry of finance's position in the budget process relative to all spending ministries. For example, a 1993 survey of Latin America and the Caribbean showed that in eighteen of twenty countries, the finance ministers wielded authority "considerably greater than that of the spending ministries on budgetary issues."[14] Despite this imbalance, ministers are still occasionally able to appeal to policy considerations when making the case for increased funds to the president or cabinet. A politically connected civilian defense minister with a clearly articulated vision of national defense would conceivably be better able to influence the MOF and the president than a minister who is active in the armed forces.

In established democracies, it is the task of the ministry of defense (MOD) to produce a policy statement outlining policies and expected outcomes, the way in which objectives will be achieved, and performance indicators to measure success. In most developed democracies, the minister's statement of policy (national security strategy or white paper) is circulated throughout the armed services so they can draw up their budgets in line with government policy. For the most part, civilians within the MOD provide strategic assessments, and military officers provide the operational details. As Pion-Berlin noted in the case of military reform: "The broad strokes of institutional reorganization must be painted by the president and his defense staff. Only then can the detail be filled in by the military."[15]

Given the recent creation of civilian ministries of defense in most new democracies, it may be unrealistic to expect the ministry to play the kind of leadership role depicted above, without the backing of the executive. In any policy area, executive leadership is particularly important when major reform is required, changes are controversial, and/or the line ministry is weak relative to the subordinate service agencies. All three of these conditions apply to defense reform in consolidating democracies, where national priorities and threat environments have changed, downsizing is often necessary, and ministries of defense are new. As Pion-Berlin has noted:

> Ultimately, it is the president that must make defense reform a priority. It is he who must instruct his minister to demand from the services full compliance with national defense policy. And it is he who must instill in the defense ministry a real sense of purpose and direction. . . . [O]rganizations in general and certainly state agencies in particular are not necessarily oriented toward the fulfillment of goals unless they receive a clear mandate from above. In the absence of such a mandate, civilian appointees within the agency feel less motivated to bring themselves up to speed on issues of national security or to hire outsiders with the expertise necessary to confidently push through controversial programs.[16]

Unfortunately, in many consolidating democracies, executives find themselves besieged with other problems that require their attention, and defense reform takes a backseat. In Brazil, for example, when President Fernando Henrique Cardoso issued a presidential directive outlining a national security strategy eleven years after the transition to democracy, this seemed to have little impact upon the military.[17] Economic crises subsequently diverted the president's attention from the issue. The discussion of the legislative branch in the next section reveals that legislators have tended to share the same preferences as the executive branch for reduced defense spending, and the same lack of interest and capacity to promote rational defense restructuring. This inattention is compounded by the fact that such a process often requires increased military expenditures in the short run (e.g., to retire personnel and to modernize equipment), even if the long-term result is a leaner defense apparatus.

Despite this general trend, civilian elites in a number of consolidating democracies are beginning to provide leadership for a comprehensive budget process founded on a debate over national security and military strategy. In some cases, civilian elites may be motivated to undertake these efforts less as a means to an end (i.e., a new national security strategy) than as a process that is valued in itself. Argentina's and Chile's governments, for example, both issued their first white papers in the mid-1990s as part of a confidence-building exercise designed to reassure the other about their military intentions and capabilities and, domestically, to increase the level of dialogue and trust between civilians and the military. (Interestingly, by reducing tensions, this activity over time may also enable the reductions in defense spending that initially motivated reforms.) The more-challenging cases to explain, given the set of incentives described above, are countries that have devoted time to developing white papers and then increased military spending in order to support the national security goals outlined therein. In Central and East European countries—despite an initial downward trend in defense spending levels in many countries after the transition to democracy—the prospect of joining NATO has forced countries to devote increased resources to a restructuring of defense capabilities in order to meet NATO standards.[18] Though in many of these countries the defense sector was not a key issue in the years immediately following the transition to democracy, with the passage of time it has assumed importance as defense reform becomes linked to the prospect of social and economic development associated with integration into the larger European community.

Stage Two: Enacting the Budget

The legislature becomes a key player in the budget process in the second stage, when the executive's proposal must be reviewed, revised, and enacted into law. Once the executive's proposed budget is submitted to the legislature, it is usually discussed in two steps: first, there is a debate and a vote on the overall amount of the budget, and then a detailed discussion of the allocation of resources among and within ministries. This discussion usually takes place within the budget committee, which calls on ministers to defend the budgets for their sectors and sometimes invites members of the other relevant congressional committees, for example, armed services or intelligence, to participate in the proceedings.[19] Centralized control by the budget committee helps ensure that legislators will take the "big picture" of the budget into account—that is, respect fiscal limits and coordinate reallocation between sectors—along with the more specific sectoral interests solicited through consultations with ministers and committees.

The ability and willingness of the legislature to modify the executive's budget proposal vary widely among countries. It is greatest in the United States, where the Congress has complete freedom to modify executive proposals and the incentives to do so (such as the prospect of shifting resources to grateful constituents). It is weakest, perhaps, in Great Britain and other parliamentary systems in the Westminster tradition, where a rejection of the budget is seen as a vote of no confidence in the government.[20] Most legislatures fall between these two extremes. For example, one survey of twenty-seven countries revealed that legislatures in seventeen of them made minor amendments to the budget. In six no changes were made, and in four the changes were "significant."[21]

Budget Rules That Constrain the Legislature's Role

The role of the legislature in the defense budget is limited by the same factors (the constitutional balance of powers or the level of party interest in national security issues, for instance) that shape its participation in overall defense policymaking.[22] This section examines how the specific rules that govern the budget process—the amount of time the legislature is allotted for debating the executive's proposal, the amount of budget information to which the legislature has access, and the powers of the legislature to change the size and allocation of the budget—affect the ability and willingness of legislators to shape the defense budget.

Time Period for Budget Review

In most countries, budget debates are charged affairs, carried out under great time pressure and with the knowledge that the proposed budget must be passed before the current one runs out, or else. The degree of pressure the legislature feels and the "or else" vary from country to country and have a noticeable impact on the ability of the legislature to make meaningful changes to the budget. Typically, the executive submits the budget two to four months before the start of the new fiscal year.[23] In some countries, however, the legislature is given less time to examine the executive's budget requests.

Most of the close examination of the budget can occur only in congressional committees; consequently, a large portion of the time that the budget is in the legislature should be devoted to the committees. In Germany, for example, the legislative stage of the budget process lasts four months, and the committee is allotted several weeks for its work. In governments where the committee is marginalized, the legislature is unlikely to have effective input into budget decisions. After the transition to democracy in South Africa, for example, the Portfolio Committee on Finance was allotted only seven days to submit a report on the budget to the National Assembly, less than one-tenth of the four months allocated to the entire legislative budget process.[24]

What happens if the budget is rejected or not passed by the legislature within the constitutionally established time frame? In most countries, the legislature still retains some leverage over the process as negotiations continue, while the executive's proposal or the prior year's budget is put into effect for an interim period or other stopgap measures are voted on by the legislature.[25] In some cases, the legislature's inability to pass the budget puts an end to the budget discussion, and either the executive's budget proposal takes effect or the previous year's budget concerning continuing expenditures is implemented.[26]

Powers to Amend the Budget

The legal powers of the legislature to amend the budget vary from country to country. At one extreme is the U.S. Congress, which has the power to increase or decrease both revenue and expenditure. In some countries, such as Great Britain, the legislature is forbidden to increase expenditures, while in others the legislature cannot increase expenditures in one sector without taking from another or raising taxes (e.g., post-1993 Argentina, Brazil, Germany, the Philippines, and Spain).[27] In many presidential systems, the president has line-item veto power (e.g., in Argentina, Brazil, and the Philippines).[28]

In countries where the legislature is unable to increase spending levels or reallocate funds, a military interested in enlarging its share of the budget would focus most of its attention on the executive branch and the formulation stage of the budget process. In other systems, it might make sense for the military to lobby the legislature for increased funds. The success of this strategy will depend on legislators' interest in participating in the debate over defense policy and, in particular, in raising defense spending, an issue discussed in more detail below.

Access to Information

Meaningful congressional input into the budget process depends on whether the legislators have sufficient information about the contents of the budget and the policy implications of their fiscal decisions. For this information, the legislature relies on data provided by the executive branch as well as research services housed in the legislature. To a certain extent, a national debate over different national security strategies and their implications for the budget is needed to inform the legislature's decisions.

The most important piece of information from the government is the budget proposal itself, which should have enough details that the legislators understand what they are approving or rejecting. In many countries, however, this is not the case, particularly with respect to the defense budget, where claims of a need for secrecy still shroud the release of information. During the first years of many new democracies, especially those where the military had played an important role under authoritarianism, the defense budget is often presented and deliberated as a lump sum. This was the case, for example, in Poland from 1989 to 1995 and in South Korea from 1987 until 1993.[29] In Mozambique the government budget did not differentiate between defense, police, and intelligence allocations until 1999.[30] From 1992 to 1996 the Russian State Duma approved a defense budget that was generally one to two pages long and consisted of only six to nine spending categories. In 1997 the details of the budget were expanded by law, but civilians in the Duma still must consider only a seventeen-category declassified budget request because, unlike their military colleagues, they lack the security clearances necessary to view the new three-hundred-line format.[31] By contrast, the U.S. military budget contains three to four thousand declassified line items, and all the relevant legislators have security clearances to view the classified items.[32]

In addition to the official budget proposal, information from the executive can also be obtained through regular contact between legislators and government ministries. In Germany, for example, the legislative budget committee interacts regularly with government departments through department briefings and expenditure reports. Within some legislatures, members of the budget committee can rely upon their own expertise, their committee staff, congressional research services, and input from sectoral committees in making their decisions. Legislators in the United States, for example, can rely upon the Congressional Budget Office in addition to well-staffed committees. Unfortunately, most legislatures in other countries lack access to this kind of specialized knowledge and expertise.[33]

Defense committees, even in countries with low levels of staffing, are likely to be more knowledgeable about the requirements of the defense sector than the members of the budget committee, and having a mechanism for their input into the budget process is important.[34] Defense committees in Eastern European legislatures, for example, influence the budget by making recommendations to the budget committee, having a decisive vote, or even presenting amendments to the floor that were rejected by the budget committee.[35] In contrast, the British budget does not have to be passed to the defense committee, and one member of the committee has noted, "As far as the budget is concerned in the UK, the Defence Committee is almost irrelevant."[36]

Ability and Willingness of Legislators to Influence the Defense Budget

In many consolidating democracies, actors in the legislature have incentives to cut the defense budget, but they have little motivation to spend their time debating defense policy in order to determine the most efficient way to downsize without undermining national security. This situation reinforces a similar trend at the level of the executive, where a strong ministry of finance can enforce budget cuts, but a weak ministry of defense fails to articulate a politically persuasive national defense strategy to mitigate or guide these cuts. This trend has been evident both in countries where organized and disciplined parties (or factions) control the legislature and, as is often the case in consolidating democracies, in countries where individual legislators have more influence in shaping the budget process.

In many new democracies, parties tend to support executive proposals for cuts in defense spending. Parties concerned with reelection will focus their platforms on economic and social issues of importance to the electorate; reduced spending for defense may be a means of fulfilling their social pledges or, for some parties, an explicit part of their platform. Although some parties might support increased military spending for ideological reasons, they rarely command a majority. Parties often fail to take into account the impact of spending cuts on national security or fail to initiate debates over national security policies; those in many consolidating democracies do not have working teams specifically assigned to develop positions on these issues.[37]

In a number of cases, the legislature may even propose additional cuts to the executive's defense budget. This seems to occur most often in cases where individual legislators with an interest in providing resources to their constituents have more influence over the budget process than do parties, and where the rules of the budget process require any increases in spending in one sector to be offset by a cut in another.[38] In Brazil, for example, where these rules hold, legislators are likely to favor shifting funds from the defense ministry to more electorally profitable ministries, such as public works.[39] In the Philippines, these considerations, as well as strong public opinion against militarization after years of martial law, led congressional committees to slash the executive's defense budget requests.[40] In Brazil and the Philippines—and indeed in most countries other than the United States—the defense budget is not a source of pork, because they either do not have domestic defense industries or these industries are geographically concentrated in small areas, and decisions affecting their operation are outside the purview of the legislature.[41] As a result, every additional dollar spent on defense is one less dollar spent on local constituencies. Even where budget rules do not force this zero-sum game, the reality of fiscal constraints means that this perception is widely shared by legislators in many countries.

Historical experience demonstrates that legislators are likely to change their preference for low levels of defense spending in the face of an immediate threat to national security. This was the case, for example, in 1995 in the Philippines when Chinese aggression against Filipino claims in the Spratly Islands led the legislature to reverse its practice of cutting the defense budget and approve a long-delayed bill granting funds for military modernization.[42] In Ecuador, the conflict with Peru in 1995 put an end to proposals to cut military spending and eliminate the practice of allotting a fixed share of revenues from oil taxes to the military. In Chile, external threats led the legislature in 1942 to institutionalize the provision of revenues from the copper industry to the military. Where informed legislators had been engaged in debates over military spending prior to the increase in threat levels (as was the case in the Philippines), the increase in spending is less likely to be made under terms that permit the military relative autonomy in the use of the funds (as occurred in Chile).[43]

Stage Three: Budget Implementation

Once the budget is approved by the legislature, funds for defense should be distributed in the manner indicated in that document. This disbursement of funds may not be feasible, however, if unforeseen needs arise (such as a natural disaster or a war) or there is a shortfall of revenues. The amount of "rectification" the budget undergoes will vary from country to country, with a great deal of tinkering occurring in France, for example, and little or none in Germany.[44] Where budget shortfalls are frequent or high inflation erodes the value of assigned funds before they reach their destination, as happens in the Philippines, ministries commonly lobby to have their funds dispensed early.[45] This can result in a modification of the allocation decisions made during the previous two stages of the budget process. In Russia, where few rules of the budget process are followed, it has been said that there are three budgets: the budget that is enacted by the Duma, the monies that the MOF disburses to the MOD, and the amount that the MOD actually spends (by some accounts, three to four times the amount budgeted to it).

Regardless of the amount of rectification, rules need to be in place for reallocating funds between spending categories and for the spending of emergency or reserve funds. In Argentina, for example, the budget can be modified on the executive's initiative, with congressional approval. Brazil's executive can modify up to 20 percent of the budget without congressional approval.[46] The Russian president's security council makes changes to the defense budget via decrees, which escape the scrutiny of the Duma.[47] Regardless of legislative participation in the making of these decisions, however, all changes in resource allocation should promptly be reported to the legislature.

Stage Four: Auditing of the Budget and Outcome Assessment

The evaluation or oversight stage of the budget process has two main purposes: first, to determine whether the money is spent as the budget says it should be (auditing); and second, to evaluate whether policy goals have been met (outcome assessment). Auditing of the budget can take one of two forms: a detailed review of individual transactions that results in holding individuals responsible for misuse of government funds, or an examination of procedures and work practices to determine whether they are effectively designed to prevent errors and to get the most value for the money. The individual audit can be valuable, especially in countries where government corruption has traditionally gone unpunished, because it holds individuals accountable for abuses. The broader, "best practices" approach, however, is especially important, and most auditing institutions have shifted their focus to this level because it fosters procedures designed to prevent wrongdoing in the first place and introduces reporting requirements that increase the likelihood of uncovering individual wrongdoing after the fact.[48] In practice, the two approaches are likely to go together—a scandal uncovered by the review of individual projects or transactions often leads to changes in the procedures that govern decision making and the spending of money.[49]

Outcome assessment is another key component of oversight, but one that is even more difficult to carry out than auditing. Its purpose is to determine whether resources spent on defense are in fact contributing to national security; if not, resources should be reallocated in the following year's budget to projects or missions that will do more to enhance national defense. Such an evaluation of policy is notoriously difficult to make in the field of defense, where, in the absence of actual conflict, the collective good being provided has few indicators of effectiveness. Whereas a ministry of public works can measure its accomplishments in terms of miles of roads built or paved, or a ministry of health in terms of clinics built and patients served, national defense outcomes short of winning a war (e.g., "number of enemies deterred") are more difficult to quantify. Officials nevertheless must openly debate this issue, establish policy objectives and indicators of effectiveness, and design spending to achieve consensually agreed-upon defense goals. Unfortunately, in many consolidating democracies leaders are not initiating this kind of debate or setting appropriate objectives, making it even more difficult to evaluate the effectiveness of defense spending.

Controlling spending and evaluating its effectiveness, both enormous tasks, are the responsibility of a wide variety of actors, starting with the institution that is charged with spending the money. The military must have internal audit procedures in place to hold its members accountable for their handling of resources. Ministries of defense should have a centralized office that monitors and evaluates spending by the individual services.

In addition to these agencies within the executive branch, most countries have nonpartisan national auditing offices that are independent of the government of the day and are responsible for reporting on government spending. In some countries, their task is limited to auditing spending; in others, it extends to evaluating whether policy goals have been met. In Great Britain, the National Audit Office carries out both tasks. The effectiveness of independent auditors, however, depends on some minimal level of accountability within the spending ministry itself. The state comptroller of Russia, for example, has complained that the military does not produce enough receipts for the sale of military property and that therefore it is impossible to monitor and control military spending.[50]

Another source of external audit is the legislature itself. Few legislatures, however, have the resources to oversee budgets independently. The U.S. Congress is a notable exception, with a strong Congressional Budget Office, congressional staffers who monitor spending on projects of interest to their legislator, and a Government Accountability Office that has evolved from an organization focused on detailed audits to one that plays a broader role in evaluating policy effectiveness.[51] In many countries, including the United States, the legislature depends heavily on information generated by the executive's internal audits and the national auditing office. It then uses legislation to require the executive to report on its spending.

In addition to such measures, the legislature often has a mandate to review reports of government and military activities produced by independent auditing agencies. Specialized committees within the legislature typically have this responsibility. In parliamentary systems, a public accounts committee frequently performs an auditing function; its lack of expertise in different subject areas, however, generally prevents it from performing an outcomes assessment. This task usually falls to the sectoral committees, such as the defense committee. For the findings of these committees to have an impact on the subsequent year's budget decisions, there needs to be a mechanism for reports to reach the budget committee (such as the integration of the public accounts committee into the budget committee) or the executive during the formulation stage. In addition, reports from the executive and independent auditors need to be received in a timely fashion so that they can be analyzed, and their findings integrated into the next year's budget.[52] For the most part, legislators in consolidating democracies have been unwilling or unable to participate constructively in a debate over national security goals and measures and how they relate to the budget.

In many policy areas, organizations in civil society can play a watchdog role, calling attention to government abuses of power or to policies that need rectifying, and can participate in national debates over security goals and measures.[53] These groups, however, tend to be weakest in the area of defense, and, in particular, members lack the expertise and access to information often necessary to monitor budget decisions.[54] In Russia, for example, the defense budget was openly published and accessible to citizens only beginning in 1998, and the amount of information supplied was minimal.[55] Just as the legislature is dependent on a certain level of executive accountability to carry out its oversight responsibilities, nongovernmental organizations (NGOs) depend on the ability of political parties and legislative committees to secure information from the executive.

In addition to domestic NGOs, the international community plays an important role in overseeing government spending in the defense realm. Adherence to treaties sponsored by international organizations like NATO, the United Nations, or the Organization of American States often requires a country to provide data on military spending and arms transfers.[56] In other cases, bilateral or multilateral agreements designed to lessen regional tensions might lead to increased transparency in defense spending (Argentina and Chile, for example, signed a 1998 agreement to fund jointly a comparison of their defense spending). To the extent that this information is made public, domestic NGOs can use it in carrying out their watchdog role. In still other cases, unilateral donor-aid recipient requirements might play a role in forcing a measure of responsibility in defense spending. U.S. legislation, for example, requires a civilian audit of military receipts and expenditures (with results reported to a civilian authority) before U.S. executive directors at international lending institutions can vote in favor of non-humanitarian assistance to any country.[57] The audit need not be publicized, however, and therefore contributes little to the ability of other organizations to monitor the government.

Off-Budget Expenditures in Defense

While consolidating democracies have made some advances in improving oversight of the formal defense budget, off-budget expenditures—that is to say, military expenditures outside the official defense budget—often pose significant challenges to democratic civilian control over the military and threaten to undermine both economic development and security. There are two main types of off-budget expenditures: military-related items hidden in the budgets of civilian ministries, and extrabudgetary expenditure, which does not appear anywhere in the government's budget. The first type is most often motivated by the executive's desire to conceal certain aspects of defense spending from the legislature or the international community.[58] The second type refers to revenue from sources other than the central treasury, which are often spent by military officials at their own discretion. Typically, there are four key sources of such revenue: (1) military business activities; (2) special funds (e.g., for arms imports) created through war levies or diversion of proceeds from state-owned companies; (3) criminal activities; and (4) foreign military assistance.[59] Not only do extrabudgetary expenditures escape the scrutiny of the general public, the legislature, and the international community (as items hidden in the civilian budget do), but they also have a number of additional negative consequences for civilian control over the military, as well as for socioeconomic development and national security.

At the very least, the existence of extrabudgetary revenue and expenditure undermines civilian control over the military. Civilians have little control over how the extrabudgetary funds are spent and cannot determine whether they are being used efficiently, effectively, or even legally. Funds may be lost through corruption, diverted to illegal paramilitary groups, or spent on programs that do not represent the priorities of the civilian leadership. In addition, to the extent that the military has an autonomous revenue stream, the influence that civilians might exercise over the military through the regular budget is greatly reduced and perhaps even nullified. Where the military is involved in business activities as a means of funding, the potentially negative impact on civilian control is even greater. As entrepreneurs, military officers can gain a level of social and economic influence within a country that may readily translate into a level of political or policy influence inappropriate for the armed forces in a democracy. This may particularly be the case at the local level, where military patron-client relations structured around the military's businesses can even supplant local political authorities. At the national level, the military may enjoy influence through its socioeconomic ties with other actors, or it may exercise untoward leverage in such key policy areas as industrial or environmental policy if the government is reluctant to regulate these areas for fear of damaging the military's economic interests.

In addition, the existence of extrabudgetary funds may undermine economic development and a nation's pursuit of its goals in other non-defense-related areas. For example, funds diverted from state enterprises to the military cannot be used to balance the budget or for investment in social and economic projects. Military entrepreneurs often enjoy special privileges, such as the use of government-funded infrastructure (trucks, buildings) for their businesses, reduced taxes, or favorable treatment when investment decisions are made. In the end, military-run businesses may unfairly crowd out competition from the private sector, to the detriment of overall economic health.

Finally, the existence of extrabudgetary funds may also undermine a nation's security in a number of ways. Military involvement in business activities may undermine military professionalism through loss of discipline; corruption; disparities in the compensation of officers involved in businesses and officers who are not; and a preference for commercial values and skills over war-fighting abilities. Neighboring states may be threatened by the uncertainty posed by extrabudgetary funds—absent information on the size of these funds and how they are being spent, it is easy for neighbors to imagine the worst and to respond aggressively. Civilian leaders are unable to assess how much money is being spent on which activities in the defense sector—a necessary first step toward determining if the armed forces are prepared to deal with threats to the nation's security and, if not, initiating reforms to build an effective force.

Most consolidating democracies have made little progress toward curbing off-budget revenues. In large part, this may be because such sources of funds often are most significant in countries where the military has a history of autonomy and usually retains the political influence to block changes.[60] Despite this lack of progress, however, successful efforts to cut levels of defense spending show that civilians often are willing to take on a privileged military if the benefit is great enough.[61] To what extent, then, might we expect to see efforts to curb off-budget expenditure?

One hypothesis is that civilians will be more likely to try to gain control over funds earmarked for the armed forces from state-owned industries than put an end to business activities run by the military itself. In many ways, civilians face the same incentives to reduce off-budget expenditures funded by state-owned companies, such as the copper industry in Chile or the oil industry in Ecuador, as they do to reduce on-budget spending. In such instances, public commercial revenue destined for the military might be reapportioned by the state to other programs, thus encouraging civilian politicians to take on the military in order to redirect those funds. (For example, the Ecuadoran Congress was on the verge of passing a law eliminating the automatic distribution of a percentage of petroleum funds to the military, until the outbreak of the Ecuador-Peru War in 1995 led members to change their minds.)[62] In contrast, civilian politicians have little incentive to put an end to the business activities of the military, given that there would be no fiscal windfall for the state treasury and a potentially large cost: the state would be forced to come up with additional funds for defense to replace those lost with the shutting down of military businesses. Under a great deal of pressure from the International Monetary Fund, the Indonesian government is seeking to rectify at least one negative aspect of military business activities—the lack of transparency—by taking steps to monitor those activities though not yet prohibiting them.

Conclusion

Despite the success of many countries in reducing the amount of money spent on defense, democratically elected civilians and their representatives have been less able to control how the money is spent or to ensure that the allocated funds meet the nation's security needs. This uneven performance can be explained by the lack, until recently, of an inclusive, civilian-led process for developing national security policy. In contrast, the fiscal and economic reforms that led to the setting of military spending limits were accompanied by extensive debates on economic policy and government spending. A sustained debate on national security issues can make a number of contributions to development of the budget: it permits indirect public participation in what is otherwise a rather closed process of budget formulation; it informs the decisions that the ministry of finance makes on allocation of resources between sectors; it guides decisions within the ministry of defense about spending among the branches of the defense sector; and it establishes the criteria necessary to evaluate whether a given resource allocation has contributed to policy objectives.

The pattern of control over spending levels but not spending choices can also be explained by variations in institutional development and interests: many consolidating democracies have been able to develop strong ministries of finance responsible for fiscal discipline, but the institutions responsible for the content of defense spending remain noticeably weaker. Civilian ministries of defense are of recent origin and in many cases have yet to develop the expertise, the procedures, or the legal powers to orchestrate a national security planning process that will inform budget decisions. Executives often find their energies devoted to solving economic or social problems (or putting out fires in the defense sphere) and lack the time or the political capital to expend on the comprehensive reform of the defense sector that is often necessary in consolidating democracies. Legislatures typically are unable and unwilling to participate meaningfully in a national debate on defense issues that might guide a budget suitable for defense restructuring. Finally, organizations in civil society, which could add a different perspective to the national debate on defense and have an interest in monitoring government spending, tend to be weak or nonexistent. Actors interested in increasing civilian control over the military and in improving the quality of national defense should contribute to a debate on national security and work to strengthen the institutions responsible for linking defense priorities to the budget process.

Notes

1. Wuyi Omitoogun, "The Processes of Budgeting for the Military Sector in Africa," in *SIPRI Yearbook 2003: Armaments, Disarmament and International Security* (Oxford: Oxford University Press, 2002), 4. Paul George provides evidence for the trend of increased underreporting of military expenditure figures. He indicates a nearly 40 percent decline in the response rate to the annual questionnaire on defense spending distributed by the UN Center for Disarmament Affairs between 1992 and 1996 (from 33 countries responding to 20). See George, "Defence Expenditures in the 1990s: Budget and Fiscal Policy Issues for Developing Countries" (paper presented at the conference "Converting Defense Resources to Human Development," Bonn International Center for Conversion, Bonn, November 9–11, 1997).

2. Dylan Hendrickson and Nicole Ball, "Off-Budget Military Expenditure and Revenue: Issues and Policy Perspectives for Donors" (CSDG [Conflict, Security, and Development Group] Occasional Papers, no. 1, King's College London for the UK Department for International Development, London, 2002), 13. The United Kingdom's Department for International Development (DFID) has been a leader in these initiatives, but others have quickly

followed suit. SIPRI (Stockholm International Peace Research Institute) commissioned a major project, Budgeting for the Military Sector in Africa, which attempted to assess budget practices in a number of African states against a standard measure of good practice. One of the early initiatives within the Stability Pact for South Eastern Europe was the Budget Transparency Initiative, focused both on making budget information available and on studying and promoting an "open, policy-oriented decision-making process."

3. See, for example, the 1995 Santiago Conference on Confidence- and Security-Building Measures, sponsored by the Organization of American States, and the Stability Pact for Southeast Europe, adopted in 1999 at the European Union's initiative.

4. This volume is an example of such an orientation. Another is Andrew Cottey, Timothy Edmunds, and Anthony Forster, eds., *Democratic Control of the Military in Postcommunist Europe: Guarding the Guards* (New York, Palgrave, 2002). Students of civil-military relations in Latin America, where transitions to democracy occurred earlier than in Central and Eastern Europe, led the way in adding emphasis on the defense budget process to the more traditional preoccupation with spending levels. See, for example, Francisco Rojas Aravena, ed., *Gasto militar en América Latina: Procesos de decisiones y actores claves* (Santiago, Chile: Centro Internacional para el Desarrollo Económico [CINDE] and Facultad Latinoamericano de Ciencias Sociales [FLACSO], 1994); David Pion-Berlin, "The Limits to Military Power: Institutions and Defense Budgeting in Democratic Argentina," *Studies in Comparative International Development* 33, no. 1 (1998); and Wendy Hunter, *Eroding Military Influence in Brazil: Politicians against Soldiers* (Chapel Hill: University of North Carolina Press, 1997).

5. In most presidential systems, with the notable exception of the United States, the MOF sets spending limits, and the president mediates any disputes between the MOF and the ministries. In parliamentary systems, countries that adhere to norms of "collective responsibility" might have a council of ministers, rather than the MOF alone, set ceilings.

6. Ceilings can be identified either at the very beginning of the process or after a first stage when preliminary budget requests are made. It is difficult to set ceilings at the very beginning if budget formulation takes a long time, because fiscal constraints frequently are not known with any certainty a full year in advance. In countries where spending ministries are not accustomed to moderating their requests to some reasonable level (e.g., an incremental increase over the previous year's spending), however, it is probably advisable to set a firm ceiling from the very beginning. See Salvatore Schiavo-Campo and Daniel Tommasi, "The Budget Preparation Process," in *Managing Government Expenditure* (Manila: Asian Development Bank, 1999), http://www.adb.org/documents/manuals/govt_expenditure/chap4.pdf.

7. Peter Batchelor and Paul Dunne, "The Peace Dividend in South Africa" (unpublished manuscript, 1997), 12.

8. David Pion-Berlin, *Through Corridors of Power: Institutions and Civil-Military Relations in Argentina* (University Park: Pennsylvania State University Press, 1997), 138–139. Similarly, the Russian military has criticized the MOF for making across-the-board cuts of 5 percent without considering increased costs in the defense sector. Guedes da Costa notes that the Planning and Budget Ministry in Brazil often makes "arbitrary" cuts to the defense budget to bring spending in line with funds. Thomaz Guedes da Costa, "Democratization and International Integration: The Role of the Armed Forces in Brazil's Grand Strategy," in *Civil-Military Relations: Building Democracy and Regional Security in Latin America, Southern Asia, and Central Europe*, ed. David R. Mares (Boulder, CO: Westview Press, 1998), 228.

9. Consuelo Cruz and Rut Diamint, "The New Military Autonomy in Latin America," *Journal of Democracy* 9, no. 4 (1998): 116. The civil-military equilibrium of a low defense budget and relative military autonomy is not a new one in Latin America. It was the case in Colombia in the 1970s and 1980s and resulted in a low level of military effectiveness. It was also the case historically in Chile. More recently, Martins and Zirker cite a Brazilian admiral who acknowledges that the military has utter freedom to spend its budget as it sees fit, as long as spending limits are respected. João R. Martins Filho and Daniel Zirker, "The Brazilian Military under Cardoso: Overcoming the Identity Crisis," *Journal of Interamerican Studies and World Affairs* 42, no. 3 (2000): 155. This was also the case at least until 1982 in Spain, where the chief of staff of the armed forces decided, with complete freedom, which weapons systems were to be acquired. Antonio Marquina, "Spanish Foreign and Defense Policy Since Democratization," in Kenneth Maxwell, ed., *Spanish Foreign and Defense Policy* (Boulder, CO: Westview Press, 1991), 28.

10. David C. Gompert, Olga Oliker, and Anga Timilsina, *Clean, Lean, and Able: A Strategy for Defense Development* (Santa Monica, CA: Rand, 2004), 9–10.

11. That is how David Betz characterizes legislative oversight of the defense budget in Hungary, Poland, Russia, and Ukraine, but it seems to apply to the budget process more generally. David Betz, "Comparing Frameworks of Parliamentary Oversight: Poland, Hungary, Russia, Ukraine" (Working Paper 115, Geneva Centre for the Democratic Control of Armed Forces [DCAF], Geneva, 2003).

12. In Chile, for example, copper funds for arms purchases are allocated not according to national security calculations but rather in equal parts to the three services, a formula established under military rule to minimize interservice rivalry. Boris Jelezov notes the historical inability of the Soviet armed forces to formulate broad strategic perspectives. Jelezov, *Defense Budgeting and Civilian Control of the Military in the Russian Federation* (Alexandria, VA: Center for

Naval Analyses, 1997), 66. Pion-Berlin makes a similar observation about the Argentine armed forces. Pion-Berlin, "The Limits to Military Power," 102.

13. This explains civilian incentives to cut defense spending but does not address the ability of the military to resist such cuts. More research is needed on the extent to which militaries are able to resist, and even undermine, more general processes of fiscal reform.

14. Budget directors in each of the twenty countries responded to the survey. See Alberto Alesina, Ricardo Hausmann, Rudolf Hommes, and Ernesto Stein, "Budget Institutions and Fiscal Performance in Latin America" (Working Paper Series 394, Inter-American Development Bank, Office of the Chief Economist, 1993), table A4.

15. Pion-Berlin, *Through Corridors of Power*, 142.

16. Ibid., 169.

17. Martins and Zirker, "The Brazilian Military," 151–152. In contrast, the 1999 appointment of a civilian minister of defense for the newly created ministry in Brazil initiated a civilian-led and inclusive discussion on national defense through the public media.

18. Even with the external requirement, consolidating democracies in Central and Eastern Europe face challenges to increasing their defense budgets. In Poland, for example, the government engaged in "creative accounting"— shifting existing budget accounts within the overall budget to inflate the level of defense spending artificially. Agnieszka Gogolewska, "Parliamentary Control of Security Policy: The Experience of Poland" (Working Paper 106, Geneva Centre for the Democratic Control of Armed Forces [DCAF], Geneva, 2003), 4–5.

19. This represents the procedure in most parliamentary and presidential systems; the United States and Great Britain are exceptions. In the United States, budget formulation is extremely decentralized and a great number of committees are involved, even after a 1974 reform to bring more coherence to the process. In Great Britain, financial powers are held directly by the House of Commons and not delegated to the budget committee, which consequently plays a reduced role.

20. In a survey of thirty-nine developing and developed countries, the vote on the budget was considered a vote of confidence in only six cases. Organisation for Economic Co operation and Development (OECD)/World Bank, "Results of the Survey on Budget Practices and Procedures, 2003" (2003), http://ocde. dyndns.org/. In Great Britain, the Parliament votes on the defense budget in its entirety, but there is no tradition of amending expenditures. This is very different from the process in the United States and Germany where individual procurement decisions are frequently the subject of great controversy. Tom Dodd, "Parliament and Defence: A Summary of Parliament's Role in

Scrutinising and Controlling Defence Policy and the Armed Forces," *RUSI Journal* 143, no. 3 (1998): 29–35.

21. Countries surveyed were members of the Organisation for Economic Co-operation and Development. Cited in International Budget Project, "Legislatures and Budget Oversight," http://www.internationalbudget.org/themes/ LEG/index.htm. In a 2003 survey of developing and developed countries, legislatures in fourteen cases generally approved the budget with no change, whereas twenty-six approved the budget with minor changes only (affecting less than 3 percent of total spending. The U.S. Congress fell into this category). The Indonesian legislature was the only one in the survey to make changes affecting more than 3 percent of the budget. OECD/World Bank, "Results of the Survey."

22. See Giraldo, chapter 2 of this volume.

23. A 1986 survey of developed and developing countries noted that the average was two months. Inter-Parliamentary Union, "Timing of the Budget," in *Parliaments of the World: A Comparative Reference Compendium*, 2nd ed., vol. 1 (New York: Facts On File, 1986), 1068. Similarly, a 2003 World Bank survey of thirty-nine developed and developing countries found that in twenty-two of the countries, the executive presented its budget to the legislature two to four months in advance of the beginning of the fiscal year. In eleven countries, legislatures received the budget with less than two months' advance notice. In five of the remaining six cases, legislatures received the budget four to six months ahead of time. (In the sixth case, the United States, the Congress received the budget more than six months in advance.) OECD/World Bank, "Results of the Survey."

24. Warren Krafchik and Joachim Wehner, "The Role of Parliament in the Budget Process" (Institute for Democracy in South Africa, Budget Information Service, n.d.), http://www.idasa.org.za.

25. In a 2003 survey of 39 developing and developed countries, the executive's proposal takes effect on an interim basis in six; the previous year's budget takes place on an interim basis in eight; and other interim measures are voted on by the legislature in ten. OECD/World Bank, "Results of the Survey."

26. In the 2003 OECD/World Bank survey, Chile and Suriname were the only two countries in which the executive's proposal took effect, with no future negotiation. In six countries, the prior year's budget concerning continuing expenditures takes effect. Ibid.

27. Alesina et al., "Budget Institutions." On Germany, see Krafchik and Wehner, "The Role of Parliament," 3. On the Philippines, see Gabriella R. Montinola, "Parties and Accountability in the Philippines," *Journal of Democracy* 10, no. 1 (1999): 136.

28. Lisa Baldez and John M. Carey, "Presidential Agenda Control and Spending Policy: Lessons from General Pinochet's Constitution," *American Journal of Political Science* 43, no. 1 (1999): 43.

29. Jong Chul Choi, "South Korea," in *China, India, Israel, Japan, South Korea, and Thailand,* vol. 1 of *Arms Procurement Decision Making,* ed. Ravinder Pal Singh, Stockholm International Peace Research Institute (London and New York: Oxford University Press, 1998), 196.

30. Martinho Chachiua, "Internal Security in Mozambique: Concerns versus Policies," *African Security Review* 9, no. 1 (2000), http://www.iss.co.za/Pubs/ASR/9No1/Contents.html.

31. Instead, military officers elected to the Duma, who have the appropriate clearances, oversee the classified details of the budget. David Betz, "No Place for a Civilian: Russian Defence Management from Yeltsin to Putin" (paper presented at the 41st annual convention of the International Studies Association, Los Angeles, March 14–18, 2000).

32. Marybeth Peterson Ulrich, *Democratizing Communist Militaries: The Cases of the Czech and Russian Armed Forces* (Ann Arbor: University of Michigan Press, 1999), 92. An excessively detailed budget proposal also can have its shortcomings, if budget lines are not grouped together into programs (or in some other fashion related to policy) so that the policy consequences of budget decisions are understandable.

33. For more on this, see Giraldo, chapter 2 of this volume.

34. The extensive legislative hearings that may accompany the debate over other pieces of legislation usually are not possible, given the time constraints and pressures of budget development. Sectoral committees within the legislature, however, should hold consultations and debates throughout the year, which would enrich their input into budget formulation. Hearings held outside the scope of the budget process itself avoid delays in getting the budget passed and might increase the chances that general policy concerns and not particular lobbies inform spending decisions.

35. See Bruce George and Alison Graham, "Defence Committees in Democratic and Democratising Legislatures" (paper presented at the Workshop of Parliamentary Scholars and Parliamentarians, Berlin, August 1994), 23–24.

36. Ibid., 18. Bruce George is the longtime chairman of the House of Commons Defence Committee.

37. Cruz and Diamint argue that this is the case in most Latin American countries. To the extent that a party has a position on the level of defense spending, it tends to be shaped by general attitudes toward the military rather than a well-articulated vision of national security. Cruz and Diamint, "The New Military Autonomy," 121.

38. Proposals for additional defense budget cuts will tend not to occur where parties are stronger, because the executive is more likely to have the support of a fairly disciplined majority party or majority coalition of parties that will support his or her budget proposal. Even if the executive does not command a majority, it is unlikely that the opposition in the legislature would cut defense spending in order to increase social spending, since the executive in such systems tends to receive credit for any government spending. In contrast, where parties are weaker, individual legislators can credibly claim to be the source of benefits for their constituencies, and thus they have incentives to push for increases in social spending.

39. Hunter, *Eroding Military Influence in Brazil*, 98.

40. Renato Cruz De Castro, "Adjusting to the Post–U.S. Bases Era: The Ordeal of the Philippine Military's Modernization Program," *Armed Forces and Society* 26, no. 1 (1999): 119–137.

41. Hunter, *Eroding Military Influence in Brazil*, 97–98.

42. Cruz De Castro, "Adjusting to the Post–U.S. Bases Era."

43. Ibid.

44. Organisation for Economic Co-operation and Development (OECD), *Budgeting and Policy Making*, SIGMA (Support for Improvement in Governance and Management in Central and Eastern European Countries) Papers, no. 8 (Paris, 1996), 85–86, http://www.sigmaweb.org/libpubs/pubs_sigpaps.htm.

45. High-ranking defense official in the Philippine government, interview by author, Naval Postgraduate School, Monterey, CA, January 14, 2001.

46. Alesina et al., "Budget Institutions."

47. Jelezov, *Defense Budgeting*, 44.

48. Larry O'Toole, "Anatomy of the Expenditure Budget," SIGMA (Support for Improvement in Governance and Management in Central and Eastern European Countries) Policy Brief 1 (1998), http://www.sigmaweb.org/libpubs/pubs_generallist.htm.

49. Procurement scandals are particularly common in the defense realm, given the large amounts of money involved and the high-profile nature of both the projects and the individuals making the decisions. On how procurement scandals have affected decision-making procedures in Great Britain and the United States, see Andrew Cox and Stephen Kirby, *Congress, Parliament and Defence: The Impact of Legislative Reform on Defence Accountability in Britain and America* (New York: St. Martin's Press, 1986). On Germany, see Regina H. E. Cowen, *Defense Procurement in the Federal Republic of Germany: Politics and Organization* (Boulder, CO: Westview Press, 1986).

50. Ulrich, *Democratizing Communist Militaries*, 92.

51. The GAO was formerly called the General Accounting Office. For a short history, see "The Background of GAO," http://www.gao.gov/about/history. html. For a more detailed analysis, see Harry Havens, "From Auditing to Policy Analysis: The Work of the General Accounting Office (GAO) of the United States," in OECD, *Budgeting and Policy Making*, 167–191.

52. Since 1982, the National Audit Office in Great Britain has published an annual Major Projects Report, focusing on arms procurement (comparing costs and dates with those projected). This report is not received by the Public Accounts Committee until twelve months after the end of the fiscal year and is not available to the rest of the Parliament and the general public for another five months. Dodd, "Parliament and Defense," 5.

53. The International Budget Project of the Center on Budget and Policy Priorities, based in Washington, DC, has an extensive Web site and is oriented especially toward groups in civil society that are interested in influencing the budget process. See http://www.internationalbudget.org for more information.

54. Even in the United States, where nongovernmental organizations are strong and information on the budget relatively accessible, the monitoring of the defense budget is a formidable challenge. For a discussion of the challenges encountered by two leading NGOs to monitor just one portion of the defense budget—spending in Latin America—see Joy Olson and Adam Isacson, "Findings and Recommendations," in *Just the Facts: A Civilian's Guide to U.S. Defense and Security Assistance to Latin America and the Caribbean* (Washington, DC: Latin American Working Group and Center for International Policy, 1998), http://www.ciponline.org/facts/find99.htm.

55. Ulrich, *Democratizing Communist Militaries*, 92.

56. For example, countries provide arms transfer data to the United Nations Register of Conventional Arms. In June 1999, members of the Organization of American States signed an Inter-American Convention on Transparency in Conventional Weapons Acquisition. Unfortunately, many of the efforts of international organizations to collect data on military expenditures are increasingly unsuccessful (see note 2 for this chapter).

57. Reference to legislation is in U.S. Department of State, "Indonesia," in *Annual Report on Military Expenditures, 1999* (2000), http://www.state.gov/www/global/arms/99_amiex2.html.

58. For example, money spent on arms in Argentina in 1995 was hidden under general treasury expenditures, since the government's official position was that it wasn't making weapons purchases. Thomas Scheetz, "Transparency, Accountability, and Rational Decision-Making in Defense Expenditures: The Case of Argentine" (paper presented at the Converting Defense Resources to Human Development conference, Bonn International Center for Conversion, Bonn, November 9–11, 1997).

59. This is a slightly modified version of the list offered by Hendrickson and Ball, "Off-Budget Military Expenditure."

60. Ibid.

61. Hunter, *Eroding Military Influence in Brazil*.

62. Some analysts argue, quite persuasively, that the Ecuadoran armed services initiated the conflict with Peru in an (ultimately successful) effort to preserve their access to the off-budget oil funds. Gabriel Marcella, *Strategic Implications for the United States and Latin America of the 1995 Ecuador-Peru War* (Carlisle, PA: Strategic Studies Institute, U.S. Army War College, 1995).

Chapter 8
Conscription or the All-Volunteer Force: Recruitment in a Democratic Society

EDWIN R. MICEWSKI

IN every political system, the way in which soldiers are recruited has a significant and long-lasting impact on civil-military relations. Unlike most dimensions of civil-military relations, however, the recruitment issue has less to do with how political elites and military leaders interact than with the way military personnel and the armed forces as a whole are embedded in the civil and political environments.[1] While a full understanding of civil-military relations must include the political aspects of power relations between government and those who control the military, and the spectrum of interaction between the armed services and society, it is this societal-military dimension rather than power politics that most influences recruitment. In Douglas Bland's analysis, liberal democratic civil-military relations inevitably involve both a "hardware" and a "software" side. In this analogy, hardware covers all issues of legal and institutional civilian control over the military, while software consists of the incorporation of democratic ideals, values, principles, and norms into the military culture of defense management, as well as the political culture of democracies.[2] In practice, although the hardware dimension (e.g., the adoption of appropriate laws and the institutionalization of democratic civilian control via civilian ministries of defense or legislative oversight committees) can be relatively easily stipulated and realized, the software side is more difficult both to implement and to assess, since it deals with people's attitudes and thought processes. This conclusion is supported by the fact that in the recent wave of democratic transformation and consolidation in Eastern and Southeastern Europe—launched, guided, and monitored primarily by NATO's Partnership for Peace initiative   civil military legislation was almost exclusively oriented toward hardware measures for arranging democratic civil-military relations. Notably, none of these countries' new leaders addressed the recruitment system, suggesting that the institutional democratic requirements of civilian control over the military can be met by both types of recruitment, conscription and volunteer.

Nevertheless, the recruitment system remains one of the most crucial factors influencing the relationship between a society and its military, because it has an immediate impact on the connection between the individual citizen and the defense of the state. This bond has historically found its expression in two models: the citizen soldier and the professional soldier. The analytical significance of both concepts is essentially the same, namely, to establish a direct and moral connection between the armed forces and society at large. Moreover, when a nation's citizens and leaders believe that the military also embodies their nation's conscience and will, the choice of whether the armed forces will depend for their recruits upon compulsory service or voluntary choice becomes of critical importance. Many believe that conscription in itself helps foster civilian democratic control of the military. When virtually all male citizens fit for service must join the armed forces, conscription guarantees a constant exchange of values and permanent interdependence between the armed forces and society at large, which in turn foster tacit civilian control over the military establishment. Irrespective of the recruitment system, however, Morris Janowitz's point that societal rather than state or institutional control may be the critical factor affecting civilian control of the military in democracies should be taken seriously.[3]

Regardless of the way they are recruited, national armed forces still appear to be a near-universal institution, with few exceptions.[4] In all nations maintaining armed forces, the choice of how to recruit soldiers for the armed forces is based on a broad range of circumstances: the security environment; geopolitical and geostrategic factors; economic conditions; cultural influences; and educational and sociopolitical interests. Whereas several European nations and the United States have worked with all-volunteer forces for decades now, in most continental European states, as well as in most of the world, the system of conscription as a primary source of enlisted and commissioned personnel predominates. Compulsory military service, in the form of national service and conscription, however, has become an ever more controversial issue in Europe in the wake of the cold war. The profound changes in the global strategic and security situation over the past decade have forced states to redefine security policies and adapt military concepts and force structures to the new circumstances. Probably the most significant measure in a number of countries has been the change from a conscript system to an all-volunteer force.[5] Those governments still relying on conscription are facing public debates and political initiatives both to change the system for various reasons and to consider a wide variety of proposals on how to meet the needs of military recruitment.

Each nation has to decide for itself which type of recruitment policy to adopt, in light of the complexities unique to it. Nevertheless, every nation can draw conclusions from the wider debate and can learn from others' historical experiences with compulsory service and all-volunteer systems. There are many reasons why abolition of the draft became a political issue in most states of the transatlantic region that hitherto never had considered the introduction of an all-volunteer force. In the first place, it appears that compulsory service and the modern manifestations of armed conflict and war no longer are compatible. Ever-evolving technological innovations in communications, equipment, and weaponry demand the best-qualified and best-trained personnel. For many nations, as one analyst notes, "The kinds of wars that are likely and the ways in which they will be waged have made the military draft obsolete."[6]

It would, however, be a gross oversimplification to analyze, judge, or decide the issue of which recruitment system to adopt based on mere functionality, that is, the exclusive examination of (presumably) measurable parameters such as geostrategy, economics, or technology. Rather, it is important to emphasize that "the military functions do not exclusively form the basis of a recruitment system, but are rather, like the recruitment system itself, also an effect of political orientation."[7] Consequently, recruitment policies appear to be less dependent on military efficiency, demographic suitability, economic strength, or technological prowess than on social forces and political developments. The increasing degree of specialization and the functional division of labor in industrialized societies translate ever more profoundly into the military sphere, decreasing the importance of compulsory military service as an equalizing force in society.[8]

It is for this reason that—in contrast to most analyses of this subject, which look at the issue from the viewpoint of functionality—this chapter examines military recruitment as a phenomenon of social science. It analyzes the military system from a theoretical and organizational viewpoint; in particular, it questions the textures of political power and societal interrelations that affect the choice of recruitment method. In this context, therefore, the chapter's focus is on how the military organization as a political and social subsystem functions in open, democratic societies. This combined theoretical and social-scientific approach, by incorporating a state's civil and political conditions in its analysis, puts them into historical perspective and clarifies the relationship between military decision making and its broader social context. Finally, the chapter will draw conclusions about the suitability and expediency of those influences and relationships.

Whereas strategic and functional considerations depend upon a nation's individual situation, this social-scientific analysis puts the issue of recruitment on a general level and outlines some major principles for reaching decisions that can be applied to all democratic political systems.

Historical Background: Some Misperceptions

In August 1793, for the first time in history, the revolutionary regime in France introduced the system of general conscription as an organized political measure to recruit soldiers. This practice of universal conscription gradually was adopted by other nations as well, and mass armies based on the draft came to characterize military organizations in most countries of Europe and Latin America in the nineteenth and twentieth centuries. The United States was more reluctant to embrace compulsory military service but finally did so during the First World War.[9] The same was true of the British, who, after extensive debate and significant resistance, were forced to adopt the draft because of manpower shortages on the western front.[10]

The debate over soldier recruitment historically has been influenced by bias not only on the part of pacifists, whose objection to compulsory service is based upon opposition to all war, but from all sides with a stake in the issue. The scientific and political discourses have been biased in two ways. First is the myth that democracy and universal conscription are complementary to each other, in the sense that the draft fosters democracy in general and ensures a more democratically inclined military force. Second is the conviction that an all-volunteer system represents a threat to democracy and promotes a "state-within-the-state" mentality in the armed forces.

The European continent has had the most consistent history of compulsory military service—more than two hundred years, including the period between 1806 and 1945 in Western Europe, and continuing until the end of the cold war in Eastern Europe—and therefore offers the best proof that conscription and democracy have often been contradictory. The first largely misleading assumption is that conscription was a democratic achievement of the French Revolution. The conscript army was in fact initially a short-term emergency measure enacted by the new republic to meet the threat of the allied armies of imperial Prussia and

Austria. The *levée en masse*, introduced in 1793, was a comprehensive mobilization of the entire nation to defend the acquisitions of the revolution against revanchist threats from the outside. Furthermore, according to revolutionary documents, standing armies and any kind of conscription, far from a hallmark of democracy, were considered to be incompatible with the dignity and freedom of the individual.

During the nineteenth century, mass armies, made possible only because of conscription, created a new dimension of warfare on the European continent. In Prussia at the time, the purpose of conscription—defense of the homeland—became corrupted internally as a kind of militarization of society, while externally the system furnished the state with an immense potential for military aggression.[11] Rather than fostering peace and democracy, conscription came to be viewed as a prerequisite to the organization of the phenomenon called total war. Against this backdrop, Helmuth von Moltke coined the term "era of national wars" *(Zeitalter der Volkskriege)* and regretfully predicted that the mass armies made possible by conscription foredoomed the art of military leadership.[12] The development also substantiated his belief that general conscription fostered the tendency for wars to become little better than "human slaughterhouses," an idea he expressed in Paris in 1871. It was just after the French had fallen victim to Prussia's conscripted mass army that the so-called Thiers law of July 27, 1872, declared military duty to be "personal and obligatory for the entire male population" of France.[13]

The emergence of mass armies was paralleled by the rise of the professional officer corps. When armies were small and the rank and file were long-term regulars, they could rely on aristocrats, who were considered to be naturally capable of military command, to serve as officers. When armies grew larger through conscription, it became necessary to create more organized, well-trained bodies of military leaders. This both reflected and reinforced a direct relation between conscription and professionalism. Career officers were needed to train and lead the constant stream of newly enlisted men. This development also tended to moderate nations' propensity toward total war by introducing a rational and calculating expertise into the political debate through a professionalized officer corps.[14]

These changes in the nature of both armies and officer corps also began to alter significantly the relations between the military organization and society. Whereas in the premodern era the rank-and-file soldiers represented an isolated group with no roots in, or connection with, the rest of society, the officers enjoyed a clearly defined status in society by virtue of their nobility. This paradigm began to reverse in the nineteenth century and is still a problem for civil-military relations in many countries today. Thanks to conscription, enlisted men came to represent a cross section of the national population—truly citizens in uniform—while career officers, though coming from all strata of society, became a distinctly separate professional group.

The degradation of conscription's original purpose continued into the twentieth century when German chancellor Adolph Hitler, repudiating Article 173 of the Versailles Treaty, reintroduced the draft to Germany in 1935. The result of welding the fascist ideology of the time to overwhelming military power—combining "blood and destiny"—which led to the use of draftees as human war matériel, is all too well known.[15] Conscription after World War II continued in European nations as a result of politics and pragmatism, in that most armies in Western Europe would not have been able to meet the force requirements of the cold war's bipolar antagonism without conscription. They also would have been unable to replenish the reservoir for the recruitment of professional soldiers of all ranks. The United States needed to maintain a large pool of draftees to deal with the wars in Korea and later Vietnam. In addition to its commitments on the continent in the face of the emerging Soviet menace after World War II, Britain required conscription to maintain its still-extensive overseas empire and great power status. In 1951 the British army stood at 433,000 soldiers, of whom 224,000 were conscripts.[16]

Although over time the reformative concept of the citizen in uniform bearing arms arguably reestablished conscription's relationship to the ideals of democracy and liberalism, the result nevertheless was not entirely desirable. In spite of the draft and a continuous mutual exchange of citizens and soldiers, the armed forces in a majority of European countries did become alienated from their political and social environment. The problems of legitimating the military, as well as finding more than tolerant approval among the citizenry, became almost insurmountable, compounded by the increasing numbers of draftees who resorted to alternative civil service rather than actual military training.

Even though the replacement of the draft by all-volunteer forces has not been an unmitigated success, the experience with an entirely professional military in the United States demonstrates that all-volunteer systems neither threaten democracy nor lead to a pervasive "state-within-the-state" mentality among service personnel.[17] The United States employed the draft for only thirty-eight of the more than two hundred years that the U.S. armed forces have been in existence, and almost entirely in wartime. Since 1973, when Congress ended the draft after nearly a quarter century of conscription, the United States has relied exclusively on volunteers, although it maintains a contingency system of mandatory registration for all eighteen-year-old males.[18] In Great Britain, where conscription had been in effect since 1949, the draft ended in 1960 and Britain's military transformed into an all-volunteer force.

Although in continental Europe the need to deter military aggression and invasion was what led to the emergence of military discipline and the system of conscription, in most of Latin America, by contrast, political leaders were not under the same pressure to protect their countries from external threat. Some Latin American militaries developed instead into enforcement institutions for social discipline, criminal detention, and penal reform.[19] Armies operated as the primary tools not only of domestic criminal justice and policing but of political power and regime protection as well. This history of internal control and political activism has been an impediment to military reform in those states to this day. Nevertheless, as Latin American societies become more democratic and liberal, the fact that the armed forces commonly performed domestic police duties and were instruments of government-legitimated internal violence puts conscription into question. In one example, the murder of a young conscripted soldier while in uniform caused a public outcry and forced Argentina to finally end compulsory military service in 1995.[20]

When the overall security interests of a nation can be met only through use of the draft, nothing can be said against conscription. Nevertheless, the preconception that generally glorifies conscription as some democratic ideal is in need of rethinking. This is not to say that a recruitment system based upon conscription cannot be effective and legitimate, but merely to say that it cannot serve as a general remedy for issues of military security and civil-military integration and, above all, should not be abused for ideological purposes.

Political Background and the Terms of the Debate

The debate over compulsory military service versus the all-volunteer system has been triggered anew by the geostrategic realities of the post–cold war world. The era of mass armies, which dominated most of the twentieth century, appears to be over. As one measure of their adaptation to these new circumstances, several European nations recognized the political necessity and demonstrated the political will to change their system of recruitment. General and technical discussions of the subject of conscription, which can prepare the way for a political decision in any country that has not yet taken this step, seem therefore to be a legitimate — and necessary — effort.

Nevertheless, democracies always face the danger of evaluating political issues, not objectively, but rather on the grounds of public attentiveness and relevance. As in all political debates dealing with controversial issues, the discourse is subject to ideological positions and party politics. Although the social-political dimension is neither the only nor the most important one, public discussion frequently supercedes governmental and military considerations. This peculiarity is a result primarily of the dynamics of daily political battle, which often is driven by subjective and partial arguments.

The question of which recruitment system to adopt, with its multiple effects on the fabric of society, nevertheless should not be disconnected from such factual considerations as appropriateness in terms of national security or democratic compatibility. That these factors are sometimes minimized may be the result of either ignorance or ideological bias or, to the particular detriment of rational decision making, the confluence of both. No matter what the character of an investigation is, however, several general, even normative aspects underlie any practical inquiry into the matter.

First, the terms "conscription" and "all-volunteer force" pertain to the method by which personnel are recruited, whether through obligation or choice, and include both the raising and the replenishment of forces. Therefore, neither method is necessarily exclusive of the other. On the one hand, a voluntary force may maintain, besides a professional component, also a reserve component such as a militia or a national guard. On the other hand, a military force based on the draft not only includes standing, reserve, and mobilization elements but also embraces a professional officer corps.

Second, neither conscription nor volunteer force embodies per se the best, optimal, and therefore only recruitment system. The most favorable system has to be the one that meets the military requirements of a nation in any given security situation in the best possible way. With this in mind, the kinds of widespread preconceptions found in both military and civilian circles detract from any public debate and often impede attempts to reach the best solutions. One such misconception is the legendary declaration by Theodor Heuss, post–World War II president of the German Federal Republic, that conscription is the "legitimate offspring of democracy." Not only is this assertion debatable from a historical viewpoint, but contemporary German social scientists also cogently add, "Conscription appears in this country by all means to be a 'legitimate offspring,' but one that stems from the Cold War; and this war is over."[21]

But it is equally questionable to try to legitimate the all-volunteer system on quasi-ethical grounds. Thus, the following statement by Allen Wallis seems hardly acceptable as a general norm: "My objections to the draft are of two kinds. First, it is immutably immoral in principle and inevitably inequitable in practice. Second, it is ineffective, inefficient, and detrimental to national security."[22] Rather, the statement appears to have been valid, if ever, only against the backdrop of U.S. politics and the Vietnam War toward the end of the 1960s, when Wallis was writing.

Third, and perhaps most important, the draft represents a considerable disruption of an individual's life. It should not, therefore, be demanded unless the management of national security interests, within the overall structure of national tasks and challenges, requires armed forces that can be mustered only by conscription. In modern societies, the benefit of military service as providing some kind of "national civic education" is hardly relevant any longer. Furthermore, given the importance of higher education and the competitiveness of career paths, taking away a year or more from a young individual's lifetime is significant.

A fourth consideration is the hierarchy of concerns that influence the choice of recruitment policy. Experts widely agree that serious debate on the recruitment issue should begin with a thorough and objective security analysis. National security challenges and interstate relations have immediate effects on the functional aspect of military effectiveness and therefore must be at the forefront of any policy decision making. This primary level of analysis comprises the geostrategic environment, a threat assessment, changes in military technology, and, last but not least, the question of whether a country is integrated into a security alliance or stands alone. These are major security paradigms, as was the bipolar paradigm that defined the cold war; now states must take into account the emerging post–cold war security environment with all its profound impacts on armed forces' strength, structure, tasks, and missions.

Although each nation must be responsible for its own security analysis, some general criteria on this level not only are important for any discussion of recruitment per se but also are closely linked to the social and political aspects of the debate.

The Primary Assessment Level: The Security Environment

The general parameters of the new security scene can be characterized by the terms "complexity," "internationalization," and "flexibility." Not only have security challenges multiplied and broadened, but their solutions are also increasingly multinational in nature. The armed forces of a large number of nations already have taken on many of these new tasks that demand system-wide flexibility and increasingly intertwined competencies. Many political as well as military representatives, however, have expressed concern that both the complexity of tasks and the scarcity of resources might overwhelm military organizations or impair their ability to succeed at classical military missions.

Security policy and military competence cannot be reduced to the probability of direct military threat. In today's internationalized and multifaceted security environment, armed forces become important actors in a civil-military defense setting that is characterized by conflict prevention, peace support, and humanitarian missions. In other words, constraining military forces to a classical national defense role is to ignore the range of security challenges confronting the modern nation. Indeed, as Shemella demonstrates in Chapter 5, classical defense is a small part of current roles and missions.

Military organizations face a broad array of new challenges and unfamiliar tasks and missions. In their efforts to focus on roles and missions of prevention and intervention, the armed services also have begun to assume a new identity in the eyes of the public. This development toward greater functionality, going far beyond the ability merely to threaten or apply violence, fosters an image of the armed forces as serving to promote stability and livable conditions not only for their own country's citizens but for all people.[23]

To emphasize the prime importance of geopolitical and strategic factors prompting the transition from a conscript to a voluntary force, Swiss military sociologist Karl Haltiner posits three conditions that make this change very likely. First, the country in question enjoys membership in a defense alliance, such as the North Atlantic Treaty Organization (NATO). Second, the territorial sovereignty of the country is not immediately endangered by military threat. And third, the country participates frequently in international peace support operations or is about to embark upon such a policy.[24]

According to this theory, if these conditions do not apply, it is much more probable that a nation will retain conscription. Haltiner cites

Finland and Switzerland as examples of nonaligned countries, and Greece and Turkey as nations confronted with a direct threat to their national sovereignty, all of which utilize the draft. He is of the opinion that both international and strategic factors will remain decisive in making the choice either to keep conscription or to move to an all-volunteer system. Even when social trends and a change of values erode support for conscription, according to Haltiner, political administrations will not relinquish conscription unless strategic factors suggest that doing so will be beneficial. The analysis undertaken in this chapter, however, contests Haltiner's point of view.

The terrorist attacks of September 11, 2001, posed a new type of challenge to national security. In doing so, they triggered a debate on the possible reintroduction of the draft in the United States. Some analysts called for conscription to meet the personnel needs of both the professional army and the National Guard as they geared up for homeland defense and the international war against al Qaeda.[25] There was a real concern among American specialists, however, that the draft would lower the quality of enlistees. Some suggested the idea of a special-skills draft in order to meet specific needs, such as for foreign-language experts or health care personnel. For the labor-intensive homeland defense field, scholar and author Charles Moskos suggested a three-part draft that would allow individuals to choose among the military, homeland security, and civil forms of service. He argued that such a system, to be called into use at short notice, ideally would not only save money and help meet the personnel requirements of the various federal agencies but also reduce the gap between military and civilian society.[26] Although this suggestion was not pursued, the discussion itself demonstrates the extent to which the system of recruitment is linked to strategic and national interests.

The Secondary Assessment Level

Further steps in the evaluation process can be taken in a meaningful manner once a thorough security assessment is in place. These steps comprise legal, economic, cultural, educational, and social factors. The secondary assessment level can best be divided into three segments: structural, economic, and social.[27]

On this secondary level, general developments in global politics, along with a new understanding of the parallels between different realms of activity, such as security and economics, can help explain the shift in the security paradigm, with its impact on military organization, structure, and perceptions of legitimacy.

Christopher Dandeker analyzes six dimensions that help explain the ongoing processes that are challenging private sector organizations, as well as the striking parallels facing armed forces. First, the diminished threat to national territorial sovereignty is paralleled by the lack of stable markets for business. Second, company downsizing is paralleled by significant reductions in the size of military establishments. Third, while companies and enterprises have to respond to an increasingly global market, the military has to address a range of missions involving extraterritorial missions other than war. Fourth, military organizations are expected to take on practices that echo civilian business models, such as contracting out functions and restructuring their hierarchies. Fifth, both military and civilian organizations have to react and find answers to the social and cultural challenges of dynamically changing societies. Sixth, both sets of organizations have to make the best use of new information technologies at all levels, from operations to personnel functions, including all dimensions of offensive and defensive "information warfare."[28]

A succinct formula for success on this secondary assessment level comes from Gordon Sullivan: "The bottom line for all this—high quality people, good discipline, good training—is decisive victory."[29] When it comes to recruitment of personnel for any organization, the question of how to enlist, employ, and retain qualified people in sufficient numbers is at the core of strategic decision making. The quality of the organization's members clearly affects all segments on this level.

Experience demonstrates that empirical processes and results on this secondary level often can be decisive for the final choice of a recruitment system. Nevertheless, this is a decision that must finally be made on the basis of democratic governance, without the interference of scientific bias or premature judgment.

Leading Aspects in Social Science

In spite of the enormous societal, strategic, and technological changes of the past few decades, the importance of the military for security has not diminished. The claim that modern industrial societies and traditional military power are essentially irreconcilable, as put forth by thinkers such as August Comte and Herbert Spencer, have turned out be untenable. In addition to the two highly mechanized world wars of the twentieth century, other, recent wars—the Persian Gulf and Afghanistan wars of 1991 and 2003 in particular, and the military interventions and peace support operations in Southeastern Europe of the 1990s—have proved this theory wrong.

More-recent international efforts at conflict resolution and conflict prevention have done nothing to lessen the importance of the military. Despite—or rather, because of—the developments of recent decades, today's democracies have proven they are willing and able to defend themselves and pursue their values. This attitude is likely to remain unchanged for the foreseeable future. The core question, however, will be the way the military integrates with society, and its answer will derive from the central issue of personnel recruitment. For volunteer forces, the challenge will be how to meet their recruitment goals and attract individuals to join the forces; for a conscription system, how to justify and legitimize this intrusive and restrictive organization.

In the realm of national security, no aspect is of greater political influence and sustained social impact than conscription, for it affects every single able-bodied and able-minded male (and in some cases, female) citizen.[30] From the point of view of the individual, the draft directly or indirectly affects all processes of socialization and education, family life, social ties, and relations of various kinds; in short, almost every aspect of a person's life. The turn to volunteer forces may be viewed as a striving for an increase in individual freedom and self-determination in modern societies. This ever-greater degree of personal and political liberty, however, is often accompanied by the phenomenon of unsettlement.[31] The stability and prosperity of any social system depend on the appropriate contributions of its members. But these contributions have to be asked for within the rational context of modern expectations. Appeals in the name of public interest, directed at the individual, must be justified by legitimate necessities and reasonable demands.

If the overall national interest demands conscription, nothing can be said against it. It is equally true, however, that no element in the nature of the state suggests the unconditional right of conscription. This right can arise only from conditions that threaten the existence of the state. In other words, the right of any state to draft its citizens depends on the existence of political circumstances that make this measure unavoidable.[32] The dynamic complexity of the modern political organization has led to the politicization of almost all civic interaction in the highly industrialized democracies. With regard to recruitment, this means that if the duty of conscription is demanded for the sake of society's well-being, its supporters must be able to demonstrate its legitimacy and benefits to the public at large.

Systems theory provides us with a way to conceptualize the relationship between society and its defense in the context of military recruitment. The objective of systems theory is to look at the modes of individual social systems—families, associations, political parties, parliaments, or military organizations, for instance—not as isolated phenomena but rather through their interdependencies within the society as a whole. The next section therefore illustrates, from the systems theory perspective, that the efficiency of the armed forces and the extent to which they are embedded in society depend on how well they meet that society's basic structural and functional requirements.[33]

The Foundation of Systems Theory

Systems theory is a product of modern scientific thinking, dating from the 1930s.[34] The core object of systems theory is to examine the organizational form of the complex relations between individual elements of a system.[35] The theory tries to answer such questions as how social, public, and communal actions are organized, and which influences and processes steer them. How are subsystems of society and state related to, and even reliant upon, each other? What gives social processes form, direction, and structure?

If one attempts to grasp modern society as an intricately interconnected system and to realize its dynamic and frequently conflictual nature, one is struck by the division of labor, the breaking up of "society" into organizational units, each of which generates a specific achievement. In their differentiated functions, these organizational entities contribute to the functionality of the overall system. In other words, the output of every organizational unit as part of a social subsystem—such as business, education, or security, for example—is at the same time input for the grand system, something that helps the entire society run smoothly.

Purpose and efficiency are the two basic requirements that any relevant organizational unit has to meet in order to be indispensable to the total system. The purpose of the organization is its dynamic contribution to the stability and functionality of the system. Efficiency is the ability of the organization to fulfill tasks and attain goals. When viewing civil-military relations in terms of integrating an organizational system—in this case the armed forces—into an open society, one becomes aware not only of how immense an impact this relationship between purpose and efficiency has on the question of recruitment, but also of how the recruitment issue influences the social and political environment. It highlights the problems that a system like the military has to face when, for instance, it must legitimize compulsory service on the emotional level, if on the material level the necessity for the draft can no longer reasonably be justified.

Functional and Structural Requirements of Societies

For our purpose, the functional demands that must be met by any organizational unit in order to be acknowledged and accepted into modern society are best represented in the structural and functional systems theory developed by Talcott Parsons.[36] Parsons seeks to connect the structures of social systems with aspects of their functionality. Further, he attempts to demonstrate the operational scope of each element, or subsystem, belonging to the overall system (that is, society). This type of analysis enables the researcher to assess the quality of a social system in terms of persistence, durability, and stability. Within "society" the military is a subsystem that contributes the fundamental structural value of "security," so that society may achieve the supreme goal of "systems maintenance."

Parsons features the notion of systems maintenance in his theory and introduces the term "self-sufficiency." This must not be confused with autarchy, as every social community is dependent upon processes of exchange with its environment (on the international level, other nations). Rather, it must be understood in terms of the capacity of a system to promote external stable relations and to control them in its own interests. In his theory, Parsons uses the term "structure" for the relatively static elements of a system (for example, the government, the judiciary, the police, the military), which are not affected by short-term upsets in the relationship between the system (a state) and its environment (global security).[37] The term "function," in contrast, relates to the dynamic aspects of a social system (such as elections, foreign policy, strategic relations), referring to all the social processes that guarantee the maintenance and stability of the system and its structures in a constantly changing environment.

The preservation of a social system—here the democratic society—is taken for granted as the foundation for the organization of society, which leads, quite understandably, to the accusation that the theory fosters and supports conservative political attitudes. Such criticism is not relevant to this discussion, however, inasmuch as—apart from the usually undoubted worthiness of democratic society to be preserved—the goal of the military subsystem, as an instrument of politics, is one of maintenance and preservation.

Both structures and functions constitute the conditions for social action. They are embedded in the two realities that make up the general social environment in which procedures take place. The first is the physical reality, made up of living organisms and material things. The second is what Parsons, borrowing from the philosophical tradition, calls final reality. This is the basic ontological orientation within a system that constitutes cultural awareness, connecting the individual personality to the overall social system.

Basic Functions and Structures and Their Application to Recruitment

For the purpose of a structural as well as functional analysis, Parsons developed the so-called AGIL scheme, which identifies the tasks and functions vital for system maintenance. Within this scheme, all social systems must fulfill four elementary functions: *A*daptation, *G*oal attainment, *I*ntegration, and *L*atent structure maintenance. These four functions correspond in turn to the four structural components that are necessary for the prosperity of any social system. This scheme applies to "society" in its entirety, as well as to every system that emerges as a subsystem or organizational unit of a subsystem. In the case of the military, these normative functional and structural requirements, and the practical processes and action patterns that flow from them to the social and organizational subsystem of the military, offer several insights into how and why given societies make the decisions they do regarding recruitment.

The adaptation function refers to both the generation and the allocation of human and material resources, such as occupational skills, information, or money. Adaptation manifests in the structural component known as roles, which are the way that individuals, or groups of individuals, participate in organizations. This function directly concerns the material and human resources that are necessary for a military organization to ensure that it can accomplish the overall societal goals of national security and defense. It has implications not only for the economy but also for the recruitment issue, primarily with respect to the structure and size of the armed forces. The legislative power of the purse plays a major role in this regard, particularly when it comes to the numbers and overall organizational design of the armed forces. The Constitution of the United States gives Congress not only the authority to declare war but also to "raise and support armies." Though typically not as explicit as the U.S.

example, in the struggle for resources within what has become a significantly changed security context, the generation and allocation of human and material capital pose a civil-military challenge to any country.

Goal attainment stands for the unity of purpose that follows from having rational interests and goals. The goal attainment function is represented by the personality as the main incentive for activities in a social system. Regardless of the kind of organization, it is predominantly the individual who is responsible for the attainment of any group's goals. This sheds light on the importance of the responsibilities the military undertakes for the sake of the common good. The goal attainment function challenges the political administration to transform its strategic assessment into a clear political mandate and then into orders for the military establishment. This affects the recruitment issue insofar as the capabilities demanded of the armed forces, on the basis of assigned missions and tasks, are closely linked to personnel recruitment. At this juncture, the strong connection between the functional necessities of national security as determined by a strategic assessment, and the "soft" dimension of societal relations in the sense of communicating security and military needs to society, becomes clear.

The integrative function signifies the collective and communal aspect and represents categories such as cultural orientation and loyalty. This function accounts for the coordination of all parts and units in a society, individuals and groupings alike. The corresponding structural quality is given by *norms*, which are preeminent qualities that must be incorporated by social subsystems in order to ensure social cohesion. For the armed forces, integration needs to be interpreted in two ways. On the one hand, it encompasses all mechanisms that support communication and cohesion within the armed services themselves. On the other hand, integration also includes all measures that help incorporate the military into the value cosmos of the entire political system.

This function touches upon the qualities of loyalty and solidarity. The appeal, for instance, to carry out national service in most societies is directed only toward the male population. Nevertheless, the normative challenge to society at large must be recognized in all cases in which an act of loyalty turns into a legal obligation. Given that individuals in modern societies usually fill a number of roles (family, parental, or occupational, for instance), transforming social loyalties into legal duties becomes a particularly intricate problem. The effort to meet the claims of every loyalty can lead to collisions not only against the backdrop of individual self-interest but also when conflicting loyalties have to be reconciled (for instance, loyalty toward one's own family or career against an appeal to serve the nation). The recruitment question is primarily concerned with the contribution of the individual, whether to accept the call of the draft by carrying out national service or to consider becoming a soldier as an occupational alternative and voluntarily joining the military.

Finally, latent structure maintenance corresponds to the securing of common cultural beliefs and convictions. Its function refers to the structural requirement of values. As the foundation of cultural legitimacy, values underlie social-normative constraints. In contrast to loyalty toward social-normative commitments such as respect for the rule of law, values provide a more profound foundation and latitude to the individual, as in belief in individual freedom. The generalization and expansion of values and value systems are an essential characteristic in modern societies. The armed forces face the challenge of maintaining their traditions while, even more importantly, holding their moral position within the overall cultural mind-set as a legitimate and accepted part of society. The degree to which basic cultural values influence individual motivations and behavior will affect the acceptability of conscription and the success of recruitment.

Functional Procedures and Action Processes

The AGIL scheme not only describes the essential functions and structures of a society but also can serve as the basis from which to draw logical inferences about the means by which any social system might attain to its goals. As shown in Figure 8.1, six procedural functions can be deduced from the AGIL design. The first, mobilization, is concerned with the use of both human and material resources. Parsons considers labor and capital—in an economic sense—to be fluid factors. The interdependencies of resources and operations demonstrate that every organization must be able to mobilize resources if it is to carry out its missions, although the way this is done differs profoundly with the type of organization or subsystem.

The prime concern for the armed forces, as for every other social system, is to secure adequate material and human resources to ensure system efficiency. The striking difference between the military organization and most other societal subsystems is that most militaries do not pursue material gain. They usually depend on public funding and, therefore, on public interest and the power constellations within the political system that control funding. The political and societal decisions that influence

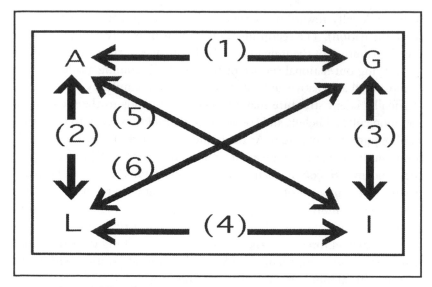

FIGURE 8.1. AGIL scheme. *Structural parameters: A*, adaptation; *G*, goal attainment; *I*, integration; *L*, latent structure maintenance. *Procedural parameters: 1*, mobilization; *2*, consumer function; *3*, decision making; *4*, value and loyalty component; *5*, allocation of resources; *6*, legitimacy. (Figure designed by Heimo Truebswasser, in Edwin R. Micewski, *Zur Frage eines Freiwilligenheeres*, Studies and Reports [Vienna: National Defense Academy, 2000], 25.)

funding levels and employment of personnel therefore play a decisive role in the final choice of how to recruit human resources.

Second, the consumer function concerns values and resultant attitudes toward the use of resources. It includes such aspects as organizational utility, productivity, and growth. It also touches on issues of organizational transparency and marketing. The consumer function constitutes a particular challenge to the armed forces, as it does for every non-profit organization. Economic subsystems—automakers, for example—generate "visible" products whose consumption and benefit manifest themselves immediately and in a measurable manner. For organizations producing "invisible" products such as security, however, marketing is much more complicated. This becomes even truer when the inputs to create the "product" include human life, in the event of conflict. While the adoption of a certain recruitment system is a significant political choice made for a variety of reasons, it is at the same time fundamentally a values-laden decision.[38] Furthermore, the armed forces, by their very nature, cannot compete with most nonmilitary organizations in pay and other compensation. To make the consumption of security attractive—in other words, to create public willingness to contribute the necessary resources—military and political organizations must make targeted efforts at both marketing and public relations (integration). If conscription is the staffing method of choice, the decisive factor may be how well military leaders have demonstrated both their organization's overall functional competence and utility to society against contemporary security challenges, and the draft's indispensability in meeting overall national security objectives.

The third function, decision making, refers to the "polity," which is a distinct subsystem of politics dedicated to the generation and allocation of power, defined by Parsons as "the generalized capacity to mobilize resources in the interest of attainment of a system goal." Because leaders of the military establishment have no direct political power, they must exert influence, which is "the ability to lead other social units to desired decisions/activities without offering benefits or threatening with consequences."[39] Through these processes, power is generated both outside and within an organization, no matter what its functional nature may be. Thus the military is not only a part of the polity that generates decision-making power but also a recipient of the power generated at higher levels of the polity. In sum, the decision function refers to the ability of the military and political leadership to formulate and execute military tasks without violating the primacy of democratic decision making.

For conscription to be acceptable within a democracy, its application must be perceived to be fair. The principle of military service equity has, however, been eroded by various political measures, ranging from a lottery system for selecting draftees to the institution of alternative service. As the attempts to achieve equity become ever more liberal, they offer the individual an almost unlimited possibility of escaping from military service, further weakening public engagement and support.[40]

The fourth function, the value and loyalty component, relates to the requirement that an organization be able to wed the loyalty and values of its members to the organization's function, goals, and tasks. Values are, from a sociological perspective, more general than goals, and they guide action rather than provide specific objectives. In this field, the policies of the armed forces generally are very close to civilian management strategies. The corporate and organizational spirit is most influential when it comes to recruiting personnel for the armed forces. In recent years, military establishments have learned that effectiveness requires them to take individual interests into account, particularly when it comes to transforming military service time into useful experience for civilian workplace demands.[41]

Fifth, the allocation function addresses the question of how an organization's resources—human and material—will be distributed and used. The function comprises both the assignment of personal or group responsibility and the distribution of financial and physical facilities. This second aspect is central, as it encompasses acquisition of physical facilities and employment of personnel. Military planning staffs must ensure the economical and purposeful use of resources in order to accomplish most effectively the tasks assigned to the services. Especially in light of the number and complexity of the missions and tasks carried out by the armed forces these days, competition for resources has come to dominate military politics and is, moreover, closely watched by the public.

The sixth function, legitimacy, regulates the relation between the subsystem (the organization) and the preferences and will of the individuals who make up society and the state. This involves issues such as the legitimate integration of the organization—with its goals, structures, and operative procedures—into society and culture. In a democracy, legitimation is a constant challenge that operates through many different kinds of mechanisms. As Parsons points out, it is the actions rather than the values of the organization that need to be legitimated, and this can take place on a variety of levels.

Questions of legitimacy challenge military philosophers, scientists, educators, and public relations experts to convey and justify the meaning and purpose of the military for security in modern, open and democratic, information-based societies. No organization is legitimized or justified by and through itself alone or by the fact of its existence. The need to explain the potentially violent nature of the military and to answer satisfactorily the ensuing questions about legitimate uses of violent political means and military force—the "management and application of violence," as Samuel Huntington has called it—remains a quasi-perennial issue at the heart of justifications for the existence of armed forces.[42] In addition, the dynamics of constantly altering security and social environments demand that legitimizing strategies quickly adapt as well.

A Few More Practical Ideas

There is no simple recipe for how to tackle the problems of recruitment—apart from the priorities that each state's leaders must consider when they assess their choices—and the apparent trend away from conscription to all-volunteer forces. No matter what choice is made, however, recruitment must be well organized according to the individual nation's circumstances. This requires an adequate financial basis and a properly functioning legal and bureaucratic structure. Soldiers—both recruits and volunteers—must believe that they are spending their time meaningfully. They must have an awareness that their service time improves and enriches their personal lives, as well as offers skills and aptitudes that can transfer from the military to the civilian sphere.

The specific challenges of military service ensure that the questions of equality and equity are a major issue in modern societies. To make conscription a fair system is not an easy task in the face of alternative service possibilities and the usual exclusion of women from conscription. Furthermore, any system of compulsory recruitment must ensure that those called up for national service are not just the poor, unlucky, or uneducated. The perceived lack of true equity has in fact often been a major criticism of compulsory service. During the U.S. mobilization for Vietnam, antiwar protesters leveled credible charges of elitism against the American draft system because of its policy of granting deferment to more or less every college student. Young men who had the money for tuition and the grades for acceptance could stay out of the service, while the poor and poorly educated had little choice but to go in. Ultimately in the case of the United States, "selection corrupted the draft."[43] The militaries of some large countries also generated public perceptions that forced service depended on chance when they found themselves unable to use all the draftees entering their military organizations. Therefore, the principle of equity demands that exemptions must clearly be legally justified and not left to luck or privilege.

In light of changes in the international security paradigm and the consequent general tendency to eschew mass armies, increasingly nations have turned away from the drafting of conscripts. The arguments that some continental European nations, such as Belgium, France, and the Netherlands, have used to explain their decisions to change from compulsory service to all-volunteer forces are illustrative:[44]

—The system of conscription is no longer commensurate with the military requirements of an ever more internationalized and cooperative security environment.

—Conscription impedes the creation of mobile, highly professional elements, able to deploy exterritorially at short notice.

—High, "state of the art" standards cannot be maintained in the military with conscript soldiers.

—The idea of conscription does not reflect the characteristics and features of modern democratic societies.

—Conscription increasingly is perceived as discriminatory and, due to fundamental changes in public perceptions, is no longer well accepted.

There is, however, one other issue in civil-military relations bearing on the recruitment debate that constitutes a kind of counterforce to the general move away from conscription. This is the social value of alternative service to the welfare of modern societies. In most of the Western-type nations still embracing the draft and offering alternative service, alternative service in itself has found appreciation to the extent that it appears to be more important to social welfare than military service. Thousands of conscripts have served in various social service and charitable organizations as well as public agencies, supporting the work of those groups as relatively inexpensive temporary employees. As a result, various political forces support conscription simply because they expect problems to arise for social service organizations if the draft were to be abolished.

Nevertheless, although consideration must be given as to how to resolve this particular social issue, it is unlikely that it will play a decisive role in the final decision on choosing the proper recruitment system. The paradox of maintaining a compulsory military service system solely for the beneficial side effect resulting from alternative service, when the main purpose of recruiting soldiers for the armed forces no longer requires conscription, is unlikely to endure in any democracy.

Conclusion and Future Prospects

This chapter has presented many of the factors and rationales that influence civil-military discourse and political decision making on the issue of military recruitment. Systems theory, as applied to social and political organizations, provides a normative framework for evaluating options for an appropriate recruitment system while allowing for the specific strategic and political situations faced by individual nations. Inferences drawn for the military establishment regarding recruitment demonstrate how intricately the topic is entangled in political and social interdependencies.

Recruitment is burdened by historical and cultural preconceptions more than most other topics in defense and civil-military relations. Perceptions of value, ideological trends, prevailing political attitudes, history, stances on matters of security and defense, and public approval or disapproval—in a word, a society's appreciation for and general reception of soldiering and military life—have a profound impact on debates and decisions concerning armed service.

Changes in international relations as well as social norms are challenging the culture of the military. While new missions work to alter the armed forces' traditional focus on national defense and war, the character of civilian society, which values individualism and the individual's desire to avoid social burdens, puts pressure on military organizations to become far more flexible than they have had to be in the past.

The future challenges of warfare, and the importance of the armed forces to political and social stability as well as security, mean that a national debate on how to recruit soldiers will be essential for almost all nations. Military service is an intricate problem that does not allow for simple answers. Within the context of security, the question of recruitment can be answered appropriately only when the entire complex of political, economic, technological, and social influences are taken into consideration. Whatever the decision on recruitment, however, political and military leaders will have to work to ensure its acceptance in society, the state, and the military itself.

Notes

1. This chapter deals only with the issues involved in the legal and constitutional recruitment of soldiers. Abuses during and after recruitment in some countries or regions, such as forced recruitment of prisoners or child soldiers, are outside the scope of this discussion.

2. Douglas L. Bland, "Patterns in Liberal Democratic Civil-Military Relations," *Armed Forces and Society* 27, no. 4 (2001): 525.

3. In reference to Morris Janowitz's influential work *The Professional Soldier*, Peter Feaver underscores this idea in his article, "The Civil-Military Problematique: Huntington, Janowitz, and the Question of Civilian Control," *Armed Forces and Society* 23, no. 2 (1996): 166.

4. Gerhard Kuemmel lists the following countries that are free of armed forces: Andorra, Costa Rica, Dominica, Grenada, Haiti, Kiribati, Liechtenstein, Maldives, Mauritius, Monaco, Nauru, Panama, Saint Lucia, Saint Vincent and the Grenadines, San Marino, Solomon Islands, Samoa, St. Kitts–Nevis,

Tuvalu, Vanuatu, and Vatican City. Gerhard Kuemmel, "The Military and Its Civilian Environment: Reflections on a Theory of Civil-Military Relations," *Connections Quarterly Journal* 1, no. 4 (2002): 63–82.

5. Belgium, for example, changed to an all-volunteer force as early as 1994; France decided in 1996 to allow conscription to expire by 2002 and thereafter to rely on a volunteer force; Spain intended, according to a governmental declaration in 1996, to introduce an all-volunteer force by 2003; the Netherlands has not drafted conscripts since 1998; in the same year, Portugal decided to abolish conscription at some indefinite point in the future; and Italy has made clear its intention to introduce an all-volunteer force by 2005.

6. Walter Y. Oi, "Historical Perspectives on the All-Volunteer Force: The Rochester Connection," in *Professionals on the Front Line: Two Decades of the All-Volunteer Force*, ed. J. Eric Fredland, Curtis Gilroy, Roger D. Little, W. S. Sellman (Washington, DC: Pergamon-Brassey's International Defense Publishers, 1996), 49.

7. Reinmar Cunis, "Rekrutierungsmodelle im demokratischen Gesellschaftssystem," in *Beiträge zur Militärsoziologie*, Kölner Zeitschrift für Soziologie Sonderheft 12, ed. René König (Cologne, 1968), 124. This and all other citations from German sources were translated by E. R. Micewski.

8. James Burk, "The Decline of Mass Armed Forces and Compulsory Military Service," *Defense Analysis* 8, no. 1 (1992): 44–49.

9. Although the U.S. Congress adopted a national draft law in 1863, only 2 percent of the Union Army were draftees. The vast majority of Civil War soldiers on both sides were volunteers. Modern conscription came to America during World War I. John Whiteclay Chambers II, "Decision for the Draft," *Magazine of History* 17 (October 2002): 26.

10. George G. Flynn, "Conscription and Equity in Western Democracies, 1940–75," *Journal of Contemporary History* 33 (January 1998): 5–20.

11. Detlef Bald, "Sechs Legenden über Wehrpflicht und Demokratie," *Blätter für Deutsche und internationale Politik* (Bonn) 6 (1997): 731–741.

12. By "national wars," Moltke was referring to the fact that only organized nation-states could maintain mass armies that were able to wage war on such a large scale. Ibid., 736.

13. Named for then-president of the French Republic Marie-Joseph-Louis-Adolphe Thiers. Flynn, "Conscription and Equity," 6.

14. For more on this, compare Samuel P. Huntington, *The Soldier and the State: The Theory and Politics of Civil-Military Relations* (1957; repr., London: Harvard University Press, 1994), 37–39.

15. Ibid.

16. Ibid., 11.

17. For a less sanguine view of elitist attitudes within the U.S. armed forces, see Guttieri, chapter 9 of this volume.

18. About 1.8 million eighteen-year-old men register in the United States each year, which represents a 91 percent compliance rate among all eligible men. Selective Service System registration information is available at http://www.sss.gov/regist.htm.

19. Peter M. Beattie, "Conscription versus Penal Servitude: Army Reform's Influence on the Brazilian State's Management of Social Control, 1870–1930," *Journal of Social History* 32, no. 4 (1999): 853.

20. Uki Goñi, "Argentina's Military Up for Sale," in *First Page for Argentina* (Buenos Aires, 1996), http://ukinet.com/media/text/military.htm.

21. Paul Klein, *Wehrpflicht und Wehrpflicht heute* (Baden-Baden: Nomos, 1991), 125.

22. W. Allen Wallis, *An Overgoverned Society* (New York: Free Press, 1976), 47.

23. Gustav Däniker, *Wende Golfkrieg: Vom Wesen und Gebrauch zukünftiger Streitkräfte* (Frankfurt: Report-Verlag, 1992), 167–188.

24. Karl Haltiner, "The Definite End of the Mass Army in Western Europe," *Armed Forces and Society* 25 (1998): 7–36.

25. See Doug Bandow, "Responding to Terrorism: Conscription Is Not the Answer," *USA Today*, January 2003, 10.

26. Ibid., 12.

27. Heinz Magenheimer, "Zur Frage der allgemeinen Wehrpflicht: Standortbestimmung-Alternativen-Konsequenzen," *Schriftenreihe der Landesverteidigungsakademie* 3 (1999): 39.

28. Christopher Dandeker, *Facing Uncertainty: Flexible Forces for the Twenty-First Century*, National Defense College, Department of Leadership (Karlstad, Sweden: Klaria Tryckeri AB, 1999), 27.

29. Gordon R. Sullivan, "The Volunteer Force and the Burden of Peace," in *Professionals on the Front Line*, ed. Fredland et al., 28.

30. Only two countries that also draft women are known to the author: Israel and Mozambique.

31. The term "unsettlement" is used by prominent communitarian Michael Walzer to describe the problematic decomposition of society into the mere coexistence of individuals. A concise account of his "Four Mobilities" leading to this unsettlement is to be found in Michael Walzer, "The Communitarian Critique of Liberalism," *Political Theory* 18, no. 1 (1990): 6–24.

32. Johannes Messner, *Das Naturrecht: Handbuch der Gesellschaftsethik, Staatsethik und Wirtschaftsethik* (Munich: Tyrolia Verlag, 1966), 884.

33. Other aspects of social order such as anthropology, ethnology, or the judiciary are of lesser importance to systems theory and are not a part of this analysis.

34. Compare Georg Kneer and Armin Nassehi, *Niklas Luhmanns Theorie sozialer Systeme: Eine Einführung* (Munich: UTB W. Fink, 1994), 21.

35. The idea of comprehending individual elements only in their distinct relationships as part of a larger whole is rooted in the philosophical tradition. Hegel, in the preface of the *Phenomenology of Mind,* for instance, emphasized that "the truth is only realized in the form of system." G. W. F. Hegel, *The Phenomenology of Mind,* trans. J. B. Baillie (London: George Allen and Unwin, [1807] 1966), 85.

36. See Talcott Parsons, *Structure and Process in Modern Societies* (Glencoe, IL: Free Press, 1960); and Parsons, *Sociological Theory and Modern Society* (New York: Free Press, 1967).

37. Talcott Parsons, *Zur Theorie sozialer Systeme* (Opladen, Germany: Westdeutscher Verlag, 1976), 168.

38. The idea that the choice of a certain form of recruitment is also a decision on values was one result of discussions at a symposium held at the Bundeswehr University Munich, July 17–19, 1996. Proceedings of the symposium: Armin A. Steinkamm and Dietmar Schoessler, eds., *Wehrhafte Demokratie 2000—Zu Wehrpflicht und Wehrstruktur* (Baden-Baden: Nomos, 1999), 173.

39. Parsons, *Structure and Process,* 41–44.

40. Spain, for example, had the largest number of conscientious objectors in the world. In 1996 the number reached a peak of more than 100,000, which was more than half of the age group drafted in that year.

41. Beth J. Asch and John T. Warner, "Should the Military Retirement System Be Reformed?" in *Professionals on the Front Line,* ed. Fredland et al., 175–206.

42. Huntington, *The Soldier and the State* (1957; Cambridge, MA: repr., 1998), 11.

43. Flynn, *Conscription and Equity,* 8.

44. Magenheimer, *Zur Frage der allgemeinen Wehrpflicht,* 83.

Chapter 9
Professional Military Education in Democracies

KAREN GUTTIERI

> *For most . . . the matter of learning is one of personal preference. But for [military] officers, the obligation to learn, to grow in their profession, is clearly a public duty.*
> GENERAL OMAR N. BRADLEY

EDUCATION is a central function of military organization. To illustrate, the basic military term "doctrine," used to refer to the principles that guide military forces in action, derives from an original meaning of "something taught; a teaching."[1] "Professional military education" (PME), a popular contemporary term, likewise emphasizes a fundamental connection between education and the military as a profession. Indeed, the establishment of formal military education both accompanied and defined the military as a recognized profession in Europe and, later, in the United States. The French were the first to develop a system of schools for their officers, beginning in the seventeenth century. Napoléon Bonaparte, himself a graduate of the Royal Military School, made education for officer candidates routine.[2] Today many military forces directly tie career advancement to completion of educational requirements. Military educational programs tend to focus on the professional officer corps, leaders within the military structure.[3]

The word "education" implies the acquisition of general knowledge and skills required for effectiveness, as opposed to "training," which implies "preparation to perform[ing] specific functions, tasks, or missions."[4] "Education" as applied to the armed services may also take on the patina of indoctrination, that is, shaping values and behavior, including those necessary for unit cohesion, morale, and—significantly—obedience to political authority. Professional military education therefore has a role to play both in civil-military relations at home and in military effectiveness abroad. Ideally, professional military education will empower the military to implement policy and at the same time discourage military leaders from seeking to make policy.

Even in states that enjoy very stable civil-military relations, what the military thinks matters in the implementation of policy and the shaping of it. Military leaders possess highly specialized knowledge unavailable to most people outside the active armed services that can give them the upper hand in debates with civilians over policy issues. Even civilian leaders who are well educated regarding military affairs tend to depend on advice from professional officers when it comes to matters directly concerning the armed forces.[5]

This chapter examines various ways that education might sustain civilian control of the military, noting that not all civilian control is democratic. In democracies, education is particularly vital as a conduit of a professional military ethos. This "objective control" and "professionalization" model, famously advanced by Samuel P. Huntington, is value laden, despite its name. Examination of professional military education in the United States, the world's most powerful democracy, highlights both benefits and costs of this approach. After two centuries, civilian control in the United States is stable, but not without other troublesome indications of a divide between the military and society in general and of policy differences with the civilian leadership in particular. Furthermore, military officers themselves declare that their education system is providing too little preparation for the kind of stability operations that constitute the bulk of America's current burden in Iraq, Afghanistan, and the Balkans and in homeland security. The requirements for civil-military synergy in modern missions, combined with a civil-military gap, suggest a need to develop professional civil-military education.

Learning to Control the Military

Civilian control—military subordination to civilian political rule—is the fundamental principle of civil-military relations and a prerequisite for functional democracy. Two primary indicators of democratic civilian control of the armed forces are, first, that an elected civilian official is commander in chief of the armed forces and, second, that military officers abstain from political activity. This separation also makes it imperative that civilians develop the expertise to manage defense issues, oversee military competence, and ensure obedience.

Some posit an inverse relationship between society's dependence on its armed forces and its control of those forces; that is, the more a society depends on its military to maintain civil order and guard against internal and external threats to its existence, the less control over the armed forces civilian leaders are likely to be able to exert without risking a revolt.[6] The dilemma of civilian control is that the more competent and powerful the military becomes—as a result of weapons procurement or education programs, for example—the more easily the military might also overthrow civilian rule.

How can civilian authorities empower the military without in turn being overpowered by it? Military *intervention* in government has been described alternatively as the result of failure by the state to govern or as the result of organizational self-preservation within the armed services. Military *obedience* has been attributed to both external and internal factors. According to one explanation, structural features of the international system—for example, the presence of some external threat—combine with a low concern about domestic challengers.[7] Other explanations emphasize beliefs and norms in the military organization, or the *culture* of the military. The theme of military professionalism, in particular, looms large in these explanations.

Education that shapes officers' beliefs and norms regarding the military's role in relation to the executive, the legislature, and civil society sets a tone for civil-military relations. Education of military officers is particularly significant in states in transition to democracy. The uncertainties that characterize the first steps toward democracy can give false appeal to the apparent certainty of military rule; education mitigates the uncertainty that derives from not knowing or understanding.

There are several ways to achieve civilian control that in turn require more or less attention to indoctrination and education. Some types of civilian control that arise in nondemocratic states involve more attention to indoctrination and ideological education than others do. Even in the United States, where professionalism is widely portrayed as the key to military subordination, ensuring obedience has not always relied on the professionalism of military officers; in fact, at first the situation was quite the reverse.

Privilege and Rank—The Traditional Model

A prominent example of nondemocratic civilian control is the traditional-aristocratic model, in which social status and military rank are comparable.[8] There is little question whether military officers will comply with civilian ruling elites if those officers are blood members of that ruling class. European nobility in the seventeenth century committed their children to military service, just as they sent others into the church and government to ensure control of those institutions by family bonds.

The founders of the United States, who shared these suspicions that a standing military force might become a danger to its government and people, were determined not to support a permanent, paid force in arms. England had garrisoned troops in Boston after the French and Indian War (1754–1763) to be sure that settlers would obey regulations and pay taxes. American distrust of standing armies that might serve as instruments of tyranny grew from this colonial experience. Firebrand revolutionary Samuel Adams declared, "A Standing Army, however necessary it may be at some times, is always dangerous to the Liberties of the People." Although an army might be needed in war, this force would be temporary. At the 1787 Constitutional Convention, Elbridge Gerry declared:

> Standing armies in time of peace are inconsistent with the principles of republican Governments, dangerous to the liberties of a free people, and generally converted into destructive engines for establishing despotism.[9]

The Americans expected that their national military force would not be professional. And in practice there was little distinction between "the professional officer and the private gentleman."[10] This is not to say, however, that officers disdained civilian political supremacy. General George Washington, supreme commander of the Continental Army and first president of the United States, firmly believed in civilian control of the military. He declared his loyalty to his civilian masters at a meeting of Continental Army leaders in Newburgh, New York, in March 1783. In doing so, he likely helped quell a movement under way by other military leaders to desert Congress and establish an alternate regime.

It once was commonplace for military officers, including such notables as Andrew Jackson and Zachary Taylor, to engage in politics, even to campaign for public office, while in uniform. Military historian Russell Weigley notes that early American gentleman-soldiers moved back and forth between political roles "without threatening civil supremacy because they were essentially civilians themselves, more than they were professional soldiers with any distinctively military outlook."[11] In this new democracy, the dual role of elites had the same net effect as the traditional-aristocratic framework of civil-military relations: it served to ensure regime loyalty and civilian control.

Penetration of Military Minds

Another means to ensure military compliance with political direction is to see that officers and enlisted personnel share the worldview of the political leadership. A "penetration," or subjective, model of political control focuses on the belief system of the officer corps. This approach—practiced in communist states, including the former Soviet Union and present-day China—depends on sociopolitical indoctrination, on the assumption that the potential for conflict is mitigated when political elites and military officers share values.[12] In an interview conducted in 1966, a lieutenant in the Vietnamese People's Liberation Army illustrated the way state-imposed ideology shaped his sense of political order: "They taught me to believe in Marxism-Leninism . . . what a peasant should do, a city-dweller should do, a worker should do."[13]

Not all communist nations indoctrinated their militaries in exactly the same way. Differences in educational emphasis can help explain the different reactions of each newly independent state's military as communism collapsed in 1989 and postcommunist regimes attempted to consolidate their rule.[14] In some Warsaw Pact states, such as Romania, military education actually put more weight on indoctrination than on professional training; this was not true, however, in Hungary or Poland. Romania's already highly politicized officer corps grew increasingly alienated from President Nicolae Ceausescu's brutal regime and played an active role in its dissolution. As material conditions for the Romanian armed forces worsened, Ceausescu sought to destabilize and divide the military through frequent shuffles in the defense establishment's leadership. Instead of weakening the will of the officer corps, however, his machinations succeeded only in radicalizing it into taking political action. In Hungary, by contrast, the more professionally trained military did not interfere when the communist government gave way peacefully to a civilian one.

In general, those communist nations that emphasized professional competence were more likely to undergo a gradual transfer of power as communist rule ended, without military interference. The reluctance of the powerful Soviet military to launch a coup between 1989 and 1991, even as the state fell apart around it, is compelling evidence that military culture matters.[15] Many factors are at play in complex regime transitions, such as prior levels of military interference in politics, the willingness of politicians to allow change to go forward, and the peacefulness or violence of popular involvement in the process of change. The experiences of the early 1990s, however, support the notion that military organizational culture also influences the decision of military leaders to intervene—or not—in politics.

Education of the Nation-in-Arms

A study of Israel suggests another model for establishing civilian control over the military that shares some characteristics of both the traditional and penetration models. Israel officially is a secular liberal state, and yet religion, traditional Jewish rites and symbols, and Hebrew biblical terminology are basic components of life in the Israeli Defense Forces (IDF).[16] More importantly, Israel is the archetype of a nation-in-arms, whose highly militarized culture permeates society as much as it indoctrinates the armed services.

Military service in Israel is universal (for men and women) and compulsory; this shared experience thus becomes part of the fabric of Israeli national identity, and military education effectively becomes social education. The military thus serves an "integrative" role, as described by mid-century theories on nation building and modernization.[17] After noting that the primary IDF mission was the security of the state, the first prime minister of Israel and later minister of defense, David Ben-Gurion, added:

> The army must also serve as an educational and pioneering nucleus for Israeli youth—for both the native-born and the newcomer. It is the duty of the army to educate a pioneer generation, healthy in body and spirit, courageous and loyal, which will weld together the exiles and disparate elements and prepare them to fulfill, through self-realization, the historic tasks of the state of Israel.[18]

At the same time that the Israeli military plays an integrative role in nation building, through public works projects and the normative effects of mandatory universal service, the IDF and the nation must respond in concert to the structural imperative of state survival in a threatening neighborhood. These circumstances prompt civilian leaders to become better informed about national security issues and also more deferential to military competence and requests for funding.

Some scholars have made a virtue of the interpenetration of the military and civilian realms in Israel, as a reciprocal relationship that built a nation and made possible civilian oversight of the military.[19] Uri Ben-Eliezer disagrees and characterizes the purposes of liberal democracy in such a state as more or less incidental relative to its raison d'être: to wage war.[20] National militarism in Israel extends to social institutions, such as a radio station that is staffed by both civilians and soldiers. Interpenetration of spheres to such a degree blurs distinctions "between the soldier and the citizen and between civilian support and the military's front line."[21] At the same time, some scholars warn that high levels of internal threat, such as the Palestinian *intifada* facing the IDF, orient the military to internal tasks, which in turn tends to politicize military officers. The nation-in-arms may be immune to a military coup but can be so militaristic as to make a coup not so much untenable as unnecessary.

Education is of very little importance in the traditional-aristocratic model of civilian control; in the penetration model, it is essential. In the nation-in-arms, education is vital, but ironically, it is the military that does the "educating" of society rather than the reverse. The education requirements for the liberal democratic model of political control, illustrated in the next section, are more complex yet just as fundamental to stability. This model depends, in a word, on professionalism.

Professionalism in Liberal Democracies

The liberal democratic model of civil-military relations dates from the emergence of democratic rule in eighteenth-century Europe and the "professionalization" of armies freshly separated from more domestically oriented civil police. At the same time, military institutions also established systems of formal instruction in the art of war. Much more recently, some countries such as the United States have instituted a military that is "all-volunteer" and hence fully professional.

The liberal democratic model requires the armed forces to accept the basic legitimacy of the state, obey civilian policy guidance, and narrowly apply martial skills to the management of conflict. Military obedience in democracies includes respect for democratic processes, whatever the outcome. In the United States, this demands legal and professional loyalty, not to a particular administration, but to the Constitution.[22]

As described by Samuel P. Huntington in his classic work, *The Soldier and the State*, the appropriate mode of political control in democracies is objective civilian control, an approach premised on separate institutional roles for political and military leaders.[23] This framework has become the "normal theory" of civil-military relations.[24] A nonpoliticized, professional military will likely be too busy with technical and operational considerations to become distracted by political affairs. Unlike subjective control methods that indoctrinate military personnel to share the leadership ideology, as was seen in the Soviet Union and other authoritarian regimes, objective control embraces differences between civilian and military realms.

The orderliness of martial life, contrasting sharply as it does with the messiness of politics, is just one measure of the somewhat rarefied world in which members of the armed forces live relative to that of their fellow citizens. A military career requires that service be provided solely to the state as long as one is in uniform, and it may involve the ultimate sacrifice of one's own life. Although remaining a full citizen, by joining the military the recruit voluntarily forgoes freedoms that most civilians take for granted, such as regular working hours at a job of choice, retirement without obligation to return to duty at need, and protection from mandatory requirements such as random drug or disease testing, which could be regarded as unconstitutional outside the armed services. Military professionalism excludes a career in politics, at least while in uniform. These differences make for a distinct military worldview, as described by Lieutenant Colonel Daniel Miltenberger:

> Certainly there is a distance, if not a divide, between military personnel and civilians in terms of how they view their jobs. In part, this distinctive outlook is a reflection of the special nature of the military as an institution—a reflection, that is, of the specific tasks it is expected to accomplish and the manner in which it organizes to accomplish them. In part, it reflects a deeper-seated set of convictions about how the world works, and a set of core values about how people ought to behave.[25]

Education plays a significant role in the professionalism of the military officer. Continuing education figures prominently on Sam Sarkesian and Robert Conner's list of elements of professionalism, described in their 1999 study of professionalism in the U.S. armed forces:

1. The organization has a defined area of competence based on expert knowledge.
2. There is a system of continuing education designed to maintain professional competence.
3. Members have an obligation to society and must fulfill it without concern for remuneration.
4. A system of values within the organization perpetuates professional character and fosters relations with society.
5. The organization has control over its system of rewards and punishments and is in a position to determine the quality of those entering the profession.[26]

The first item, expert knowledge, and the fourth, a system of values, depend on the existence of a system of education to foster these qualities, while the second supposes that military education continues throughout the career of the professional officer.

The so-called objective model of civilian control actually depends on a value-laden set of cultural norms. The argument in favor of objective control is circular and is about internalization of a principle: once military officers internalize the norm of civilian control, such control has de facto been established.[27] Professionalism is likewise defined as a commitment to a set of shared values specific to the profession, inculcated through specialized education or training. Don Snider, Robert Priest, and Felisa Lewis thus describe "a moral obligation" among military personnel to serve society: "Called to their profession and its stewardship of the knowledge of war, and motivated by their social obligation and pursuit of excellence, officers are committed to a career of continuous study and learning."[28]

Professionalization is often portrayed as a panacea against military intervention in politics, but experience shows that this is not necessarily the case. U.S. policy encouraged Latin American governments to make their militaries professional in the 1960s and 1970s, but some of those that did were overthrown anyway.[29] U.S. policymakers, however, had violated another of Huntington's proscriptions by persuading these same militaries to assume constabulary roles and orient themselves toward internal defense.[30]

Some observers blame military interventions in Latin America in the 1960s and 1970s on the civilian leaders themselves. Elected leaders, they suggested, might have manipulated—and thus politicized—the officer corps to win support for partisan agendas, or they might simply have failed to address pressing socioeconomic problems. The highly institutionalized military, believing itself more capable of enforcing reforms, would have been strongly tempted to step in and "put things right."[31] If an actual or perceived imbalance between military and civilian capability matters, so does the education and indoctrination of the military. Steven Angerthal notes: "The implication contained in this approach is that military training that frames political competence and government legitimacy as issues that deserve military attention would be interventionist."[32]

There is reason to think that military attitudes toward civil society make a difference in how well officers accept the principle of civilian control. Argentine military officers who supported the successful 1976 military coup against elected president Isabel Perón defined their patriotic values in terms of "protecting the nation and its security concerns," but those who did not support the coup cited "esteem for civil society and respect for the popular interest."[33] A military education system that frames the actions of an elected government as dangerous to the nation, as Angerthal describes in the Argentine case, implicitly promotes military intervention. By the same token, professional military education that fails to recognize and bridge a potential culture gap between the military and society is, by implication, negligent.

What then is the appropriate role of professional military education in a liberal democracy? Significant differences of opinion stem from different views about the desirability of interpenetration between the civil and military spheres.

Schools of Thought on Military Education

In 1957, the same year that Huntington published *The Soldier and the State*, John Masland and Laurence Radway published *Soldiers and Scholars: Military Education and National Policy*.[34] The two books drew very different conclusions. Huntington maintained that the soldier should be limited to "professional" tasks in order to ensure civilian supremacy, while Masland and Radway countered that military officers with a fuller understanding of policy would be better able to implement it and less likely to challenge civilian authority.

These views form the basis of two general approaches to military education: that it should either be confined to narrow technical subjects in segregated military academies or be open to include a solid liberal education in the company of civilians. The first approach requires that boundaries be drawn around purely military-technical knowledge, a model that is both difficult and unwise. Civilian control depends on educated civilians as well as military officers, and it depends on effective communication between the two. Civilians must understand military matters if they are to manage national security policy competently, and military officers must understand policies in order to implement them effectively. Segregating military education physically and intellectually is counterproductive to these aims.

A military that becomes too alienated from its parent society is in danger of losing legitimacy and support.[35] For this reason, civilian values must be supreme within the military as well as society in general. In those cases where civilian values preclude military effectiveness (such as the value of civil liberties versus the need to obey orders), civilian leaders should be the ones who decide to what degree democratic freedoms are limited within the military. To maintain the armed forces' political legitimacy, military culture must reflect the values of the larger society.[36] The evidence is increasing that all-volunteer armed services even in the most stable democracies may be susceptible to elitism and a growing sense of separation from civil society by virtue of the very kinds of indoctrination that foster effectiveness and cohesion as a professional fighting force.

An apparently growing civil-military divide in the United States troubles some analysts who participated in a Triangle Institute for Security Studies (TISS) study. Through an extensive survey conducted between 1998 and 2000, these scholars intended to capture American civilian and military perspectives on society, national security, military professionalism, and the civil-military relationship. The project led the researchers to the conclusion that "numerous schisms and trends have undermined civil-military cooperation and in some circumstances harmed military effectiveness; they will, if not addressed, continue to do so and with worsening consequences."[37] For example, although the civilian elites surveyed were evenly divided in political loyalty between the Democratic and Republican parties, military respondents identified with the Republican party by margins of six to one or greater. As Ole Holsti observes, "Military elites are clearly abandoning non-partisanship; whereas in the 1976 FPLP [Foreign Policy Leadership Project] survey, 55 percent identified their party affiliations as 'independents,' 'other,' or 'none,' the comparable figure in the TISS survey was only 28 percent for the elite military and 27 percent for active reservists."[38]

Partisan political activity is also on the rise, though it is not confined to members of the Republican party. Examples include public endorsements and criticisms of government policy by both serving and retired military officers and, in one instance, an unprecedented display of military weaponry—at a cost of hundreds of thousands of dollars—to delegates of the 2000 Republican National Convention in Philadelphia.[39]

The culture gap thesis is generally concerned with whether the public might cease to support the military. The problem in the United States, however, is not public confidence in the armed forces but the reverse. The American people consistently express higher confidence in the armed services than in most other government institutions.[40] The sentiment is not reciprocated. Thomas Ricks in 1997 noted with alarm that the U.S. Marine Corps was manifesting real alienation from society: "New Marines seemed to experience a moment of private loathing for public America." He cited retired admiral Stanley Arthur, a commander of U.S.

naval forces during the 1991 Gulf War who also warned of changes in recent years: "Today the armed forces are no longer representative of the people they serve. More and more, enlisted [men and women] as well as officers are beginning to feel that they are special, better than the society they serve. This is not healthy in an armed force serving a democracy."[41] The Triangle Institute survey confirmed Ricks's findings. Analysts Paul Gronke and Peter Feaver report, "Few of the elite military officers agreed with any positive statements about society at all; the elite military's negative assessment of the moral state of civilian society is widely shared, at least among respondents to our survey."[42]

This evidence of military disdain for civilian culture in a firmly rooted democracy is disturbing. It might be much more troubling in a nation in democratic transition. A military without respect for society and democratic norms of national leadership is vulnerable to manipulation by ideologues with antidemocratic agendas and can become a means of repression against the population it is intended to protect.

After the Vietnam War, the United States ended conscription. An increased reliance on reserve forces was developed in part to mitigate the social gap opened by professionalization, but separateness lingers. Today military distinctiveness sometimes manifests as military elitism and must be judged for its compatibility with America's societal and global security interests.

Military Education in the United States

In the United States, appreciation of the value of a broad education for officers developed only over time. Congress established the U.S. Military Academy at West Point on the Hudson River in 1802, but this still did not signal a full commitment to military education. West Point began with a narrow focus on engineering, as would the U.S. Naval School, later known as the U.S. Naval Academy, founded in 1845 at Annapolis, Maryland. Before the Civil War, when the traditional-aristocratic system of nepotism and patronage prevailed, a powerful name and family connections were much more likely than professional education to determine a young man's service prospects. As Samuel Huntington noted, the prestige of West Point did not develop immediately: "Of the Army's thirty-seven generals from 1802 to 1861, not one was a West Pointer; twenty-three were virtually without military experience and eleven others entered the service at the grade of captain or higher."[43] Congress continued to resist the establishment of a professional army based on formal military education. William Eustis, the secretary of war between 1808 and 1813, refused even to call newly appointed academy cadets to active duty.[44]

Huntington maintained that professionalization began at a time when the U.S. Army was relatively isolated from civil society, following the Civil War. Education became the means by which the officer corps were professionalized and separated from their social base. Once rank at birth ceased to determine one's potential rank as an officer, military service became attractive as a means for members of the laboring classes to improve their station in life. The services, now isolated organizationally and reduced in number by Congress, focused on the development of their officers' professional character.

This forced isolation marked the beginning of a transition from the citizen-soldier to a professional with conservative values largely at odds with those of American society. It created a sense of separateness and professionalism that Huntington considered vital to military effectiveness in the global wars of the next century.[45]

General William T. Sherman, commanding general of the U.S. Army, promoted a system of military education that would provide both the fundamentals of a liberal education and opportunities for advanced professional development. This program included indoctrination in liberal democratic values that embraced military subordination to civilian control and an avoidance of politics that included refraining from any expression of political opinion. When asked whether he would consider serving in public office, Sherman answered, "I will not accept if nominated, and will not serve if elected."[46] The worldview espoused by Sherman was based on a strict separation of spheres; this outlook explained his strong objections to the use of the army as a police force. If education would teach officers the workings of democracy, indoctrination would make it clear that democratic procedures had no place within military organizations.

Sherman, looking to other nations as models for a system of professional military education in the United States, appointed West Point graduate Emory Upton to study the armies of Asia and Europe.[47] Upton subsequently introduced reforms into U.S. military education that mirrored the much-admired Prussian system. Beginning with a broad general education in public schools or military-run cadet houses, this system then formally linked levels of instruction with the progression of an officer's military career. This tiered system allowed each new level of learning to build upon those that came before, as well as on the experience of the student. These linkages remain evident today in the rank-based progression that U.S. military education follows in the teaching of contemporary policy.[48]

The U.S. system today encompasses five levels of military education related to the five phases of an officer's career, as specified in the Chairman of the Joint Chiefs of Staff (CJCS) Joint Professional Military Education Framework. The first stage prepares the candidate to become a commissioned officer. This primary-level study takes place at branch, warfare, or staff specialty schools and focuses on tactics and preparation for that branch or specialty. Intermediate-level education of midgrade officers—majors and lieutenant commanders with more than eleven years of service—widens the focus to the operational as well as the tactical level of war.[49] The senior program includes study at the strategic level, along with an examination of other instruments of national power (diplomatic, economic, and informational). Finally, all those achieving the rank of general officer/field officer must complete a six-week capstone course within two years of confirmation. The next sections examine two of these levels, the precommissioning and senior programs.

Precommissioning Education

Although the service academies—West Point, Annapolis, and the Air Force Academy at Colorado Springs—are the most well-known precommissioning programs in the U.S. military, they are not the only or even the most common path to a commission. Officer Candidate Schools (OCSs) enable selected enlisted personnel and noncommissioned officers to gain entry to the officer corps, and they serve as the primary route for commissioning in the Marine Corps. Some services require a college degree to participate in the fourteen-week OCS course.

The Reserve Officer Training Corps (ROTC), offered as two-to-four-year programs in military instruction at civilian colleges and universities, is the largest source of officers in the U.S. armed forces.[50] Generals Colin Powell (national security adviser, chairman of the Joint Chiefs of Staff, and later secretary of state) and John Shalikashvili (chairman of the Joint Chiefs of Staff) participated in ROTC programs. The ROTC solution to a shortage of officers after the Civil War once again was a reflection of America's cultural distrust of standing armies. Congress sought to train more officers without expanding West Point, fearing that a larger, better-funded academy would make it impossible to reduce the army's size at will later on. At the same time, it was equally evident that the increasingly diverse national economy needed a broader and more accessible public system of higher education. The 1862 Land-Grant Act gave federally controlled public lands to states so that they might sell them in order to endow colleges that would include military tactics among the areas of study.[51] In this way, a nation that was only reluctantly supplanting a citizen-based militia with a permanent professional force found a way to foster and sustain cultural links between society and the officer corps. This system of public support became more regularized in the National Defense Act of 1916, which formally established the ROTC. The act also created federal military scholarships—a program it expanded in 1964— as incentives for military study, thus setting a precedent for the extensive use of educational incentives in military recruiting today.

In 1997 a study group on professional military education chaired by former U.S. defense secretary (and later vice president) Richard Cheney rejected an argument that OCS and ROTC can supplant the service academies. Aside from their role as institutions of professional learning, the academies have been described as "the repositories of service ethos."[52] Admission to the four-year academy programs after high school is extremely competitive and very expensive for the taxpayer, but academy-trained officers tend to stay in service longer and rise higher in rank. Although the academies produced only 14 percent of the total officer pool in 1989, academy graduates included 30 percent of army and air force generals and 45 percent of navy admirals.

Some critics, however, regard the pervasiveness of academy graduates in the upper ranks as the result of an "old boy" network that has persisted to a greater or lesser degree since the academies were founded, rather than being a testament to the value of the academies themselves. The military as an institution has in general been an integrative force in America. Future U.S. civil-military relations will be affected by the degree to which the services demonstrate respect for and equal opportunity for women and ethnic minorities, including opportunities for equal education and promotion.

Volker Franke's study of West Point cadets in 1997 concluded that the inculcation of warrior values came at the expense of "learning peace"—that is, preparing for the peacekeeping and stability operations so prevalent in modern conflict.[53] Even so, Snider and his colleagues found that academy students were less likely than their ROTC counterparts at Duke University to see the military role in black-and-white terms. Less promising was respondents' surprising willingness (ranging from 30 to 50 percent of those polled) to be actively involved in political activities such as lobbying for public support of the military's positions on policy, influencing the decision whether to intervene militarily in other nations, or setting public policy goals. According to the researchers, the results showed "serious misunderstandings on the part of both sets of students as to what constitutes proper civil-military relations."[54]

The responsibility of officers to advise political leaders on military matters and then execute policy highlights the importance of undergraduate education in international security for the officer corps. Daniel J. Kaufman asserts that the service academies should "prepare graduates . . . for positions of responsibility in both operational and policymaking assignments."[55] The line between advice and advocacy in modern war planning, however, is not clearly drawn. This concern is greater still for the senior-level courses.

Senior-Level Programs

Senior-level one-year programs are available to officers at the rank of o-5 to o-6 (lieutenant colonel and colonel in the army, air force, and marine corps; commander and captain in the navy) from a number of institutions. The faculty of war colleges that provide these programs are mostly active-duty military officers with master's degrees. Enrolled officers may also have earned accredited graduate degrees from civilian universities or the Naval Postgraduate School, where the majority of faculty hold PhD degrees.

The service war colleges owe their creation to Secretary of War Elihu Root, whose General Order 155 established a War College Board in 1901. Root also founded the Army General Staff in 1903, with the Army War College to serve as an adjunct for planning and policy advising.[56] The naval and air war colleges and a small Marine War College came later.

Current official U.S. policy directs the war colleges to "emphasize analysis, foster critical examination, encourage creativity, and provide a progressively broader educational experience."[57] A 2003 report by the National Center for Public Policy and Higher Education seemed to demonstrate these goals are at least to some degree being met. The center's report on student reactions to the impending war in Iraq at the National Defense University and its two colleges, the National War College and the Industrial College of the Armed Forces, observed a heated debate over the invasion of Iraq that came as something of a surprise even to students. The report cited one student's estimate that "only about half of his classmates in the school's prestigious Industrial College of the Armed Forces favored military action in Iraq."[58]

The attention given to civil-military relations varies among the service war colleges, with some, but not all, paying particular attention to ethics. A study by Judith Stiehm, asking whether ethical instruction at the war colleges teaches subordination to civilian political leaders or noncompliance, found that many students held some disturbing attitudes toward the relationship between the country's military and civilian institutions. A survey of officers found them more likely to refuse an "unethical but legal" request than an "unwise but legal" request, causing Stiehm to speculate that "individual judgment is being accorded more importance than either the law or the military hierarchy." [59] Students commonly expressed the belief that society is in decay; that, in order to be respected as commander in chief, the president must have served in uniform; and that the military should advocate for or insist on policy choices rather than sticking to an advisory role.

Education and U.S. Military Effectiveness

Since effectiveness can be a matter of life or death, military organizations have a strong incentive to invest in improvements, such as the latest weaponry and better education for officers. As obvious as the benefits of education may seem, we also know that learning fosters changes in perception and outlook, making education a potentially risky investment for an organization such as the military that depends on strict obedience and complete loyalty. Nevertheless, the risks of a good education are offset by the benefits of competitive advantage in the international security arena, where survival can depend on informed risk-taking and innovation. The current military predominance of the United States is commonly attributed to its investment in military education. General Edward "Shy" Meyer offered his own opinion on the superiority of the U.S. model: "Churchill said that World War II was won in the classrooms of U.S. military schools in the 1920s and 1930s. . . . And I think Desert Storm and the Cold War were won in the military classrooms and training centers during the 1970s and 1980s." [60]

It is surprising then that few scholars have carried out any comparative analyses between the U.S. system and others. Data on global military expenditures, for example, offer no separate information on the percentages of defense spending devoted to military education.

Demoralized after Vietnam, the U.S. Army innovated in peacetime, launching a "doctrinal renaissance" in the 1970s. This was a time when the Soviet Union's armed forces were looking increasingly capable of successfully fighting a conventional war in Europe, while Vietnam had badly shaken America's sense of invulnerability.[61] With prompting by civilian leaders, the U.S. military shifted its focus to warfare of the future, created requirements for intensive joint service training, and began a tectonic shift in the way U.S. military forces prepared for war in general.[62] The training revolution extended to the military schools, creating incentives for professional military education and prompting the development of training and simulation exercises, particularly at the multiservice or joint level. In 1995 the Chairman of the Joint Chiefs of Staff Review Panel Report recommended that war colleges reorient their curricula to reward critical thinking as well as the ability to absorb information, and that the colleges prepare their students for new strategic challenges.[63]

The military-technical revolution is not the only "transformation" in warfare in the latter part of the twentieth century. Today planning for organized combat between uniformed armies on battlefields has become less relevant, and civil-military operations more prominent, than in previous times.[64] Civilians tend to occupy both old and new roles in conflict: as victims, belligerents, audiences, and sometimes uneasy partners to intervening military forces. Nonprofit relief workers and other noncombatants operate in conflict zones alongside soldiers. The military may at times be compelled to handle civilian problems in the event that local government or international agencies cannot or will not do so, as happened in Bosnia and Kosovo.

The nature of current missions in Iraq, Afghanistan, and elsewhere requires military officers to appreciate the nuances of national policy and to work closely with civilian officials, other militaries, and civilians from intergovernmental and nongovernmental agencies. Expanded military roles and missions to support stability operations—also known as military operations other than war, or MOOTW—are a source of tension in the U.S. civil-military relationship, but these so-called nonmilitary tasks are vital to military effectiveness in modern war.

There are indications that the implementation of certain changes, such as those required by the Goldwater-Nichols Act of 1986, have not gone far enough. The U.S. Army Peacekeeping Institute's after-action report on U.S. operations in Bosnia cited serious problems, in particular compartmentalization across headquarters and "stovepiped" planning processes among services, international militaries, and civilian agencies.[65] These kinds of problems can be traced to continuing weaknesses in the education system. General William Crouch, who led the Implementation Force into Bosnia, recalls, "I was on my own. I'd certainly never trained for something like this."[66] In 2002 a Rand report for the army noted that the curricula of the Command and General Staff College and the Army War College did not pay sufficient attention to MOOTW, or stability operations, such as stemming terrorism, providing humanitarian assistance, managing internal defense for countries in conflict, and handling peace operations.[67] The army, in short, was not educating its people for the most likely missions, including the combined-arms cohesion that must be achieved quickly among disparate elements in peacekeeping and stability operations.

Frequent forays in peacekeeping and stability operations, however, create an imperative for learning. The actions of even junior officers in these settings can affect mission success and, potentially, national policy. In 2001 the Army Training and Leader Development Panel reported concerns that the officer education system does not provide "the skills for success in full spectrum operations."[68] In late 2002, in the midst of a major operation in Afghanistan and the ramp-up for war in Iraq, the army proposed to close down the U.S. Army Peacekeeping Institute. After considerable outside lobbying, it gained a new lease on life in 2003 as the Peacekeeping and Stability Operations Institute.

The United States armed forces spent many months in Iraq before putting together effective training packages to teach cultural awareness and management of civilian disturbances. Revelations of American abuses of detainees at Iraq's Abu Ghraib prison, made public in 2004, indicate serious shortcomings in the way military police were prepared for the environment. A recent and very superficial review of courses at the National War College, the Army War College, and the Marine Corps Expeditionary Warfare School identified a smattering of lectures and few course electives on peacekeeping.[69] This finding comes even though a "broad intellectual background" was identified by general officers in a U.S. Institute of Peace study as a key asset in peace operations.[70] This level of preparedness will not be achieved in a two-hour lecture or even a semester-long course.

The Naval Postgraduate School (NPS) in Monterey presents an alternate model. NPS is staffed largely by civilian academics and populated by U.S. and international officers and civilian government officials. Thus, professional civil-military education at NPS provides some civilian influence in the education environment, and yet it also has a depth of course offerings on military affairs unimaginable at civilian institutions. NPS developed an entire master's track in stabilization and reconstruction studies that offers courses specifically focused on regional studies, stability operations, and the political, economic, social, and judicial dimensions of postconflict reconstruction. The stabilization and reconstruction program predates the 2004 Defense Science Board call for U.S. military schools to develop study programs and expertise in this field.[71] Although the first cohort of students who graduated in December 2003 were entirely international, reflecting again the challenges faced by those who believe the American military services should prepare for stability operations, American enrollment should grow as troops return from theaters in Afghanistan and Iraq, and Congress presses the military to prepare for postconflict transitions.

More changes can be expected as the lessons of war shape our understanding of military effectiveness. Education, recruitment demographics and methods, and experience in modern war are combining to transform the self-image of the military. The typical officer has progressed from combat leader to managerial technician and now to the "soldier-scholar," giving civilian degrees new significance for career military personnel.[72] In the words of Charles Moskos and colleagues, this is the era of a "post-modern military."[73] Such changes wreak havoc with the traditional assumption of a clear differentiation between the military and civilian spheres that Huntington saw as vital to stable civil-military relations in a previous era, but such changes may be vital today. It is clear that the educational preparation of officers will matter not only to U.S. military effectiveness but also to the future stability of U.S. civil-military relations.

Conclusion

In a world of rapid change, the competitive edge is gained through the ability to learn, and to do so more quickly than the adversary. Rapid technological advances in war fighting would be both inconceivable and impossible to implement without a long-term investment in the minds of those who put their lives at risk for their nation. Future discussions of professional military education should expand to embrace more fully the larger educational and training context that includes doctrinal development, simulation, and field exercises.

Much of professional military education is focused on doctrinal development and the conduct of analysis relevant to operations, because these kinds of studies make the military smarter as it prepares for and wages war. Doctrine and operations will not be effective in the end, however, if they are ill-suited to policy directives coming from the civilian government. Military education must aim to complement, rather than compete with, liberal democratic leadership and a participatory civil society. Although military indoctrination understandably teaches pride in the distinctiveness of armed service and the esprit de corps that promotes cohesiveness in the field, military education must inculcate loyalty to civil society, respect for the supremacy of civilian leadership, and patience with the messiness of democratic processes.

The importance of military effectiveness offers both a rationale for military education and a potential danger to the democracy the armed forces are expected to defend. In some developing nations, the danger of military effectiveness has been made all too apparent when military leaders decided that because their organizations were comparatively more highly institutionalized and competent than the civilian government, they were "obliged" to stage a coup. Officers who disdain disorder or are unable to resist the blandishments of civilians seeking to politicize the armed forces have taken the reins of government into their own hands, often with disastrous results for the entire country. The challenge for democracies in any stage of development is to teach their military officers an appreciation for, or at the very least a tolerance of, the institutions of democratic governance.

The U.S. military, once regarded as a "hotbed of anti-intellectualism," now invests heavily in the education of its officers. Education has played a vital role in boosting U.S. military effectiveness by fostering the integration of new technologies in battle, shaping unit cohesion, and enhancing multiservice and multinational war fighting. Furthermore, the use of educational inducements attracts and sustains a smart force. American professional military education, however, has not prevented nor overcome the emergence of some troubling cultural divisions between the American military and society at large that must be addressed.

Samuel Huntington promoted a model of objective control that implies a separate and specialized system of education for military officers. The continued viability of this model is questionable, however, given the nature of war today. To remain relevant, professional military education not only must prepare officers for the challenges of new environments but also must address the complex changes in civil-military relations that accompany new modes of war fighting. Effective implementation of policy requires military officers to understand the strategic environment and the purposes of military action as defined by political leaders. In stable democracies, changing roles and missions give the educational system added significance for civil-military coordination. Civilian involvement in professional military education, such as putting nonmilitary instructors and students in the same classroom with officers, in particular seems a valuable approach to keeping military minds both competitive against adversaries and cooperative within liberal democracies.

Notes

The epigraph to this chapter is quoted in Richard B. Cheney, *Professional Military Education: An Asset for Peace and Progress*, ed. Bill Taylor (Washington, DC: Center for Strategic and International Studies, 1997), 17.

1. *American Heritage Dictionary of the English Language*, 4th ed., s.v. "doctrine," http://www.bartleby.com/am/. See also Barry R. Posen, *The Sources of Military Doctrine: France, Britain, and Germany between the Wars* (Ithaca, NY: Cornell University Press, 1984), 13.

2. In the nineteenth century these schools attracted American army officers who came to Europe to study the French system firsthand. See William E. Simons, "Introduction: A PME Panorama," in *Professional Military Education in the United States: A Historical Dictionary*, ed. William E. Simons (Westport, CT.: Greenwood Press, 2000), 1–17.

3. Samuel P. Huntington, *The Soldier and the State: The Theory and Politics of Civil-Military Relations* (1957; repr., Cambridge, MA.: Belknap Press of Harvard University Press, 2002), 3.

4. U.S. Chairman of the Joint Chiefs of Staff, "Officer Professional Military Education Policy," Chairman of the Joint Chiefs of Staff Instruction CJCSI 1800.01A (December 1, 2000), GL-8.

5. See Colin Gray, *Strategic Studies: An Assessment* (Westport, CT: Greenwood Press, 1982).

6. M. D. Feld, "Professionalism and Politicization: Notes on the Military and Civilian Control," in *The Perceived Role of the Military*, ed. M. R. Van Gils (Rotterdam: Rotterdam University Press, 1971), 267–276, esp. 275.

7. Huntington and Finer emphasize the problem of domestic institutional failure's leading to military intervention. See Samuel P. Huntington, *Political Order in Changing Societies* (New Haven, CT: Yale University Press, 1968); and S. E. Finer, *The Man on Horseback: The Role of the Military in Politics*, 2nd ed. (Boulder, CO: Westview Press, 1988). Eric A. Nordlinger, in *Soldiers in Politics: Military Coups and Governments* (Englewood Cliffs, NJ: Prentice-Hall, 1977); and William R. Thompson, in *The Grievances of Military Coup-Makers* (Beverly Hills, CA: Sage Publications, 1973), emphasize the corporate interests of the military. Brian D. Taylor offers military culture as an alternative in "The Soviet Military and the Disintegration of the USSR," *Journal of Cold War Studies* 5, no. 1 (2003): 17–66. For a structural argument, see Michael

Desch, *Civilian Control of the Military: The Changing Security Environment* (Baltimore: Johns Hopkins University Press, 1999).

8. Nordlinger, *Soldiers in Politics*.

9. Cited in Michael F. Cairo, "Civilian Control of the Military," Democracy Papers, U.S. Department of State International Information Programs, http://usinfo.state.gov/products/pubs/democracy/dmpaper12.htm.

10. Sam C. Sarkesian and Robert E. Connor Jr., *The U.S. Military Profession into the Twenty-first Century* (London: Frank Cass, 1999), 34.

11. Russell Weigley, "The American Military and the Principle of Civilian Control from McClellan to Powell," *Journal of Military History* 57 (October 1993): 36.

12. Stephen D. Wesbrook, "Sociopolitical Training in the Military: A Framework for Analysis," in *The Political Education of Soldiers*, ed. Morris Janowitz and Stephen D. Wesbrook (Beverly Hills, CA: Sage Publications, 1982), 15–54.

13. Cited in Wm. Darryl Henderson, "The Vietnamese Army," in Janowitz and Wesbrook, *The Political Education of Soldiers*, 158.

14. Zoltan Barany, "Democratic Consolidation and the Military: The East European Experience," *Comparative Politics* 30, no. 1 (1997): 21–43.

15. Taylor, "The Soviet Military." Taylor's study of *Voennyi Vestnik*, the main journal of the Soviet ground forces, for the years 1980–1991 found a continuing preoccupation with external tasks, so much so that even as the state was on the verge of collapse in 1990–1991, a mere 1 percent of the articles focused on internal security.

16. Stuart A. Cohen, "From Integration to Segregation: The Role of Religion in the IDF," *Armed Forces and Society* 25, no. 3 (1999).

17. Lucien W. Pie, "Armies in the Process of Political Modernization," in *The Role of the Military in Underdeveloped Countries*, ed. John J. Johnson (Princeton, NJ: Princeton University Press, 1962), 69–89.

18. Cited in Amos Perlmutter, "The Israeli Army in Politics: The Persistence of the Civilian over the Military," *World Politics* 20, no. 4 (1968): 623.

19. See Fritz Stern, *The Citizen Army, Key to Defense in the Atomic Age* (New York: St. Martin's Press, 1957); and Dan Horowitz and Moshe Lissak, *Out of Utopia* (Albany: State University of New York Press, 1989).

20. Uri Ben-Eliezer, "A Nation-in-Arms: State, Nation, and Militarism in Israel's First Years," *Comparative Studies in Society and History* 37, no. 2 (1995).

21. Ibid., 285.

22. Don M. Snider, Robert F. Priest, and Felisa Lewis, "The Civil-Military Gap and Professional Military Education at the Precommissioning Level," *Armed Forces and Society* 27, no. 2 (2001): 257.

23. Huntington, *The Soldier and the State*, 31.

24. See Eliot A. Cohen, *Supreme Command: Soldiers, Statesmen, and Leadership in Wartime* (New York: Free Press, 2002).

25. Daniel T. Miltenberger, "The Military," part 3 of *Guide to IGOs, NGOs, and the Military in Peace and Relief Operations*, ed. Pamela Aall, Lieutenant Colonel Daniel T. Miltenberger, and Thomas G. Weiss (Washington, DC: United States Institute of Peace Press, 2000), 207.

26. Sarkesian and Connor, *The U.S. Military Profession*, 21.

27. Finer, *Man on Horseback*, 24–27. See also Bengt Abrahamsson, *Military Professionalism and Political Power* (Beverly Hills, CA: Sage Publications, 1972).

28. Snider et al., "The Civil-Military Gap," 256.

29. Brazil experienced twenty-one years of military rule (1964–1985); Argentina, fourteen years (1966–1973 and 1976–1983); Chile, twelve years (1968–1980); and Uruguay, twelve years (1973–1985). Talukder Miniruzzaman, "Arms Transfers, Military Coups, and Military Rule in Developing States," *Journal of Conflict Resolution* 36, no. 4 (1992): 749.

30. Alfred Stepan, "The New Professionalism of Internal Warfare and Military Role Expansion," in *Armies and Politics in Latin America*, rev. ed., ed. Abraham F. Lowenthal and J. Samuel Fitch (New York and London: Holmes and Meier, 1986), 136.

31. Juan J. Linz and Alfred Stepan, eds., *The Breakdown of Democratic Regimes* (Baltimore: Johns Hopkins University Press, 1978); Guillermo O'Donnell, *Bureaucratic Authoritarianism: Argentina 1966–1973 in Comparative Perspective*, trans. James McGuire with Rae Flory (Berkeley and Los Angeles: University of California Press, 1988).

32. Steven Angerthal, "Officer Training and Democracy: A Study of Argentina" (PhD diss., University of Wisconsin–Madison, 1999), 144–147.

33. Ibid.

34. Huntington, *The Soldier and the State*; John W. Masland and Laurence I. Radway, *Soldiers and Scholars: Military Education and National Policy* (Princeton, NJ: Princeton University Press, 1957). These works were reviewed together by Roger Hilsman in *American Political Science Review* 51, no. 4 (1957): 1091–1094. See also Gene M. Lyons and John W. Masland, *Education and Military Leadership: A Study of the ROTC* (Princeton, NJ: Princeton University Press, 1959).

35. Morris Janowitz in the 1960s and, more recently, Rebecca Schiff, for example, argue for more-integrated civil-military relations. See Morris Janowitz, *The Professional Soldier: A Social and Political Portrait* (Glencoe, IL: Free Press, 1960), 148; and Rebecca L. Schiff, "Civil-Military Relations Reconsidered: A Theory of Concordance," *Armed Forces and Society* 22, no. 1 (1995).

36. The complete list of principles for U.S. civil-military relations from Snider et al., "The Civil-Military Gap," 257, reads as follows:

   1. The military exists for the defense of the state.

   2. The military profession is subordinate to, but delegated limited autonomy by, the political leaders and institutions of government.

   3. Civilian values are supreme, including within the military. In those cases where civilian values preclude military effectiveness, civilian leaders should decide if they are to be limited within the military.

   4. The military must be sufficiently reflective of society and its values to maintain political legitimacy.

   5. Politics is beyond the competence of professional military officers; the officer corps is to remain unpoliticized, particularly in partisan politics.

   6. The responsibilities of the military professional to the state are threefold: representative, advisory, and executive (to carry out the orders of civilian leaders). The military has no advocacy role in political decisions; professionalism and absolute candor must prevail in all such advice and representation.

37. Peter D. Feaver, Richard H. Kohn, and Lindsay Cohn, "The Gap between Military and Civilian in the United States in Perspective," in *Soldiers and Civilians: The Civil-Military Gap and American National Security*, ed. Peter D. Feaver and Richard H. Kohn (Cambridge, MA: MIT Press, 2001), 11.

38. Ole Holsti, "Of Chasms and Convergences," in Feaver and Kohn, *Soldiers and Civilians*, 98.

39. See Steven Lee Myers, "The 2000 Campaign: The Convention; Pentagon Taking Opportunity for Show," *New York Times*, July 28, 2000, A1.

40. Gallup survey as cited by Paul Gronke and Peter D. Feaver, "Uncertain Confidence: Civilian and Military Attitudes about Civil-Military Relations," in Feaver and Kohn, *Soldiers and Civilians*, 134.

41. Thomas E. Ricks, "The Widening Gap between the Military and Society," *Atlantic Monthly*, July 1997, 66, 68.

42. Gronke and Feaver, "Uncertain Confidence," 134.

43. Huntington, *The Soldier and the State*, 206.

44. Simons, "Introduction," 2.

45. Huntington, *The Soldier and the State*, 229.

46. W. T. Sherman, *Memoirs of General W. T. Sherman* (New York: Charles Webster, 1892).

47. E. Upton, *The Armies of Asia and Europe* (New York: D. Appleton, 1878).

48. "In 1973, only 24 percent of all officers had earned advanced degrees; by 1996, that number had increased to 38 percent . . . over 80 percent of Army officers selected for promotion to brigadier general have earned advanced degrees, as compared with approximately 20 percent of their contemporaries in the corporate world." Cheney, *Professional Military Education*, 16.

49. The schools providing this level of education are the Air Command and Staff College, Army Command and General Staff College, College of Naval Command and Staff, Marine Corps Command and Staff College, Marine Corps College of Continuing Education, Joint and Combined Staff Officer School, and the Joint Forces Staff College, as well as international military colleges.

50. In 1995, the ROTC produced 6,400 active-duty commissions; the service academies produced 3,070; and OCSs produced 2,700. Cheney, *Professional Military Education*, 22.

51. Simons, "Introduction," 7–8.

52. Hans Spier, "Review of Masland and Radway," *American Sociological Review* 23, no. 3 (1958): 335–336.

53. Volker Franke, *Preparing for Peace: Military Identity, Value Orientations, and Professional Military Education* (Westport, CT: Praeger, 1999).

54. Snider et al., "The Civil-Military Gap," 270.

55. Daniel J. Kaufman, "Military Undergraduate Security Education for the New Millennium," in *Educating International Security Practitioners: Preparing to Face the Demands of the 21st Century International Security Environment*, ed. James M. Smith, Daniel J. Kaufman, Robert H. Dorff, and Linda P. Brady (Carlisle Barracks, PA: U.S. Army War College, 2001), 8.

56. Samuel J. Newland, "A Centennial History of the U.S. Army War College," *Parameters* (Autumn 2001): 34–42.

57. U.S. Chairman of the Joint Chiefs of Staff, "Officer Professional Military Education Policy", A-B-4.

58. See Kathy Witkowsky, "The Military's Next Generation: Prestigious National Defense University Seeks to Create Strategic Thinkers," *National CrossTalk* 11, no. 2 (2003): 1, 15.

59. Judith Hicks Stiehm, "Civil-Military Relations in War College Curricula," *Armed Forces and Society* 27, no. 2 (2001): 273–294, esp. 286.

60. Cheney, *Professional Military Education*, 16.

61. John L. Romjue, *American Army Doctrine for the Post–Cold War* (Fort Monroe, VA: Office of the Command Historian, U.S. Army Training and Doctrine Command, 1996).

62. Anne W. Chapman, *The Origins and Development of the National Training Center, 1976–1984* (Fort Monroe, VA: Office of the Command Historian, U.S. Training and Doctrine Command, 1992).

63. See Richard Chilcoat, "The Revolution in Military Education," *Joint Forces Quarterly* (Summer 1999): 59–63.

64. See Kalevi J. Holsti, *The State, War, and the State of War* (Cambridge: Cambridge University Press, 1996), 27; Martin van Creveld, *The Transformation of War* (New York: Free Press, 1991); Edward N. Luttwak, "Toward Post-Heroic Warfare," *Foreign Affairs* 74, no. 3 (1995): 109; and Christopher Bellamy, "From Total War to Local War: It's a Revolution," *Independent*, July 23, 1996, 14.

65. See U.S. Army Peacekeeping Institute, *Bosnia-Herzegovina After Action Review Conference Report* (Carlisle Barracks, PA: U.S. Army War College, 1996).

66. Cited in Howard Olsen and John Davis, *Training U.S. Army Officers for Peace Operations: Lessons from Bosnia*, Special Report (Washington, DC: United States Institute of Peace, 1999), 2.

67. David E. Johnson, *Preparing Potential Senior Army Leaders for the Future: An Assessment of Leader Development Efforts in the Post–Cold War Era* (Santa Monica, CA: Rand, 2002). See also U.S. Department of the Army, *The Army Training and Leader Development Panel (ATLDP) Officer Study Report to the Army*, http://www.army.mil/features/ATLD/ATLD.htm. According to Army FM 3-0, "Stability operations promote and protect U.S. national interests by influencing the threat, political, and information dimensions of the operational environment. They include developmental, cooperative activities during peacetime and coercive actions in response to crisis." U.S. Department of the Army, *Operations*, 9-1.

68. U.S. Department of the Army, *ATLDP Officer Study Report to the Army*, oS-2. See also William M. Steele and Robert P. Walters, "Training and Developing Army Leaders," *Military Review* (July–August 2001).

69. Leigh C. Caraher's chapter on military education in Binnendijk and Johnson's *Transforming for Stabilization and Reconstruction Operations* misses many education and training programs outside the National Defense University orbit, including courses at the U.S. Army Peacekeeping and Stability Operations Institute and the Naval Postgraduate School (NPS). Caraher complains of inadequate attention to conflict causes and postconflict reconstruction, but NPS devotes several courses to these topics in a program that includes six courses specifically designed to address issues in postconflict environments. Leigh C. Caraher, "Adapting Culture through Professional Military Education," in *Transforming for Stabilization and Reconstruction Operations*, ed. Hans Binnendijk and Stuart E. Johnson (Washington, DC: National Defense University Press, 2003), 85–92.

70. Olsen and Davis, *Training U.S. Army Officers*, 6.

71. U.S. Office of the Under Secretary of Defense for Acquisition, Technology, and Logistics, *Transition to and from Hostilities*, Defense Science Board 2004 Summer Study (Washington, D.C., 2004), 52.

72. Charles C. Moskos, John Allen Williams, and David R. Segal, "Armed Forces after the Cold War," in *The Postmodern Military: Armed Forces after the Cold War*, ed. Charles C. Moskos, John Allen Williams, and David R. Segal (New York: Oxford University Press, 2000), 1.

73. Five organizational changes characterize the new military form: (1) increased coordination and communication between the civilian and military spheres; (2) a lessening of the rigid differences within the services regarding rank and regarding combat versus service support roles; (3) a shift in understanding of the military's purpose, to include stabilization and peace operations; (4) the need to seek legitimation of missions by the United Nations, NATO, or other supranational organization; and (5) internationalization of military forces as nations increasingly seek to build coalitions to solve international problems. Moskos et al., "Armed Forces after the Cold War," 1.

Conclusion

THOMAS C. BRUNEAU AND SCOTT D. TOLLEFSON

THIS book stands out from the existing literature on civil-military relations, which up until now has focused largely on theory—principal-agent framework or cultural determinism, for example—or single-country case studies, or a combination of these. The contributors to this volume instead have sought to strike an analytical balance between abstract theory and the empirical findings of their own extensive fieldwork around the world in new democracies. Basing our analyses on the New Institutionalist framework, we have tried to locate our theory of civil-military relations in the middle ground between empiricism and abstraction by examining specific institutions of democratic civilian control such as ministries of defense, legislative defense committees, and military budgeting. The orientation of New Institutionalism directed our attention to the proper level of analysis and allowed us to identify the most critical factors that help ensure democratic civilian control of the military.

Two major themes weave through the chapters in this book. First is the importance of civilian interest and expertise in exerting control over the armed forces in a democracy. Second is the need to ensure the military's effectiveness as it attempts to fulfill the roles and missions selected by civilian leaders from the broad spectrum of possibilities available to them. It is important to understand the dynamic relationship between these two core ideas under democracy: far from demanding a trade-off, we maintain that democratic civilian control and military effectiveness actually reinforce one another, echoing Eliot Cohen's thesis on the importance of civilian leaders in waging wars.[1]

The Importance of Civilian Expertise

Some five hundred years ago Niccolo Machiavelli, in his masterful treatise on the art of rule, *The Prince*, emphasized the necessity for civilian leaders to be involved with and develop expertise in matters pertaining to the use of armed force, not only in wartime but also in times of peace.

In the chapter "Military Duties of the Prince," Machiavelli expounds on the need for heads of state to become experts in warfare if they are to be successful rulers.

> A prince . . . should have no other object, no other thought, no other subject of study, than war, its rules and disciplines; this is the only art for a man who commands, and it is of such value [virtù] that it not only keeps born princes in place, but often raises men from private citizens to princely fortune. . . . The quickest way to lose a state is to neglect this art; the quickest way to get one is to study it. . . . Therefore, a prince should never turn his mind from the study of war; in time of peace he should think about it even more than in wartime.[2]

Unlike the hypothetical autocrat of sixteenth-century Europe, democratic leaders in the modern world must of course have many other objects, thoughts, and subjects of study than warfare alone, but a president or a prime minister who ignores the subject altogether may be risking his or her country's security or sovereignty itself.

Our emphasis on the role of civilian expertise may initially seem at odds with the book's overarching focus on the institutional bases of democratic civilian control of the armed forces. Every chapter has maintained that only via democratically established institutions can the armed guardians of a state's security be guarded from their own organizational impulse to take over the reins of government. Yet while academic analysts and international policy scholars can designate the *creation* of a certain set of institutions as the most indispensable element for ensuring democratic civilian control of the military, it is only through the effective *design and use* of these institutions that civilians may actually assert control. It is indeed the case that "the devil is in the details," and it is only civilians with an understanding of these details who will be able to craft and maintain institutions in such a way as to play a central role in the policymaking process.

The curricula at the Center for Civil-Military Relations raise the concept of "institutional engineering" to encourage civilian officials and military officers in its varied seminar programs to think about the best ways to create institutions that will promote not only democratic control over, but also the effectiveness of, the armed forces for ensuring national security and defense. Just as there is a rich literature on creating democratic political institutions, we believe there is a need for a similar body of scholarship on how to create responsive military institutions and the democratic means for their control. It is difficult to see how civilians can exert effective control when they lack access to the necessary expertise for good decision making. Unless a sufficient cadre of well-prepared civilian experts is available to advise political leaders on military questions, civilian control will remain little more than a charade. This situation is evident in many of the countries that CCMR members have visited, such as Taiwan, Indonesia, Guatemala, and Algeria. People entering the military gain the advantages of a professional organization that include an institutionalized body of expertise, a strong corporate identity, and a narrowly delineated code of ethics, as well as varied opportunities for specialized education and training at home and abroad. By contrast, civilians in organizations that deal with national security and defense cannot draw on a comparable sense of identity or corporate knowledge—unless they have served in the military themselves—and they usually lack other opportunities to develop their expertise.

As Jeanne Giraldo pointed out in Chapter 2, there are a number of reasons why politicians are seldom interested in becoming experts in national security and matters pertaining to the armed forces. Furthermore, most countries lack an institutionalized civil service that can offer experts in national security and defense issues the career continuity and stability that would encourage them to fill positions in the executive branch (primarily, but not exclusively, in a ministry of defense) and the legislature. Consequently, civilian control of the armed forces in most Third World democracies is more of an aspiration than a reality.

Military Effectiveness

In Chapter 5, Paul Shemella gave us an idea of the broad range of roles and missions with which governments presently task their militaries. The variety and complexity of those tasks in turn make it difficult to assess the military's actual effectiveness and may even entail a trade-off between flexibility and capability. In the process of organizing themselves to meet the demands of one kind of mission, the armed services may jeopardize their effectiveness in another area. For example, military support to civilian authorities may have negative consequences for peace support operations or territorial defense.

What makes assessing military effectiveness even more difficult is the challenge of finding appropriate and accurate "measures of merit." Unlike a business whose managers can point to profits as an empirical indicator of how well the firm is doing, few government activities can rely on some bottom line that indicates operational effectiveness. In contrast to the fields of education, transport, or agriculture, militaries have no intermediate measures such as number of degrees awarded, kilometers of roads paved, or bushels of grain harvested to which they can point when asked to justify themselves. In the best scenario, a military has proven itself effective as a deterrent to potential aggressors if it has no war to fight. But even if deterrence is the yardstick, how does one measure the real contribution of the military against other variables such as international pressure or diplomacy? To use another example, how do we evaluate the effectiveness of a country's contribution to a peace support operation when its motives for doing so may include winning international favor, receiving money from the United Nations, getting equipment and training from richer and more-developed countries, or promoting the value of the military back home? Which of these goals marks "success," and to whom?

The field of intelligence provides another telling example of this conundrum. An intelligence organization is considered "effective" when nothing happens—at least nothing that those outside the intelligence circle are aware of. It is precisely when the intelligence community acts, in Sherlock Holmes's phrase, as "the dog that didn't bark," that it is considered most effective. In short, when measuring military effectiveness, we often find ourselves struggling to prove the value of a negative, even if roles and missions are clearly defined—a condition that, as Douglas Porch noted in Chapter 4, is seldom the case. It also is important to consider the possible implications of this problem—evaluating effectiveness—for civilian control and expertise. Does the military need civilian allies to ensure its political and societal relevance? If such is the case, do military leaders themselves fully recognize and appreciate the need for civilian allies, or is it a ploy used to persuade them to work with civilians?

The great range of military roles and missions these days has not only enhanced the need for active civilian involvement in national security decision making but also increased the possibility that civilians without military experience might develop the expertise necessary to play a leading role in the national security realm. In some operations, such as military support to civilian authorities and intelligence analysis, civilian experts can easily be as knowledgeable as military officers. In others, such as peace support operations, military tasks are highly specialized at the operational level, but the missions' foreign policy, economic, and social implications mean that civilians have a critically important part to play in their success. It is generally only in traditional territorial defense and at the high end of the combat spectrum that civilians often lack the knowledge and experience boasted by members of the military. Yet military officers we encounter in our programs often refer to these ultimate (yet extremely rare) tasks to belittle the expertise of the civilians they must work with. This tendency indicates there might be as much of a need to deprogram the military from thinking that civilians cannot ever be competent in national security matters as there is to educate the civilians themselves. The best way to ensure such a change in outlook among members of the military will be, as Karen Guttieri explains in Chapter 9, to make sure the military education system inculcates the values and norms of democratic civilian leadership along with more traditional studies.

Civilian policymakers and lawmakers must fulfill two conditions if they are to overcome any lingering, credible military resistance to cooperation. The first is to interest and educate civilians in these issues, and the second is to institutionalize a system of public service in which these specialists can find stable employment where their expertise will be valued. The education of civilians can be accomplished through training, both in-country and abroad. The establishment of a professional civil service is a more difficult hurdle, but one approach might be for other nations to offer foreign military assistance specifically to create and even temporarily fund such positions. CCMR is involved in just such a project with the Colombian Ministry of Defense. Rather than detracting from military effectiveness, the contributors to this volume find that civilian involvement and control will actually enhance it. As we have demonstrated, the perspective must be broad and comprehensive enough to embrace both roles and missions and the institutional bases of civilian control.

At the international level, civilian control in democracies is now virtually expected and makes interaction in military matters between the smaller and larger states, including the United States, easier. Many international military missions must take into account civilian governmental and nongovernmental organizations and the media, tasks civilians generally have an easier time with than do military officers. Domestically, civilian involvement and control in defense issues can enhance perceptions of legitimacy for the military and lead to improvements in such key areas as funding and recruitment. If a democracy's population views the army as alien from civil society, a holdover from the bad old days, or as fulfilling no real purpose, it will be no surprise that the armed services have trouble recruiting high-quality officers and obtaining resources for equipment, training, and operations. Elected officials in the executive and the legislature, supported by a cadre of expert advisers, must be interested in and informed about national security and defense if they are to maintain control over an effective military organization.

Future Work

This book, focusing on the utility of New Institutionalism for analyzing civil-military relations in new democracies, is the first of a planned series of volumes on civil-military relations. Given unlimited space and time, we would have liked to include two other topics in the present analysis: the officer promotion process, which is a basic tool of civilian control of the armed forces, and the complex interaction of the domestic economy and the armed forces, as both producer and consumer, respectively, of goods and services in a society. Both of these topics are the subject of heated disputes in the third-wave democracies and could benefit from examination through the prism of New Institutionalism.

The next book in the series, already in the works, will apply New Institutionalism to the question of how democracies seek to control their intelligence services while ensuring that the nation's intelligence and counterintelligence requirements will be met. The control of intelligence services, which by their very nature must operate with a high level of secrecy, is a major challenge in any democracy. It is even more so in new democracies because in most cases the intelligence services under the previous regimes had functioned primarily as organs of internal state security to intimidate and control their own people. Given the present emphasis on counterterrorism and international crimes such as drug and human trafficking, money laundering, and the like, most countries recognize that they require an effective intelligence service to protect national security. And they are being pressured by other states to establish such effective services. The upcoming volume will use several case studies to explore how different countries are seeking to reform their intelligence services in order to bring them under democratic civilian control while simultaneously ensuring their ability to do the job of intelligence gathering and analysis.

The third book will apply an assessment framework to a set of country case studies to determine how their military organizations fit within the overall context of state and society. The framework consists of a list of questions that address five relevant areas: the political system, the constitutional and legal arrangements regarding the military, the nature and organization of military institutions, the allocation of defense resources, and the anatomy of civil society.

The fourth book, also applying New Institutionalism, will use a set of case studies on civil-military relations in the United States to demonstrate how things *really* work in one of the world's most stable democracies.

Many members of CCMR can offer insights into the system—gained from years of experience in the military, in Washington, or both—that are not typically found in the scholarly literature. In our work abroad we often find that young American officers and inexperienced civilians working in embassies or nongovernmental organizations advise their foreign hosts about civil-military relations based implicitly or explicitly on a model of the United States that is more imaginary than realistic. This book is intended to show that the actual model of American civil-military relations, far more complex than many imagine, can nonetheless illustrate how the military may undertake a broad variety of tasks without challenging civilian control and can be considered a legitimate and necessary asset to the nation and democracy. The U.S. system of democratic civil-military relations works, and works well, but not for the reasons that the uninitiated seem to assume.

As an addition to this series, we envision monographs that analyze specific institutions in individual countries. These might include the founding, establishment, and current roles of the ministry of defense in Brazil and Bulgaria; why Central American republics are embracing peacekeeping operations as a primary mission; the establishment of a national security council in Indonesia; and the means whereby the military generates popular support in Mongolia. The common thread of these studies will be how individual countries found, establish, and operate institutions of democratic civilian control and military effectiveness.

Last but far from least will be a study to describe and analyze the myriad international actors that seek to influence the direction of other countries' national security and defense policies, particularly in the area of civil-military relations. Although there is now a broad literature on the "export of democracy," hardly any focus on the defense and security arenas.[3] Our goal is to develop a research strategy that will allow us to describe and gain an understanding of these complex multinational relationships.

As the world grows smaller through global communications networks, interdependent financial markets, and increasingly powerful trade protocols, democratic nations find themselves and their domestic institutions expected to cooperate ever more closely in the military arena, through peace and stability support operations, shared intelligence, international police actions, and coalition warfare. To act as effective partners, these countries must share an ethos of democratic civilian control over the armed forces and promote the internal structures that will allow them to do so. The better we understand the reasons why good civil-military relations flourish or fail, the better the older, stabler democracies will be able to assist their newer counterparts to forge institutions that will enable them to succeed at this challenging task.

Notes

1. Eliot A. Cohen, *Supreme Command: Soldiers, Statesmen, and Leadership in Wartime* (New York; Free Press, 2002).

2. Niccolo Machiavelli, *The Prince*, trans. and ed. by Robert M. Adams (New York: W. W. Norton and Co., 1977), 42.

3. The most notable exception is Marybeth Peterson Ulrich, *Democratizing Communist Militaries: The Cases of the Czech and Russian Armed Forces* (Ann Arbor: University of Michigan Press, 1999).

Bibliography

Aall, P., D. T. Miltenberger, and T. G. Weiss, eds. 2000. *Guide to IGOs, NGOs, and the Military in Peace and Relief Operations*. Washington, DC: United States Institute of Peace Press.

Abenheim, D. 1988. *Reforging the Iron Cross: The Search for Tradition in the German Armed Forces*. Princeton, NJ: Princeton University Press.

Abrahamsson, B. 1972. *Military Professionalization and Political Power*. Beverly Hills, CA: Sage Publications.

Agüera, M. 2001. "Ambitious Goals, Weak Means? Germany's Project 'Future Bundeswehr' Is Facing Many Hurdles." *Defense Analysis* 17(3).

Aguero, F. 1995. *Soldiers, Civilians, and Democracy: Post-Franco Spain in Comparative Perspective*. Baltimore: Johns Hopkins University Press.

Alesina, A., R. Hausmann, R. Hommes, and E. Stein. 1993. "Budget Institutions and Fiscal Performance in Latin America." Working Paper Series 394, Inter-American Development Bank, Office of the Chief Economist, Washington, DC.

Allmayer-Beck, J. C., and E. Lessing. 1974. *Die K. u. K. Armee, 1848–1914*. Vienna: Prisma Verlag.

Andrew, C. 1995. *For the President's Eyes Only: Secret Intelligence and the American Presidency from Washington to Bush*. New York: Harper Collins.

Andrew, C., and V. Mitrokhin. 1999. *The Sword and the Shield: The Mitrokhin Archive and the Secret History of the KGB*. New York: Basic Books.

Angerthal, S. 1999. "Officer Training and Democracy: A Study of Argentina." PhD diss., University of Wisconsin–Madison.

Antunes, Priscila, and Marco A. C. Cepik. 2003. "The New Brazilian Intelligence System: An Institutional Assessment." *International Journal of Intelligence and Counterintelligence* 16(2).

Arbatov, A. G. 1997. "Military Reform in Russia: Dilemmas, Obstacles, and Prospects." Working Paper (September), International Security Program, Belfer Center for Science and International Affairs, Harvard University, Cambridge, MA.

Arquilla, J., D. Ronfeldt, and M. Zanini. 1999. "Networks, Netwar, and Information-Age Terrorism." In *Countering the New Terrorism*, ed. Ian O. Lesser, Bruce Hoffman, John Arquilla, David F. Ronfeldt, Michele Zanini, and Brian Michael Jenkins. Santa Monica, CA: RAND.

Art, R. J., V. Davis, and S. P. Huntington, eds. 1985. *Reorganizing America's Defense: Leadership in War and Peace*. Washington, DC: Pergamon-Brassey's International Defense Publishers.

Asch, B. J., and J. T. Warner. 1996. "Should the Military Retirement System Be Reformed?" In Fredland et al., *Professionals on the Front Line*.

Asprey, R. B. 1959. *The Panther's Feast*. New York: Putnam's Sons.

Avant, D. D. 1994. *Political Institutions and Military Change: Lessons from Peripheral Wars*. Ithaca, NY: Cornell University Press.

Bald, D. 1997. "Sechs Legenden über Wehrpflicht und Demokratie." *Blätter für Deutsche und internationale Politik* (Bonn) 6.

Baldez, L., and J. M. Carey. 1999. "Presidential Agenda Control and Spending Policy: Lessons from General Pinochet's Constitution." *American Journal of Political Science* 43(1).

Bandow, D. 2003. "Responding to Terrorism: Conscription Is Not the Answer." *USA Today*, January.

Barany, Z. 1997. "Democratic Consolidation and the Military: The East European Experience." *Comparative Politics* 30(1).

Bar-Joseph, U. 1995. *Intelligence Intervention in the Politics of Democratic States: The United States, Israel, and Britain*. University Park: Pennsylvania State University Press.

Barletta, M., and H. Trinkunas. 2004. "Regime Type and Regional Security in Latin America: Toward a 'Balance of Identity' Theory." In *Balance of Power: Theory and Practice in the 21st Century*, ed. T. V. Paul, J. J. Wirtz, and M. Fortman. Stanford, CA: Stanford University Press.

Barnett, C. 1975. *The Sword Barriers: Supreme Command in the First World War*. Bloomington: Indiana University Press.

———. 1991. *Engage the Enemy More Closely: The Royal Navy in the Second World War*. New York: W. W. Norton and Co.

Barrett, A. 2001. Goldwater-Nichols Act Readings: Legislative Activities and Documents Leading to the Passage of the Goldwater-Nichols Department of Defense Reorganization Act of 1986. Unpublished class materials. Naval Postgraduate School, Monterey, CA.

Batchelor, P., and P. Dunne. 1997. "The Peace Dividend in South Africa." Chap. 2 in *Dymystifying the Peace Dividend*, ed. Joern Broemmelhorster. Bonn: Bonn International Center for Conversion; Baden-Baden: Nomos Verlagsgesellschaft.

Beattie, P. M. 1999. "Conscription versus Penal Servitude: Army Reform's Influence on the Brazilian State's Management of Social Control, 1870–1930." *Journal of Social History* 32(4).

Beesley, A. H. 1913. *The Gracchi, Marius, and Sulla.* New York: Scribner's.

Bellamy, C. 1996. "From Total War to Local War: It's a Revolution." *Independent,* July 23.

Ben-Eliezer, U. 1995. "A Nation-in-Arms: State, Nation, and Militarism in Israel's First Years." *Comparative Studies in Society and History* 37(2).

Bergerud, E. M. 1991. *The Dynamics of Defeat: The Vietnam War in Hau Nghia Province.* Boulder, CO: Westview Press.

Bergin, A., R. Hall, R. Jones, and I. McAllister. 1993. "The Ethnic Composition of the Australian Defence Force: Management, Attitudes, and Strategies." Working Paper 11, Australian Defence Studies Centre, Australian Defence Force Academy, Canberra.

Betts, R. K. 2001–2002. "The Trouble with Strategy: Bridging Policy and Operations." *Joint Forces Quarterly* (Winter).

Betz, B., and J. Lowenhardt, eds. 2001. *Army and State in Postcommunist Europe.* London: Frank Cass.

Betz, D. 2000. "No Place for a Civilian: Russian Defence Management from Yeltsin to Putin." Paper presented at the 41st annual convention of the International Studies Association, Los Angeles, March 14–18.

———. 2003. "Comparing Frameworks of Parliamentary Oversight: Poland, Hungary, Russia, Ukraine." Geneva Centre for the Democratic Control of Armed Forces (DCAF), Working Paper 115, Geneva.

Binnendijk, H., and S. E. Johnson, eds. 2003. *Transforming for Stabilization and Reconstruction Operations.* Washington, DC: National Defense University Press.

Bissell, R. M., Jr., with J. E. Lewis and F. T. Pudlo. 1996. *Reflections of a Cold Warrior: From Yalta to the Bay of Pigs.* New Haven, CT: Yale University Press.

Bland, D. L. 1995. *Chiefs of Defence: Government and the Unified Command of the Canadian Armed Forces.* Toronto: Canadian Institute of Strategic Studies.

———. 1997. *National Defence Headquarters: Centre for Decision.* Study prepared for the Commission of Inquiry into the Deployment of Canadian Forces to Somalia. Ottawa: Minister of Public Works and Government Services.

———. 1999. "A Unified Theory of Civil-Military Relations." *Armed Forces and Society* 26(1).

————. 2001. "Patterns in Liberal Democratic Civil-Military Relations." *Armed Forces and Society* 27(4).

Blechman, B. M. 1991. "The Congressional Role in U.S. Military Policy." *Political Science Quarterly* 106(1).

Blischke, W. 1981. "Parliamentary Staffs in the German Bundestag." *Legislative Studies Quarterly* 6(4).

Bloch, M. 1968. *Strange Defeat: A Statement of Evidence Written in 1940.* New York: W. W. Norton and Co.

Born, H. 2002. "Between Efficiency and Legitimacy: Democratic Accountability of the Military in the U.S., France, Sweden, and Switzerland." Geneva Centre for the Democratic Control of Armed Forces (DCAF), Working Paper 102, Geneva. http://www.dcaf.ch/publications/Working_Papers/102.pdf.

————. 2002. *An Inventory of Actors: Strengthening Parliamentary Oversight of the Security Sector in Transition Countries.* Geneva: Geneva Centre for the Democratic Control of Armed Forces (DCAF). http://www.dcaf.ch/PCAF/inventory.pdf.

————. 2002. "Learning from Best Practices of Parliamentary Oversight of the Security Sector." Geneva Centre for the Democratic Control of Armed Forces (DCAF), Working Paper 1, Geneva. http://www.dcaf.ch/publications/Working_Papers/01(e).pdf.

Born, H., P. Fluri, and A. Johnsson, eds. 2003. *Parliamentary Oversight of the Security Sector: Principles, Mechanisms, and Practices.* Handbook for Parliamentarians, no. 5. Geneva: Inter-Parliamentary Union/Geneva Centre for the Democratic Control of Armed Forces.

Bozeman, A. 1988. "Political Intelligence in Non-Western Societies: Suggestions for Comparative Research." In *Comparing Foreign Intelligence: The U.S., the USSR, the UK, and the Third World,* ed. R. Godson. Washington, DC: Pergamon-Brassey's International Defense Publishers.

Bruce, G. M. P., and J. D. Morgan. 1999. "Parliamentary Scrutiny of Defense." *Journal of Legislative Studies* 5(1).

Bruneau, T. C. 2001. "Controlling Intelligence in New Democracies." *International Journal of Intelligence and Counterintelligence* 14(3).

Bruneau, T. C., P. N. Diamandouros, R. Gunther, A. Liphart, L. Morlino, and R. A. Brooks. 2001. "Democracy, Southern Style." In *Parties, Politics, and Democracy in the New Southern Europe,* ed. P. N. Diamandouros and R. Gunther. Baltimore: Johns Hopkins University Press.

Burk, J. 1992. "The Decline of Mass Armed Forces and Compulsory Military Service." *Defense Analysis* 8(1).

Busza, E. 1996. "Transition and Civil-Military Relations in Poland and Russia." *Communist and Post-Communist Studies* 29(2).

Cairo, M. F. "Civilian Control of the Military." Democracy Papers, U.S. Department of State International Information Programs. http://usinfo.state.gov/products/pubs/democracy/dmpaper12.htm.

Cajina, R. 1996. *Transición política y reconversión militar en Nicaragua, 1990–1995*. Managua: CRIES.

Calland, R., ed. 1999. *The First Five Years: A Review of South Africa's Democratic Parliament*. Cape Town: IDASA.

Caparini, M. 2002. "Challenges of Control and Oversight of Intelligence Services in a Liberal Democracy." Paper presented at the workshop "Democratic and Parliamentary Oversight of Intelligence Services," Geneva Centre for the Democratic Control of Armed Forces, Geneva, October 3/-5. http://www.dcaf.ch/news/Intelligence%20Oversight_051002/ws_papers/caparini.pdf.

Caraher, Leigh C. 2003. "Adapting Culture through Professional Military Education." In *Transforming for Stabilization and Reconstruction Operations*, ed. Hans Binnendijk and Stuart E. Johnson. Washington, DC: National Defense University Press.

Carsten, F. L. 1966. *The Reichswehr and Politics, 1918–1933*. Berkeley and Los Angeles: University of California Press.

Chachiua, M. 2000. "Internal Security in Mozambique: Concerns versus Policies." *African Security Review* 9(1). http://www.iss.co.za/Pubs/ASR/9No1/Contents.html.

Chambers, J. W., II. 2002. "Decision for the Draft." *Magazine of History* 17 (October).

Chapman, A. W. 1992. *The Origins and Development of the National Training Center, 1976–1984*. Fort Monroe, VA: Office of the Command Historian, U.S. Training and Doctrine Command.

Cheney, R. B. 1997. *Professional Military Education: An Asset for Peace and Progress*. Ed. B. Taylor. Washington, DC: Center for Strategic and International Studies.

Chickering, R. 1998. *Imperial Germany and the Great War, 1914–1918*. Cambridge: Cambridge University Press.

Chilcoat, R. "The Revolution in Military Education." *Joint Forces Quarterly* (Summer 1999): 59–63.

Choi, J. C. 1998. "South Korea." In *China, India, Israel, Japan, South Korea, and Thailand*, vol. 1 of *Arms Procurement Decision Making*, ed. R. P. Singh. Stockholm International Peace Research Institute. London and New York: Oxford University Press.

CIA (Central Intelligence Agency). 1995. *A Consumer's Guide to Intelligence.* PAS 95-00010. Washington, DC: CIA Public Affairs Staff.

Clark, W. K. 2001. *Waging Modern War: Bosnia, Kosovo, and the Future of Combat.* New York: Public Affairs Press.

Clausewitz, C. von. 1984. *On War.* Ed. and trans. Sir M. Howard and P. Paret. Princeton, NJ: Princeton University Press.

Cohen, E. A. 2001. "The Unequal Dialogue: The Theory and Reality of Civil-Military Relations and the Use of Force." In Feaver and Kohn, *Soldiers and Civilians.*

———. 2002. *Supreme Command: Soldiers, Statesmen, and Leadership in Wartime.* New York: Free Press.

Cohen, S. A. 1999. "From Integration to Segregation: The Role of Religion in the IDF." *Armed Forces and Society* 25(3).

Copeland, G. W., and S. C. Patterson, eds. 1994. *Parliaments in the Modern World: Changing Institutions.* Ann Arbor: University of Michigan Press.

Cottey, A., T. Edmunds, and A. Forster. 2000. "The Second Generation Problematic: Rethinking Democratic Control of Armed Forces in Central and Eastern Europe." Civil-Military Relations in Central and Eastern Europe. http://www.bristol.ac.uk/Depts/GRC/CMR/TCMR%20Papers/TCMR%201.7.htm.

———, eds. 2002. *Democratic Control of the Military in Postcommunist Europe: Guarding the Guards.* Basingstoke, UK, and New York: Palgrave.

———. 2002. "Introduction: The Challenge of Democratic Control of Armed Forces in Postcommunist Europe." In *Democratic Control of the Military in Postcommunist Europe: Guarding the Guards,* ed. A. Cottey, T. Edmunds, and A. Forster. New York: Palgrave.

Cowen, R. H. E. 1986. *Defense Procurement in the Federal Republic of Germany: Politics and Organization.* Boulder, CO: Westview Press.

Cox, A., and S. Kirby. 1986. *Congress, Parliament, and Defence: The Impact of Legislative Reform on Defence Accountability in Britain and America.* New York: St. Martin's Press.

Crane, B., and P. Shemella. 1988. "Between Peace and War: Comprehending Low Intensity Conflict." National Security Program Discussion Paper, ser. 88-02. Cambridge, MA: John F. Kennedy School of Government, Harvard University.

Crutcher, M. H., ed. 2000. *The Russian Armed Forces at the Dawn of the Millennium.* Carlisle Barracks, PA: U.S. Army War College.

Cruz, C., and R. Diamint. 1998. "The New Military Autonomy in Latin America." *Journal of Democracy* 9(4).

Cruz De Castro, R. 1999. "Adjusting to the Post–U.S. Bases Era: The Ordeal of the Philippine Military's Modernization Program." *Armed Forces and Society* 26(1).

Cunis, R. 1968. "Rekrutierungsmodelle im demokratischen Gesellschaftssystem." In *Beiträge zur Militärsoziologie*. Kölner Zeitschrift für Soziologie Sonderheft 12, ed. René König, Cologne.

Dandeker, C. 1999. *Facing Uncertainty: Flexible Forces for the Twenty-first Century*. National Defense College, Department of Leadership. Karlstad, Sweden: Klaria Tryckeri AB.

Däniker, G. 1992. *Wende Golfkrieg: Vom Wesen und Gebrauch zukünftiger Streitkräfte*. Frankfurt: Report-Verlag.

Danopoulos, C. P. 1992. *From Military to Civilian Rule*. Frankfurt: Regina.

Danopoulos, C. P., and C. Watson, eds. 1996. *The Political Role of the Military: An International Handbook*. Westport, CT: Greenwood Press.

Danopoulos, C. P., and D. C. Zirker. 1996. *Civil-Military Relations in the Soviet and Yugoslav Successor States*. Boulder, CO: Westview Press.

Davidson, P. B. 1989. *Vietnam at War: The History, 1946–1973*. Novato, CA: Presidio Press.

Delbrück, H. 1975. *Warfare in Antiquity*. Vol. 1 of *History of the Art of War*. Trans. W. J. Renfroe Jr. Lincoln: University of Nebraska Press.

Desch, M. C. 1999. *Civilian Control of the Military: The Changing Security Environment*. Baltimore: Johns Hopkins University Press.

———. 1999. "Structural Theory of Civil-Military Relations." In *Civilian Control of the Military: The Changing Security Environment*. Baltimore: Johns Hopkins University Press.

Diamandouros, P. N., and R. Gunther, eds. 2001. *Parties, Politics, and Democracy in the New Southern Europe*. Baltimore: Johns Hopkins University Press.

Diamint, R., ed. 1999. *Control civil y fuerzas armadas en las nuevas democracias latinoamericanas*. Buenos Aires: Grupo Editor Latinoamericano SRL.

Diamond, L., and M. F. Plattner, eds. 1993. *The Global Resurgence of Democracy*. Baltimore: Johns Hopkins University Press.

———, eds. 1996. *Civil-Military Relations and Democracy*. Baltimore: Johns Hopkins University Press.

Dodd, T. 1998. "Parliament and Defence: A Summary of Parliament's Role in Scrutinising and Controlling Defence Policy and the Armed Forces." *RUSI Journal* 143(3).

Döring, H. 2001. "Parliamentary Agenda Control and Legislative Outcomes in Western Europe." *Legislative Studies Quarterly* 26(1).

Downes, C. 1991. *Special Trust and Confidence: The Making of an Officer.* London: Frank Cass.

————. 1997. "Ethos-Directed Armed Forces for the 21st Century." Paper presented to General Dennis Riemer, Chief of Staff, U.S. Army, Washington, DC, November.

————. 2001. "Leadership Challenges of RMA Technologies, and Their Familiar and New Battlespaces." Paper presented at the annual conference of the Australian Defence College, Canberra. May 10.

Druetta, Gustavo, E. Estévez, E. López, and J. E. Miguens, eds. 1990. *Defensa y democracia: Un debate entre civiles y militares.* Buenos Aires: Puntosur Editores.

Duiker, W. J. 1981. *The Communist Road to Power in Vietnam.* Boulder, CO: Westview Press.

Dunlap, C. 1992. "The Origins of the American Military Coup of 2012." National War College Paper. Reprinted in *Parameters* (Winter 1992–1993).

————. 1996. "Melancholy Reunion." Institute for National Security Studies Occasional Paper, U.S. Air Force Academy, Colorado Springs.

Duus, P., ed. 1988. *The Twentieth Century.* Vol. 6 of *The Cambridge History of Japan.* Cambridge: Cambridge University Press.

Dziak, J. J. 1988. *Chekisty: A History of the KGB.* Lexington, MA: Lexington Books.

Edmonds, M. 1985. *Central Organizations of Defense.* Boulder, CO: Westview Press.

————. 1988. *Armed Forces and Society.* Leicester, UK: Leicester University Press.

Eksteins, M. 1998. "Memory and the Great War." In *The Oxford Illustrated History of the First World War*, ed. H. Strachan. Oxford: Oxford University Press.

Falk, S., and I. Shapiro. 1999. *A Guide to Budget Work: A Systematic Overview of the Different Aspects of Effective Budget Analysis.* September. http://www.internationalbudget.org/resources/guide/.

Feaver, P. D. 1996. "The Civil-Military Problematique: Huntington, Janowitz, and the Question of Civilian Control." *Armed Forces and Society* 23(2).

————. 1999. "Civil-Military Relations." *Annual Review of Political Science* 2.

————. 2003. *Armed Servants: Agency, Oversight, and Civil-Military Relations.* Cambridge, MA: Harvard University Press.

Feaver, P. D., and R. H. Kohn, eds. 2001. *Soldiers and Civilians: The Civil-Military Gap and American National Security.* Cambridge, MA: MIT Press.

Feaver, P. D., R. H. Kohn, and L. Cohn. 2001. "The Gap between Military and Civilian in the United States in Perspective." In Feaver and Kohn, *Soldiers and Civilians.*

Feld, M. D. 1971. "Professionalism and Politicization: Notes on the Military and Civilian Control." In *The Perceived Role of the Military*, ed. M. R. Van Gils. Rotterdam: Rotterdam University Press.

Finer, S. E. 1962. *The Man on Horseback: The Role of the Military in Politics.* London: Pall Mall Press; New York: Praeger.

————. 1988. *The Man on Horseback: The Role of the Military in Politics.* 2nd ed. Boulder, CO: Westview Press.

Fitch, S. J. 1998. *The Armed Forces and Democracy in Latin America.* Baltimore: Johns Hopkins University Press.

Flynn, G. G. 1998. "Conscription and Equity in Western Democracies, 1940–75." *Journal of Contemporary History* 33 (January).

Forster, A., T. Edmunds, and A. Cottey. 2002. "Introduction: The Professionalisation of Armed Forces in Central and Eastern Europe." In *The Challenge of Military Reform in Central and Eastern Europe: Building Professional Armed Forces*, ed. A. Forster, T. Edmunds, and A. Cottey. Basingstoke, UK: Palgrave.

Franke, V. 1999. *Preparing for Peace: Military Identity, Value Orientations, and Professional Military Education.* Westport, CT: Praeger.

Fredland, J. E., C. Gilroy, R. D. Little, and W. S. Sellman, eds. 1996. *Professionals on the Front Line: Two Decades of the All-Volunteer Force.* Washington, DC: Pergamon-Brassey's International Defense Publishers.

Freedman, L. 1998. "The Revolution in Strategic Affairs." Adelphi Paper 318, Oxford University Press for the International Institute for Strategic Studies, London.

Freedman, L., and V. Gamba-Stonehouse. 1991. *Signals of War: The Falkland Islands Conflict of 1982.* Princeton, NJ: Princeton University Press.

George, B., and A. Graham. 1994. "Defence Committees in Democratic and Democratising Legislatures." Paper presented at the Workshop of Parliamentary Scholars and Parliamentarians, Berlin, August.

George, P. 1997. "Defence Expenditures in the 1990s: Budget and Fiscal Policy Issues for Developing Countries." Paper presented at the Bonn

International Center for Conversion conference "Converting Defence Resources to Human Development," Bonn, November 9–11. http://www.bicc.de.

Gerth, H. H., and C. W. Mills. 1958. *From Max Weber: Essays in Sociology*. New York: Oxford University Press.

"Getting Even." 1985. *Newsweek*, October 21.

Gibson, C. P., and D. M. Snider. 1999. "Civil-Military Relations and the Potential to Influence: A Look at the National Security Decision-Making Process." *Armed Forces and Society* (Winter).

Gilbert, F., ed. 1975. *The Historical Essays of Otto Hintze*. New York: Oxford University Press.

Gill, P. 1994. *Policing Politics: Security Intelligence and the Liberal Democratic State*. London: Frank Cass.

Giménez-Salinas, A. 2003. "The Spanish Intelligence Services." In *Democracy, Law, and Security: Internal Security Services in Contemporary Europe*, ed. J.-P. Brodeur, P. Gill, and D. Töllborg. Aldershot, UK: Ashgate.

Giraldo, J. K. 2001. "Democratizing Civil-Military Relations: What Do Countries Legislate?" Center for Civil-Military Relations, Occasional Paper 7, Monterey, California.

Godson, R. F. 1986. "Intelligence and Policy: An Introduction." In *Intelligence Requirements for the 1980's: Intelligence and Policy*, ed. R. F. Godson. Lexington, MA: Lexington Books.

———. 1995. *Dirty Tricks or Trump Cards: American Counterintelligence and Covert Action*. Washington, DC: Pergamon-Brassey's International Defense Publishers.

Goerlitz, W. 1963. *History of the German General Staff, 1657–1945*. New York: Frederick A. Praeger.

Gogolewska, A. 2003. "Parliamentary Control of Security Policy: The Experience of Poland." Geneva Centre for the Democratic Control of Armed Forces (DCAF), Working Paper 106, Geneva.

Gompert, D. C., R. L. Kugler, and M. C. Libicki. 1999. *Mind the Gap: Promoting a Transatlantic Revolution in Military Affairs*. Washington, DC: National Defense University Press.

Gompert, D. C., O. Oliker, and A. Timilsina. 2004. *Clean, Lean, and Able: A Strategy for Defense Development*. Santa Monica, CA: Rand.

Goñi, U. 1996. "Argentina's Military Up for Sale." *First Page for Argentina* (Buenos Aires). http://ukinet.com/media/text/military.htm.

Gordon, M. R., and B. E. Trainor. 1995. *The Generals' War: The Inside Story of the Conflict in the Gulf*. Boston: Little, Brown.

Gott, R. 2000. *In the Shadow of the Liberator: The Impact of Hugo Chavez on Venezuela and Latin America.* London: Verso.

Graham, L. S. 1993. *The Portuguese Military and the State: Rethinking Transitions in Europe and Latin America.* Boulder, CO: Westview Press.

Gray, C. 1982. *Strategic Studies: An Assessment.* Westport, CT: Greenwood Press.

Gronke, P., and P. D. Feaver. 2001. "Uncertain Confidence: Civilian and Military Attitudes about Civil-Military Relations." In Feaver and Kohn, *Soldiers and Civilians.*

Guedes da Costa, T. 1998. "Democratization and International Integration: The Role of the Armed Forces in Brazil's Grand Strategy." In *Civil-Military Relations: Building Democracy and Regional Security in Latin America, Southern Asia, and Central Europe,* ed. D. R. Mares. Boulder, CO: Westview Press.

Ha, Y.-S. 1997. "Public Finance and Budgeting in Korea under Democracy: A Critical Appraisal." *Public Budgeting and Finance* (Spring).

Hadley, A. 1986. *The Straw Giant.* New York: Random House.

Haggard, S., and M. D. McCubbins, eds. 2001. *Presidents, Parliaments, and Policy.* Cambridge: Cambridge University Press.

Halberstam, D. 1972. *The Best and the Brightest.* New York: Random House.

Hall, P. A., and R. C. R. Taylor. 1996. "Political Science and the Three New Institutionalisms." *Political Studies* 44.

Haltiner, K. 1998. "The Definite End of the Mass Army in Western Europe." *Armed Forces and Society* 25.

Hammond, S. W. 1996. "Recent Research on Legislative Staffs." *Legislative Studies Quarterly* 21(4).

Handel, M. I., ed. 1989. *Leaders and Intelligence.* London: Frank Cass.

———. 2001. *Masters of War: Classical Strategic Thought.* London: Frank Cass.

Harries, M., and S. Harries. 1992. *Soldiers of the Sun: The Rise and Fall of the Imperial Japanese Army.* New York: Random House.

Harrison, A. 1989. *Challenging De Gaulle: The OAS and the Counterrevolution in Algeria, 1954–1962.* New York: Praeger.

Harrison, M. M. 1981. *The Reluctant Ally: France and Atlantic Security.* Baltimore: Johns Hopkins University Press.

Hastedt, G. 1991. "Controlling Intelligence: Defining the Problem." In *Controlling Intelligence,* ed. G. Hastedt. London: Frank Cass.

Hastings, M., and S. Jenkins. 1983. *The Battle for the Falklands*. New York: W. W. Norton and Co.

Havens, H. S. 1996. "Budgeting and Policy-Making by the Legislature in the United States." In Organisation for Economic Co-operation and Development (OECD), *Budgeting and Policy Making*.

———. 1996. "From Auditing to Policy Analysis: The Work of the General Accounting Office (GAO) of the United States." In Organisation for Economic Co-operation and Development (OECD), *Budgeting and Policy Making*.

Hegel, G. W. F. [1807] 1966. *The Phenomenology of Mind*. Trans. J. B. Baillie. London: George Allen and Unwin.

Henderson, W. D. 1982. "The Vietnamese Army." In Janowitz and Wesbrook, *The Political Education of Soldiers*.

Hendrickson, D., and N. Ball. 2002. "Off-Budget Military Expenditure and Revenue: Issues and Policy Perspectives for Donors." CSDG Occasional Papers, no. 1. King's College London for the UK Department for International Development, London.

Herman, M. 1996. *Intelligence Power in Peace and War*. Cambridge: Cambridge University Press.

Herring, G. C. 1986. *America's Longest War: The United States and Vietnam, 1950–1975*. New York: McGraw Hill.

Herspring, D. R. 1990. *Soviet High Command, 1967–1989: Personalities and Politics*. Princeton, NJ: Princeton University Press.

———. 1998. *Requiem for an Army: The Case of the East German Military*. Lanham, MD: Rowman and Littlefield Publishers.

———. 2001. *Soldiers, Commissars, and Chaplains*. Lanham, MD: Rowman and Littlefield.

Herspring, D. R., and I. Volgyes, eds. 1978. *Civil-Military Relations in Communist Systems*. Boulder, CO: Westview Press.

Heymann, P. B. 2001. "Controlling Intelligence Agencies." Working Paper Series on Internal Security Reform, Project on Justice in Times of Transition, Kennedy School of Government, Harvard University. http://www.ksg.harvard.edu/justiceproject/workingpapers.htm.

Higley, J., and R. Gunther, eds. 1992. *Elites and Democratic Consolidation in Latin America and Southern Europe*. Cambridge: Cambridge University Press.

Hilsman, R. 1957. Review of *The Soldier and the State*, by Samuel P. Huntington, and *Soldiers and Scholars: Military Education and National Policy*, by Laurence I. Radway. *American Political Science Review* 51(4).

The History of the U.S. Army Corps of Engineers. 1998. Alexandria, Virginia: Office of History, Headquarters, U.S. Army Corps of Engineers.

Hittle, J. D. 1961. *The Military Staff: Its History and Development.* Harrisburg, PA: Military Service Division, Stackpole Co.

Hogan, M. J. 1998. *A Cross of Iron: Harry S. Truman and the Origins of the National Security State, 1945–1954.* New York and Cambridge: Cambridge University Press.

Holsti, K. J. 1996. *The State, War, and the State of War.* Cambridge: Cambridge University Press.

Holsti, O. 2001. "Of Chasms and Convergences." In Feaver and Kohn, *Soldiers and Civilians.*

Holt, P. M. 1995. *Secret Intelligence and Public Policy: A Dilemma of Democracy.* Washington, DC: CQ Press.

Horowitz, D., and M. Lissak. 1989. *Out of Utopia.* Albany: State University of New York Press.

Howard, M. 1984. "The Forgotten Dimensions of Strategy." In *The Causes of Wars and Other Essays.* Cambridge, MA.: Harvard University Press.

Hunter, W. 1997. "Continuity or Change? Civil-Military Relations in Democratic Argentina, Chile, and Peru." *Political Science Quarterly* 112(3).

———. 1997. *Eroding Military Influence in Brazil: Politicians against Soldiers.* Chapel Hill: University of North Carolina Press.

Huntington, S. P. 1957. *The Soldier and the State: The Theory and Politics of Civil-Military Relations.* Cambridge, MA, and London: Belknap Press of Harvard University Press. Various reprint editions are cited in notes to the text.

———. 1968. *Political Order in Changing Societies.* New Haven, CT: Yale University Press.

———. 1991. "Why?" Chap. 2 in *The Third Wave: Democratization in the Late Twentieth Century.* Norman: University of Oklahoma Press.

International Budget Project. N. d. "Legislatures and Budget Oversight." http://www.internationalbudget.org/themes/LEG/index.htm.

Inter-Parliamentary Union. 1986. "Timing of the Budget." In *Parliaments of the World: A Comparative Reference Compendium,* 2nd ed., vol. 1. New York: Facts On File.

Isaacs, A. 1993. *Military Rule and Transition in Ecuador, 1972–92.* Pittsburgh: University of Pittsburgh Press.

Jackson, P. 2003. "Warlords as Alternative Forms of Governance." *Small Wars and Insurgencies* 14(2).

Janowitz, M. 1960. *The Professional Soldier: A Social and Political Portrait.* New York and Glencoe, IL: Free Press.

Janowitz, M., and S. D. Wesbrook, eds. 1982. *The Political Education of Soldiers.* Beverly Hills, CA: Sage Publications.

Jelezov, B. 1997. *Defense Budgeting and Civilian Control of the Military in the Russian Federation.* Alexandria, VA: Center for Naval Analyses.

Johnson, D. E. 1997. *Modern U.S. Civil-Military Relations: Wielding the Terrible Swift Sword.* Washington, DC: National Defense University Press.

———. 2002. *Preparing Potential Senior Army Leaders for the Future: An Assessment of Leader Development Efforts in the Post–Cold War Era.* Santa Monica, CA: RAND.

Johnson, J. J., ed. 1962. *The Role of the Military in Underdeveloped Countries.* Princeton, NJ: Princeton University Press.

Johnson, L. K. 1980. "The U.S. Congress and the CIA: Monitoring the Dark Side of Government." *Legislative Studies Quarterly* 5.

———. 1996. *Secret Agencies: U.S. Intelligence in a Hostile World.* New Haven, CT: Yale University Press.

Johnson, L. K., and K. J. Scheid. 1997. "Spenging for Spies: Intelligence Budgeting in the Aftermath of the Cold War." *Public Budgeting and Finance* (Winter).

Johnston, A. I. 1995. *Cultural Realism: Strategic Culture and Grand Strategy in Chinese History.* Princeton, NJ: Princeton University Press.

Joo, R. 1996. "The Democratic Control of Armed Forces: The Experience of Hungary." Chaillot Paper 23, Institute for Security Studies, WEU, Paris.

Kaufman, D. J. 2001. "Military Undergraduate Security Education for the New Millennium." In *Educating International Security Practitioners: Preparing to Face the Demands of the 21st Century International Security Environment,* ed. J. M. Smith, D. J. Kaufman, R. H. Dorff, and L. P. Brady. Carlisle Barracks, PA: U.S. Army War College.

Keaveney, A. 1982. *Sulla, the Last Republican.* Dover, NH: Croom Helm.

Kelleher, C. M. 1985. "Defense Organization in Germany: A Twice Told Tale." In *Reorganizing America's Defense: Leadership in War and Peace,* ed. R. J. Art, V. Davis, and S. P. Huntington. Washington, DC: Pergamon-Brassey's International Defense Publishers.

Keller, W. W. 1989. *The Liberals and J. Edgar Hoover: Rise and Fall of a Domestic Intelligence State.* Princeton, NJ: Princeton University Press.

Kier, E. 1997. *Imagining War: French and British Military Doctrine between the Wars.* Princeton, NJ: Princeton University Press.

Kincaid, A. D. 2000. "Demilitarization and Security in El Salvador and Guatemala: Convergences of Success and Crisis." *Journal of Interamerican Studies and World Affairs* (Winter).

Kinnard, A. D. 1977. *The War Managers*. Hanover, NH: University Press of New England.

Klein, P. 1991. *Wehrpflicht und Wehrpflicht heute*. Baden-Baden: Nomos.

Kneer, G., and A. Nassehi. 1994. *Niklas Luhmanns Theorie sozialer Systeme: Eine Einführung*. Munich: UTB W. Fink.

Kohn, R. H. 1997. "How Democracies Control the Military." *Journal of Democracy* 8(4).

Krafchik, W., and J. Wehner. N. d. "The Role of Parliament in the Budget Process." Institute for Democracy in South Africa, Budget Information Service. http://www.idasa.org.za.

Krepinevich, A. F., Jr. 1986. *The Army in Vietnam*. Baltimore: Johns Hopkins University Press.

Kuemmel, G. 2002. "The Military and Its Civilian Environment: Reflections on a Theory of Civil-Military Relations." *Connections Quarterly Journal* 1(4).

Kuhlmann, J., and J. Callaghan, eds. 2000. *Military and Society in 21st Century Europe: A Comparative Analysis*. Piscataway, NJ: Transaction Publishers.

Laqueur, W. 1995. *The Uses and Limits of Intelligence*. New Brunswick, NJ: Transaction Publishers.

Lasswell, H. 1941. "The Garrison State." *American Journal of Sociology* 46(4).

Lesser, I. O., B. Hoffman, J. Arquilla, D. F. Ronfeldt, M. Zanini, and B. M. Jenkins, eds. 1999. *Countering the New Terrorism*. Santa Monica, CA: RAND.

Lindsay, J. M. 2000. "Legislative Control of the Military: Lessons from the American Experience." Occasional Paper 12, Center for Civil-Military Relations, Naval Postgraduate School, Monterey, California.

Linz, J. J. 2000. *Totalitarian and Authoritarian Regimes*. Boulder, CO: Lynne Rienner.

Linz, J. J., and A. Stepan, eds. 1978. *The Breakdown of Democratic Regimes*. Baltimore: Johns Hopkins University Press.

———. 1996. *Problems of Democratic Transition and Consolidation: Southern Europe, South America, and Post-Communist Europe*. Baltimore: Johns Hopkins University Press.

Locher, J. R., III. 2002. *Victory on the Potomac: The Goldwater-Nichols Act Unifies the Pentagon*. College Station: Texas A&M University Press.

Longley, L. D., and R. H. Davidson, eds. 1998. *The New Roles of Parliamentary Committees*. London: Frank Cass and Co.

Loveman, B. 1999. *For la Patria: Politics and the Armed Forces in Latin America*. Wilmington, DE: Scholarly Resources.

Lowenthal, A. F., and J. S. Fitch, eds. 1986. *Armies and Politics in Latin America*. Rev. ed. New York: Holmes and Meier.

Lowenthal, M. M. 1992. "Tribal Tongues: Intelligence Consumers, Intelligence Producers." *Washington Quarterly* (Winter).

————. 2003. *Intelligence: From Secrets to Policy*. 2nd ed. Washington, DC: CQ Press.

Luttwak, E. N. 1987. *Strategy: The Logic of War and Peace*. Cambridge, MA: Belknap Press of Harvard University Press.

————. 1995. "Toward Post-Heroic Warfare." *Foreign Affairs* 74(3).

Lyons, G. M., and J. W. Masland. 1959. *Education and Military Leadership: A Study of the ROTC*. Princeton, NJ: Princeton University Press.

MacFarling, I. 1996. *The Dual Function of the Indonesian Armed Forces: Military Politics in Indonesia*. Canberra: Australian Defence Studies Centre, Australian Defence Force Academy.

Machiavelli, N. 1977. *The Prince*. Trans. and ed. Robert M. Adams. New York: W. W. Norton and Co.

Macmillan, H. 1984. *War Diaries: Politics and War in the Mediterranean, 1943–1945*. New York: St. Martin's Press.

Magenheimer, H. 1999. "Zur Frage der allgemeinen Wehrpflicht: Standortbestimmung-Alternativen-Konsequenzen." *Schriftenreihe der Landesverteidigungsakademie* 3.

Mainwaring, S., and C. Welna, eds. 2003. *Democratic Accountability in Latin America*. Oxford: Oxford University Press.

Mainwaring, S., G. O'Donnell, and J. S. Valenzuela. 1992. *Issues in Democratic Consolidation: The New South American Democracies in Comparative Perspective*. Notre Dame, IN: University of Notre Dame Press.

Marcella, G. 1995. *Strategic Implications for the United States and Latin America of the 1995 Ecuador-Peru War*. Carlisle, PA: Strategic Studies Institute, U.S. Army War College.

Mares, D. R., ed. 1998. *Civil-Military Relations: Building Democracy and Regional Security in Latin America, Southern Asia, and Central Europe*. Boulder, CO: Westview Press.

Marquina, A. 1991. "Spanish Foreign and Defense Policy since Democratization." In *Spanish Foreign and Defense Policy*, ed. Kenneth Maxwell. Boulder, CO: Westview Press.

Martins Filho, J. R., and D. Zirker. 2000. "The Brazilian Military under Cardoso: Overcoming the Identity Crisis." *Journal of Interamerican Studies and World Affairs* 42(3).

Masland, J. W., and L. I. Radway. 1957. *Soldiers and Scholars: Military Education and National Policy.* Princeton, NJ: Princeton University Press.

Maurer, L. M. 1999. "Parliamentary Influence in a New Democracy: The Spanish Congress." *Journal of Legislative Studies* 5(2).

Maxwell, K., ed. 1991. *Spanish Foreign and Defense Policy.* Boulder, CO: Westview Press.

McCarthy, S. 1996. "South Africa's Intelligence Reformation." *International Journal of Intelligence and Counterintelligence* 9(1).

Merari, A. 1993. "Terrorism as a Strategy of Insurgency." *Terrorism and Political Violence* 5(4).

Messner, J. 1966. *Das Naturrecht: Handbuch der Gesellschaftsethik, Staatsethik, und Wirtschaftsethik.* Munich: Tyrolia Verlag.

Meyers, R. T., ed. 1999. *Handbook of Government Budgeting.* San Francisco: Jossey-Bass.

Micewski, E. R. 2000. *Zur Frage eines Freiwilligenheeres.* Studies and Reports. Vienna: National Defense Academy.

———, ed. 2003. *Civil-Military Aspects of Military Ethics.* Vol. 1. Vienna: National Defense Academy Printing Office.

Millotat, C. O. 1992. *Understanding the Prussian-German General Staff System.* Carlisle Barracks, PA: Strategic Studies Institute.

Miltenberger, D. T. 2000. "The Military." Part 3 of *Guide to IGOs, NGOs, and the Military in Peace and Relief Operations,* ed. Pamela Aall, Lieutenant Colonel Daniel T. Miltenberger, and Thomas G. Weiss. Washington, DC: United States Institute of Peace Press, 2000.

Miniruzzaman, T. 1992. "Arms Transfers, Military Coups, and Military Rule in Developing States." *Journal of Conflict Resolution* 36(4).

Mollo, L. S. 2000. "Negotiating for Civilian Control: Strategy and Tactics of Umkhonto We Sizwe (MK) in the Democratic Transition of South Africa." Master's thesis, Naval Postgraduate School, Monterey, CA.

Montinola, G. R. 1999. "Parties and Accountability in the Philippines," *Journal of Democracy* 10(1).

Moran, J. 1998. "The Role of Security Services in Democratization: An Analysis of South Korea's Agency for National Security Planning." *Intelligence and National Security* 13(4).

Moreno, E., B. F. Crisp, and M. S. Shugart. 2003. "The Accountability Deficit in Latin America." In Mainwaring and Welna, *Democratic Accountability in Latin America.*

Morgenstern, S., and L. Manzetti. 2003. "Legislative Oversight: Interests and Institutions in the United States and Argentina." In Mainwaring and Welna, *Democratic Accountability in Latin America.*

Morgenstern, S. and B. Nacif, eds. 2002. *Legislative Politics in Latin America.* Cambridge: Cambridge University Press.

Moskos, C. C., J. A. Williams, and D. R. Segal. 2000. "Armed Forces after the Cold War." In *The Postmodern Military: Armed Forces after the Cold War,* ed. C. C. Moskos, J. A. Williams, and D. R. Segal. New York: Oxford University Press.

————, eds. 2000. *The Postmodern Military: Armed Forces after the Cold War.* New York: Oxford University Press.

Myers, S. L. 2000. "The 2000 Campaign: The Convention; Pentagon Taking Opportunity for Show." *New York Times,* July 28, A1.

National Democratic Institute for International Affairs (NDI). 1996. "Committees in Legislatures: A Division of Labor." Legislative Research Series, Paper 2, Washington, D.C.

Nelson, D. N. 1998. "Civil Armies, Civil Societies, and NATO's Enlargement." *Armed Forces and Society* 28(2).

Newland, S. J. 2001. "A Centennial History of the U.S. Army War College." *Parameters* (Autumn).

Norden, D. L. 1996. *Military Rebellion in Argentina.* Lincoln: University of Nebraska Press.

————. 1996. "Redefining Political-Military Relations in Latin America: Issues of the New Democratic Era." *Armed Forces and Society* (Spring).

Nordlinger, E. A. 1977. *Soldiers in Politics: Military Coups and Governments.* Englewood Cliffs, NJ: Prentice-Hall.

Norton, P., and D. M. Olson. 1996. "Parliaments in Adolescence." In *The New Parliaments of Central and Eastern Europe,* ed. D. M. Olson and P. Norton. London: Frank Cass.

Nye, J. S., Jr. 1996. "Epilogue: The Liberal Tradition." In *Civil-Military Relations and Democracy,* ed. Larry Diamond and Marc F. Plattner. Baltimore: Johns Hopkins University Press.

O'Brian, P. 1996. *The Yellow Admiral.* New York: W. W. Norton and Co.

O'Donnell, G. 1988. *Bureaucratic Authoritarianism: Argentina 1966–1973 in Comparative Perspective.* Trans. J. McGuire with K. Flory. Berkeley and Los Angeles: University of California Press.

Oi, W. Y. 1996. "Historical Perspectives on the All-Volunteer Force: The Rochester Connection." In Fredland et al., *Professionals on the Front Line.*

Olsen, H., and J. Davis. 1999. *Training U.S. Army Officers for Peace Operations: Lessons from Bosnia.* Special Report. Washington, DC: United States Institute of Peace.

Olson, D. M. 1994. *Democratic Legislative Institutions: A Comparative View.* Armonk, NY: M. E. Sharpe.

Olson, J., and A. Isacson. 1998. "Findings and Recommendations." In *Just the Facts: A Civilian's Guide to U.S. Defense and Security Assistance to Latin America and the Caribbean.* Washington, DC: Latin American Working Group and Center for International Policy. http://www.ciponline.org/facts/find99.htm.

Omitoogun, W. 2002. "The Processes of Budgeting for the Military Sector in Africa." In *SIPRI Yearbook 2003: Armaments, Disarmament, and International Security.* Oxford: Oxford University Press.

Organisation for Economic Co-operation and Development (OECD). 1996. *Budgeting and Policy Making.* SIGMA (Support for Improvement in Governance and Management in Central and Eastern European Countries) Papers, no. 8. Paris: OECD. http://www.sigmaweb.org/libpubs/pubs_sigpaps.htm.

Organisation for Economic Co-operation and Development (OECD)/World Bank. 2003. "Results of the Survey on Budget Practices and Procedures, 2003." http://ocde.dyndns.org/.

Ostrow, J. M. 1998. "Procedural Breakdown and Deadlock in the Russian State Duma: The Problems of an Unlinked and Dual-Channel Institutional Design." *Europe-Asia Studies* 50(5).

O'Toole, L. 1998. "Anatomy of the Expenditure Budget." SIGMA (Support for Improvement in Governance and Management in Central and Eastern European Countries) Policy Brief 1. http://www.sigmaweb.org/libpubs/pubs_generallist.htm.

Pantev, P., ed. 2001. *Civil-Military Relations in South-East Europe: A Survey of the National Perspectives and of the Adaptation Process to the Partnership for Peace Standards.* Vienna: Institut fur Internationale Friedenssicherung; Sofia: Institute for Security and International Studies; in cooperation with the PfP Consortium.

Pape, R. A. 1990. "Coercive Air Power in the Vietnam War." *International Security* 15(2).

Park, C. W. 1998. "The National Assembly of the Republic of Korea." *Journal of Legislative Studies* 4(4).

Parsons, T. 1960. *Structure and Process in Modern Societies.* Glencoe, IL: Free Press.

———. 1967. *Sociological Theory and Modern Society*. New York: Free Press.

———. 1976. *Zur Theorie sozialer Systeme*. Opladen, Germany: Westdeutscher Verlag.

Perlmutter, A. 1968. "The Israeli Army in Politics: The Persistence of the Civilian over the Military." *World Politics* 20(4).

Pie, L. W. 1962. "Armies in the Process of Political Modernization." In *The Role of the Military in Underdeveloped Countries*, ed. J. J. Johnson. Princeton, NJ: Princeton University Press.

Pion-Berlin, D. 1997. *Through Corridors of Power: Institutions and Civil-Military Relations in Argentina*. University Park: Pennsylvania State University Press.

———. 1998. "The Limits to Military Power: Institutions and Defense Budgeting in Democratic Argentina." *Studies in Comparative International Development* 33(1).

———, ed. 2001. *Civil-Military Relations in Latin America: New Analytical Perspectives*. Chapel Hill: University of North Carolina Press.

Porch, D. 1977. "Colonies and Coups: Portugal's Colonial Wars." In *The Portuguese Armed Forces and the Revolution*, 28–60. London: Croom Helm.

Posen, B. R. 1984. *The Sources of Military Doctrine: France, Britain, and Germany between the Wars*. Ithaca, NY: Cornell University Press.

Powell, C., and E. S. Leland. 1993. "1993 Report on the Roles, Missions, and Functions of the Armed Forces." Transcript of news briefing, February 12. Available from Federation of American Scientists, http://www.fas.org/man/docs/corm93/brief.htm.

Pridham, G., ed. 1995. *Transitions to Democracy*. Aldershot, UK: Dartmouth.

Przeworski, A. 1991. *Democracy and the Market: Political and Economic Reforms in Eastern Europe and Latin America*. New York and Cambridge: Cambridge University Press.

Quiñónez, J. M. 2000. *El gasto de defensa en Nicaragua: La toma de decisiones en la asignación de recursos*. Managua: Centro de Estudios Estratégicos de Nicaragua and the National Democratic Institute.

Rasmussen, M. J. M. 1999. "The Military Role in Internal Defense and Security: Some Problems." CCMR Occasional Paper 6 (October), Center for Civil-Military Relations, Monterey, CA.

Remmer, K. L. 1989. *Military Rule in Latin America*. Boston: Unwin Hyman.

Ricks, T. E. 1997. "The Widening Gap between the Military and Society." *Atlantic Monthly*, July.

Roberts, A. "NATO, Secrecy, and the Right to Information." *East European Constitutional Review* (Fall 2002/Winter 2003).

Robertson, K. G. 1998. "Recent Reform of Intelligence in the UK: Democratization or Risk Management?" *Intelligence and National Security* 13(2).

Robinson, T. W., ed. 1990. *Democracy and Development in East Asia: Taiwan, South Korea, and the Philippines*. Lanham, MD: University Press of America.

Rojas Aravena, F., ed. 1994. *Gasto militar en América Latina: Procesos de decisiones y actores claves*. Santiago, Chile: Centro Internacional para el Desarrollo Económico (CINDE) and Facultad Latinoamericano de Ciencias Sociales (FLACSO).

Roman, P. J., and D. W. Tarr. 2001. "Military Professionalism and Policymaking: Is There a Civil-Military Gap at the Top? Does It Matter?" In Feaver and Kohn, *Soldiers and Civilians*.

Romjue, J. L. 1996. *American Army Doctrine for the Post–Cold War*. Fort Monroe, VA: Office of the Command Historian, U.S. Army Training and Doctrine Command.

Rouquie, A. 1987. *The Military and the State in Latin America*. Trans. Paul Sigmund. Berkeley and Los Angeles: University of California Press.

Russett, B. 1993. *Grasping the Democratic Peace: Principles for a Post–Cold War World*. Princeton, NJ: Princeton University Press.

Sarkesian, S. C., and R. E. Connor Jr. 1999. *The U.S. Military Profession into the Twenty-first Century*. London: Frank Cass.

Schafer, H., and C. von Stechow. 1990. "Control of Security Policy." In Thaysen et al., *The U.S. Congress and the German Bundestag*.

Scheetz, T. 1997. "Transparency, Accountability, and Rational Decision-Making in Defense Expenditures: The Case of Argentine." Paper presented at the Converting Defense Resources to Human Development conference, Bonn International Center for Conversion (BICC), Bonn, November 9–11.

Schiavo-Campo, S., and D. Tommasi. 1999. "The Budget Preparation Process." In *Managing Government Expenditure*. Manila: Asian Development Bank. http://www.adb.org/documents/manuals/govt_expenditure/chap4.pdf.

Schiff, R. L. 1995. "Civil-Military Relations Reconsidered: A Theory of Concordance." *Armed Forces and Society* 22(1).

Schmitter, P. C. 1995. "The Consolidation of Political Democracies: Processes, Rhythms, Sequences, and Types." In *Transitions to Democracy*, ed. G. Pridham. Aldershot: Dartmouth.

Schmitter, P. C., and T. L. Karl. 1993. "What Democracy Is . . . and Is Not." In *The Global Resurgence of Democracy*, ed. L. Diamond and M. F. Plattner. Baltimore: Johns Hopkins University Press.

Schulz, D. E., ed. 1998. *The Role of the Armed Forces in the Americas: Civil-Military Relations for the 21st Century*. Conference report. Carlisle Barracks, PA: Strategic Studies Institute.

Schüttemeyer, S. S. 1994. "Hierarchy and Efficiency in the Bundestag: The German Answer for Institutionalizing Parliament." In *Parliaments in the Modern World: Changing Institutions*, ed. G. W. Copeland and S. C. Patterson. Ann Arbor: University of Michigan Press.

Scott, W. R. 1995. *Institutions and Organizations*. Thousand Oaks, CA: Sage Publications.

SEEDON (South Eastern Europe Documentation Network. http://www.seedon.org.

Shaw, M. 1979. "Conclusions." In *Committees in Legislatures: A Comparative Analysis*, ed. J. D. Lees and M. Shaw. Oxford: Martin Robertson.

Shay, R. P. 1977. *British Rearmament in the 1930s: Politics and Profits*. Princeton, NJ: Princeton University Press.

Sherman, W. T. 1892. *Memoirs of General W. T. Sherman*. New York: Charles Webster.

Shin, D. C. 1994. "On the Third Wave of Democratization: A Synthesis and Evaluation of Recent Theory and Research." *World Politics* (October).

Shope, V. C., comp. 1999. "Civil-Military Relations: A Selected Bibliography." Carlisle Barracks, PA: U.S. Army War College Library. http://www.carlisle.army.mil/library/bibs/civmil.htm.

Shulsky, A. N. 1993. *Silent Warfare: Understanding the World of Intelligence*. Revised by G. J. Schmitt. Washington, DC: Pergamon-Brassey's International Defense Publishers.

Simon, J. 1996. *NATO Enlargement and Central Europe: A Study in Civil-Military Relations*. Washington, DC: National Defense University Press.

Simons, W. E. 2000. "Introduction: A PME Panorama." In *Professional Military Education in the United States: A Historical Dictionary*, ed. W. E. Simons. Westport, CT: Greenwood Press.

Singh, R. P., ed. 1998. *China, India, Israel, Japan, South Korea, and Thailand.* Vol. 1 of *Arms Procurement Decision Making.* New York: Oxford University Press.

Snider, D. M., and M. A. Carlton-Carew. 1995. "U.S. Civil-Military Relations." Washington, DC: Center for Strategic and International Studies.

Snider, D. M., R. F. Priest, and F. Lewis. 2001. "The Civil-Military Gap and Professional Military Education at the Precommissioning Level." *Armed Forces and Society* 27(2).

Snider, L. B. 1997. *Sharing Secrets with Lawmakers: Congress as a User of Intelligence.* Washington, DC: Center for the Study of Intelligence.

Sondhaus, L. 1990. *In the Service of the Emperor: Italians in the Austrian Armed Forces, 1814–1918.* Boulder, CO: East European Monographs; distributed by Columbia University Press.

Spier, H. 1958. "Review of Masland and Radway." *American Sociological Review* 23(3).

Steele, W. M., and R. P. Walters. 2001. "Training and Developing Army Leaders." *Military Review* (July–August).

Steffani, W. "Parties (Parliamentary Groups) and Committees in the Bundestag." In Thaysen et al., *The U.S. Congress and the German Bundestag.*

Steinkamm, A. A., and D. Schoessler, eds. 1999. *Wehrhafte Demokratie 2000—Zu Wehrpflicht und Wehrstruktur.* Baden-Baden: Nomos.

Steinmo, S., K. Thelen, and F. Longstreth, eds. 1992. *Structuring Politics: Historical Institutionalism in Comparative Analysis.* New York and Cambridge: Cambridge University Press.

Stepan, A. 1971. *The Military in Politics: Changing Patterns in Brazil.* Princeton, NJ: Princeton University Press.

———. 1986. "The New Professionalism of Internal Warfare and Military Role Expansion." In *Armies and Politics in Latin America,* rev. ed., ed. A. F. Lowenthal and J. S. Fitch. New York and London: Holmes and Meier.

———. 1988. "The Brazilian Intelligence System in Comparative Perspective." Chap. 2 in *Rethinking Military Politics: Brazil and the Southern Cone.* Princeton, NJ: Princeton University Press.

———. 1988. *Rethinking Military Politics: Brazil and the Southern Cone.* Princeton, NJ: Princeton University Press.

Stern, F. 1957. *The Citizen Army, Key to Defense in the Atomic Age.* New York: St. Martin's Press.

Stiehm, J. H. 2001. "Civil-Military Relations in War College Curricula." *Armed Forces and Society* 27(2).

Strachan, H. 1997. *The Politics of the British Army.* New York and Oxford: Oxford University Press.

Strom, K. 1998. "Parliamentary Committees in European Democracies." In *The New Roles of Parliamentary Committees,* ed. Lawrence D. Longley and Roger H. Davidson. London: Frank Cass and Co.

Stueck, W. 1995. *The Korean War: An International History.* Princeton, NJ: Princeton University Press.

Sullivan, G. R. 1996. "The Volunteer Force and the Burden of Peace." In Fredland et al., *Professionals on the Front Line.*

Swaine, M. D. 1999. *Taiwan's National Security, Defense Policy, and Weapons Procurement Processes.* Santa Monica, CA: RAND.

Taylor, B. D. 2003. *Politics and the Russian Army: Civil-Military Relations, 1689–2000.* Cambridge: Cambridge University Press.

———. 2003. "The Soviet Military and the Disintegration of the USSR." *Journal of Cold War Studies* 5(1).

Thaysen, U., R. H. Davidson, and R. G. Livingston, eds. 1990. *The U.S. Congress and the German Bundestag.* Boulder, CO: Westview Press.

Thelen, K., and S. Steinmo. 1992. "Historical Institutionalism in Comparative Politics." In *Structuring Politics: Historical Institutionalism in Comparative Analysis,* ed. S. Steinmo, K. Thelen, and F. Longstreth. Cambridge: Cambridge University Press.

Thompson, N. 2001. Review of *War in a Time of Peace,* by David Halberstam. *Washington Monthly* (September).

Thompson, W. R. 1973. *The Grievances of Military Coup-Makers.* Beverly Hills, CA: Sage Publications.

Treverton, G. F. 1987. *Covert Action: The Limits of Intervention in the Postwar World.* New York: Basic Books.

Trinkunas, H. 2000. "Crafting Civilian Control in Emerging Democracies: Argentina and Venezuela." *Journal of Interamerican Studies and World Affairs* 42(3).

Tsypkin, M. 2000. "The Russian Military, Politics, and Security Policy in the 1990s." In *The Russian Armed Forces at the Dawn of the Millennium,* ed. Michael H. Crutcher. Carlisle Barracks, PA: U.S. Army War College, 2000.

Turner, S. 1985. *Secrecy and Democracy: The CIA in Transition.* Boston: Houghton Mifflin.

Tzu, S. 1971. *The Art of War.* New York: Oxford University Press.

Ugarte, J. M. 1990. "La Comisión de Defensa Nacional: Un rol casi inédito." In *Defensa y democracia: Un debate entre civiles y militares,* ed. G. Druetta, E. Estévez, E. López, and J. E. Miguens. Buenos Aires: Puntosur Editores.

———. 2000. *Legislación de inteligencia: Legimidad y eficacia.* Guatemala City: WOLA (Washington Office on Latin America).

Ulrich, M. P. 1999. *Democratizing Communist Militaries: The Cases of the Czech and Russian Armed Forces.* Ann Arbor: University of Michigan Press.

Upton, E. 1878. *The Armies of Asia and Europe.* New York: D. Appleton.

USAID (U.S. Agency for International Development). 2000. *Avaliação estratégica do programa de democracia e governação.* Angola.

U.S. Army Peacekeeping Institute. 1996. *Bosnia-Herzegovina After Action Review Conference Report.* Carlisle Barracks, PA: U.S. Army War College.

U.S. Chairman of the Joint Chiefs of Staff. 2000. "Officer Professional Military Education Policy." Chairman of the Joint Chiefs of Staff Instruction CJCSI 1800.01A, December 1.

U.S. Department of the Army. 2001. *The Army Training and Leader Development Panel (ATLDP) Officer Study Report to the Army.* http://www.army.mil/features/ATLD/ATLD.htm.

———. 2001. *Operations.* Field Manual FM 3-0. Washington, DC: Headquarters, U.S. Department of the Army.

U.S. Department of State. 2000. "Indonesia." In *Annual Report on Military Expenditures, 1999.* http://www.state.gov/www/global/arms/99_amiex2.html.

U.S. Office of the Under Secretary of Defense for Acquisition, Technology, and Logistics. 2004. *Transition to and from Hostilities.* Defense Science Board 2004 Summer Study. Washington, D.C.

Van Creveld, M. 1985. *Command in War.* Cambridge, MA: Harvard University Press.

———. 1991. *The Transformation of War.* New York: Free Press.

van Eekelen, W. F. 2002. "Democratic Control of Armed Forces: The National and International Parliamentary Dimension." Geneva Centre for the Democratic Control of Armed Forces (DCAF), Occasional Paper 2, Geneva. http://www.dcaf.ch/publications/publications%20new/occasional_papers/2.pdf.

Van Gils, M. R., ed. 1971. *The Perceived Role of the Military.* Rotterdam: Rotterdam University Press.

Von Mettenheim, K., ed. 1997. *Presidential Institutions and Democratic Politics: Comparing Regional and National Contexts.* Baltimore: Johns Hopkins University Press.

Waller, J. M. 1994. *Secret Empire: The KGB in Russia Today.* Boulder, CO: Westview Press.

Wallis, W. A. 1976. *An Overgoverned Society.* New York: Free Press.

Walzer, M. 1990. "The Communitarian Critique of Liberalism." *Political Theory* 18(1).

Watson, C. A. 2000. "Civil-Military Relations in Colombia: A Workable Relationship or a Case for Fundamental Reform?" *Third World Quarterly* 21(3).

Weigley, R. 1993. "The American Military and the Principle of Civilian Control from McClellan to Powell." *Journal of Military History* 57.

Weigley, R. F. 1967. *History of the United States Army.* New York: Macmillan.

Wesbrook, S. D. 1982. "Sociopolitical Training in the Military: A Framework for Analysis." In Janowitz and Wesbrook, *The Political Education of Soldiers.*

Westwood, J. N. 1986. *Russia against Japan, 1904–1905: A New Look at the Russo-Japanese War.* London: Macmillan.

Whitford, J., and T.-D. Young. 1996. "Command Authorities and Multinationality in NATO: The Response of the Central Region Armies." In *Command in NATO after the Cold War: Alliance, National, and Multinational Considerations,* ed. T.-D. Young. Carlisle Barracks, PA: Strategic Studies Institute.

Williams, K., and D. Deletant. 2001. *Security Intelligence Services in New Democracies: The Czech Republic, Slovakia, and Romania.* London: Palgrave.

Williams, M. C. 1998. *Civil-Military Relations and Peacekeeping.* New York: Oxford University Press.

Williams, P., and K. Walter. 1997. *Militarization and Demilitarization in El Salvador's Transition to Democracy.* Pittsburgh: University of Pittsburgh Press.

Wilson, G. 2002. *This War Really Matters: Inside the Fight for Defense Dollars.* Washington, DC: Congressional Quarterly Press.

Witkowsky, K. 2003. "The Military's Next Generation: Prestigious National Defense University Seeks to Create Strategic Thinkers." *National CrossTalk* 11(2).

Woodward, B. 1991. *The Commanders.* New York: Simon and Schuster.

Worley, D. R. 2001. *W(h)ither Corps?* Carlisle Barracks, PA: Strategic Studies Institute.

Wright, P., with P. Greengrass. 1987. *Spycatcher: The Candid Autobiography of a Senior Intelligence Officer.* New York: Viking.

Young, T.-D., ed. 1996. *Command in NATO after the Cold War: Alliance, National, and Multinational Considerations.* Carlisle Barracks, PA: Strategic Studies Institute.

————. 1996. "Defense Planning and the Bundeswehr's New Search for Legitimacy." In *Force, Statecraft, and German Unity: The Struggle to Adapt Institutions and Practices.* Carlisle Barracks, PA: Strategic Studies Institute.

————. 1997. *Multinational Land Formations and NATO: Reforming Practices and Structures.* Carlisle Barracks, PA: Strategic Studies Institute.

————. 2000. "Multinational Land Forces and the NATO Force Structure Review." *Royal United Services Institute Journal* 145(4).

Zaverucha, J. 1993. "The Degree of Military Political Autonomy during the Spanish, Argentine, and Brazilian Transitions." *Journal of Latin American Studies* 25.

————. 1998. "The 1988 Brazilian Constitution and Its Authoritarian Legacy: Formalizing Democracy while Gutting Its Essence." *Journal of Third World Studies* 15(1).

Zegart, A. B. 1999. *Flawed by Design: The Evolution of the CIA, JCS, and NSC.* Stanford, CA: Stanford University Press.

About the Editors and Contributors

Editors

Thomas C. Bruneau joined the Department of National Security Affairs (NSA) at the Naval Postgraduate School (NPS), Monterey, California, in 1987. He earned his PhD from the University of California at Berkeley and, before coming to NPS, taught in the Department of Political Science at McGill University, Montreal. Dr. Bruneau has served both as chairman of NSA and director of the Center for Civil-Military Relations (CCMR) at NPS. He has researched and written extensively on Portugal and Latin America, especially Brazil. Dr. Bruneau has published more than a dozen books in English and Portuguese, as well as articles in numerous journals. His latest articles are "Controlling Intelligence in New Democracies," in *International Journal of Intelligence and Counterintelligence* 14, no. 3 (2001), and "Civil-Military Relations in Latin America: The Hedgehog and the Fox Revisited," in *Revista Fuerzas Armadas y Sociedad 19, no. 1–2 (2005).*

Scott D. Tollefson earned his graduate and postgraduate degrees from Johns Hopkins University and the Paul H. Nitze School of Advanced International Studies (PhD, 1991). He was the director of the Master of Arts program in Political Science at Kansas State University. His research focuses on international relations in Brazil and civil-military relations in Argentina, Brazil, and Chile. He was an assistant professor in the Department of National Security Affairs at the Naval Postgraduate School from 1991 to 1998. He is the author of numerous chapters and articles on the above topics. He is currently a teacher with Saudi Aramco Schools in Dhahran, Saudi Arabia.

Contributors

Kenneth R. Dombroski earned his MA in international studies from the University of South Carolina and his PhD in world politics at the Catholic University of America. He is a lecturer with CCMR, where he develops curricula for in-residence, distance-learning, and mobile education team courses and teaches graduate courses in peacekeeping and the role of intelligence agencies in democracies for NSA. A retired military intelligence officer, Mr. Dombroski served in strategic intelligence assignments with the Defense Intelligence Agency and with the U.S. Central Command during Operation Desert Storm.

Jeanne Kinney Giraldo earned her Bachelor's degree in Politics from Princeton University and her Master's degree in Government from Harvard University, where she is currently completing her PhD. She began teaching in NSA in 1999, where her current research focuses on coalition politics in Chile, changes in political representation in Latin America, counter–drug efforts, and civil-military relations. Professor Giraldo's publications include "Development and Democracy in Chile: Finance Minister Alejandro Foxley and the Concertación's Project for the 1990s," in *Technopols: Freeing Politics and Markets in Latin America in the 1990s*, ed. Jorge I. Domínguez (University Park: Pennsylvania State University Press, 1997); and "Parties, Institutions, and Market Reforms in Constructing Democracies" (with Jorge Domínguez), in *Constructing Democratic Governance: Latin America and the Caribbean in the 1990s—Themes and Issues*, ed. Jorge I. Domínguez and Abraham F. Lowenthal (Baltimore: Johns Hopkins University Press, 1996).

Richard B. Goetze Jr., Major General USAF (retired), earned a Master of Arts degree in Latin American Studies and a PhD from the American University in Washington, DC. Since his retirement after thirty years of service, he has written and consulted extensively on international affairs, particularly regarding security issues related to Latin America. In addition to his work with the Naval Postgraduate School, he is an adjunct faculty member with the Naval War College, teaching a course on National Security Decision Making to members of congressional staffs. General Goetze was Chairman of the Board of Trustees of the Aerospace Education Foundation, a Trustee of the University Aviation Association, and Chairman of the Board of Directors of the American Public University System.

Karen Guttieri is an assistant professor in NSA. She joined the school in 2001 after conducting postdoctoral research at Stanford's Center for International Security and Cooperation, where she studied the intersection of politics and technology in the revolution in military affairs. Her research focuses on military operations in civilian environments, including the effectiveness of civil-military operations, military organizational learning from peace operations, and civil-military relations in peace implementation. Dr. Guttieri is coauthor of "Archival Analysis of Thinking and Decision-Making: Assessing Integrative Complexity at Distance," in *The Psychological Assessment of Political Leaders: Method and Application* (Ann Arbor: University of Michigan Press, 2003). She also has published articles in several journals, including the *Journal of Conflict Resolution* and *International Insights*.

Edwin R. Micewski is a Brigadier General in the Austrian Armed Forces and Director of the Institute for Humanities and Social Sciences at the National Defense Academy, Vienna. He specializes in political theory and social philosophy, particularly the philosophy of law and state, the use of force, and the ethics of the military. He has lectured widely at the National Defense Academy, Vienna, at the University of Vienna and the University of Linz, and has served as a research fellow and guest professor with NSA. His publications include *Grenzen der Gewalt—Grenzen der Gewaltlosigkeit* [Limits of Violence—Limits of Nonviolence] (Frankfurt: Peter Lang, 1998); *Ethics and International Relations* (Vienna: Literas, 2001); and *Protection of Cultural Property in the Event of Armed Conflict—A Challenge in Peace Support Operations* (Vienna: NDA Publication Series, 2002).

Douglas Porch earned his PhD from Corpus Christi College, Cambridge University, and joined the faculty of NSA in 1996. A specialist in military history, Dr. Porch has served as Professor of Strategy at the Naval War College in Newport, Rhode Island, and is also a frequent lecturer at the United States Marine Corps University at Quantico, Virginia, and the U.S. Army War College in Carlisle, Pennsylvania. His books include *The French Secret Services: From the Dreyfus Affair to Desert Storm* (New York: Farrar, Straus, and Giroux, 1995); and *The French Foreign Legion: A Complete History of the Legendary Fighting Force* (New York: Harper-Collins, 1991), which won prizes both in the United States and in France. *Wars of Empire*, part of the Cassell History of Warfare series (London), appeared in October 2000, and *The Path to Victory: The Mediterranean Theater in World War II* (New York: Farrar, Straus, Giroux) in 2004.

Paul Shemella, Captain, USN (retired), is a graduate of the U.S. Naval Academy and the Naval Postgraduate School, with operational experience in Latin America and Europe. He served in the Navy's Special Operations division and is an expert in policy and strategy development. He currently manages programs in Combating Terrorism and Defense Restructuring for CCMR. Captain Shemella's publications include "Frost and Fire: The Maritime LNG Sabotage Threat," Naval Postgraduate School thesis (1982); "Between Peace and War: Comprehending Low Intensity Conflict," Kennedy School of Government (Cambridge, MA: Harvard University, 1988); and "Sheltering the Genie: The LIC Threat to Nuclear Systems" (Washington, DC: Defense Nuclear Agency, 1990).

Thomas-Durell Young received his PhD and DES from the Institut Universitaire de Hautes Etudes Internationales, Université de Genève, Geneva, and is a 1990 graduate of the U.S. Army War College. He currently serves as European Program Manager in CCMR, where he oversees marketing, development, and execution of a large number of technical assistance projects throughout Central and Eastern Europe. Prior to taking this position in March 2000, he was a Research Professor at the Strategic Studies Institute of the U.S. Army War College. He has authored five books and monographs and numerous articles and book reviews. His latest book, coauthored with the late John Borawski, is *NATO after 2000: The Future of the Euro-Atlantic Alliance* (Westport, CT: Praeger, 2001). He is coeditor of the journal *Small Wars and Insurgencies* and sits on the editorial boards of *Defense and Security Analysis* and the *Australian Army Journal*.

Index